Contents

Section C – Environment

Unit 6 – Domestic Environment

Unit 7 – International Environment

Appendices

Applied Business Questions (ABQs)

COMPULSORY QUESTION FOR 80 MARKS (HIGHER LEVEL ONLY)

Section 2 of the Leaving Certificate Business Examination Paper Higher Level is a compulsory Applied Business Question for 80 marks (i.e. 20% of the total marks of 400). Each Applied Business Question is based on three units of the syllabus. The units to be examined will vary each year. Leaving Certificate Applied Business Questions are at the end of each appropriate unit:

End of			Page
Chapter 8	Leaving Certificate 2004 and 2009	Units 1, 2, 3	111
Chapter 12	Leaving Certificate 2005 and 2010	Units 2, 3, 4	204
Chapter 17	Leaving Certificate 2006 and 2011	Units 3, 4, 5	278
Chapter 22	Leaving Certificate 2007 and 2012	Units 4, 5, 6	340
Chapter 25	Leaving Certificate 2008 and 2013	Units 5, 6, 7	388

LEAVING CERTIFICATE

Global Business
Revised Edition

John O'Connor

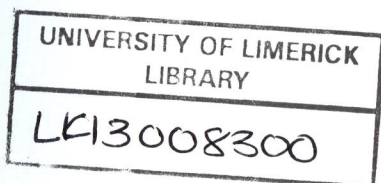

Editor

Frieda Donohoe

Design

Melanie Gradtke

Layout

Paula Byrne

Set in Garamond 12 pt

Cover Design

Melanie Gradtke

Picture Research

Sarah Deegan

ISBN 1-84131-663-6

Produced in Ireland by Folens Publishers, Hibernian Industrial Estate, Greenhills Road, Tallaght, Dublin 24.

Preface

Global Business Revised Edition is a textbook for students of Leaving Certificate Business at both Higher and Ordinary levels.

The aims of the Leaving Certificate Business syllabus include:

- To contribute to a balanced and appropriate general education, leading to the personal and social development of students through a study of Business and Enterprise.
- To develop a clear understanding of the role of Enterprise.
- To encourage the development of appropriate Enterprise learning skills.
- To develop a critical understanding of the overall environment in which business functions.

The objectives of the syllabus include:

- To develop an understanding of the structures, institutions, processes and management of Business.
- To promote a positive awareness of cultural and social diversity in International Business.

Global Business Revised Edition meets the aims and objectives of the business syllabus.
A special word of thanks to the many business teachers in different branches of the BSTAI who advised and assisted me in preparing this edition of the book. In particular, I would like to thank Kevin Lawlor, Marian College, Ballsbridge and Paddy Brennan, Scoil Mhuire, Clane for their invaluable advice and reports on the final draft of this book.

Finally I would like to acknowledge the outstanding editorial and design work of Frieda Donohoe and Paula Byrne. Their professionalism and enthusiasm greatly enhanced the book.

John O'Connor
April 2005

Acknowledgements

The Publisher wishes to thank the following for permission to reproduce material: the Audiovisual Library of the European Commission; Toyota Ireland; Capt. Phil Devitt, Harbour Master, Kinsale harbour, Co. Cork; Microsoft; eircom plc; Shannon Estuary Ports; Kerry Group plc; Coillte Teoranta; Office of the Revenue Commissioners; Slide File; Coca-Cola Ireland; Bank of Scotland; Shell; Irish Life; Allied Irish Bank; Intel Ireland; Bank of Ireland; The Consumers' Association of Ireland; The Director of Consumer Affairs; The Ombudsman; Fáilte Ireland; Irish Management Institute; Irish Farmers' Association; Irish Congress of Trade Unions; PA News; Labour Relations Commission; Labour Court; BSK Photo; IDA Ireland; Enterprise Ireland; IPA Magazines; Harland and Wolff; McDonalds; Dairygold; Irish League of Credit Unions; Bord Gáis; Bord na Móna; Bus Éireann; ESB; Louth County Enterprise Board; FÁS; EPIC; Office for Official Publications of the European Communities, 1999 (Photos taken from Serving the European Union); World Trade Organisation; CCE; Alamy; Corbis; Pat Mulhall; Provision; George Munday and the Irish Image Collection; Central Statistics Office; Camera Press; Getty Images; Brian Parsons; Photocall Ireland; Galway County and City Enterprise Board; Sligo County Enterprise Board.

Leaving Certificate Business Syllabus

Section A	People in Business	Unit 1
Section B	Enterprise	Units 2, 3, 4, 5
Section C	Environment	Units 6, 7

Leaving Certificate Business Examination Paper Higher Level

400 Marks 3 Hour Examination

Students are required to answer the following:

    (a) Eight questions out of ten from Section 1 (80 marks)

and

    (b) The Applied Business Question in Section 2 (80 marks)

and

    (c) Four questions from Section 3 as follows:

- One question from **Part 1** and
- Two questions from **Part 2** and
- **One other question** from either **Part 1** or **Part 2**

N.B. All questions in Section 3 carry 60 marks each.

Calculators may be used

Part 1: Contains three questions from Units 1, 6, 7
Part 2: Contains four questions from Units 2, 3, 4, 5

Leaving Certificate Business Examination Paper Ordinary Level

400 Marks 2½ Hour Examination

Students are required to answer the following:

    (a) Ten questions out of fifteen from Section 1 (100 marks)

and

    (b) Four questions from Section 2 as follows:

- One question from **Part 1** and
- Two questions from **Part 2** and
- **One other question** from either **Part 1** or **Part 2**

All questions from Section 2 carry equal marks (75 marks)

Introduction to People in Business

Objectives

The following topics from **Unit 1** of the syllabus are covered in this chapter:
- What is Business?
- Who are the People in Business?
- Interest Groups in Ireland
- Stakeholders
- Relationships in Business: Co-operative and Competitive

What is Business?

A business is an organisation set up to provide goods or services to potential customers. Businesses come under two categories: commercial and non-commercial. A commercial firm's main objective is to make profit.

Business
↓
goods/services to consumers

Whether the commercial firm is small or large, local or national, profit is the main objective, e.g. local shops (newsagents, chemists, boutiques), large supermarket chains (Dunnes Stores) and banks (AIB PLC). A non-commercial firm's main objective is to provide a service, e.g. Fáilte Ireland is a State agency that promotes tourism in Ireland. Charities, e.g. GOAL, also provide a non-commercial service.

Who are the People in Business?

1. Entrepreneurs (Risk-takers)

A person who starts up a new business is an entrepreneur. This person has the initiative and courage to start up a new business, hoping to make profit. Every entrepreneur requires the following:

- managerial skill
- organisational skill
- financial resources

➡ **Entrepreneur**

A person who sets up a new business is an entrepreneur.

If the business is a success, the entrepreneur will make profit. (Why else would you invest money in a business?) If the business fails, the entrepreneur will lose the money invested.

It is not possible to insure against the risk of a business losing money and having to close down.

In 2003, 2,142 businesses closed down in Ireland due to financial losses.

Being enterprising involves taking a risk by organising a profit or non-profit business venture.

Not every entrepreneur has a profit motive – some people are prepared to invest money and time in setting up non-profit organisations, e.g. a local sports club, a charity, etc. John O'Shea set up GOAL as an international charity to provide food, shelter and aid to people in underdeveloped countries.

2. Investors

Some entrepreneurs lack adequate finance to develop their business and so additional financial support is required. This money can be obtained from bank loans, grants from State agencies or from private investors. The bank would require security for the loan. Private investors may require shares in the business in order to receive a share of future profits. **Investors take a financial risk, whereas entrepreneurs take a commercial risk.**

> *The entrepreneur has a business idea. Investors provide some of the finance to turn the idea into a business reality, in order to earn a return on the investment (ROI).*

3. Consumers

Consumers purchase goods and services which are provided by entrepreneurs, i.e. they are the customers. Consumers' aims are as follows:

(a) To obtain high quality products or services at the lowest price possible.

(b) To be guaranteed a reliable after-sales service (if relevant), e.g. with a dishwasher, TV etc.

(c) To have a choice when buying a product, e.g. a car.

4. Producers/Suppliers

Producers manufacture goods for the market, e.g. Jacobs produce biscuits. There is a business link between producers and consumers. This link can be both co-operative and competitive.

> Producers would not survive without consumers. It is important to keep the customer happy with:
> • top quality goods
> • good prices
> • good service

Co-operative Relationships between Producers and Consumers

Co-operation between them exists in the following areas:

(a) Brand Loyalty

- Producers promote a brand image in order to increase sales.

- Consumers support brand image when they are happy with quality and price.

(b) Profit level and Selling Price

- When consumers are happy to pay the producers selling price, then both sides are co-operating with each other.

Competitive Relationships between Producers and Consumers

Competition (disagreement) between producers and consumers may exist in the following areas:

(a) Quality of the Product

If consumers are not happy with the quality of goods on sale, they may stop supporting the supplier and shop elsewhere.

(b) Overpriced Goods

In a competitive market where consumers have a choice, consumers will stop supporting a firm that is overcharging.

5. Employers

Employers employ staff to perform different tasks. Employers have obligations to their employees in many ways:

(a) To provide proper working conditions.

(b) To pay agreed wages.

(c) To provide contracts of employment.

(d) To treat all employees fairly and without discrimination.

> Employers have rights and responsibilities.

6. Employees

Employees work for their employers and carry out the tasks given to them, e.g. they perform the duties of machine operators and sales representatives in return for wages. They are a valued resource of every business.

Employees' rights include the following:

(a) To be paid the agreed wages.

(b) To receive an employment contract.

(c) To join a trade union.

(d) To have safe and healthy working conditions.

> Even though they work for the same firm, there can be competition amongst employees in areas such as promotion, reaching sales targets, etc.

Employees' responsibilities include the following:

(a) To do an honest day's work.

(b) To accept and carry out reasonable instructions from supervisors and management.

(c) To adhere to the terms and conditions in the contract of employment.

> A good co-operative relationship between employers and employees is essential for the successful running of every business. Skilled employees can give a firm a competitive edge.

7. Service Trader or Service Provider

These are firms that offer services required by entrepreneurs, for example:

(a) Financial Services – banks, insurance companies etc.

(b) Distribution Services – wholesalers, retailers etc.

(c) Information Services – market research firms etc.

(d) Legal Services – solicitors provide legal advice to help solve some disputes.

8. Interest Groups

Interest Groups (also called Pressure Groups)

(a) The role of interest groups in Ireland is to influence decisions made by organisations such as the Government, EU, IBEC, etc.
Example: The ICTU (Irish Congress of Trade Unions) is an interest group that tries to influence the Government on wage levels, taxation and government policy. It is one of the social partners involved when centralised wage agreements are negotiated between the government and employers.

> *Interest groups are not elected organisations. Their aim is to influence decisions.*

(b) They are not elected organisations but they have strength in numbers and so can affect business in the following ways:

(i) By boycotting firms.
Example: The IFA (Irish Farmers' Association) once used their strength in numbers to boycott meat processors until a major problem over prices was resolved in their favour.

(ii) They can encourage consumers not to support certain firms. Environmental groups encourage consumers not to support firms that do not sell reusable products.

(c) Lobbying is one of the aims of interest groups. This involves trying to influence decision makers usually through a high profile organised campaign of discussion and debates in the public media.
Example: In 2004, the Irish Vintners Association strongly lobbied the Government not to introduce the 'No Smoking' legislation. They failed in their aim as the Government introduced the legislation.

How does Business respond to Pressure Groups?

Business would be very foolish to ignore the aims of pressure groups. They should respond in the following ways:

(a) Positive response by agreeing with some of their wishes. This will help to restore goodwill with those who support the interest group.

(b) Use Public Relations (PR) to persuade the consumer market that the aims of the interest group are unreasonable.

Interest Groups in Ireland

The following interest groups exist:

(a)	IBEC	(e)	ICMSA
(b)	ICTU	(f)	IMI
(c)	CAI	(g)	PG
(d)	IFA	(h)	BIG

Employers' Interest Group
IBEC (Irish Business and Employers Confederation)
This is a business association whose main objective is to provide one voice which advises and represents employers on industrial relations matters. It has a membership of 6,000 employers. It negotiates on behalf of its members with the Government and the ICTU on industrial matters such as wage agreements. It advises its members where relevant, e.g. effects of new EU legislation.

Employees' Interest Group
ICTU (Irish Congress of Trade Unions)
The ICTU is the main vehicle of the trade union organisation in Ireland. In 2005 there were 61 unions in Ireland, of which 57 were affiliated to this body. The biggest trade union in Ireland is SIPTU (Services, Industrial, Professional and Technical Union) and in 2005 it had over 200,000 members. The ICTU uses its influence to further the interests of its members. It has enough influence to safeguard and improve the wages and working conditions of its members.

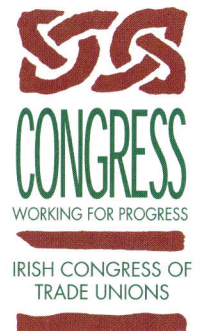

Consumers' Interest Group
CAI (Consumers' Association of Ireland)
The CAI was set up in 1966 as an independent, non-profit organisation. Its members are ordinary consumers solely interested in promoting and protecting the interests of consumers in Ireland.

  It publishes a monthly magazine entitled *Consumer Choice,* through which it informs and updates its members on issues, e.g. EU legislation relevant to consumers.

Farmers' Interest Groups

IFA (Irish Farmers' Association)
ICMSA (Irish Creamery Milk Suppliers Association)
Both associations protect their members' interests by negotiating and lobbying the Government and the EU on agricultural (agri-) issues.

Management Interest Group

IMI (Irish Management Institute)
The IMI is known as the voice of business managers in Ireland. Its objective is to raise the standard of management in Ireland. This objective is achieved by holding seminars and conferences and providing training services for its members.

IRISH MANAGEMENT INSTITUTE

Protection Groups (PG)

These are set up for a specific reason and usually disband once the aim has been achieved, e.g. a residents' group may be set up to oppose the establishment of a new factory which could cause pollution problems in an area.

Business Interest Group (BIG)

A Chamber of Commerce is a voluntary association made up of business people in an area. Its aim is to promote and protect the business interests of all its members. It also tries to attract new industry to local areas.

Stakeholders

All the people in business are stakeholders. The main aim of management is to serve all the stakeholders. In different ways, the stakeholders are affected by how a firm is run by its management. To a certain extent, the stakeholders depend on each other and so a decision by one section of the business can influence the reaction of another. For example, a strike by employees could lead to a fall in profits, so investors will not be happy. Some investors might react by withdrawing their investment.

For a business to succeed, it is important for co-operation to exist between all members of the stakeholder team. The co-operation of the workers is essential so that top quality goods are produced, goods which satisfy consumers and lead to sales and profits for the business. Adequate profit levels will, in turn, satisfy the entrepreneur and thus enable investors to earn and receive a return on their investment.

Interest groups are not stakeholders as they have no direct involvement in running a business. Their role can, however, have an impact on each stakeholder because their actions may influence some business decisions.

> All the stakeholders have an interest in the business. A decision by one stakeholder can affect the interest of another.

Analysis of Impact on Stakeholders

Fashion Manufacturer Ltd is more successful in the marketplace than its competitors. This affects its various stakeholders as follows:

1.	Big sales and profits enable management to	Pay high dividends to the shareholders.
2.	Achieving big profits enables management to	Pay bonuses to directors and management.
3.	Since the business is doing well, it enables management to	Employ more staff and give wage increases and bonuses to existing employees.
4.	Since the business is profitable, it enables management to	Pay all creditors and expenses on time, thus maintaining and improving its credit rating with suppliers.
5.	Big sales and profits enable the business to	Give some price reductions to its customers.
6.	Because the business is profitable, it enables management to	(a) Reinvest some profits to finance future expansion. (b) Support local community groups with sponsorship.

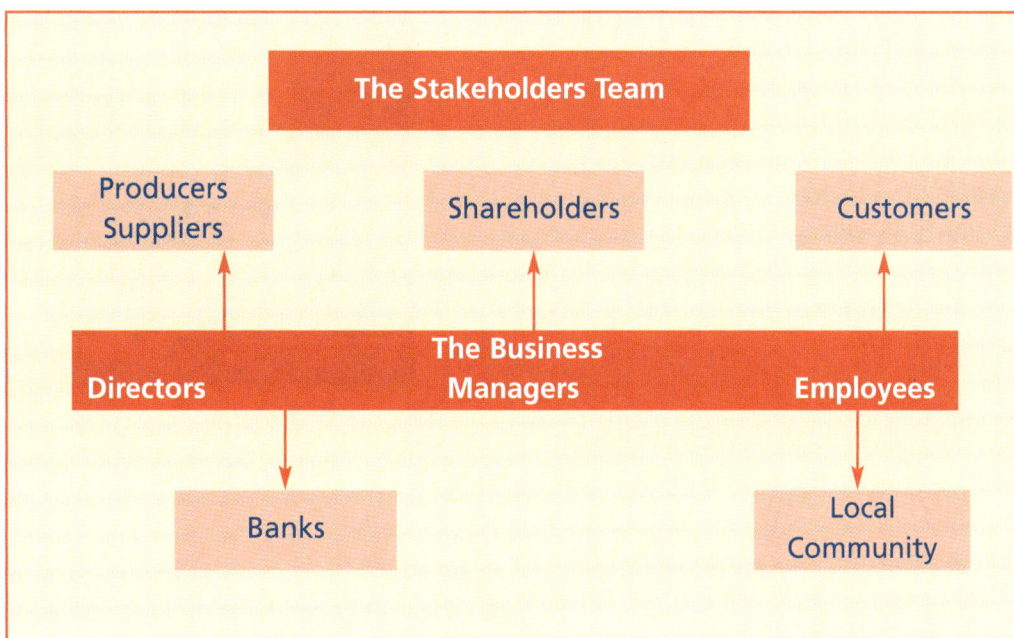

The Stakeholders Team

Producers Suppliers

Shareholders

Customers

The Business
Directors **Managers** **Employees**

Banks

Local Community

7

Relationships in Business: Co-operative and Competitive *(Higher Level Only)*

In business there can be both co-operation and competition between the members of the stakeholder team:

1.	Between Employers and Employees	2.	Between Businesses

1. Relationship between Employers and Employees

Co-operation between Employers and Employees

Co-operation in the following areas must exist for a business to be efficient and successful:

(a) Wages, Profit-Sharing, Share Options

Employers may have both a wages and a bonus system in operation. As well as being paid a basic wage, every employee can earn an additional bonus if they reach agreed targets, e.g. output. The existence of a bonus system provides an extra incentive for employees to be productive and efficient. Some firms have a profit-sharing scheme, where an agreed percentage of the profits is paid to the employees. Some public limited companies (PLCs) have a share option scheme, whereby employees can purchase shares at a preferential price, e.g. Irish Distillers.

Employees of firms with profit-sharing schemes take an interest in sales figures and profits.

(b) Industrial Democracy

Allowing a workers' representative on the board of directors is good for employer/employee relationships. Giving the workers a say in the management of the firm will enable both sides to have a better understanding of each other's viewpoint.

Industrial democracy ensures that employees feel fully involved in the company.

(c) Empowerment of Employees

This involves giving responsibility to employees to make decisions when dealing with customers in certain areas. This is good for staff morale and will lead to a better service to customers.

(d) Union Recognition

Employers must recognise the employees' right to join a trade union. By willingly accepting their right in this area there should be a good industrial relations climate in the business.

(e) Training

Providing sufficient resources for training will enable employees to improve their skills and do a better job for the firm.

Competition between Employers and Employees

In some cases there can be a competitive relationship between employers and employees and they may disagree on vital issues, for example:

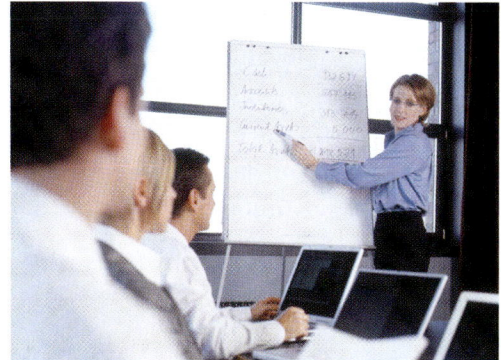

Employees update their skills at an in-house training course.

(a) Bonus Payments

They may disagree on the issue of realistic targets for bonus payments. Employees may feel that the targets set by management are too high and will not be achieved.

(b) Flexibility

Employers will want employees to be flexible on working hours, overtime and demarcation, so that the firm is in a position to react to market changes. Employees may require wage increases in return for this flexibility.

(c) Job Security

Employers will want the business to be profitable and will take necessary steps (as they see fit) to maintain profit levels. Investing in new machinery may lead to some redundancies.

2. Relationship between Businesses: Co-operative and Competitive *(Higher Level Only)*

A co-operative relationship between businesses exists when they combine their efforts for their mutual benefit, i.e. to promote local economic development. This co-operation leads to job creation and brings benefits to the business community.

A competitive relationship between businesses exists all the time. There is ongoing competition in many areas, for example:

  (a) Sales to customers.
  (b) Selling prices charged, especially between supermarkets.
  (c) Quality of goods and services provided.
  (d) Employing staff.
  (e) Sales promotion campaigns.

Exercises

1. (a) What is a business? State five examples of a business in your area.

    (b) State two examples of businesses that have a national identity rather than a local identity.

2. (a) What is the main difference between a commercial business and a non-commercial business? Give one example of each.

    (b) Give three reasons why a person would want to become an entrepreneur?

3. (a) How does an investor differ from an entrepreneur?

    (b) What is a consumer? What are the main requirements of a consumer?

4. Discuss briefly the role of each of the following in business:

    (a) Producers (b) Employers (c) Employees

5. (a) What are interest groups? Give two examples.

    (b) What is the relationship between interest groups and producers?

    (c) Describe what is meant by stakeholders in business.

6. (a) Explain the relationship between employers and employees.

    (b) Why might there be a lack of co-operation between employers and employees?

7. (a) By means of a diagram, show what is meant by the stakeholder team in business.

    (b) 'The entrepreneur is the most important member of the stakeholder team.' Give reasons for agreeing or disagreeing with this statement.

    (c) Indicate the co-operation and competition that can exist between producers and consumers.

8. Describe a co-operative and a competitive relationship that exists between businesses in an area.

2 Resolving Conflict: Non-legislative Methods

Objectives
The following topics from **Unit 1** of the syllabus are covered in this chapter:
- What is Conflict?
- Conflict Resolution
- Non-legislative Methods
- The Law of Contract

What is Conflict?

Conflict occurs when people disagree. There can be conflict between directors at board level, between management and unions, or between the business and its customers. In today's business world, customers do not suffer for long: they simply move on and deal with a competitor. Customers are aware of their rights and are more demanding as a result.

Management and staff often disagree though they both mean well.

Sources and Causes of Conflict

Sources of conflict in business include the following:

1. Directors and Managers Disagree
The board of directors want maximum profit, whereas management might be demanding extra finance for new machinery, extra staff etc. In this case, the cause of the conflict relates to acceptable profit levels for the different parties.

2. Different Objectives of Business and Customer
Conflicts here usually relate to quality, price, after-sales service etc. Customers require high quality and low prices. The seller will always want to provide high quality, but at prices higher than consumers want to pay. In this case, the cause of the conflict is the selling price.

An autocratic approach to leadership can cause conflict with staff.

3. Leadership Style of Managers
A dictatorial or autocratic style of leadership can lead to conflict with staff. This type of leader tries to make changes without consultation. Staff often react against this style of decision making. In this case, the cause of the conflict is the management style used to make changes.

4. Industrial Relations Issues
There may be conflicts between employers and employees on issues such as wages, working conditions, level of output (productivity) etc. In this case, the cause of the conflict is the different opinions generated by the union's demands for its members.

Conflicts can arise between a business and its supplier.

5. Disputes between Business and Suppliers
There may be conflicts on issues such as delivery dates, quality of goods supplied, discounts, length of credit etc. In this case, the cause of the conflict is normal differences between a business and its supplier.

Conflict Resolution

Conflicts must be resolved, otherwise the business and the employees lose out. Ignoring a conflict, hoping it will go away, is no way to resolve any issue. If a conflict is not sorted out, the business will lose sales, employees may lose some wages and customers may shop elsewhere. Conflicts can be resolved by non-legislative or legislative methods.

Non-legislative Methods

The following methods may be used to resolve a conflict without using the law:

1. Negotiating a Solution

- This involves trying to solve the problem by getting all parties to the dispute to sit down, discuss the issues and agree an acceptable solution.

- This approach may necessitate both sides agreeing to compromise a little in order to resolve the conflict.

- Early negotiation to resolve a conflict is advisable as it stops a small problem becoming a big one.

2. Conciliation

- This is an attempt by a third party to settle a dispute by hearing the submissions of both sides and suggesting a solution for settling the issue.

- The major weakness of conciliation is that the recommendation to settle the dispute is not binding for either side.

Early negotiation can prevent serious problems arising in the future.

3. Arbitration

- This is where both parties to the dispute request a third party to investigate the issues and make a recommendation. Both sides have agreed in advance to accept this recommendation.

- This method of resolving a dispute is rarely used as there is a general reluctance to agree in advance to accept recommendations.

The main benefits of arbitration include the following:

(a) The conflict is going to be resolved as both sides have agreed in advance to accept the decision of the arbitrator.

(b) It is usually a quick way to resolve a conflict.

(c) It is cheaper than having a dispute resolved in a court of law. No fees for solicitors and barristers are incurred.

> One way to resolve a dispute is for both sides to agree to an arbitrator. This ensures a resolution as both sides have agreed in advance to accept the decision of the arbitrator.

4. Collective Bargaining

Negotiations over wages between employers and unions are called collective bargaining. When both sides agree, a collective agreement is drawn up. This is a voluntary agreement and is not, therefore, legally binding on either side. This is the major weakness of this method of resolving a conflict. Wage negotiations are often conducted in a win/lose situation.

The merits of collective bargaining are as follows:

(a) It is a very flexible and informal way to resolve an industrial conflict.

(b) The negotiators are not influenced or pressurised by outside parties to resolve the conflict. They negotiate among themselves and try to come up with a solution that will be acceptable to all sides.

5. Ombudsman

The word 'Ombudsman' is Swedish in origin and means a representative or agent of the people.

What does the Ombudsman do?

The job of the Ombudsman is to investigate complaints from members of the public who feel that they have been unfairly treated by certain public bodies, e.g. An Post, local authorities and health boards. The office of the Ombudsman is impartial and completely independent of the Government. The Ombudsman is regarded as a mediator or a conciliator on behalf of individual citizens. Before contacting the Ombudsman, the person must try to solve the problem with the public body concerned. It is only when the person has failed in this that the Ombudsman should be contacted.

The Ombudsman investigates the complaint in private and will issue a recommendation to solve the problem. The Ombudsman does not have the authority to force a body to accept its recommendation. The service is provided free of charge.

> On 1 June 2003, Emily O'Reilly was appointed Ireland's third Ombudsman.

A large number of valid complaints are received by the Ombudsman every year. In 2003, for example, over 3,000 valid complaints were received.

The consistency of the large number of complaints clearly indicates how highly rated the Ombudsman's Office is by the public.

Insurance Ombudsman of Ireland

An Ombudsman scheme also exists for the insurance industry in order to resolve conflicts between insurance companies and its customers. The Office of the Insurance Ombudsman is financed by the insurance industry and its recommendations are binding on both sides.

Ombudsman for Credit Institutions

This office deals with conflicts between financial institutions (e.g. banks and building societies) and their customers. This office is financed by the financial institutions and its recommendations are binding on both sides.

Overall, it is true to say that the various Ombudsman schemes play an important role in resolving conflict (problems) for consumers.

The Law of Contract

What is a Contract?

A contract is a legally binding agreement that is enforceable by law. In the business world, contracts are being made daily, e.g. a contract to buy a house, a contract with the bank to obtain a loan.

> There are two parties to every contract – the Offerer and the Offeree.
> The Offerer is the person who makes the offer.
> The Offeree is the person who receives the offer, e.g. Brenda Dixon offers €200,000 to James Ryan for his house, which was advertised for sale. James Ryan accepts the offer of €200,000.
> In this example, Brenda Dixon is the Offerer and James Ryan is the Offeree.

Elements of a Valid Contract

The following common elements must be present in order to have a valid contract:

1.	Agreement, i.e. offer and acceptance
2.	Consideration
3.	Intention
4.	Capacity
5.	Consent
6.	Legality of form

1. Agreement

Every contract is based on agreement. In order to find out if agreement was reached by the parties, it is essential to analyse the negotiations into 'offer' and 'acceptance'. An 'offer' is not a contract, it is a commitment by the person making the offer to be bound by a contract if the offer is accepted. The offer must be clear, complete and unconditional. The 'acceptance' must be identical to the offer and must be communicated to the offeree in the time specified in order for it to be legally effective.

The offer and acceptance can be oral, in writing or by conduct.

Oral	At a public auction a person makes an oral offer for a house. The auctioneer orally accepts the offer.
Writing	Certain contracts must be in writing, e.g. HP agreements and sale of property house, land etc.
Conduct	In a supermarket, the customer who brings goods to the check-out area is offering to buy these goods by his/her action (conduct). When the check-out person accepts the money from the customer, the offer has been accepted by conduct on behalf of the business.

Termination of an Offer

An offer is not a contract. It is made with the intention of entering into a contract. An offer can be rejected – this usually happens at public auctions.

Invitation to Treat

An advertisement in a newspaper by a shopkeeper offering goods for sale at a stated price is not an offer. It is regarded as an **Invitation to Treat**, i.e. an invitation to the public to make an offer to buy the goods at the advertised price. The shop owner is free to accept or reject any offer for those goods.

An offer lapses or ceases to exist under the following circumstances:

   (a) If either party dies before acceptance.

   (b) If it is not accepted within the time specified by the offerer.

   (c) If it is withdrawn or revoked before it is accepted.

   (d) If the offeree makes a conditional acceptance (i.e. a counter offer).

2. Consideration

This is the money value of a legally binding contract. It is the value agreed by the parties to a contract, e.g. Peter Doyle sold his car to Kevin Hogan for €18,000 – the €18,000 was the consideration.

3. Intention

It must be the intention of both parties that a legal contract exists. Where business negotiations are taking place, it is assumed by both parties that when discussions are finished, an agreement, i.e. contract, will be finalised.

4. Capacity

The parties must have the capacity to enter into a contract, i.e. they must have reached the age whereby they are capable of entering into a contract. The age of majority in Ireland is 18. A person or firm should not enter into a contract with an infant (under 18) because such a person is not legally bound to fulfil the contract. It is possible for a company to enter into a contract once it does so within the terms specified in its Memorandum of Association. If the company directors authorise actions not covered in the Memorandum of Association, they are acting outside their authority – they are acting *ultra vires.*

5. Consent

Both parties to a contract must consent to the agreement. Neither party must be put under pressure to sign the contract. If there is no consent, there is no contract.

6. Legality

Some contracts must be in writing in order to be legally valid, e.g. contract for the sale of a house.

  Unless the contract is legal, it is not binding.

Example: A written or oral agreement between an accountant and a client which enables the customer to evade tax is illegal. The client cannot sue the accountant in this case.

> It is the existence of all these elements that enables a contract to be agreed, signed and enforced.

Termination of a Contract

There are two parties to every contract and it can be terminated in the following ways:

1.	By Performance
2.	By Agreement
3.	By Breach of Contract
4.	By Frustration

1. By Performance

If both parties to the contract perform their obligations, the contract has been completely performed, e.g. Building Ltd have a contract to build a house for Mary Ryan for an agreed consideration of €120,000. When the house is built to her satisfaction and the €120,000 is paid over, the contract has been fully performed.

2. By Agreement

Both parties to the contract may, by mutual consent, bring it to an end, e.g. a contract of employment may include a clause whereby if the employer gives the employee one month's notice, the employment contract is then ended by agreement.

3. By Breach of Contract

This means that one party to the agreement failed to fulfil his/her side of the deal. The other side may choose to repudiate the contract and bring it to an end. They may also be able to sue for damages. In such a case the fundamental condition of a contract was broken.

4. By Frustration

If some unforeseen event occurs making it impossible to carry out the remainder of the contract, then the contract can be terminated. For example, if:

(a) goods to be delivered were stolen or destroyed by fire.

(b) either party to the contract dies.

(c) the bankruptcy of either party to the contract occurs.

Remedies for Breach of Contract

1.	Damages
2.	Specific performance
3.	Rescind the contract

1. Damages

The normal remedy for breach of contract is financial compensation for the loss suffered due to the breach.

2. Specific Performance

The court may order that the contract be carried out in accordance with the terms of the agreed contract. This kind of decision would be relevant where there was a dispute over the sale of premises or land.

3. Rescind the Contract

If the contract is rescinded (cancelled), the injured party may sue for compensation for damages or loss incurred.

Exercises

1. (a) Why is there conflict in business?

   (b) Discuss three different conflicts that may arise in business.

2. State and explain three non-legislative methods of resolving conflict in business.

3. (a) Why are conflicts not always settled by arbitration?

   (b) Why might there be conflict between a business and its customers?

4. (a) What is an Ombudsman?

   (b) Why do consumers bring their complaints to the Ombudsman?

5. (a) Explain what is meant by a contract. (b) Discuss the elements of a valid contract.

6. (a) Discuss the different ways a contract can be terminated.

   (b) Outline the remedies for a breach of contract.

7. (a) How does an offer differ from a contract?

   (b) Using an example, show your understanding of invitation to treat.

3 Resolving Conflict:
Legislative Methods

Objectives

The following topics from **Unit 1** of the syllabus are covered in this chapter:

- Resolving Consumer Conflict
- Sale of Goods and Supply of Services Act 1980
- Conditions and Warranties
- Consumer Information Act 1978
- Industrial Relations Act 1990
- Resolving Industrial Conflict
- Unfair Dismissals Act 1977–1993
- Labour Court
- LRC

What are Legislative Methods?

Consumers and employees have rights. When conflict arises, the problem must be resolved. If conflicts are not resolved to the satisfaction of the person making the complaint, then it may be necessary for that person to resort to using the law.

Resolving Consumer Conflict

It is not just the seller who has responsibilities in the marketplace. The old legal term *caveat emptor* – let the buyer beware – still applies to contracts of sale because the buyer has a responsibility to use common sense when making decisions. Even if the buyer has been careful, conflicts can still arise. The range of problems facing consumers include the following:

1. Inferior quality goods; usually associated with mass production.
2. Inadequate after-sales service.
3. Misleading advertising, e.g. selling prices.

> ➡ **Caveat Emptor**
>
> *Let the Buyer Beware. Do not spend your money by means that you will later on regard as unfair.*

Sale of Goods and Supply of Services Act 1980

This Act was passed to protect the consumer. The rights of consumers under the Sale of Goods and Supply of Services Act, 1980 include the following:

1. Goods

A. Merchantable Quality

It is implied that all goods for sale must be of merchantable quality, i.e. fit for their normal use. For example, when you purchase a colour TV you should get a colour picture and not a black and white one.

B. Fit for the Purpose

If the buyer indicates to the seller a particular use for the goods requested, then the buyer must be able to rely on the seller's knowledge and the goods received must be for the stated purpose.

C. Sale by Description

If the goods are sold by description, then there is an implied condition that the items purchased must accurately correspond to the description.

D. Sale by Sample

If the goods are sold by sample, there is an implied condition that the bulk quantity of the goods must correspond to the sample. If any serious fault exists in the goods supplied, which was not obvious from any reasonable examination of the sample, the buyer may take action against the seller for a breach of the implied condition.

E. Ownership and Quiet Possession

The buyer relies on the seller having a proper title and claim on the goods, i.e. he/she trusts that the seller has the legal right to sell.

F. Contract for the Sale of Vehicles

When a vehicle is delivered, it must be free from any defect which would make it a danger for the public. A certificate of 'road worthiness' must be given to the buyer except in the following circumstances:

(i) If the buyer is a 'dealer' in vehicles.

(ii) If both parties agree that the vehicle requires repairs before use.

An implied warranty exists to the effect that spare parts and an adequate after-sales service will be available from the seller for the period of time stated in any advertisements.

G. Guarantees

Under the Act, a retailer is responsible for a manufacturer's guarantee and the dissatisfied consumer can claim against either or both. The 'guarantee' is an extra protection for the consumer. The Act states that a guarantee applies not only to the buyer or hirer, but to anybody who owns the goods during the period of the guarantee. A person who receives goods as a present (e.g. a dishwasher) can claim under the guarantee as if he/she were the buyer, as long as the goods are still within the guarantee period.

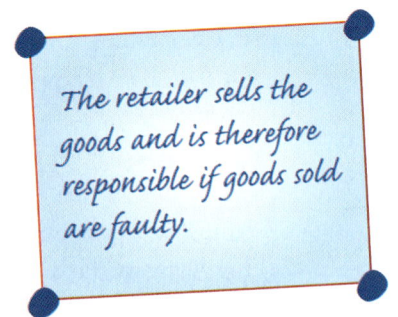

The retailer sells the goods and is therefore responsible if goods sold are faulty.

H. Unsolicited Goods

'Inertia selling' is a relatively new selling technique. It consists of sending goods to people who have not ordered them and seeking payment later for the unsolicited goods. The Sale of Goods and Supply of Services Act 1980 has a number of provisions relating to unsolicited goods.

A person who receives such goods may keep them without payment in the following circumstances:

(i) At the end of six months, provided the consumer has not unreasonably prevented the supplier from collecting them (during this period this customer should not use the goods and should take reasonable care of them).

or

(ii) Thirty days after the consumer gives written notice to the sender of the fact that the goods are unsolicited and informs the sender of the name and address of the consumer and the place where the goods can be collected. It is illegal to demand payment for unsolicited goods.

I. Conditions and Warranties

Conditions

All the points mentioned above are regarded as a 'condition of contract'. The 'condition' in law is a vital and fundamental part of the contract. If the 'condition' is not adhered to, then the buyer may repudiate the contract in full. For example, if goods are sold by sample and the bulk quantity supplied does not correspond to the sample, the buyer may refuse to accept the goods purchased and the contract can be terminated.

Warranty

A 'warranty' is an element or statement of fact that is specifically contained in a contract. If the warranty is broken, the buyer cannot repudiate the contract, but can claim for damages in court. It is a minor part of a contract.

> **Example:**
> K. McKenna Ltd purchased new machinery costing €250,000. It was agreed in the sale contract that the machinery was to be delivered and installed during the first week of March 2000. The machinery was not delivered until mid-May 2000 – 10 weeks later than agreed in the contract. In this case, the buyer must accept delivery of the machinery but will be able to sue for loss of production (sales/profits) due to the late delivery by the supplier. In practice, there is usually an agreed penalty clause in such contracts to compensate the buyer – this eliminates the hassle and costs of going to court.

2. Services

For the purpose of the Sale of Goods and Supply of Services Act 1980, services are treated similarly to goods. The following implied terms exist in relation to services offered:

(a) That the supplier has the appropriate qualification and skill required to provide the service, e.g. it is implied that an accountant advertising financial services is fully qualified.

(b) That the service will be provided with due care and attention.

(c) That the materials used will be of merchantable quality.

3. Retailer is Responsible

The responsibility for sorting out a complaint from a consumer rests with the retailer (seller). If a customer's complaint is valid, a credit note is not an adequate remedy unless the customer is willing to accept it. A consumer is entitled to the choice of a credit note, a refund or an exchange in the event of the goods being faulty. The notices below may no longer be displayed in shops:

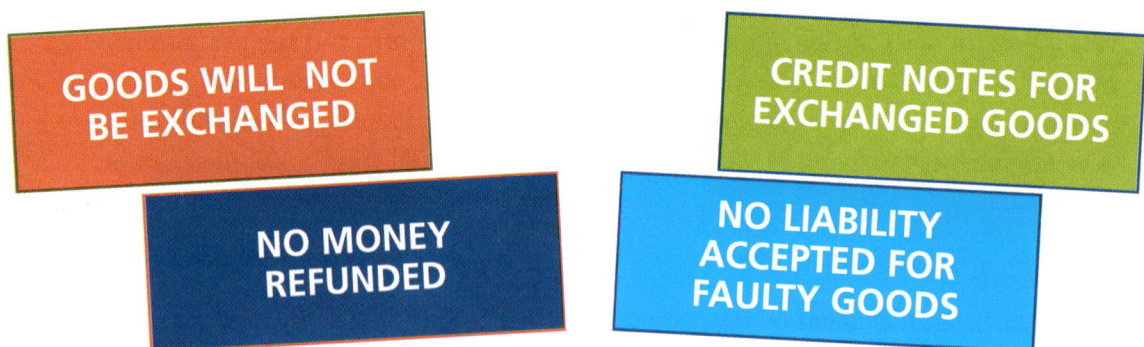

GOODS WILL NOT BE EXCHANGED

CREDIT NOTES FOR EXCHANGED GOODS

NO MONEY REFUNDED

NO LIABILITY ACCEPTED FOR FAULTY GOODS

Such statements give the impression that the customer has no rights. Any dealer using such statements is liable for prosecution under the Sale of Goods and Supply of Services Act 1980.

4. Redress for the Consumer

If goods do not work properly from the time they are purchased (i.e. they are faulty), the consumer has different forms of redress. For example they can:

(a) Request a full cash refund.

(b) Agree to accept a credit note to be used against future purchases.

(c) Insist on replacement goods.

At all times, the consumer must react promptly after discovering the fault, otherwise the right to object will be lost.

5. Enforcement of the Sale of Goods and Supply of Services Act 1980

> The Director of Consumer Affairs is responsible for monitoring the enforcement of the Act and can prosecute sellers who deny consumers their rights.

Consumer Information Act 1978

The objective of this Act is to give more information to the consumer about goods or services advertised by sellers.

The important features of this Act are as follows:

1. If a trade description is false or misleading, the trader is guilty of an offence.

2. Trade descriptions must be accurate, i.e. descriptions of the contents, quality, weight etc.

3. Advertising must not be misleading, e.g. if a trader advertises that goods are reduced from €100 to €60, the goods must have been on sale at the higher price for at least 28 successive days in the preceding three months. Traders advertising misleading information are liable to a fine.

   - False trade descriptions are illegal.
   - Inaccurate trade descriptions are illegal.
   - Misleading advertising is illegal.

4. The Act provides for the appointment of a Director of Consumer Affairs to monitor the provisions of the Act, initiate proceedings for breaches and order advertisers of misleading information to cease advertising.

The Office of the Director of Consumer Affairs

Appointed under the Consumer Information Act 1978, the functions of the Director of Consumer Affairs include the following:

1. To enforce the provisions of the Act and to promote better standards of advertising.

2. To instigate legal proceedings against any trader involved in misleading advertising.

3. To investigate complaints received from consumers or other interested parties.

4. To request, where relevant, an advertiser to cease advertising. If this request is ignored, to apply to the High Court for an injunction to stop the false advertising.

5. To monitor legislation and EU consumer directives and to inform the public of their consumer rights.

6. To present an annual report to the Minister for Enterprise, Trade and Employment.

The role of the Director of Consumer Affairs is very important to consumers. If the Director of Consumer Affairs didn't promote good advertising practice, it is likely that consumers would be misled, thus losing out on quality, value and legal rights.

Small Claims Court

1. The small claims procedure is a service set out in the Act for consumers who have claims for faulty goods or services, where the size of the claim does not exceed €1,270.

2. The person making the claim is called the Applicant, the person against whom the claim is made is called the Respondent.

3. The aim of the Small Claims Court is the accessible, speedy, low cost and fair resolution of minor disputes without the need for costly legal representation.

A small claim is made on a special application form which can be obtained from the Small Claims Registrar in the District Court. The applicant pays an application fee of €9. The Small Claims Registrar will try to solve the problem. If they are unsuccessful, the case will be heard by the District Court.

The main weakness of the Small Claims Court is that it cannot enforce a judgement. It has, however, been successful in having almost 90 per cent of its recommendations accepted. If its recommendation is rejected by the Respondent, the Applicant has the option of having the case heard by the District Court.

Which Legislative Method is Best for Consumers?

The most important Act regarding the customer–business relationship is the Sale of Goods and Supply of Services Act 1980. The reasons are as follows:

1. This Act affects every consumer in the country.

2. Under this Act, goods and services must do what they claim to do. If goods are not of merchantable quality, a consumer is entitled to a cash refund, a replacement or a credit note.

3. It gives statutory rights to consumers which cannot be limited by guarantees from the manufacturer or retailer.

4. It places responsibility with the retailer, which makes it easier for a consumer when seeking redress for receiving faulty goods.

5. Under this Act, motor vehicles are implied to be free from potentially dangerous defects.

6. Suppliers are aware of consumers rights, so they should take great care to meet consumers' requirements.

Industrial Relations Act 1990

This Act became law in July 1990. It repealed and replaced the Trade Disputes Act 1906 and various other Acts. The main provisions of the Act are as follows:

Uimhir 19 de 1990
Number 19 of 1990
AN TACHT CAIDRIMH THIONSCAIL, 1990
INDUSTRIAL RELATIONS ACT, 1990

1. Immunity

The Act provides immunity for trade unions and workers from claims arising from industrial action as part of a trade dispute. Before an immunity applies, the following conditions must be met:

(a) There must be a trade dispute as defined by the Industrial Relations Act 1990.

(b) The proposal to take industrial action must have been voted upon by secret ballot and a majority must have voted in favour of the proposed action.

(c) If only one worker is involved in the dispute, then all agreed procedures must have been used (e.g. a Rights Commissioner).

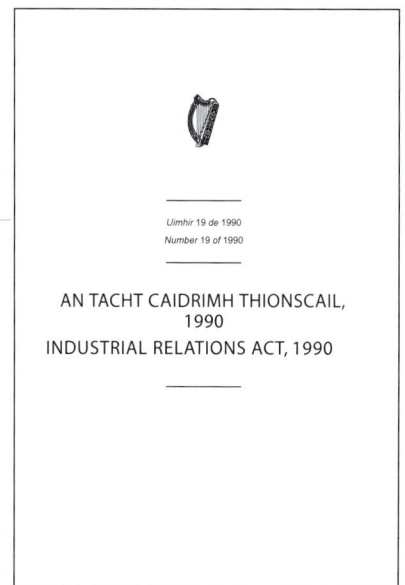

2. Trade Dispute

> ➡ **Definition of a Trade Dispute**
>
> *Any dispute between employers and workers which is connected with the employment or non-employment or the terms or conditions of employment of any person.*

Unions and workers cannot be sued for taking industrial action when there is a proper trade dispute and voting is by secret ballot.

N.B. A dispute between workers is no longer regarded as a trade dispute.

3. Minimum Notice

Under the Act, the union must give employers a minimum of one week's notice of their intention to go on strike.

4. Secret Ballot

Every trade union must contain a provision in its rules requiring a secret ballot before a strike can be authorised. Failure to carry out this ballot will mean that workers will not be legally protected if they go on strike.

5. Legitimate Trade Dispute

Under the Act, the following issues are valid for a trade dispute:

A. Dismissal or Suspension

No matter what reason management have for dismissing or suspending a worker, the issue will usually cause unrest and, in some cases, lead to a strike.

B. Trade Union Recognition

Management must recognise the right of workers to join or be represented by a trade union. In 1990, a threatened strike in Ryanair Airlines was called off at the last moment when management agreed to recognise the union.

C. Pay and Conditions of Employment

Issues here include the following:

wages/overtime	holiday	safe working practices
demarcation	redundancy payments	minimum notice

D. Discrimination

Under the Employment Equality Act 1998, it is illegal for persons to be treated differently in employment on the grounds of their sex or marital status. For example, a decision not to promote a woman because she is pregnant would be grounds for a claim on the basis of discrimination. It is also grounds for a claim of unfair dismissal.

E. Illegal Trade Disputes

A trade dispute centred around any of the following issues is illegal and the strikers are therefore not protected from being sued by the employer for losses suffered etc:

(i) An attempt to enforce a 'closed shop' agreement. A 'closed shop' is a workplace where a worker can obtain a job only if he/she is a member of a specific union.

(ii) A dispute of a political nature.

(iii) A disagreement between workers and management about how the business should be run.

6. Labour Relations Commission

The Act established the Labour Relations Commission (LRC) to resolve industrial disputes.

7. Requirements to form a Trade Union

The Act lays out the requirements to form a trade union. There must be 1,000 members (minimum) and a sliding scale deposit ranging from a minimum of €20,000 to a maximum of €60,000.

Resolving Industrial Conflict

The following organisations and individuals can be involved in resolving conflicts:

1.	The Labour Relations Commission (LRC)
2.	The Labour Court
3.	Rights Commissioner
4.	Employment Equality Act
5.	Employment Appeals Tribunal

1. Labour Relations Commission (LRC)

Role of the LRC

(a) To promote improved industrial relations, policies, procedures and practice.

(b) To assist in settling trade disputes.

(c) To reduce the number of industrial disputes coming before the Labour Court.

Functions of the LRC

(a) To provide an industrial relations conciliation service (not arbitration). The LRC will appoint an Industrial Relations Officer who will try to resolve the dispute between the employer and employees. As a general rule, a dispute should first be heard by the LRC before it is referred to the Labour Court.

(b) To provide an industrial relations advisory, development and research service to highlight the issues that cause problems in the workplace and try to resolve them.

(c) To prepare codes of practice for industrial relations in consultation with the ICTU and IBEC and to offer guidance on their implementation. Such codes of practice are not legally binding.

(d) To nominate a Rights Commissioner to investigate a certain type of dispute, e.g. where only one worker is in dispute.

(e) To appoint Equality Officers to investigate disputes covered by the Employment Equality Act 1998. An Equality Officer is an Officer of the LRC who has a specialised knowledge of equality law.

(f) To assist Joint Labour Committees (JLCs) and Joint Industrial Councils in carrying out their functions.

(g) To conduct ongoing research and monitor developments in industrial relations matters.

The LRC plays a very important role in Industrial Relations in Ireland. It provides a forum where the dispute can be discussed – 'A Talk Out is better than a Walk Out'. In 2003, the LRC held 2,988 conciliation meetings and its success rate was 92 per cent. Its success has greatly reduced the number of cases being referred to the Labour Court, which is an industrial court of last resort.

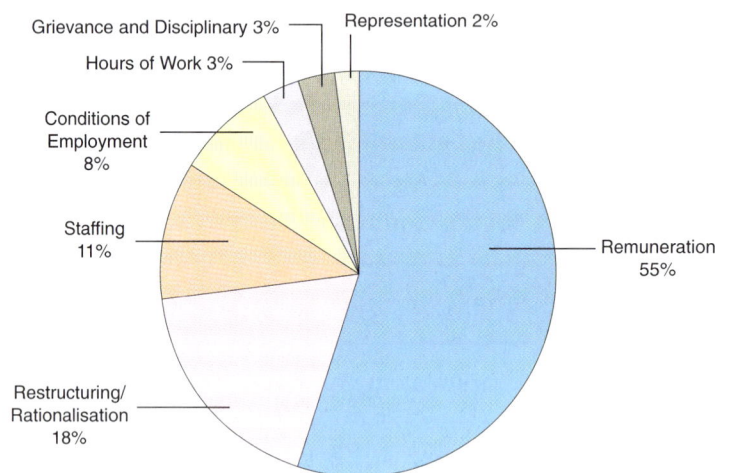

Disputes referred to Conciliation in 2003

2. The Labour Court (Court of Last Resort)

Under the Industrial Relations Act 1990, the Labour Court has the following functions:

(a) To investigate trade disputes and issue recommendations for their settlement. This function can be specifically requested by the Minister for Enterprise, Trade and Employment if the prolonging of a dispute is against the public interest. The Labour Court may decide to intervene themselves if they deem it appropriate.

Labour Court Functions:
- To investigate trade disputes and try to solve them.
- To investigate a trade dispute with no LRC involvement.
- To sometimes issue a binding recommendation.
- To establish JLCs.
- To register agreements.

(b) To investigate a trade dispute where the LRC has notified the Labour Court of its intention to waive its involvement in a particular dispute and the parties to the dispute have requested the intervention of the Labour Court.

(c) To issue a binding recommendation if either party to a dispute has rejected the recommendation of a Rights Commissioner or an Equality Officer.

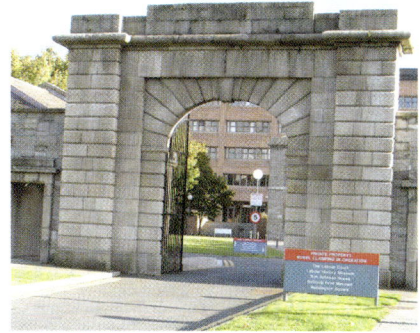

The Labour Court

(d) To establish Joint Labour Committees (JLCs) and to assist them in preparing Employment Regulations Orders. The aim of the JLCs is to recommend wage levels and conditions of employment in areas where workers are in a weak bargaining position, e.g. workers in many hotels where unions don't exist.

(e) To register employment agreements and to take the necessary steps to ensure they are implemented.

3. Rights Commissioner

(a) Rights Commissioners deal with problems involving individual workers as distinct from all the workers.

(b) The Rights Commissioner is appointed under the Industrial Relations Act 1990.

(c) The Rights Commissioner privately investigates a trade dispute when requested to do so by one of the parties to the dispute, provided that the other party does not object.

> **Disputes investigated by Rights Commissioners in 2003:**
> - 18% re unfair dismissals.
> - 4% re terms of employment.
> - 27% re payment of wages.
> - 31% re breaches of Industrial Relations Act 1990.

(d) Having investigated the dispute, the Rights Commissioner will make a recommendation which either party is able to reject and then appeal in the Labour Court.

4. Employment Equality Act 1998

> **➡ Definition of Employment Equality Act 1998**
>
> *This Act described discrimination as the treatment of one person in a less favourable way than another person is, has been or would be treated.*

This Act covers employees in both the public and private sector.

The nine grounds on which discrimination is unlawful under the Act are outlined below:

1. Gender, i.e. male/female.
2. Marital status, i.e. single/married/separated/widowed.
3. Family status, i.e. pregnant.
4. Religion, i.e. people with different religious beliefs.
5. Age, i.e. people over 18 and under 65.
6. Race, i.e. people of different colour, nationality, or ethnicity.
7. Disability, i.e. where one person has a disability and another person doesn't.
8. Traveller community, i.e. where one person is a member of a travelling community and another person is not.
9. Sexual orientation, i.e. homosexual, etc.

All aspects of employment are covered, i.e.
- equal pay
- promotion
- dismissal
- conditions

Equality Authority

The Equality Authority is an independent body set up under the Employment Equality Act 1998.

Functions of the Equality Authority

(a) To work towards the elimination of discrimination in relation to the nine grounds outlined in the Employment Equality Act 1998.

(b) To promote equality of opportunity in employment in relation to the nine grounds outlined in the Employment Equality 1998.

(c) To provide information to the public on the working of the Employment Equality Act 1998.

(d) To monitor and review the operations of the Employment Equality Act 1998.

Office of Director of Equality Investigation (ODEI – Equality Tribunal)

The ODEI – Equality Tribunal is separate to the Equality Authority. It was set up under the Employment Equality Act 1998.

Functions of the ODEI – Equality Tribunal

(a) To investigate complaints taken under the Employment Equality Act 1998.

(b) To appoint Equality Officers and Equality Mediation Officers to assist in investigating complaints of discrimination in the workplace and try to resolve the issues.

(c) To submit a yearly report to the Minister for Justice, Equality and Law Reform on the activities of the Office.

Unfair Dismissals Act 1977–1993

(a) The purpose of the Act, which was amended in 2001, is to protect employees from being unfairly dismissed by an employer.

(b) The Act applies to all employees aged between 16 and 66 who have had at least one year's continuous service with the same employer.

(c) The Act provides that every dismissal of an employee will be presumed to be unfair, unless the employer can show substantial grounds to justify the dismissal.

Grounds for a Fair Dismissal

A dismissal is fair if it is based wholly or mainly on one of the following grounds:

(a) Capability, competence or qualification for the job, i.e. the employee may be incapable of doing the job due to long-term illness.

(b) Misconduct, e.g. theft

(c) Redundancy

Grounds for an Unfair Dismissal

Under this Act, a worker cannot be dismissed due to reasons arising from any of the following:

(a) Trade Union membership

(b) Pregnancy

(c) Race

(d) Religion

(e) Being a member of a travelling community

(f) Suing the employer

(g) Going on strike

Constructive Dismissal

A constructive dismissal would occur where the working conditions of an employee are made so intolerable by the employer that the employee has to leave.

> EXAMPLE:
> An employee in the Customer Service department of a travel agency complained to her boss that she was being 'bullied' by her colleagues. She complained to management who ignored her comments. She walked out of the job saying that she was 'forced out' because management ignored her complaint. A Rights Commissiner found that she had been unfairly dismissed and awarded her six months' wages.

Procedure for Dismissal

Before being dismissed, the employee must be given the reason for the dismissal, the evidence which the employer has to justify the dismissal and a fair opportunity to respond to the allegations. The following is the standard procedure to be implemented by an employer when taking disciplinary action against an employee:

(a) Counsel the employee – point out what is wrong and outline what the employee should now do to rectify the situation.

(b) If counselling fails, the employee should be given a verbal warning.

(c) A written warning follows the verbal warning.

(d) A final written warning is then given.

(e) Suspension from work is confirmed in writing, with or without pay.

(f) Finally, the employee is dismissed.

The onus is on the employer to follow the above procedure and ensure the employee is made aware of the consequences at each stage in the disciplinary procedure.

Employees' Right to Appeal

If an employee is of the opinion that the dismissal was unfair, a claim for unfair dismissal can be made to the Rights Commissioner, then to the Employment Appeals Tribunal or to the Circuit Court or High Court. The redress awarded to the employee who was unfairly dismissed could be of three types:

> *The most common reason that employers face time-consuming and costly Employment Tribunal cases is their failure to follow proper procedures.*

(a) The employee is reinstated in the job as if nothing had occurred.

(b) The employee is given another job in the firm under acceptable conditions.

(c) Financial compensation up to a maximum of two years' salary is awarded.

5. Employment Appeals Tribunal (EAT)

(a) The Employment Appeals Tribunal is an independent body in Ireland, responsible for implementing your rights under protective employment law.

(b) The EAT consists of three people:

   (i) A chairperson who has legal qualifications

   (ii) One representative from the trade unions

   (iii) One representative from an employers' organisation

(c) This Tribunal hears a wide range of disputes, e.g. unfair dimissals.

(d) The decision of the EAT is called a determination and is legally binding. In some cases, the determination may be appealed to the High Court by either party but only on a point of law.

Trade Unions

A trade union is an association whose main functions include the following:

1. To protect its members and strive to ensure the security of their jobs.

2. To gain improvements in wages and working conditions for its members.

3. To negotiate on behalf of its members when a trade dispute occurs.

4. To co-operate with IBEC and the Government in centralised wage agreements.

Examples of Trade Unions in Ireland:

- ASTI (Association of Secondary Teachers in Ireland)

- TUI (Teachers Union of Ireland)

Industrial Action by Trade Unions

Notice of Industrial Action

Under the Industrial Relations Act 1990, one week's notice of the intention to go on strike must be given by the union to the employer.

Picketing

There are two types of picketing:

1. Primary Picketing – picketing the employer involved in the dispute. This form of picketing is legal under the Industrial Relations Act 1990.

2. Secondary Picketing – picketing another employer in order to make the strike more effective. Another employer could, for example, be delivering goods to the 'strike hit' firm in an attempt to help the affected employer. This form of picketing is illegal.

Strikes

A strike is where workers withdraw their labour in order to force the employer to meet their demands on some specified issue, e.g. a wage increase. There are different kinds of strikes or disputes:

1. **An Official Strike** – this strike is properly organised, i.e. the union organises the secret ballot and gives the employer one week's notice.

2. **An Unofficial Strike** – this is where the workers decide to go on strike without the approval of their union. The LRC refuses to intervene in unofficial disputes.

3. **Work to Rule** – a 'go-slow' is an alternative to going on strike. The workers do the minimum, output is greatly reduced but wages still have to be paid. Management must react to resolve this type of dispute.

Data Protection Act 1988

This Act applies to personal information on computers. It does not cover personal information maintained on manual files. Important terms in the Act are as follows:

1. **Data** – information in a form which can be processed.
2. **Data Subject** – is an individual who is the subject of personal data.
3. **Data Controller** – the person who has and controls the content and use of personal data.
4. **Data Processor** – the person who processes personal information on behalf of a data controller.

> The Data Protection (Amendment) Act 2003 includes personal information on computers and on manual files.

Rights of Data Subjects

These are laid out in the Act and include:

1. A person's right to have access to the data on the computer.
2. A person's right to insist on any incorrect data being corrected or deleted.
3. A person's right to complain to the Data Protection Commissioner if a Data Controller is in breach of the Act.
4. A person's right to compensation resulting from incorrect information being used by the Data Controller.

Obligations of Data Controllers

The obligations under the Act are as follows:

1. To obtain the information in an accurate and lawful manner.
2. To ensure that the information must only be used for the specific purpose for which it was obtained.
3. To keep the data in a safe and secure place and to delete it when it is no longer required.
4. To supply a person on request with a copy of the stored data.

Enforcement

The Office of the Data Protection Commissioner was set up under the Data Protection Act 1988 to supervise and monitor the Act. Functions of the Office include:

1. To maintain a register of Data Controllers and Data Processors.
2. To prepare and publish codes of practice in the area of data protection.
3. To issue Enforcement Notices on those who are in breach of the Act.
4. To give permission for authorised officers to enter a premises and obtain the data on file.
5. To instigate legal proceedings against those who are in breach of the Act.

Exercises

1. (a) State three problems facing consumers when buying goods.

    (b) Explain what is meant by the following terms:

    (i) Merchantable Quality (ii) Sale by Description

2. Outline the rights of consumers under the Sale of Goods and Supply of Services Act 1980.

3. Distinguish clearly between 'Conditions' and 'Warranties' in the Sale of Goods and Supply of Services Act 1980.

4. (a) Outline the functions of the Director of Consumer Affairs.

    (b) Discuss the role and importance of the Small Claims Court.

5. 'The day of the *caveat emptor* is gone because the consumer is well protected, so the responsibility for consumer satisfaction rests with the seller.'

    (a) Explain what *caveat emptor* means.

    (b) Outline the important provisions of the Consumer Information Act 1978.

6. Read the following information and answer the questions which follow:
    Joan Ryan purchased a pair of shoes for €180. The second time she wore them the sole came off one of the shoes. She contacted the shop manager where she purchased the shoes. The shop manager said that the shoes were of merchantable quality when she purchased them, refused to replace the shoes and suggested that she make direct contact with the manufacturer.

    (a) Explain what is meant by merchantable quality.

    (b) Name the law that protects Joan Ryan in this case.

    (c) Outline one non-legislative method of solving the above problem.

    (d) What legal rights does Joan Ryan have in this case?

    (e) What duties does the shop have in this case?

    (f) What advice would you give the shop manager regarding the handling of complaints from customers.

7. (a) Under what Act was the Labour Relations Commission established?

    (b) State three functions of the LRC.

    (c) Why do workers want to join a trade union?

4 Enterprise and Entrepreneurs

Objectives

The following topics from **Unit 2** of the syllabus are covered in this chapter:

- What is Enterprise?
- Characteristics of Entrepreneurs
- Intrapreneurs
- Enterprise Skills
- Planning
- SWOT Analysis
- Enterprise in Action
- Why Become an Entrepreneur?
- The Role of the Entrepreneur

What is Enterprise?

→ **Definition of Enterprise**

Enterprise involves people using their initiative to come up with ideas that they can turn into a business. When they take the risk to set up the business, they become an entrepreneur.

Entrepreneurs are individuals with the ability and initiative to notice such opportunities, as well as the willingness to take advantage of them, e.g. Denis O'Brien set up ESAT.

Without entrepreneurs there would be no enterprise. Entrepreneurs are the leaders in industry and commerce. They are self-confident and have tireless energy, which they harness in their drive to achieve the goal of creating a successful business in their lifetime.

Each business generation produces successful entrepreneurs. In 1997 Eddie O'Connor founded Airtricity. By 2005, his firm was the largest provider of renewable energy in Ireland. In 2004 the firm had sales of €130m. It has 30,000 customers in Ireland with operational wind farms in Donegal, Sligo, Cavan and Wicklow.

Eddie O'Connor had the foresight to see the potential in his business – he was a **Risk-taker.**

> Every business owner is an entrepreneur who has:
> - skill
> - initiative
> - the ability to take a risk
> - a wish to make a profit

Louise Kennedy, Veuve Cliquot Business Woman of the Year, 2003.

Denis O'Brien, Chairman of the Board and CEO of ESAT Telecom.

Eddie O'Connor, CEO of Airtricity.

Characteristics of Entrepreneurs (Risk-takers)

Entrepreneurs have certain characteristics which set them apart from other people. These characteristics are innate personal qualities which they have from natural ability. These qualities cannot be learned – you either have them or you don't, e.g. being determined, being confident, being cautious, etc. Not all entrepreneurs have the same characteristics. Characteristics of entrepreneurs include the following:

1.	Risk-taking	They are prepared to take financial and personal risk in a business venture. The financial risk can be reduced by operating the business as a limited company so as to have limited liability.
2.	Decision-making	They are able to 'decide on the spot', i.e. make speedy decisions as situations arise and be decisive.
3.	Need for success	They are independent-minded people who are determined to succeed.
4.	In control	They like to control the situation and require regular updating in order to stay in control.
5.	Self-confidence	They make the decisions because, having invested in the enterprise, they are confident that they understand the problems and can solve them. They see problems and temporary hiccups that can be solved.
6.	Realism	They are realistic when assessing the potential of the business and what can realistically be achieved.
7.	Resilience	They are determined to succeed, are motivated to keep going, can overcome mishaps and are confident of success, even if it takes longer than expected.
8.	Leadership	They lead by example, get on well with employees and respond positively to constructive comments or criticism.
9.	Flexibility	Priorities may change as situations change.

These characteristics are inherent in an entrepreneur's personality. A person may have a good idea, but if they are afraid to take a risk for fear of failure, they cannot be called an entrepreneur. Enterprise only exists when people have initiative, are creative, have confidence and are determined to succeed.

Characteristics of entrepreneurs:
- confident
- creative
- flexible
- good communicator
- realistic
- innovative
- a risk-taker
- highly motivated
- decisive

Enterprise Skills

Skills can be learned through training or acquired from experience. The following enterprise skills are necessary in business:

1. Leadership

> Leading by example and motivating and encouraging the staff.

Effective leadership is essential to the smooth running of a business.

2. Planning

> Planning the future of the business and predicting future problems and potential solutions.

Preparing a short-term plan (a tactical plan), while biding time to prepare a long-term plan (a strategic plan). It may involve preparing a SWOT analysis.

3. Problem Solving

> Having the ability to decide how to resolve the different problems that may arise.

For example, financial or distribution problems.

4. Human Relations

> Getting on well with people.

Managing people can have a positive impact on employees regarding their attitude, output etc. This area is very important in business.

5. Time Management

Effective use of time by management.

Time should be spent on important issues and not wasted on small matters.

6. Delegation

Delegating work to other people and trusting that they will perform their tasks efficiently.

One person cannot do everything in a business.

7. Innovation

Suggesting new business opportunities that should be considered by the business.

Such ideas may be the result of specialised training or experience.

8. Reality-Perception Skills

Ensuring that common sense prevails when solving a problem and making a decision.

This involves being realistic and unemotional when making decisions, e.g. making an employee redundant due to a decline in business.

9. Risk-taking

Measuring the potential risk involved and how that risk can be managed.

For example, if a firm fails to sell all its stocks, then someone may need to decide how much the firm would lose if unsold stock were reduced in price. This information is very important if costly stocks are involved, e.g. fashion clothes.

Enterprise in Action

Enterprise is not only about noticing a potential business opportunity and taking a risk to profitably exploit that opportunity. It is also related to assessing different situations and deciding what to do. Leadership is an important enterprise skill as it enables a person to make decisions and motivate staff. Enterprise is relevant in many areas, for example:

Enterprise in action:
- In business
- At home
- In school
- In the local community
- In Government
- In work

1. In New Business

Every business is started by an entrepreneur who sees a potential business opportunity, e.g. Feargal Quinn saw a potential market for a new supermarket. In 2005, his chain of supermarkets with a turnover of €140m and 800 employees was sold for €350m.

2. In Existing Business

A forward-looking managing director may decide to expand a firm's sales into the foreign market, i.e. exports. This person is showing initiative and enterprise in expanding the business by exporting.

3. In the Home

It is important to manage the household finances so that income will be equal to or greater than expenditure. Preparing a household cash budget is sensible and enterprising because decisions will be made based on the information available, e.g. is it profitable to operate a B&B service? Parents that grow their own vegetables are home entrepreneurs.

4. In School

Organising a fundraising venture amongst the students in order to raise finance for a school tour is a sign of enterprise in the school.

5. In the Local Community

A person who establishes a youth club to provide facilities for the young people in an area is showing enterprise. Profit is not the motive in this case.

6. In the Public Sector

The public sector includes the following:

(a) Government Departments, e.g. Department of Enterprise, Trade and Employment

(b) Government Agencies, e.g. Enterprise Ireland

(c) State Sponsored Bodies, e.g. Bord na Móna

(d) Local Authorities

Civil servants employed in the public sector who come up with practical new ideas to help industry by job creation are displaying enterprise skills.

7. In Work

Employees who show initiative and are creative are usually promoted. They are referred to as intrapreneurs because they have shown the characteristics of an entrepreneur.

> **EXAMPLE:**
> As he sat at his desk in his secure civil service job, Declan Boland pondered about his future. Since graduating from college in 1990 with a Business degree, he had worked in the Department of Finance in Dublin. He had been promoted twice and his wages were €45,000. His friend James Jones had dropped out of college after one year and had become a very successful businessman. Declan Boland decided to resign from his secure job and start up a business. He was confident that he had good ideas that he could turn into a profitable business.

Why become an Entrepreneur?

Why did Declan Boland want to become an entrepreneur? This question is relevant to every person who wants to set up a business.

Profit – without it a business will not survive.

People become entrepreneurs for the following reasons:

1. To make a profit from the business that is more substantial than the wages to be earned from a secure job.

2. To be their own boss, with the freedom and flexibility to make decisions and be independent, i.e to be self-employed.

3. To implement a new business idea and see if it is successful and profitable.

4. To be as successful as other people who have set up a business.

5. To take the risk because they can afford to set up a business and hope for the best.

6. To expand the established family business by diversifying or opening a new branch.

The Role of the Entrepreneur

The role of the entrepreneur in business includes the following:

1. To create an idea that would work in business.
2. To take the risk in starting up a new business.
3. To invest capital in the business.
4. To manage the firm at the beginning and oversee its expansion.
5. To employ suitable staff to work in the business.
6. To ensure that the customers are satisfied with the firm's products.

If I want to be my own boss, I must become an entrepreneur.

Intrapreneurs

Within big firms, it is important to have an entrepreneurial attitude. The intrapreneur works within an organisation, displaying entrepreneurial qualities such as flair, drive and initiative. They come up with creative ideas, e.g. new product ideas or cost-cutting measures, impress top management and are promoted to positions in management.

Enterprise in Ireland

In 2004, the results of a survey on enterprise in 21 countries were published. This survey paints a very poor picture of enterprise in Ireland. The following are some of the results from this survey:

1. Only one out of every 100 adults in Ireland wants to set up a business.
2. In Brazil, 12 per cent of adults want to set up a business.
3. In 2004, Japan was the only country where there were fewer entrepreneurs than in Ireland (1 in 2,000 people).
4. Ireland was best in terms of Government support for new and expanding firms.
5. In Ireland, new business activity is highly concentrated in Dublin and a couple of major cities and large towns.

Revision of Important Terms	
• Enterprise	• Business Strategy
• Entrepreneur	• Planning
• Enterprise skills	• SWOT Analysis
• Intrapreneurs	• Delegation

Exercises

1. (a) What is an entrepreneur?

   (b) List seven characteristics of entrepreneurs.

2. (a) Why do entrepreneurs take risks?

   (b) Explain what is meant by an intrapreneur.

3. (a) What skills are required to become an entrepreneur?

   (b) State two differences between an entrepreneur and an intrapreneur.

4. 'Enterprise is not confined to business; it is also relevant in the home, in school, in work and in the local community.' Discuss.

5. 'A person with a secure job doesn't have the worries of an entrepreneur.'

   (a) Why do some people prefer to have a job rather than be their own boss in business?

   (b) Why do some people prefer to be an entrepreneur rather than have a secure job?

6. May and Kevin Collins plan to open a boutique in Cork city.

   (a) Identify five enterprise skills that they might possess.

   (b) State two possible business opportunities that might arise for them.

   (c) Indicate three business risks of which they should be aware.

   (d) Identify three rewards they would be expected to receive by becoming entrepreneurs.

5 Management and Management Skills

Objectives

The following topics from **Unit 3** of the syllabus are covered in this chapter:

- What is Management?
- Management in Action
- Characteristics of Managers
- How Does Enterprise Differ from Management?
- Three Management Skills
  - Leading
  - Motivating
  - Communicating

What is Management?

The term management is usually associated with business management. In fact, it is required in all forms of organisations and organised activities, e.g.

1. In school – with the board of management.
2. In a football club – the club manager.
3. In a company – the managing director.
4. In the home – parents are the home managers.

Management will always be required where people work together to achieve some stated objective. The process of management involves bringing together all the resources available to an organisation in order to get the work done.

> Management Resources = People + Finance + Machinery + Materials

There is no one standard definition of management. The following is the definition of famous management people, Koontz and O'Donnell, in 1976.

> **➡ Definition of Management**
>
> *Management is an operational process which involves analysing the essential managerial functions of planning, organisation, staffing, directing and controlling.*

The work of management can be divided into management activities and management skills:

Management Activities	Management Skills
(a) Planning	(a) Leading
(b) Organising	(b) Motivating
(c) Controlling	(c) Communicating

Types of Business Manager

1. Sales Manager	Responsible for managing the sales department.
2. Distribution Manager	Responsible for managing the distribution department.

Types of Non-business Manager

1. School Principal	Responsible for managing the school.
2. Chairperson of a sports club	Responsible for running the club.

Characteristics of Managers

The successful manager is a good leader, who has a business instinct and can inspire others. Other characteristics of an effective manager include the following:

1. Good Organiser and Delegator

Arranging work in a simple and sensible manner is part of being a good organiser. In a large firm, every department must realise the importance of co-operating with other departments and with management. Effective organising requires a lot of co-operation. A particularly important trait for a good organiser is the ability to delegate work efficiently. This involves sharing out the workload in a fair manner.

Managers work:
- In business
- In Government
- In the local community
- At home
- At school

2. Decisive

It is not only important to be able to make fast decisions, but also to be consistent and to accept responsibility for the outcome of implementing decisions. A clear-thinking person is needed to manage a crisis. Such a person is a leader in business.

3. Hard Worker

Applying the necessary effort to every task and continuing when problems arise shows commitment to the job. This sets a good example for the employees.

4. High Standards

Attaining high standards involves having honesty in all dealings, always acting with integrity and showing support and loyalty to employees.

5. Human Relations

All employees should be treated fairly and with understanding. Staff problems should not be ignored; staff are an important element of the business.

6. Initiative

A manager's initiative causes him or her to act confidently and without prompt to lead the firm, encourage the staff and solve problems as they arise. This creates great confidence in the business.

7. Time Management

> **→ Definition of Time Management**
>
> *Time management involves making the most effective use of the time available to effectively complete a task.*

In business, **Time is Money** – if a job takes longer than it should, this is an additional cost to the business. Time cannot be replaced: once finished, it is gone forever.

(a) Time management involves the most effective use of the time available to complete a task. This is necessary in business in order that management time is not wasted.

(b) It involves the following:

  (i) Listing the tasks to be done in order of importance.

  (ii) Setting a 'time target' for each task and monitoring it regularly.

  (iii) Where necessary, delegating some tasks to others.

Benefits of Time Management to Business

(a) Effective time management will ensure that costs are controlled. This is necessary for business to be efficient and to have a competitive advantage.

(b) Poor and costly management decisions, due to work pressure, are avoided.

Management in Action

Managers are at work in many spheres of life, for example:

1. Business

> Starting up a business, ensuring the products are produced and sold, employing staff etc.

As the business expands, they must delegate work to other managers.

2. Government

> Administering Government Departments which provide services for the public.

Each Government Department is managed by a minister and civil servants. Each Department must ensure that the relevant Government policy is carried out.

3. In the Local Community

> Setting up a sports club.

This will involve setting up a committee, organising fund-raising activities, receiving subscriptions from members, operating a club bank account and monitoring the ongoing activities.

4. At Home

> Controlling the finance of the home.

This involves preparing the household budget for expenses and income. Decision making on spending is very important in the home.

5. At School

> Running the school.

For example, employing teachers, arranging the class timetable, communicating with teachers, pupils, parents and the Department of Education and Science. This is done by the Board of Management and school Principal.

How does Enterprise differ from Management?
(Higher Level Only)

Enterprise results from the generation of ideas from many sources. It includes the element of risk-taking. Some entrepreneurs may be very good at creating new ideas and raising the money to finance them, but they may not be capable of implementing them. They may have no interest in running a business or indeed lack the skills to do so. If this is the case, they employ managers to take over this responsibility.

   Management involves managing people, controlling resources and developing and implementing the ideas of entrepreneurs in an organised manner, i.e. converting the idea into a business reality. It involves setting targets and making decisions when required.

> Enterprise involves risk-taking – management involves less risk-taking.

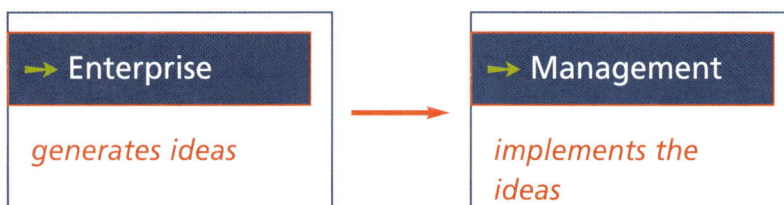

➡ Enterprise	➡ Management
generates ideas	*implements the ideas*

To be successful, a good manager must be enterprising enough to achieve the aims of the business.

> A good manager might not be a good entrepreneur.

Management Skills

A skill is the ability to carry out certain tasks in a highly efficient manner. Some people have natural skills, others acquire skills from training courses.

The following are the management skills required in business:

1.	Leadership	2.	Motivating	3.	Communicating

1. Leadership

> **→ Definition of Leadership**
>
> *Leadership has been defined as the means by which individuals or groups of people are persuaded to work towards the achievement of agreed objectives.*

A leader is a person who has the power to effectively exercise control over people. Leadership is practised, not so much in words, but in attitude and action.
  Businesses succeed where

  (a) The leaders are visible and their authority is accepted.

  (b) The leaders have a clear vision of the firm's aims and can communicate them to others.

  (c) Subordinates have clear objectives and adequate resources.

The effective manager 'leads from the front' and is able to get the rest of the management team and staff to follow by example. The level of real co-operation will depend on the style of leadership. The different styles of leadership are as follows:

  (a) Autocratic or Authoritarian (dictatorial)

  (b) Democratic

  (c) Laissez-Faire

A. Autocratic or Authoritarian Leadership
The characteristics of this type of leadership include the following:

  (i)   The manager does not discuss or consult with staff when giving instructions.

  (ii) The manager expects orders to be carried out immediately without questions. Employees do not question the 'boss' and just do what they are told.

  (iii) Communication in the business is one way – from the top down. The manager is the only person contributing to decision making.

  (iv) It is successful in the short term when the 'leader' is an expert in a specialised area.

Implications of Autocratic Leadership for a Business

    (i) Employees do not like a 'dictator' type of boss so in time their support will diminish.

   (ii) The boss cannot always be right, so the approach of not consulting with employees means that important opinions are not considered in decision making. In time, morale will decline and key employees may leave.

  (iii) From a buiness viewpint, the work is done quicker.

The autocratic style of leadership is not always appropriate in modern business. It is a style of leadership associated with the army or police force. Sometimes, however, this style has to be used in business.

B. Democratic Leadership

The characteristics of this type of leadership include the following:

    (i) It allows for and encourages workers to give their opinions and contribute to the decision-making process.

   (ii) By taking employees' views into account, it is a more inclusive form of leadership.

  (iii) It encourages a good atmosphere in the workplace, so job satisfaction and motivation levels are high.

  (iv) There will be a two-way system of communication in the business, i.e. management down to staff and staff up to management.

   (v) It encourages employees to become intrapreneurs.

Implications of Democratic Leadership for a Business

    (i) Consulting with the staff is time-consuming and a business opportunity may be lost due to a late decision.

   (ii) Trying to accommodate the viewpoints of employees may result in a poor final decision.

  (iii) It is good for staff morale, so output levels should be high.

C. Laissez-Faire (a French word for "Leave to Do")

The characteristics of this type of leadership include the following:

    (i) The main objectives of the business are made known to all the management and staff.

   (ii) It is up to the staff to organise their work and make decisions without checking with management.

  (iii) It is a non-interfering and non-involvement form of leadership.

  (iv) In the absence of clear directions and guidelines from the top, it is wrong to expect that correct decisions will always be made.

(v) Communication will be difficult in a business where this style of leadership (management) exists.

(vi) It is an unsuitable form of leadership in modern business because it leads to inconsistency and inefficiency.

This style of leadership would be appropriate in a multinational environmental firm where individuals are highly trained and self-directed, e.g. scientific researcher.

Delegating

Delegation involves getting subordinates to do work. In a large firm, the managing director will appoint people in charge of different areas of the business, i.e. a sales manager, an accountant, an R&D manager etc. Each manager is given the authority to run his or her department and will report directly to the managing director.

Delegation is very important. If a manager tries to do too much, there will be problems in the business. Abdication is not a form of delegation.

Delegation is essential in business for the following reasons:

(a) To ensure proper standards of work and efficiency.

(b) In some areas, specialists are required to do certain work, e.g. a computer operator.

(c) Delegation of authority gives managerial experience to subordinates. This is good management practice and allows for promotion from within when future vacancies arise; this is good for staff morale.

(d) It avoids the situation where management is overloaded with work.

ORGANISATION CHART IN BUSINESS

This chart provides information for both management and staff on the formal management structure of a business, e.g. Line Management.

LINE MANAGEMENT STRUCTURE OF A BUSINESS

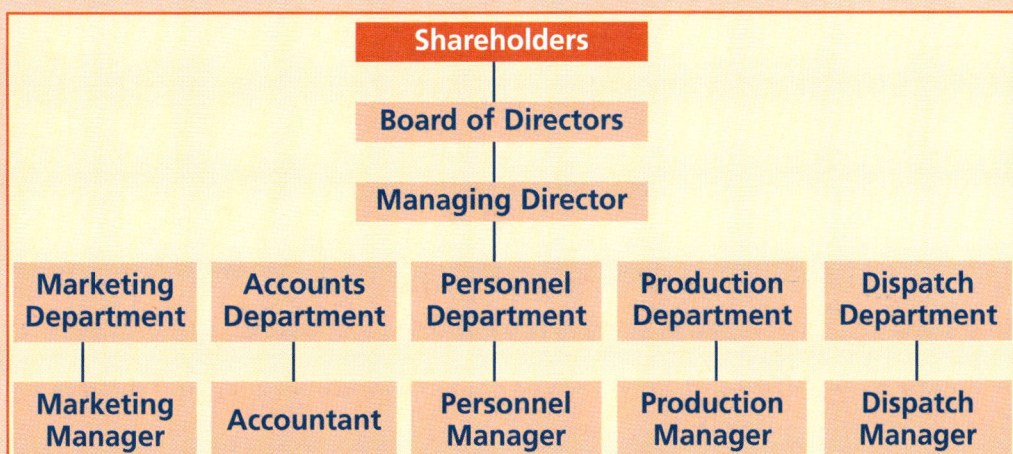

Shareholders
Board of Directors
Managing Director

Marketing Department	Accounts Department	Personnel Department	Production Department	Dispatch Department
Marketing Manager	Accountant	Personnel Manager	Production Manager	Dispatch Manager

Even though delegation is essential, it is only successful when there is authority, responsibility and accountability.

> ### AUTHORITY AND RESPONSIBILITY
>
> A manager can delegate authority but can never delegate ultimate responsibility. A manager must be careful in his/her attitude to delegation because, no matter what happens, the 'buck stops on the desk of the managing director'. The delegator should not be an absconder or an abdicator and should always follow up delegated work.
>
> ### ACCOUNTABILITY
>
> A department manager is responsible for the actions and performance of that department. Each 'sub-manager' must submit regular reports to the managing director. If results are not as good as expected, reasons must be stated, e.g. sales are 20 per cent below budget because of new competition.

2. Motivating

> ### ➡ Definition of Motivation
>
> *Motivation is the set of forces that cause people to behave in certain ways.*

Workers must be motivated to find their work interesting. This is necessary in order to ensure efficiency in the firm. Management need to develop good morale in the workplace. Morale reflects an employee's attitude towards work, colleagues and the employer.

High morale will exist in a firm under the following circumstances:

(a) When employees receive satisfaction from the work they do.

(b) When employees take pride in their work.

(c) When employees co-operate with and respect colleagues and superiors.

(d) When employees feel that they are part of the firm and are making a contribution to its success.

The biggest mistake a boss can make is not to say "well done" to employees.

A firm with high morale has a motivated and hard-working staff, so management will not have problems with absenteeism; productivity will be high and the firm will be as profitable as possible.

Non-Financial Motivation

Some people are motivated to work by more than just money. Once a satisfactory income is achieved, the wages are of secondary importance. The following are some of the non-financial factors that motivate people:

(a) Security of employment – employees in big firms have secure jobs.

(b) Status – some professions, e.g. medicine, have a greater status in the public eye than others.

(c) Aspiration – some employees are motivated by a desire to be promoted in the future.

(d) Praise – everybody likes praise and recognition for a job well done.

Theories of Motivation

(a) Maslow's Theory of Motivation

Abraham Maslow (1908–70) was a social scientist who published a book entitled *A Theory of Human Motivation.* Maslow believed that people in organisations were motivated by a tiered hierarchy of needs, i.e. from low needs to high needs. Low needs, essentials like food, shelter and safety, must be met before high needs, such as social acceptance or esteem, can be satisfied. He believed that every person had the same needs.

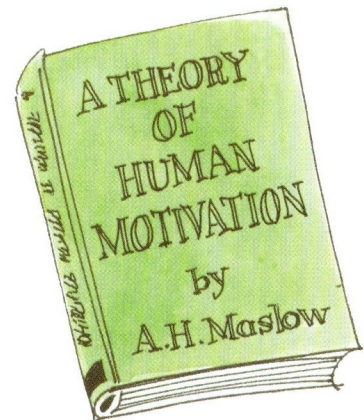

Maslow's Theory referred to the following:

(i) Every person has needs which must be satisfied. As a need is satisfied, it is no longer dominant and so another need becomes a motivating factor.

(ii) A person's needs are arranged in progressive levels – a hierarchy of relative importance.

(iii) A person's job can help to satisfy these needs.

(iv) The different needs are called the hierarchy of needs and include the following:

- Physiological needs (essential needs): food, drink, clothes, wages etc.

- Security needs: job security, employment contract, pension etc.

- Social needs: friendship, social club membership etc.

- Esteem needs: status – job title, promotion etc.

- Self-actualisation needs: being ambitious, being given more responsibility at work, becoming an entrepreneur etc.

Maslow's Hierarchy
of Needs

Organisational Example

Self-
actualisation
Needs
(Ambitions) → Challenging Job

Esteem
(Status) → Job Title

Social Needs
(Friendship, Acceptance) → Friends at Work

Safety/Security
(Job Security) → Pension Plan

Physiological Needs
(Food, Drink, Wages) → Basic Salary

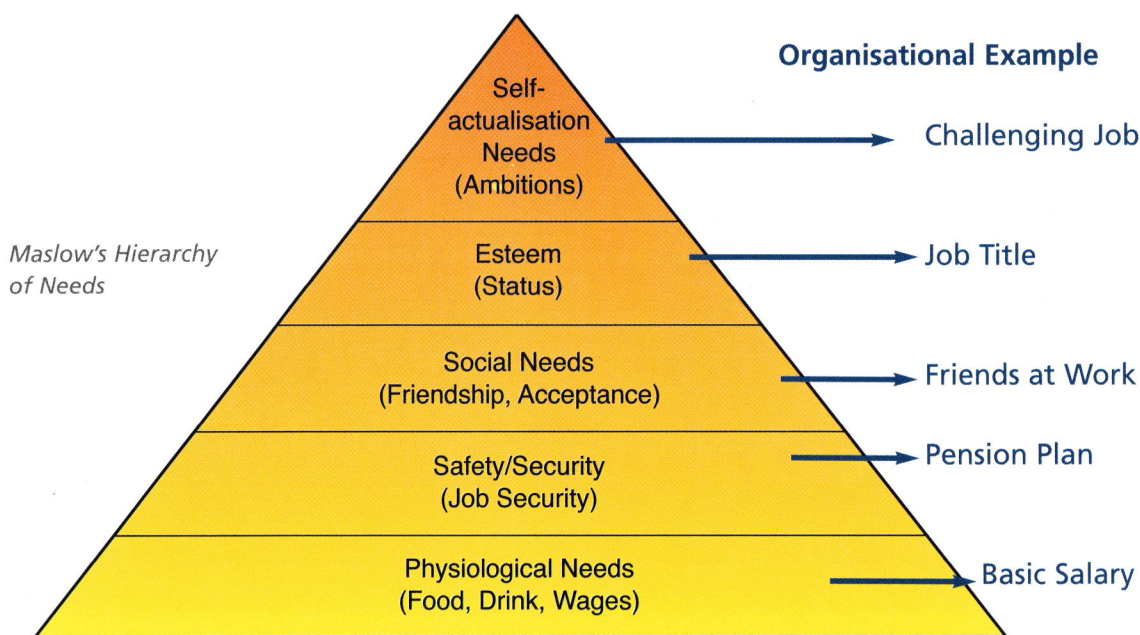

What are the Implications of Maslow's Theory and Findings for Business?
The implications are as follows:

(i) Once financial needs (wage levels) are satisfied, additional rewards will be sought in order to satisfy some higher needs, e.g. promotion to fulfil esteem needs.

(ii) Employees' attitudes and effort in work will be related to the success of management in satisfying their non-financial needs.

(iii) Morale will be low if the work is boring, regardless of the levels of pay. A firm with low morale will have problems with absenteeism. Efficiency levels will be low and profits will fall.

(b) McGregor's Theory X and Theory Y

Douglas McGregor (1906–64) was an American social psychologist and management consultant. He analysed the way in which employers and employees looked at work:

Employer: is the boss, pays the wages, gives instructions, doesn't like unions.
Employee: does the job, takes the wages, accepts no responsibility.

While managing different firms, he noticed two contrasting styles of management; these became known as Theory X and Theory Y. He claimed that large firms tend to be run based on one of these totally opposite approaches.

Theory X – Assumptions

(i) Most employees are lazy and will not work hard unless they are closely supervised – they don't like working.

(ii) Management must offer incentives, e.g. a bonus, to motivate the 'lazy' employees.

(iii) Most employees require safety and security needs as a priority.

(iv) Most employees lack ambition so they must be motivated to 'pull their weight' in the job.

(v) Most employees will resist changes in work practice and are easily influenced by others.

> **Theory X – McGregor**
> • Most employees are lazy.
> • Most workers lack ambition.
> • Most employees don't want change.

Theory X is associated with an autocratic style of management. The dictatorial style of boss will issue orders and expect them to be carried out without any reaction from the 'lazy', uninterested employees.

Theory Y – Assumptions

(i) Employees enjoy working and are willing to work and accept responsibility, as a result of a positive attitude adopted by management.

(ii) Employees are able to motivate themselves, so strict supervision is not required.

(iii) Satisfying the self-actualisation needs of individuals, e.g. giving them more responsibility and allowing them to work independently, is a very good way of getting them fully committed to their work.

(iv) All employees in a firm should receive suitable training so they can use their knowledge and initiative to solve problems which arise.

> **Theory Y – McGregor**
> • Workers enjoy working.
> • Workers can motivate themselves.
> • Training is important.
> • Workers' skills are not always maximised.

(v) The abilities of many employees are not fully used to the benefit of the firm – available talent, knowledge or aptitude is not fully utilised and so is a loss to the firm.

Theory Y is associated with a democratic style of management, which treats the employees in a proper manner, encourages them to get involved and contribute ideas and ensures that morale in the workplace is good.

Both Maslow and McGregor's theories are related to human relations. Maslow's theory is seen as the better one as it is a hierarchy of needs which is based on a series of human needs that range from the instinctive to the ambitious. His theory can be applied in practice to areas such as consumer behaviour and organisational behaviour.

Exercises

1. (a) What is management?

   (b) Name two types of business manager and two types of non-business manager.

   (c) The work of a manager is not confined to running a business. Outline the non-business areas in which managers are involved.

2. (a) 'A good manager is a good leader.' What are the characteristics of a good manager?

   (b) How does enterprise differ from management?

3. (a) State and outline three management skills.

   (b) Explain what is meant by delegation.

   (c) Why is delegation important in business?

4. (a) Outline Maslow's Theory of Motivation.

   (b) Do you think Maslow's Theory of Motivation is relevant to business today? Give two reasons for your answer.

5. (a) Outline McGregor's Theory X and Theory Y.

   (b) How do McGregor's Theory X and Theory Y differ from Maslow's Theory?

6. (a) Outline the various skills necessary for effective communication in business.

   (b) Illustrate how a person can be enterprising in a sports club.

7. Apply Maslow's Theory of Motivation to the following circumstances:

   (a) Part-time jobs in a supermarket.

   (b) Employees working in a high-tech plant.

6 Management Skills – Communicating

Objectives

The following topics from **Unit 3** of the syllabus are covered in this chapter:

- What is Communication?
- Effective Communication – Barriers to Effective Communication
- Which Medium of Communication Should be Used?
- Methods of Communication
- Types of Communication
- Meetings
- The Application of Communications in Business

What is Communication?

Communication is a two-way process which involves the transferring of information from one person to another in a manner which ensures that the receiver will understand the message from the sender. No business can be effectively run without an effective system of communication between management, staff, customers, suppliers, etc.

Communication Skills

The following four skills are essential for communication to be effective:

1. Listening – important so that information can be received.

2. Reading – important in order to know what information has been received.

3. Speaking – clarity of speech will make it possible for the message to be heard and understood.

4. Writing – in business it is important that letters, names, notices are written in a clear manner.

The Objectives of Communication

The four objectives of communication are as follows:

1. For the message to be received.

2. For the message to be understood.

3. For the message to be accepted.

4. To get a response, i.e. action.

Effective Communication

Effective communication is important for the efficient running of business. It is essential when doing business with suppliers and customers.
To be effective, communication requires the following:

1. A person who wishes to send the information.

2. A clear and concise message to be sent.

3. An appropriate medium for relaying the message, e.g. e-mail, phone, fax, etc.

4. A person to receive the information and keep a record of it, if necessary.

5. A response which indicates that the message has been received.

How can Good Communication in a Firm be Maintained and Improved?

Since communication is so important, it is essential that it be maintained and improved. This can be achieved by taking the following measures:

1. Ensuring that both management and staff are properly trained in the communication skills of listening, reading, writing and speaking.

2. Making sure that a welcoming and warm style of management exists. This will require confidence and openness from both management and staff.

3. Making sure that staff are motivated to work as a team. This is important since they are all working for the same employer.

4. Having regular contact between management and staff, e.g. briefing sessions.

5. Establishing agreed procedures and making sure that they are clearly explained and understood by both management and staff.

6. Always making sure that the most appropriate form of communication is used, e.g. confidential information for the managing director should be given orally.

Barriers to Effective Communication
What are they? How can they be overcome?

The barriers to effective communication are a threat to business. These barriers must be highlighted, so that steps can be taken to overcome them. The barriers to effective communication and some solutions to overcome them are as follows:

1. Language

The person giving the information should not use technical terms which the receiver may not understand, e.g. an accountant telling a client that his business is overtrading when the client does not know what this means.

Solution

The accountant should use simple terms that the client will understand.

2. Authority

Too many people may be giving instructions, perhaps contradicting each other.

Solution

A proper system of authority and delegation should exist. People will then understand who is in charge. The chain of command should be clear for all employees.

3. Noise

If people cannot clearly hear the oral message, then it is likely to be misinterpreted. This may lead to bad decisions being made.

Solution

Deliver the oral message when the listeners are silent and in a noise-free area.

4. Time

The receiver may not be given enough time to read/listen, understand and respond to the message from the sender.

Solution

The sender should not expect an immediate response. The receiver of the information should be given an adequate amount of time to fully understand the message and then give an appropriate answer.

5. Information Overload

A person may be receiving too many messages over a short time period. This can lead to confusion if the receiver is so busy that even important messages are not being responded to.

Solution

Reduce the volume of messages/queries being sent to the person, so that those being received will be dealt with effectively.

6. No Record

If important messages are not written, there may be no record of what was said. This situation may lead to future disagreements between the sender and the receiver of the information.

Solution

Make sure that a written record of important messages exists. This will avoid problems resulting from confusion over the information sent.

Implications of Bad Communication for a Firm

Ineffective communication can cause many problems, for example:

1. Poor industrial relations: caused by ineffective communication between management and unions. It can result in absenteeism, a go-slow by staff etc.

2. Bad public image: due to a failure to respond to queries from customers. This can lead to lost sales.

3. Lost sales: due to a stock shortage caused by failure on the part of the warehouse manager to inform the purchasing department that stock levels were low. This lack of teamwork is a sign of low morale.

4. Lost opportunities: caused by the failure of management and staff to have an effective system of communication.

Which Medium of Communication should be used?

The following factors should be considered before deciding which medium of communication to use.

1.	Urgency	How urgent is the information that has to be communicated?
2.	Efficiency	Are some forms of communication more efficient than others?
3.	Secrecy	How confidential is the information to both the sender and the receiver?
4.	Legal Requirements	Certain forms of communication must be in writing.
5.	Time	What time is it? This is important when telecommunicating to other countries, e.g. Australia.
6.	Cost	How much will it cost to communicate the information?
7.	Speed	How fast can the information be communicated to the receiver?
8.	Content	Is the information to be communicated good news or bad news, e.g. if a bank manager has decided to 'stop' a business cheque, how should the firm be informed?
9.	Technology	What technology is available to effectively transmit the information?
10.	To Whom	Is the information for internal or external use?

Methods of Communication in Business

Formal communication channels are those that are officially established, known and agreed by management. An organisational chart which shows the chain of command in business enables formal communication to take place.

Informal communication channels are commonly called the 'grapevine'. This form of communication is not liked by management as some of the information may be inaccurate and of a gossipy nature.

Internal Communication

This form of formal communication is normal in business, e.g. a management–staff meeting could only be internal. A memo on a notice board is only for internal use. The various forms of internal communication are as follows:

1.	Newsletter	7.	Intercom
2.	Telephone	8.	E-mail
3.	Notice Board	9.	Text Message
4.	Meeting	10.	Person to Person
5.	Memo	11.	Closed-circuit TV
6.	Suggestion Box	12.	Grapevine

External Communication

This form of communication is concerned with conveying information about the business to the public, suppliers and customers. The various forms include the following:

1.	Newspapers, national and local	6.	Intercom
2.	Radio and television	7.	E-mail
3.	Telephone	8.	Text Message
4.	Fax	9.	Person to Person
5.	Letter	10.	Closed-circuit TV

Types of Communication

The three main types of communication are as follows:

1.	Verbal Communication: the spoken word
2.	Written Communication: the written word
3.	Visual Communication: what is seen

1. Verbal Communication

This is a direct form of communication, e.g. one-to-one discussion, telephone discussion, a lecturer addressing a group of people or a sales manager discussing topics at a sales meeting.

Advantages of Verbal Communication

(a) It is regarded by many as the best means of communication. It gives both parties the opportunity to discuss the issues, examine documents, observe each other's attitude etc.

(b) It is possible to clarify and elaborate where necessary and mistakes can be rectified immediately.

(c) An agreement can be reached more quickly. This is especially true and important for a union negotiating an agreement on behalf of its members. An oral agreement can be reached to resolve an immediate problem.

Disadvantages of Verbal Communication

(a) It can be very time-consuming for management.

(b) No record of the communication exists for future proof or reference.

(c) A speaker may not be very convincing, so the impact of the message may be lost.

2. Written Communication

There are times when the information to be communicated should be in writing:

(a) To have a permanent record of what was said or agreed, e.g. a contract of employment must be in writing.

(b) To eliminate any misunderstanding over what was said – very important in matters involving conflict, discussions and agreement.

(c) If the receiver is located a long distance away, e.g. 100 miles.

(d) If the message is complex and requires careful interpretation.

(e) When it is standard practice in a business, e.g. orders and invoices should be in writing.

Short clear sentences are the key to effective written communication.

Summary of Written and Verbal Communication Methods	
Written	**Verbal**
Letter	Face-to-face conversation
Business document	Telephone
E-mail	Intercom
Computer print-out	Meeting
Fax	Public address system
Memo	Conference/Seminar
Report	Lecture/Presentation

3. Visual Communication

'One picture is worth ten thousand words'

In a large firm, management will have a lot of information on issues such as purchases, sales, profits, stock levels etc. It is normal practice to have this information presented, not only in writing, but also in a visual form, e.g. diagrams and charts.

Reasons for Presenting Information in Graphical Form

(a) By looking at a chart, people can immediately get a complete picture of the information under discussion.

(b) Information in graphical form adds weight when highlighting any point. Immediate action may be taken if a worrying trend is showing on a graph.

(c) Visual information can be absorbed faster than written information. It makes the message easier to understand.

(d) Some issues in business may be difficult to describe in writing but easy to illustrate. This is especially true where statistical information is involved.

(e) Graphs are sometimes used as a back-up to an oral or written presentation of information.

Different Forms of Presenting Visual Information

(a)	Bar chart	(e)	Histogram
(b)	Pie chart	(f)	Gannt chart
(c)	Pictogram	(g)	Break-even chart
(d)	Line Graph	(h)	Table

(a) Bar Chart

The main visual advantage of this type of chart is that it emphasises quantities. It is shown in the form of a column diagram. It has a good visual impact.

EXAMPLE

The following information is available from the sales manager of 'Rent a Video' store for January 2005:

Week 1   January 1–7   Number of videos rented   550
Week 2   January 8–14   Number of videos rented   280
Week 3   January 15–21   Number of videos rented   340
Week 4   January 22–28   Number of videos rented   250

You are required to illustrate the above information in a Bar Chart.

SOLUTION

Videos Rented during January 2005

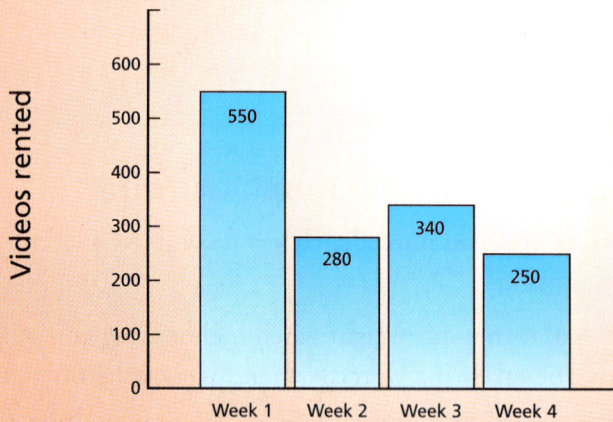

The number of videos rented out each week can clearly be seen on the Bar Chart. The trend is also clear, in particular, that most rentals occurred in the first week in January.

(b) Pie Chart

(i) This diagram is in the form of a circular pie (360 degrees).

(ii) It is divided into sectors which correspond in size to the different items being displayed so that comparisons can be made.

(iii) It has considerable visual impact because the message is visually clear.

(iv) It can be used to show the proportion of the total figure that relates to each component.

(v) Each section of the Pie Chart relates to the individual components' contribution to the total amount.

EXAMPLE 1

The following information relates to the cost of a unit of production in a manufacturing firm:

Cost Category	€
Materials	40
Wages	30
General Expenses	20
Profit	10
Selling Price	100

You are required to illustrate the above information in a Pie Chart.

SOLUTION

Unit cost of Production

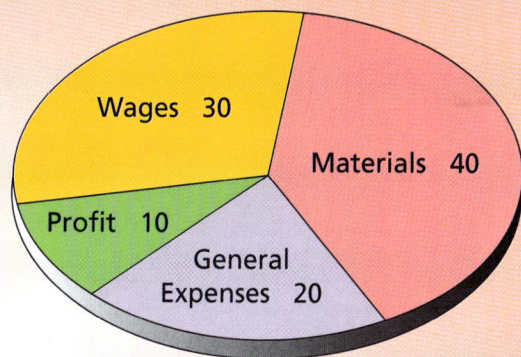

EXAMPLE 2

The following information was provided by the sales manager of a cleaning firm:

Province	No. of Customers
Connaught	100
Munster	200
Ulster	100
Leinster	600

You are required to illustrate the above information in a Pie Chart.

SOLUTION

Number of Customers

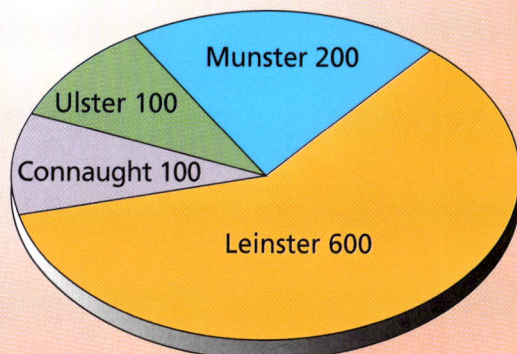

(c) Pictogram

(i)   This diagram is used to illustrate changes in the form of figures as shown in similar units (see diagram).

(ii) It is the representation of information using pictures and it shows trends and comparisons.

(iii) It is an effective way of presenting information once the information is in even numbers and can be calculated by a scale.

EXAMPLE 1

At a sales conference the following pictogram was presented.

Video Sales

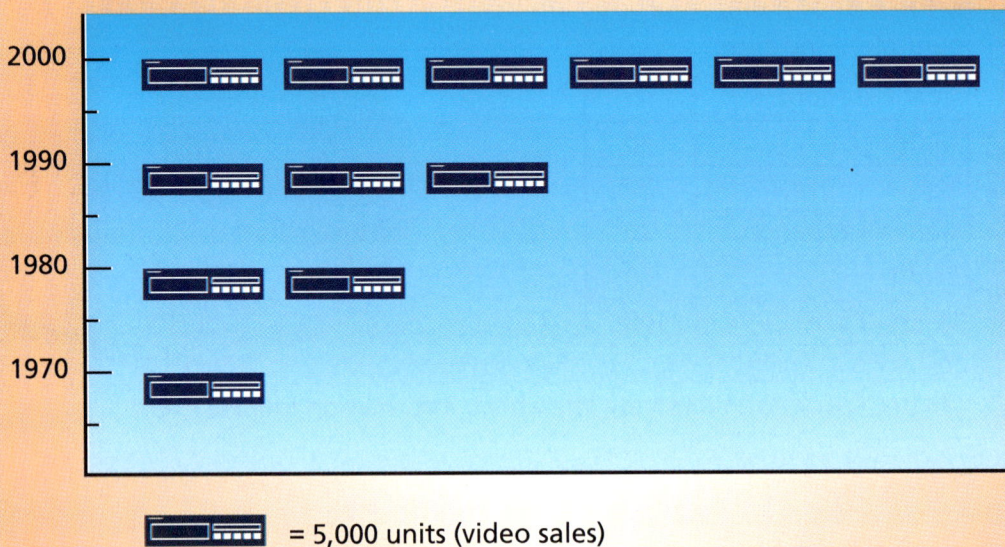

= 5,000 units (video sales)

Videos Sold

It is obvious from looking at the above pictogram that
(i)   5,000 videos were sold in 1970.
(ii)   The trend of sales since 1970 is improving.
(iii) 30,000 videos were sold in 2000.

(d) Line Graph

(i) The collected data is plotted against a vertical and horizontal axis.

(ii) It highlights trends so it is easy to make comparisons with different sets of figures.

EXAMPLE

The board of directors have requested the sales manager to illustrate the sales pattern for the decade 1990–99. The following table has been produced by the sales manager:

Year	1990	1991	1992	1993	1994	1995	1996	1997	1998	1999
Sales	100k	200k	250k	300k	400k	420k	400k	500k	700k	1 million

You are required to illustrate the above information in a Line Graph.

SOLUTION

By looking at this Line Graph, it is very easy to see the trend of sales over a 10-year period.

Sales 1990–1999

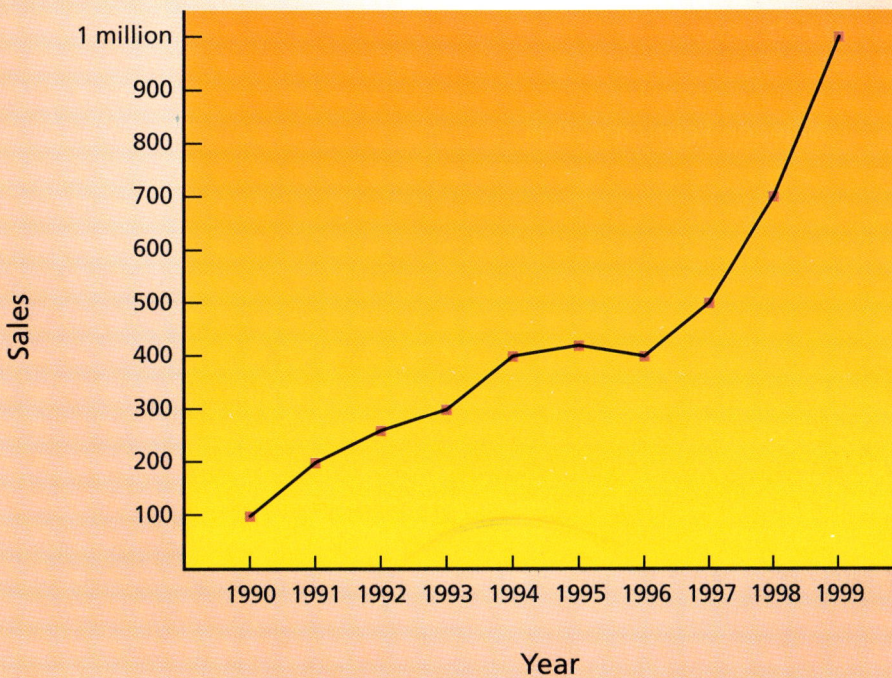

(e) Histogram

(i) Similar in layout to a bar chart but there are no gaps between the bars and only one topic is dealt with.

(ii) The diagram shows the frequency of occurrence of the one subject under discussion within clearly defined limits (called class limits).

EXAMPLE

The following table shows the mileage recorded by the firm's sales representatives during the month of February 2005:

Miles	Sales Reps
400–450	1
450–500	2
500–550	3
550–600	4
600–650	5

You are required to illustrate the above information in a Histogram.

SOLUTION

By looking at this histogram, it is very easy to see the trend of sales reps' mileage in February.

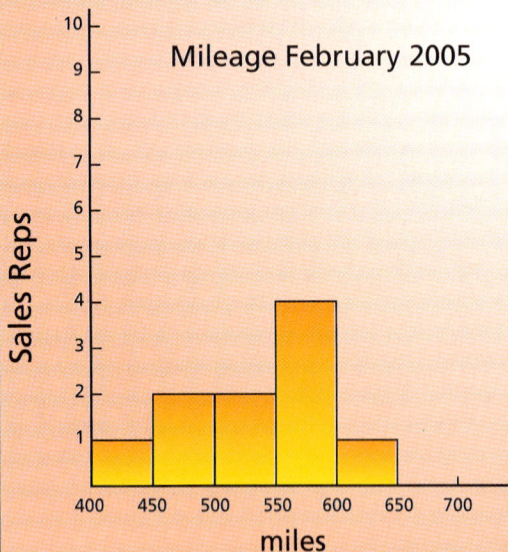

(f) Gannt Chart (also called a Progress Chart)

    (i) This chart is used to compare actual results against projected results (budget).

    (ii) It shows whether the results are on target.

EXAMPLE

The following are the projected and actual sales of a new project for the first three months.

	January	February	March
Projected	1,000	2,000	3,000
Actual	1,500	3,000	2,000

You are required to illustrate the above information in a Gannt Chart.

SOLUTION

Projected versus Actual Sales

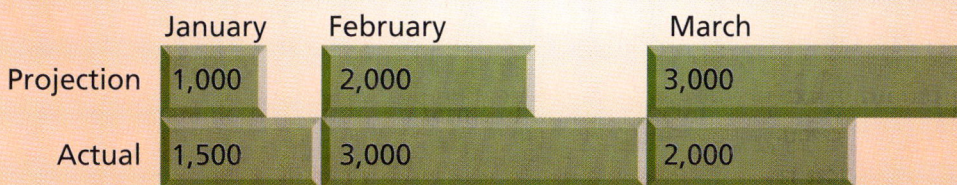

	January	February		March
Projection	1,000	2,000		3,000
Actual	1,500	3,000		2,000

(g) Break-Even Chart
(See Chapter 14 for an example of a Break-Even Chart)

    (i) This chart shows the level of output required to break even (B/E), i.e. when Revenue = Costs: when no profit is earned or loss incurred. This is the break-even point.

    (ii) Until the B/E point is reached, the firm is not making profit.

    (iii) It shows the relationship between outputs, revenue, costs and profits.

    (iv) B/E charts are widely used in business as management always want to know what sales level is required to break even.

Meetings

Meetings are very common as a means of communication. A meeting is defined as the coming together of at least two people for a lawful purpose. Meetings can involve small to large numbers of people congregating for different reasons, e.g. an AGM of a company, a club meeting and a union management meeting.

● The Reasons for Meetings

Meetings are held to achieve some or all of the following:

1. To give and receive information about a particular topic. This will enable those attending to clarify issues.
2. To bring experienced people together to discuss and solve a problem which has arisen.
3. To facilitate direct contact between a group of people. The group (employees, club members etc.) can be informed of some issue and their reactions can be assessed.
4. To develop greater co-operation between different departments in a business.
5. To make decisions regarding the future of a firm, e.g. board meetings.
6. To adhere to legal requirements, e.g. by law, every company must hold an AGM.

● Different Types of Meeting

1.	Statutory meeting	Every Public Limited Company (PLC) must hold a general meeting of all its shareholders within 13 months of the date of receiving the Trading Certificate. This is called a Statutory Meeting.
2.	Ad hoc meeting	This type of meeting is arranged to deal with a 'one-off' problem or situation. An ad hoc committee is formed and, upon completion of its specific work, it is disbanded.
3.	Annual general meeting (AGM)	Every company, club and organisation holds a special yearly meeting called the AGM, where members are entitled to attend and to speak and vote on issues under discussion.
4.	Formal meeting	Every company holds regular board meetings. These are formal meetings.

● The Agenda

This is a document sent by the secretary to all members/shareholders stating the topics to be discussed at a meeting and the order in which they will come. The Agenda is the programme (menu) for a meeting.

The Chairperson

If no one has the authority to act as a chairperson, the first thing that must be done at a meeting is to appoint someone.

Duties of a Chairperson
The duties of a chairperson include the following:
1. To act as a spokesperson for the firm, club etc., setting out its views/opinions to the general public.
2. To have a thorough knowledge of the rules governing the organisation, e.g. to be aware of the contents of the company's Memorandum and Articles of Association.
3. To invite, welcome, introduce and thank special guests who attend meetings.

Functions of a Chairperson
1. To ensure that his/her appointment is in order, i.e. that he/she was properly elected.
2. To see that the meeting was properly convened according to the rules of the organisation.
3. To ensure that a quorum is present before the meeting commences. A quorum is the minimum number of people (as stated in the rules) which must be present before a meeting can commence to discuss the items on the agenda.
4. To have the minutes of the previous meeting read by the secretary. If accepted, the minutes are proposed and adopted and signed by the chairperson.
5. To keep order at the meeting so as to allow each topic on the agenda to be discussed.
6. To allow speakers a reasonable time to make relevant contributions to the meeting.
7. To put motions to a vote and announce the results.
8. To bring the meeting to a close.

Characteristics of a Chairperson
A chairperson must ensure that a meeting is sensibly run and that the issues on the agenda are properly discussed. The characteristics of a chairperson include the following:
1. Totally impartial.
2. Firm in ensuring that the issues on the agenda are discussed in a relevant manner.
3. Able to delegate issues to committees.
4. Clear and accurate when making comments, announcing decisions etc.
5. Able to create the proper atmosphere at a meeting. This will have a positive impact on others present at the meeting.

The Secretary

The functions of the secretary include the following:

1. To call meetings, i.e. to arrange the meeting and to send the notice, agenda and relevant documentation to every person entitled to attend the meeting.

2. To read out the minutes of the previous meeting when requested to do so by the chairperson.

3. To read out any written correspondence received.

4. To take written notes at meetings and to write up the minutes afterwards.

5. To carry out certain legal requirements, e.g. a company secretary must ensure that changes in share ownership are properly recorded in the Companies Registration Office. The company secretary is also responsible for ensuring that the annual returns are submitted to the Registrar of Companies.

Characteristics of a Secretary

The characteristics of an efficient secretary of a meeting include the following:

1. Good organiser – both before and during the meeting.

2. Realises the importance of a speedy and accurate response to correspondence and queries received from members/shareholders etc.

3. Able to prepare different types of letters, reports, i.e., have accurate word-processing skills.

4. Understands the topics being discussed and is able to summarise.

The Treasurer

Every club and voluntary organisation has a treasurer whose job includes the following:

1. Keeping proper books of accounts, e.g. Cash Receipt Book to record subscriptions received from members and Cheque Payments Book to record all payments made.

2. Lodging all money received to the bank account.

3. Paying all the bills on behalf of the organisation.

4. Preparing a financial report for the AGM and providing copies of same for all the members.

Terms Associated with Meetings

1.	Standing Orders	The rules which exist for the conduct of meetings. If referred to at a meeting, it is usually to move a resolution that they be suspended.
2.	Motion	The topic under discussion at a meeting.
3.	Quorum	The minimum number of people which must be present before a meeting can commence.
4.	A Proxy	A person who is authorised to represent a shareholder at an AGM and to vote in accordance with the instructions given by the shareholder.
5.	In camera	Held in private: a meeting which the public and press are not allowed to attend.
6.	Voting by poll	Those entitled to vote must sign a form which has two headings, 'For' and 'Against' a motion.
7.	Voting by ballot	Each voter indicates a choice on a special paper, which is then put into a special ballot box. This is the voting procedure for a general election.
8.	Voting by a show of hands	Members are asked to vote by raising a hand. The teller or chairperson counts the votes and announces the result.

Annual General Meeting (AGM) of a Business

The reasons for holding the AGM of a company include the following:

1. To enable the board of directors to explain to the shareholders the financial position of the firm, the size of the profits and the amount of dividends to be proposed.

2. To meet the requirements of the law, i.e. the Companies Acts 1963–1999 require an AGM to be held.

3. To give the shareholders the opportunity to 'cross-examine' the directors regarding the firm's performance during the year.

4. To consider the auditor's report on the financial position of the company.

The company secretary should inform the shareholders about the AGM. The notice sent to the shareholders should contain the following:

1. The name of the company.

2. The venue for the meeting.

3. The date on which the meeting will be held.

4. The time that the meeting will begin.

5. The agenda for the meeting.

> A shareholder entitled to attend and vote is entitled to appoint a Proxy (who need not be a shareholder) to attend, speak and vote instead of him/her.

The following is an Agenda for the AGM of a private limited company:

Electrical Company Ltd

Notice of the Annual General Meeting of the Electrical Company Ltd.

Notice is hereby given that the tenth Annual General Meeting of the company will be held at the registered office of the company – 18 Main Street, Navan at 2 p.m. on 1 May 2005, for the following purposes:

(a) Minutes of the previous AGM.
(b) Matters arising from the minutes.
(c) Chairperson's report of the year.
(d) Auditor's report.
(e) Proposal of dividend to the shareholders.
(f) To appoint auditors for the following year.
(g) To elect two directors to replace J. Doyle and K. Moran, who are obliged to resign in accordance with the Articles of Association.
(h) To authorise the board of directors to fix the auditor's fees.
(i) To agree on directors' remuneration.
(j) A.O.B. (Any Other Business).

By Order of the Board
J. Treacy (Secretary)
J. Treacy

18 Main Street
Navan
4 April, 2005

The following is a sample Agenda of a club:

Notice of the Annual General Meeting of the Western Sports Club

Notice is hereby given that the third Annual General Meeting of the Western Sports Club will be held in the Clubhouse, Salthill, Galway at 7.30 p.m. on Sunday, 28 March 2005.

Agenda

1. Minutes of the AGM held in 2004 and matters arising from them.
2. Chairperson's report for the season.
3. Treasurer's report for the season.
4. Election of officers for the coming season.
5. Discussion on the size of the yearly subscription.
6. Amendments to Rule number 5, which prohibits people under 25 from joining the club.
7. A.O.B.

Matt Molloy
Matt Molloy (Secretary)

Here are the minutes of the AGM of the Electrical Company Ltd:

Electrical Company Ltd

Minutes of the AGM of the Electrical Company Ltd held on 1 May 2005 in the Registered Office, 18 Main Street, Navan.

Present: All directors, 50 shareholders and the auditor.

(a) The meeting commenced at 2.05 p.m. and the minutes of the 2004 AGM were read and adopted.

(b) Since there were no matters existing from the minutes they were signed by the chairperson, Bernard Hopkins.

(c) The chairperson, Bernard Hopkins, addressed the meeting. He expressed satisfaction at the financial position of the company and spoke with hope for future expansion by opening new branches in Donegal, Galway and Portlaoise. He forecast an increase in profits in the coming year and assured shareholders of the safety of their investment. He said that he expected the share price to increase by 60 per cent in the coming year.

(d) The auditor's report showed a profit after tax of €73,000.

(e) The directors proposed a dividend of 20 per cent and this was accepted by a majority of 4:1.

(f) The auditing firm of J. Carey & Co. was reappointed.

(g) P. Molloy and P. Gleeson were elected to the board of directors, replacing J. Doyle and K. Moran who retired in accordance with the Articles of Association.

(h) The board of directors was given the authority to agree a fee with the auditors.

(i) It was agreed to grant the directors an increase in directors' fees of 25 per cent.

(j) As there was no other business to be discussed, the chairperson brought the meeting to a close at 4.45 p.m.

J. Treacy
J. Treacy (Secretary)

The Application of Communications in Business

1.	Memorandum
2.	Report Writing
3.	Business Letters

1. Memorandum (Memo)

A memo is an important method of internal communication. It provides a written record of communication. The memo message should be kept short and it usually deals with only one item.

Why are Memos used?

(a) To convey information to the recipient, e.g. new instructions from the chief executive to the managing director.

Memo:
- Short
- Written
- Internal

(b) To circulate information to many people, e.g. memo to all staff about holidays from the managing director.

(c) To update people on developments relevant to the business, e.g. moving to a new location.

(d) To confirm information on an issue relevant to employees, e.g. holiday arrangements.

The style of a memo will vary a lot. A directive from the managing director to the managers will be written in formal, impersonal language, e.g. a memo regarding a staff bonus.

MEMO

To: All Staff
From: Niamh Burke, Managing Director
Date: 24 March 2004
Re: Staff Bonus

Each employee will be paid a bonus of €1,000 due to the success of the firm in receiving the Q Mark. The bonus will be included in the pay cheque due on 30 March.

Niamh Burke

2. Report Writing

A report is defined as a document in which some problem is examined for the purpose of finding out information, reporting findings, putting forward ideas and making recommendations if requested, e.g. the board of directors may ask the human resource manager to prepare a report as to the reasons why five key employees resigned.

Different Types of Reports

(a)	Individual Report
(b)	General Report

(a) Individual Report

This is an internal report and is produced by someone in authority, e.g. a sales report would be prepared by the sales manager.

(b) General Report

This is a formal report and may be for external publication. It is usually fairly detailed.

Rules of Report Writing

The rules of report writing are as follows:

A	Accuracy
B	Brevity
C	Clarity
D	Simplicity
E	Effectiveness

The Writing of Reports

The following points should be considered when writing a report:

(a) The purpose of the report.

(b) The terms of reference given to the report writer, i.e. the instructions given to the report writer by whoever commissioned the report.

(c) The report's recipient, i.e. who will receive and read the report?

(d) Timing, i.e. when is the final report required?

(e) Arranging the format of the final report.

(f) It must be signed by the report writer.

Benefits of Reports

(a) Reports present the conclusions of experts on the topics to be investigated.

(b) The conclusions and recommendations of a report serve as guidelines for future actions. Such actions can be justified on the basis of the report.

(c) Reports may highlight the causes of problems in a firm, so steps can be taken to ensure efficiency in the future. This will help a firm to achieve its objectives.

(d) Annual reports are a guide to directors and shareholders in decision-making.

(e) Reports can justify the causes of certain interest groups (minority or majority groups).

Formal Report Structure

In order to produce a good report the following points should be considered by the report writer:

(a)	Title	There should be a proper title on the report. The title should clearly indicate the subject matter of the report, e.g. export sales.
(b)	Names	The names of the report writers should be listed.
(c)	Who is the Report for?	The report should state the person(s) for whom the report is intended, e.g. the board of directors.
(d)	Table of Contents	The contents should indicate the various sections and chapter headings in the report and the corresponding page numbers.
(e)	Terms of Reference	These are the instructions given to the report writer by those instigating the report.
(f)	Introduction	This should state the objectives of the report, the problems to be solved and the assumptions made by the report writer.
(g)	Body of Report	This contains the facts, i.e. the various sections and chapters in the report and its findings.
(h)	Recommendations	The report writer must ensure that any recommendations made are relevant to the facts available.
(i)	Acknowledgements	This includes people who helped the report writer with information for the report.
(j)	Appendices	These contain statistical data, definitions of technical terms and copies of relevant documents and photographs.
(k)	Summary and Conclusions	This section should contain the following: (i) A brief summary of the contents of the main section. (ii) A summary restating the conclusions and recommendations. It should also state what action should be taken based on the recommendations and by whom.
(l)	Index	Laid out in alphabetical order, this contains important words, terms and phrases and their relevant page numbers.

Example of a Formal Report

The Board of Directors of Cosmetic Products Ltd have requested the managing director to prepare a formal report on the benefits and challenges to the business from installing information technology (IT) applications.

REPORT FROM THE MANAGING DIRECTOR TO THE BOARD OF DIRECTORS

Title: Report on the benefits and challenges of installing IT applications in the company.

From: Sheila Collins, Managing Director

To: Board of Directors of Cosmetic Products Ltd

Terms of Reference: To prepare a report on the benefits and challenges to the business of installing IT applications

Date: 1 May 2005

Table of Contents: Section A: Terms of Reference, Page 3
Section B: Summary, Page 4–7

Body of Report:
The benefits include the following:
1. It will speed up the downloading of information from IT network.
2. It will facilitate the use of e-mail for internal communication with management and staff and for external communication with suppliers and customers.
3. It will speed up the payroll system in the business.
4. There will be greater accuracy and speed in keeping customer records.
5. Advertising on the Internet will help increase sales and profits.
6. If all employees acquire IT skills, then fewer clerical staff will be required.

The challenges include the following:
1. Major capital expenditure costs will have to be incurred in the provision of hardware and software.
2. A major programme for IT training for staff will have to take place.
3. Less middle management will be required. This will lead to seven redundancies at an estimated cost of €100,000.
4. A specialist IT person will have to be employed to provide back-up support and maintenance.

Recommendation:
Since the firm is in a very competitive industry, it is essential to invest in the most modern IT applications.

3. Business Letters

Apart from using a firm's products or services and reading advertisements, the only direct and individual contact some people have with a firm is a business letter. The main objective of a letter is to convey a message, e.g. complaint, apology or enquiry.

The important points to keep in mind when writing letters are as follows:

(a) Be clearly focused on the message to be conveyed in the letter.

(b) Keep in mind the position of the receiver of the letter and how that person will respond or react.

(c) The letter is a written and permanent record, so take care that the contents are accurate, clear and fair.

(d) Since some people don't like to receive long letters, make the letter as brief as possible so that it will achieve the following:

(i)	Attention	Immediately capture the reader's attention.
(ii)	Interest	Make the receiver interested in the information/message in the letter.
(iii)	Desire	Immediately create a desire in the reader's mind to enquire more about what is being read.
(iv)	Action	Ensure that the reader will know what steps or action to take.

The Structure and Layout of a Business Letter

Business letters are usually written on stationery with a printed letterhead. The layout is as follows:

(a) The heading which shows the name, address, telephone, fax and e-mail address of the company, e.g.

Folens
Hibernian Industrial Estate
Greenhills Road
Tallaght
Dublin 24
Ireland

Folens
Publishers

Phone: 01 4137200 **Fax**: *Sales*: 01 4137282 *Accounts*: 01 4137274 *Editorial*: 01 4137276 *Management*: 01 4137280 **E-mail**: info@folens.ie

(b) The date on which the letter is written.

(c) The salutation, e.g. Dear Sir.

(d) The opening paragraphs. These should state the subject matter of the letter. A short opening sentence will usually attract the attention of the reader, e.g. I regret ...

(e) The closing paragraph. This should be short and bring the letter to an end.

(f) The close, e.g. Yours sincerely.

(g) The signature and title of the sender, e.g. Maureen McConigley, Managing Director.

Example of a Business Letter

Draft a letter to the Human Resource Manager of Euro Services Ltd, Raheny, Dublin 5, setting out four characteristics which an interviewer looks for in candidates applying for management positions.

21 Baker Street
Templeogue
Dublin 16

Phone (01) 4943 425
5 September 2005

Human Resource Manager
Euro Services ltd,
Raheny,
Dublin 5.

Dear Ms Smith,

The following characteristics are essential in candidates for management positions:

1. **Self–Confidence:**
A person who is indecisive would be unsuitable if difficult decisions have to be made.

2. **Human Relations:**
It is important that the new manager is comfortable working with people. This person must be able to listen to subordinates, rather than always dictate to them.

3. **Initiative:**
A person with initiative will always 'bring something extra' to the job. Having the ability to show leadership qualities will have spin-off benefits on others in the business.

4. **Delegation:**
A good delegator will realise the importance of recognising the ability of others to perform certain tasks.

Yours sincerely,
Deirdre Brennan

Deirdre Brennan

Revision of Important Terms		
• Communication	• Break-even Chart	• Club Treasurer
• Barriers to Communication	• Histogram	• A Proxy
• Internal Communication	• Gannt Chart	• Memo
• External Communication	• Ad Hoc Meeting	• Minutes
• Visual Communication	• Agenda	• Report Writing
• Bar Chart	• Chairperson	
• Pie Chart	• Secretary	

Exercises

1. (a) What is meant by communication?

   (b) 'Effective communication is essential in business.' How can good communication in a firm be achieved?

2. (a) What are the barriers to effective communication in business?

   (b) How can these barriers be overcome?

3. (a) Outline the factors to be considered before deciding which medium of communication to use.

   (b) Using examples, distinguish between internal and external means of communication.

4. Oral, written and visual are the three main types of communication.

   (a) Outline the benefits of oral communication.

   (b) When is written communication suitable in business?

   (c) Why is information sometimes presented in a visual form?

5. Using an example in each case, describe the following methods of presenting information:

   (a) Pie Chart (b) Pictogram (c) Bar Chart

6. (a) Why are meetings an important form of communication?

   (b) Explain each of the following terms: (i) Agenda (ii) Ad Hoc Meeting
       (iii) Minutes of a Meeting

7. (a) Outline the duties and functions of a chairperson at a meeting.

   (b) Discuss the functions of each of the following:
       (i) The secretary of a social club (ii) The treasurer of a social club

8. (a) Draft a memo to all department managers changing the day and time for the
       weekly managers' meeting from Monday at 10 a.m. to Friday at 11 a.m.

   (b) Why are memos used as a form of internal communication?

9. (a) Outline the structure of a report.

   (b) What factors should be considered when writing a report?

10. Draft a report from the sales manager to the board of directors outlining the
    potential benefits to the firm of developing an export market.

11. Draft a letter from the sales manager to the firm's customers informing them of a
    price increase in the firm's product of 10 per cent.

12. The AGM of the Connaught Hockey Club is due to be held on 18 December.

    (a) You are required to draft a suitable agenda for the AGM to send to the club
        members. The agenda should contain six items for discussion at the meeting.

    (b) Write up the minutes of the AGM.

13. (a) Draft the notice of the agenda of the AGM of Patricia Hogan Ltd. It should
        contain six items.

    (b) Write up the minutes of the AGM.

14. (a) State four duties of a secretary at the AGM of a sports club.

    (b) How does a memo differ from a business letter?

    (c) State three barriers to effective communication in business. How can each
        barrier (problem) be solved?

15. The following information relates to the cost of a unit of production in a firm:

Materials used in production	€100
Wages	€60
General Expenses	€40
Profit	€100
Selling Price	€300

(a) Illustrate the above information in the form of a Pie Chart.

(b) Why is a Pie Chart suitable for showing information in visual form?

16. The following information is available from the accounts of Reading Books Ltd:

Product	Books	Magazines	Newspapers	CDs	Tapes	Sundries
Sales €	30,000	15,000	10,000	7,000	5,000	3,000

Show how the above information can be presented:

(a) In a Pie Chart   (b) In a Bar Chart

Why is a Bar Chart suitable for showing information in visual form?

17. The following net profit figures are available from the accounts of Fashion Boutique Ltd:

Year	2004	2003	2002	2001	2000
Net Profit	€60,000	€50,000	€40,000	€35,000	€25,000

Illustrate the above information using a Bar Chart.

18. Sean Smith is a car dealer selling new and used cars. The number of cars sold for the first six months of 2004 are given below:

Month	Cars Sold
January	20
February	18
March	16
April	17
May	15
June	10

Illustrate the car sales figures in a histogram.

7 Management Activities

Objectives

The following topics from **Unit 3** of the syllabus are covered in this chapter:

- Management Activities
  - Tactical, Strategic, Operational
- Organising
  - Line Authority, Staffing, Span of Control
- Controlling
  - Stock Control, Credit Control, Quality Control, Financial Control

Management Activities

The management activities involved in running a business are as follows:

1.	Planning
2.	Organising
3.	Controlling

1. Planning

→ **Definition of Planning**

Planning is the process of deciding the objectives of the business and how they are going to be effectively achieved.

What is Planning?

- A plan is a predetermined course of action.
- In business, a manager prepares a plan and then chooses the best way to operate the business and achieve the aims of the plan.
- Setting a sales target is a form of planning in business. If the sales target is reached, the plan has worked. If the sales target is not reached, it is important to find out why, e.g. absenteeism of employees, poor quality goods, new competition, etc.

Is Business Planning Necessary?

In today's competitive business world, planning is of crucial importance. If a business does not plan, it will not survive. Many firms have failed in the past because of poor planning. Fatal errors were made in many areas, for example:

Planning is essential if business is to be efficient.

- Over-estimating the size of the potential market.
- Poor location of the business.
- Failing to react to market trends influenced by competitors or new legislation.
- Poor management.

Planning is necessary if firms are to be prepared to react to changes that affect business. These changes include the following:

(a) Business operates in a **dynamic environment** with ongoing changes occurring.

(b) Firms must keep up to date with **changes in technology**. If not, competitors who have will increase their market share. Modern technology has led to the mass production of some goods. This lowers the unit cost of production, e.g. the Biro pen can be produced in Hong Kong 50 per cent cheaper than in England.

(c) It is important to make decisions based on **consumer patterns** of spending. For example, there is now a large increase in the use of branded and pre-packed goods. Every firm must plan in order to satisfy customer requirements.

(d) Business has become very competitive. Planning is a vital tool which can be used to sustain market share and assist the business to react to **new challenges from competitors**, i.e. plan for the future, not the present.

(e) Staff must be trained if the firm's efficiency is to be maintained. **Training** is a form of planning which increases the firm's attractiveness to customers. Ongoing staff planning must take place in order to update employees' skills.

Benefits of Business Planning

(a) When planning, it is necessary to take stock of all resources available to the firm. By doing so, weaknesses become apparent and steps can be taken to remedy them, thus making the business competitive.

(b) If all the management and staff are given an input in the business plan, the final plan will have everyone's full support.

(c) Involving the workers in the plan will give them greater knowledge of their place in the firm and will help them understand the importance of their contribution.

> Planning ensures that the scarce resources available to an organisation are effectively used.

(d) Planning helps to create positive thinking amongst the employees. They are more willing to accept change, which in turn leads to greater efficiency for the firm.

(e) The existence of a business plan will streamline the operation of a business.

(f) Planning is necessary to qualify for bank, Government and EU loans.

(g) If plans are accurate, sales and profits should be on target with projections.

Principles of Planning

    (a) All plans must be based on definite agreed **objectives,** i.e. identify the goals of management for the firm.

    (b) The plans must be **precise** and easy to understand – eliminating the possibility of misinterpretation.

    (c) It must be possible to **achieve** the plan, otherwise employees will be frustrated and inefficiency will arise. In other words, the plan must be sensible and realistic.

    (d) The plan must be **flexible** enough to allow for unexpected changes where necessary. It may be necessary to make changes to the plan because of changing circumstances.

> **Keywords for Planning:**
> - Objectives
> - Precise
> - Achieve
> - Flexible
> - Control
> - Communication

    (e) The plan should include **control** procedures, so that performance can be checked against the projected standard, thus ensuring that proper standards are reached.

    (f) There must be proper **communication** with those involved in operating the plan.

Types of Planning

    (a) Tactical Planning or Functional Planning

    (b) Strategic Planning

    (c) Operational Planning

(a) Tactical Planning or Functional Planning

This is short-term planning (for one or two years) and is designed to achieve some stated short-term goals, for example:

- Developing an export sales market to test reaction to the firm's existing products.

- Achieving a certain profit figure.

- Financing the purchase of stock by 'leaning on the trade', i.e. using creditors and insisting on 60 days' credit.

> *A tactical plan is short-term.*
> *A strategic plan is long-term.*

(b) Strategic Planning

A strategy is a means used to achieve an end. It is not just any plan but is unified, comprehensive, integrated and covers all parts of the business.

This involves long-term planning (two to six years). Such plans are called corporate plans as they include all activities of the firm, for example:

- The Marketing Plan

- The Production Plan

- The Human Resource Plan

Strategic planning is important for coping with both internal and external changes. Strategic plans are formulated by the board of directors and implemented by the managing director and the management team.

Most firms tend to set long-term objectives in the following areas:

(i)   Profit

(ii) Market share

(iii) Sales

(iv) Capital expenditure (e.g. new machinery)

(v)   Diversification

An effective strategic plan does three things:

(i)   It assesses the strengths and weaknesses both inside and outside the firm.

(ii) It identifies key trends and opportunities for the business.

(iii) It makes clear decisions which are definite about what, how and when things are to be done.

Issues involved in Strategic Planning

(i)   It is necessary to clarify the long-term objective of the business. This is called the firm's Mission Statement, i.e. what the business was set up to achieve. It includes some 'company goals' as a means of giving more detail to explain and clarify the mission.

➡ **Mission Statement**

Defining the Mission of an organisation is the starting point for all planning. The Mission Statement is the reason why an organisation exists, i.e. why a business was set up – what it hopes to achieve. The Mission Statement is a statement of intent by a business. It provides a vision for the future direction, a sense of purpose for the firm's existence. It does not indicate how the aims will be achieved.

(ii) The internal analysis of a firm should examine the following areas:

Finance	How much internal finance will be available and how much is required?
Financial targets	Existing sales and profit levels should be assessed to assist in finding budgeted figures for the future.
Premises and plant equipment	Is the existing capacity adequate for future expansion?
Research and development	Is the current level of R&D adequate? Are changes required for the future?

(iii) The external analysis of a firm should examine the following areas:

Macroeconomic trends	Economic, social, demographic and lifestyle trends that affect the business need to be studied.
Financial targets	What are they doing in areas such as new products, selling prices etc.?
Advances in technology	Are competitors more advanced in the area of technological development?
Legislation	What impact will new legislation have on the business? For example, legislation banning smoking in pubs, hotels, etc. has resulted in a sales decline for cigarette companies.

Benefits of Strategic Planning

(i) It offers guidance to management and staff in coping with the future.

(ii) It enables management to be more alert to changes, threats and opportunities.

(iii) It allows for a better allocation of resources within the firm.

(iv) It unifies decision making across the organisation.

SWOT Analysis

A SWOT analysis is a vital part of strategic planning.

> The objective of a SWOT analysis is to enable a firm to profitably avail of possible future opportunities.

➡ SWOT ANALYSIS

INTERNAL
Strengths (Positive)
Weaknesses (Negative)

EXTERNAL
Opportunities (Positive)
Threats (Negative)

A firm should see its strengths and weaknesses as being part of the current situation and opportunities and threats as being part of the future. A SWOT analysis examines the internal strengths and weaknesses and the external opportunities and threats (risks). Many Japanese businesses believe in doing a SOT analysis as they claim that they have no weaknesses.

They pursue a policy of Total Quality Management (TQM). A firm should consider the following:

1. Strengths	• Location of business • Good product • Skills of employees	• Top management • Up-to-date technology • Modern selling techniques
2. Weaknesses	• Giving too much credit • Cash flow problems • Obsolete production methods	• No future plans • Poor management skills • No marketing strategy
3. Opportunities	• Scope for expansion into new market (exports) • New products to meet changing demands of customers • To diversify into a different type of business	
4. Threats	• Competition due to free trade • New consumer laws	• New marketing inventions, e.g. Internet

This analysis is important because it should be considered by a firm in order to maximise its ability to compete and achieve its main objective – profit.

The business strategy for the future should involve building on strengths, eliminating weaknesses that make the business vulnerable, availing of new opportunities and taking steps to reduce future threats.

Multinational firms commonly refer to the SWOT as their Planning Balance Sheet.

(c) Operational Planning

This is short-term and involves planning for the weeks and months ahead, e.g. weekly sales forecasts and monthly budgets.

Policies

The policies of a firm are the means by which a firm hopes to achieve its objectives. The policy of a business is formulated by:

(i) The board of directors, who decide the main policies.

(ii) The managing director, who is responsible for implementing the decisions of the board of directors.

(iii) External influences such as Government legislation or EU directives which could force a change in company policy.

A firm may have the following policies:

(i) Dividend Policy	How much of the profits are to be paid in dividends? It is a function of the board of directors to make a recommendation to the shareholders at the AGM.
(ii) Marketing Policy	What level of credit is to be given to customers and what selling price is to be charged (more or less than competitors)?
(iii) Capital Expenditure Policy	How is new machinery to be paid for, e.g. borrowed, leased or paid for from the business resources?
(iv) Stock Level Policy	Are stock levels to be kept at maximum or minimum levels?

2. Organising

> **Definition of Organising**

Organising involves ensuring that there is a clear structure within the firm to facilitate the smooth running of the business, e.g. a simple organisational (management) structure should be in place.

Unless there is proper organisation within a large firm, there will be chaos. It is necessary to have a management structure in every firm for the following reasons:

(a) To identify all the tasks that have to be done.

(b) To ensure that the necessary financial and human resources are made available to carry out the tasks.

(c) To ensure that the firm is efficiently run.

The Structure of Organisations

The formal structure is developed in order to enable an organisation to organise its activities so that it can be efficiently run. The following organisational chart shows the line management structure in a large company:

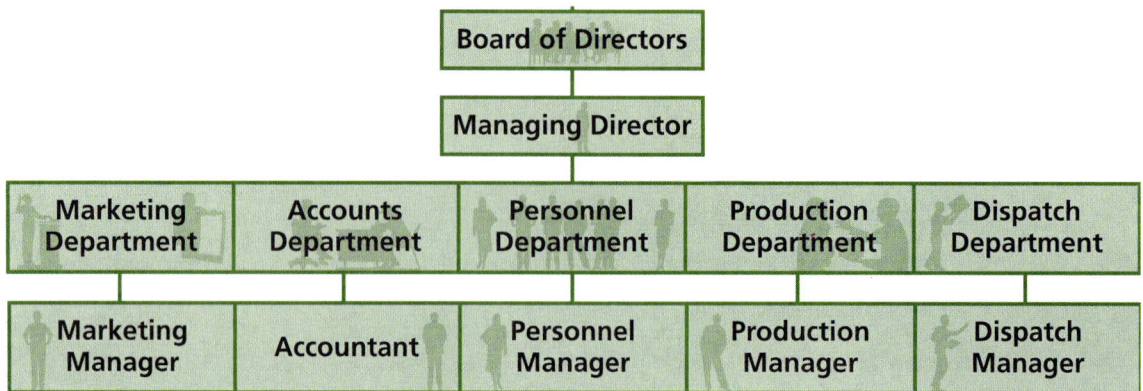

Line Management

Line Authority and Responsibility

   (a) The above organisational chart shows the chain of command in the firm, i.e. how authority is organised.

   (b) The board of directors appoints the managing director, who is responsible for setting up the various departments and appointing a manager to each department.

   (c) This structure is called a 'line relationship'. It can be seen on the chart that the managing director has authority over each department below him/her.

   (d) Each department on the horizontal line should co-operate with the others. No one department in the line has authority over another department – they are all on the same level.

Benefits of a Line Organisation

The benefits of a line organisation structure in a big firm include the following:

   (a) It makes it possible to manage the firm efficiently since all responsibilities are clarified.

   (b) It eliminates bottlenecks and communication problems.

   (c) It prevents management from being overloaded.

   (d) The management structure is easy to understand. Employees in each department know that they are responsible to their line manager.

> *Line organisation helps to prevent management from being overloaded.*

Line and Staff Authority

Both line and staff are terms which describe the type of relationship that exists between management and staff.

Line authority shows the authority that a manager would have over a subordinate, e.g. sales manager over a sales person.

Staff authority shows what function a manager has with other departments, e.g. a new IT department would provide advice to all line departments.

Staffing

Efficient staff are essential for the smooth running and progress of every firm. In a large firm the human resource manager will play an important role in this area. It is essential that skilled staff be employed and, where possible, promotional vacancies should be filled from within the firm.

Span of Control (also called Span of Management)

The span of control relates to the number of subordinates who report to one supervisor or manager. If a manager has responsibility for ten subordinates, then the span of control is ten. The size of the span of control will vary from firm to firm. In many firms, there is less middle management, so the span of control is wider. In practice, the average number is between four and sixteen.

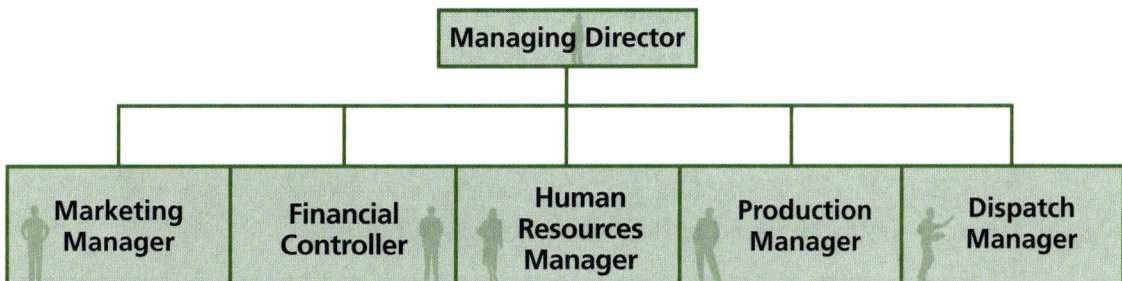

In this example, the span of control is five.

Factors that affect the size of the span of control include the following:

(a)	The type of work	If the job is simple, the span of control can be wide. If the job is difficult and requires skill and expertise, the span of control should be small.
(b)	The expertise of the manager	A skilful manager will be able to supervise a large number of employees.
(c)	The ability of the employees	If the employees are skilled and motivated, a large span of control is possible.
(d)	The nature of the product	If a firm is producing high cost and high quality products, then a small span of control may be appropriate.

3. Controlling

> → **Definition of Controlling**
>
> *Controlling is a management activity that involves measuring performances to make sure the required standards are being reached.*

If there are deviations from the required standards, then corrective action must be taken.

Principles of Effective Control

The principles of effective control include the following:

(a) Controls must be set up according to the nature of the job to be carried out, e.g. budgets, profit ratios.

(b) It must be possible to measure and record the actual output and this must be compared to the expected output.

(c) All deviations, no matter how small, must be recorded and reported immediately to the manager in charge. He/she must take appropriate action to identify and eliminate the cause of the deviation, e.g. are the increases in wage costs caused by unplanned overtime? If so, the reason for this overtime should be investigated.

Enterprise Controls

Controls should be found in the following areas of business:

Finance	Profits must be checked and the cash flow of the firm must be monitored.
Production	Output levels, quality and wastage must be monitored.
Marketing	Cost of sales, level of credit to customers and number of complaints must be monitored.
Human Resources	A firm with a high labour turnover (staff leaving) or a high level of absenteeism should investigate the reasons for such problems.
Stocks	A firm should have a policy on stock levels and any deviation should be brought to the attention of the purchasing manager.

Stock Control (Inventory Control)

The objective of stock control is to ensure that stock levels are adequate to meet the needs of customers, while at the same time keeping them to a minimum. This reduces storage and administration costs.

Stock Control involves controlling stock levels, maximum or minimum.

Different firms have different policies on stock levels:

- Maximum stock levels
- Minimum stock levels

Wholesalers carry large stocks of goods in their warehouses. This is necessary due to the wide range of goods required by traders and also the necessity to 'bulk buy' to obtain big discounts from manufacturers.

Cost of Carrying Stock

The cost of holding high stock levels:

(a) Money tied up in the stock is not available for alternative uses, such as earning interest in a deposit account.

(b) Valuable storage space, security and insurance must be maintained.

(c) There is a greater risk of some stock becoming stale and unsaleable.

The cost of understocking, i.e. out-of-stock costs:

(a) Sales to customers who will not wait for the goods to arrive will be lost.

(b) Profits will be lost due to the empty space.

(c) Future sales may be lost if some customers lose confidence in the firm and trade with competitors instead.

(d) Idle space in the warehouse still incurs costs, e.g. security.

Minimum Stock Level

This is the level below which stock levels should not fall. Buffer Stock is the name given to the minimum level to which stocks should fall.

The following factors should be considered when deciding on a policy of minimum stock levels:

(a) The lead time, i.e. the normal time allowed for delivery by the supplier. The shorter the lead time, the easier it is to keep stock levels low.

(b) How easy is it to obtain supplies? If there are several potential suppliers, then there is no need to have big stock levels.

> ➡ LEAD TIME
>
> *Normal delivery time by the supplier – it is important to know how reliable it is.*

(c) The storage space available. If it is small, then the firm may have no option but to operate with small stock levels.

(d) The level of normal sales. If low, then there is no need to carry big stock levels.

(e) The nature of the product in question. For example, fashions change on a regular basis, so it may be unwise for a retail fashion store to carry large stocks.

Just-In-Time (JIT)

From the viewpoint of a production manager, this means making goods to order just before they are required. Goods are ordered a short time before they are required, i.e. a short lead time. This avoids the cost of having to carry high stock levels. It also improves the cash flow because money is not tied up in stock.

This system will only apply when the purchaser has an ongoing business arrangement with a preferred supplier who has the ability and track record of supplying high quality goods on time. This system puts the pressure and costs back onto the supplier. From the viewpoint of the buyer, it means that the cost benefits of bulk buying are lost.

Credit Control

Credit control is a term applied to the means employed by a firm for controlling the amount of credit it allows. Firms sell goods on credit but they want to be sure of payment in the future (e.g. 30 days' credit). The firms or persons to whom goods are sold on credit are called debtors.

Why sell on credit to customers?
To increase sales and profit.

Why do Firms sell Goods on Credit?

The following are examples of reasons for allowing credit:

    (a) To attract new customers and to increase sales to existing customers.

    (b) Historical circumstances; credit may always have been granted to customers.

    (c) To give the seller a major advantage over competitors who do not allow credit.

    (d) To increase sales and profits.

Credit Controller

Some firms have a policy of giving credit to all their major customers. A firm with an annual sales turnover of €12m may have debtors at the end of each month of €1m. It is important to keep control of the debts and ensure that debtors are paying on time. The person responsible for this is the credit controller.

Functions of the Credit Controller

    (a) To decide if credit should be given to a new customer.

    (b) To review the credit limits of existing customers – this is usually done on an annual basis.

    (c) To ensure that agreed credit limits are not exceeded by customers.

    (d) To offer incentives to debtors to pay on time, e.g. extra discount.

    (e) To ensure that all goods are sold with a Reservation of Title, i.e. it is a condition of sale that ownership of the goods remains with the seller until

Reservation of Title

The seller owns the goods sold on credit until they are paid for.

they are paid for. If the debtor goes bankrupt, the seller has the legal right to take back the goods from the customer's shop or warehouse.

(f) To make sure that the customer has a written copy of the trading terms and conditions. These include:

(i) The length of credit allowed, e.g. 30 days.

(ii) The seller's right to charge interest on overdue balances.

(iii) The size of the credit limit, e.g. €20,000.

Investigating Credit Status

Granting credit is a risk for the seller, so it is important to keep this risk to a minimum. An investigation into the credit status of a new customer may be carried out in the following ways:

(a) The customer may be asked for a bank reference.

(b) The customer may be asked to provide a trade reference, e.g. from other suppliers.

(c) The service of a Status Enquiry Agency (e.g. The Trade Protection Agency in Dublin) can be used to find information about the customer. The Agency charges a fee of about €100 for each enquiry. The Agency will give a report on the management of the firm, its trading history, its credit status in the industry and its own recommendations.

(d) Check the following in the Companies Registration Office:

(i) Is the company properly registered?

(ii) Have accounts been filed?

(iii) Have any debts (charges) been registered against the company?

(e) Interview the customer and question them about the financial backing for the business, the existence of a business plan, the number of employees etc.

(f) The sales people may be asked for their opinion on the credit rating of some customers.

Bad Debts ('The Cheque is in the Post')

Bad debts arise when debtors go bankrupt. One of the functions of the credit controller is to ensure that a firm is aware which customers are creditworthy. The following methods may be used to reduce the losses due to bad debts or delayed payments:

(a) Have an efficient credit control department:

(i) Make sure that invoices are sent out on time.

(ii) If the account is overdue, make contact by phone or arrange for a sales representative to call to the customer.

(iii) If the customer is still in business, then instigate legal proceedings for the recovery of the debt. Under the Bankruptcy Act 1988, bankruptcy proceedings can be initiated if the debt is at least €1,500.

(b) Offer financial inducements such as attractive discounts for early payment of the debt.

(c) Employ the services of a debt collection agency to collect the money from the debtor. They charge a percentage fee for this service but, if successful, it is cost effective.

(d) Charge interest on the overdue balance. This would only be done if the debtor was regularly late in paying bills.

(e) Have an insurance policy against bad debts.

(f) Make sure that all goods were sold with Reservation of Title.

Quality Control

One of the functions of a sales manager is to decide the selling price of a new product. Research has clearly shown that for certain products, quality is more important than price. To reduce the number of faulty goods being sold, it is essential to have an effective quality control system. A firm must know what quality standard is required by the market, e.g. a €30,000 car will have to be a high quality car.

What is Quality?

> ➡ **Definition of Quality**
>
> *Quality is a degree of excellence that meets the customer's requirements on all issues except price.*

Quality will always be remembered long after the price is forgotten. Good quality control leads to efficiency in the firm. The firm is then able to advertise with confidence that its products will have zero defects. High quality must exist at each stage of the production process. This includes insisting on high standards of raw materials from suppliers. It also means that all staff are properly trained in their work. Good planning, as well as ongoing monitoring and testing, will help to produce a quality product for consumers.

The Quality Mark (Q mark)

Many firms now display the Quality Mark (Q Mark). Firms aim to acquire the Q Mark as it represents a stamp of quality which can give them a competitive advantage. The Q Mark is obtained from Excellence Ireland.

Benefits of having the Q Mark

    (a) It signifies that the firm has a high standard of quality control. This fact has been established by the Irish Quality Association, which is an independent organisation.

    (b) It is good for staff morale as their contribution to the firm's attainment of high quality is recognised. Without the support of the staff, the Q Mark would not be obtained.

    (c) A firm with the Q Mark has a marketing advantage over a competitor that has not achieved it. Some purchasers will not deal with suppliers that do not have the Q Mark.

    (d) It is an important step towards achieving one of the ISO 9000 standards, which are International Quality Management standards that are essential for big manufacturers and exporters.

nsai

I.S. EN ISO 9002

ISO 9000 Series

The ISO 9000 is a recognised international series of standards for quality management systems. It was developed by the International Standards Organisation and is administered by the National Standards Authority of Ireland (NSAI). In order to obtain the ISO 9000, a firm would initially have to be thoroughly audited. It would then have to implement the changes recommended, allow ongoing assessment of its standards and be subject to at least four unscheduled audits a year by the NSAI.

Benefits of having the ISO 9000

    (a) It is evidence to the public of high levels of efficiency in the firm.

    (b) To attain the award there is an elimination of wasteful expenditure and duplication of work, so the operations of the firm become more streamlined and efficient.

    (c) The workforce are more focused and effective.

    (d) Increased productivity makes the firm more competitive and gives a competitive advantage over firms that do not have the ISO 9000.

    (e) It enables the firm to tender for Government contracts, which are only given to firms with the ISO 9000.

    (f) Overall sales and profits should increase.

    (g) Firms who do not have the ISO 9000 will not qualify for certain Government grants and may have difficulty obtaining bank loans.

Financial Control

Budgeting

A budget is a financial plan for a specified period which is agreed in advance. It shows how much money is required for spending and where this money is going to come from.

Objectives of a Budget

   (a) To prepare a financial plan for the future.

   (b) To indicate to the appropriate people the targets that have to be met.

   (c) To control the activities of each department, e.g. ensure that each department operates within its allocated budget.

   (d) To motivate people to achieve the budgetary targets, e.g. sales targets.

   (e) The existence of a budget will impress potential lenders of finance.

The managing director is responsible for submitting the budget to the board of directors. A budget is required for each department, i.e. sales, production, R&D, accounts etc. The combination of the budgets for each department in the business makes up the firm's budget for the year. The total budget is called the master budget.

Budgets

Budgetary Control

If a business is to succeed it must operate within budgets and be in control of its financial situation. Each manager must monitor the activities and costs of the department.

The Sales Budget

The sales budget is usually divided into monthly, quarterly and annual amounts. At the end of each quarter, the actual sales can be compared to the budgeted sales and the difference is called a variance. If the variance is large, the reasons for this should be explored.

Sales Budget January – March		
Budgeted Sales	**Actual Sales**	**Variance**
€100,000	€82,000	(€18,000)

In the example above, sales are €18,000 below budget, i.e. a negative variance. The sales manager should enquire into the reasons for the variance. It may be due to any of the following:

   (a) New competition in the market.

   (b) Customers reacted against a price increase.

(c) Price reductions by competitors.

(d) An over-optimistic budget was submitted.

Benefits of Budgetary Control to a Firm

(a) A negative deviation (variance) can be observed and appropriate action taken, e.g. if sales are 10 per cent below budget, a new marketing strategy may be required. It is better to be aware of the problem at an earlier rather than a later stage.

(b) There is a financial control on each department, so it is possible to identify which department is not keeping within its budget.

(c) It is possible to judge the performance of each department against the target set in the budget.

Revision of Important Terms	
• Management Activities	• Just-in-Time
• Planning	• Credit Control
• Tactical Planning	• ISO 9000
• Policies	• Maximum Stock Level
• Organising	• Strategic Planning
• Span of Control	• Line Authority
• Stock Control	

Exercises

1. (a) Name three management activities in business.

   (b) Name three management skills required in business.

   (c) Outline the importance of one management activity of your choice.

2. (a) What are the differences between tactical planning and strategic planning?

   (b) Why is planning important to business?

3. (a) Explain four different policies a firm may have.

   (b) How is business policy implemented?

4. (a) 'The lack of a proper organisation system in a firm will lead to chaos.' Discuss.

   (b) Illustrate by means of a diagram an organisation structure in a big firm.

5. (a) Explain what is meant by the span of control.

   (b) Outline the factors that affect the size of the span of control.

6. (a) Why is controlling an important management activity?

   (b) Indicate four different types of control to be found in an enterprise.

7. Explain each of the following:

   (a) Minimum Stock Level

   (b) Just-in-Time

   (c) Maximum Stock Level

   (d) Credit Control

8. 'Selling goods on credit may be a risk for business.'

   (a) How may the credit status (rating) of a customer be assessed?

   (b) What steps can be taken to reduce losses due to bad debts?

9. 'Consumers require high quality products and services.' Discuss the importance of each of the following in relation to quality:

   (a) Q Mark

   (b) ISO 9000

10. The following information is available in relation to Multy Products Ltd.

    2004 Budgeted Sales   €450,000

    2004 Actual Sales   €390,000

    (a) Calculate the variance. Is it positive or negative?

    (b) Outline possible reasons for the variance.

8 Information and Communications Technology (ICT)

Objectives

The following topics from **Unit 3** of the syllabus are covered in this chapter:

- Information Technology
- Electronic Data Interchange (EDI)
- Integrated Services Digital Network (ISDN)
- The Internet
- Electronic Mail (E-mail)
- Information Superhighway
- E-Commerce and Shopping online
- World Wide Web (WWW) and Websites

→ **Definition of Information Technology**

Information Technology (IT) is defined as the computer hardware and software used to store, analyse and communicate business data.

It is usually called ICT (Information and Communications Technology).

For a business to succeed in the business world, it should have access to the following methods of electronic communcation where relevant:

1.	The Internet	4.	Laptop Computers
2.	E-Mail	5.	Broadband
3.	Video-Conferencing	6.	EPOS

Importance of ICT in Business

1. Accurate up-to-date information can be speedily received and transmitted worldwide, e.g. through e-mail.

2. Management can be kept informed, on an ongoing basis, of developments in other areas of the business relevant to their area and decisions are therefore more reliable. Managers can be more confident in their approach to decision making when they have all the most up-to-date facts.

3. The growth of the use of ICT in business has reduced the levels of management hierarchy and increased the span of control.

4. Some employees can work from home through teleworking.

103

5. Important management time can be saved by the use of video-conferencing.

6. EPOS (Electronic Point of Sale) equipment is now at the centre of data collection by retailers. The laser scanning systems automatically gather data from bar codes. This enables the computer to accurately record sales. It also forms the basis for stock control.

Electronic Data Interchange (EDI)

1. This is a form of computer-to-computer interchange of data. It is really a form of structured e-mail.

2. The important aspect of EDI is that there is a structured system for the transfer of data and agreed standardised transaction formats.

3. Each side of the transaction must be able to understand and recognise these agreed formats if the electronic transfer of documents etc. can be made.

4. Purchase orders, invoices, etc. can be transferred between the computers of different firms using the agreed formats, thus saving time and money. **Example**: Tesco has an automated system whereby orders, invoices and payments are automatically triggered when sales are scanned at the checkout. Sales are automatically recorded to assist in regulating stock levels and, from that, stock control.

Benefits of EDI for Business

1. Reduction in Costs

There is a cost benefit in the reduction in paperwork, personnel time in administration work, stock levels and mistakes. Built-in program checks ensure minimum errors.

2. Competitive Advantage

There should be an increase in sales and market share as the business finds it easier and quicker to deal with its suppliers and customers.

3. Service to its Customers

An improved service to customers will improve the image of the business, which in turn will lead to further increases in sales and profits.

4. Improved Communication

EDI enables the wholesalers and retailers to communicate with their suppliers (manufacturers) with the minimum use of staff. Orders are sent, received, acknowledged and dispatched in a speedy manner through the use of computer systems. All the documents involved are exchanged electronically.

5. Improved Cash Flow

Because invoices are sent electronically and in time, there is no room for the old argument by the customer that the invoice was 'lost in the post'.

Problems with EDI

1. Costs

The high capital expenditure costs can only be justified if the volume of business can be predicted to increase sufficiently.

2. Compatibility

It is necessary for EDI standards and message formats to be agreed.

3. Agreement with Customers

A manufacturer will have problems if some customers do not have the technology necessary to participate in electronic business. Provision would have to be made for these customers to be dealt with in the old way.

4. Fraud

As it is possible to automate procedures with EDI, it is also possible for people with the skill and knowledge to generate fraudulent transactions, which might not be detected for some time.

Integrated Services Digital Network (ISDN)

This is a high-speed telecommunications service that enables a business to send and receive voice, video, and data transmission. It carries large amounts with a much larger capacity using a network of telephone lines. The measure of a line's ability to carry data is called bandwidth.

ISDN Uses

1. File Transfer

Computer files can be speedily transferred in a secure and low-cost manner.

2. Video-conferencing

A conference link-up is possible whereby people can discuss issues using computer or television screens. This is a very cost-effective way for management decisions to be clarified and implemented.

3. Teleworking

The ISDN can connect a home computer to a business, thus enabling a manager to perform business tasks as if he/she were in the workplace.

Broadband

Presently, the fastest connection between phone users and the World Wide Web (WWW) is called broadband. Typically, this system is 10 times faster than the dial-up system. This speed allows transactions (such as ordering online, downloading software, catalogues, etc.) to take place at speeds which make the web more practical for consumers and businesses to use. As a result, it is expected that broadband will increase the use of the Web for business. The music industry, in particular, exploits the speed of broadband by making large song files available for download. Increasingly, people are downloading films and TV programmes.

Due to its speed, broadband allows multiple users to share one phone line. This requires a switch ('router') which can also be a wireless system. This allows a household or business to have many people accessing the web using laptops which have no cables attached to the phone system.

The Internet

The Internet (Net) is a global network, where millions of computers are connected together (through phone lines, ISDN, broadband cables, wireless links, etc), in order to share information. A personal computer (PC) which has a modem can be connected to the Internet through an Internet Service Provider (ISP), e.g. Indigo or eircom. The modem converts information from a computer into a format suitable for transmitting across a network. The ISP acts as a router, sending information to and from the PC. If the user wishes to view a website, or send e-mail, their PC

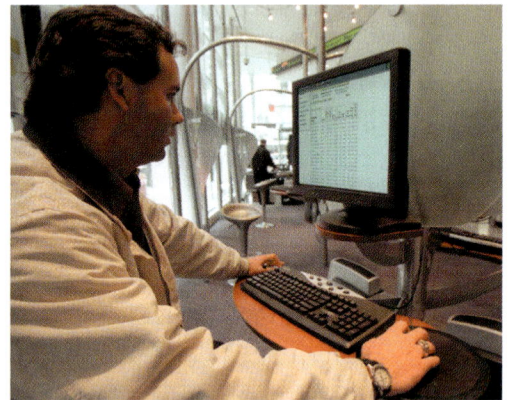

Clients of E-Trade do their investing at the E-Trade Investor Centre.

sends the information to their ISP; the ISP then forwards the information on to the relevant server (a computer dedicated to managing networks), e.g. an e-mail server, or the server where the website they wish to view is hosted. The two most common uses of the Internet are e-mail and the World Wide Web (WWW).

Networks

The Internet is the largest network in the world, crossing the entire planet. A network is a number of computers connected together, usually for the purpose of sharing information. Once the computers are connected, they are able to "talk" to each other, sending and receiving information, whether it is via e-mail, a website, video-conferencing, etc.

When a computer wishes to send information to another computer, anywhere in the world, via the Internet, it first breaks up the information into smaller pieces, called packets, and then transmits the packets through the modem. In order to ensure the packets reach the right destination, the computer uses IP (Internet Protocol) addresses. All computers connected to the Internet have a unique IP address. The computer consults a server called a Domain Name Server (DNS), of which there are many, in order to locate the destination computer. The packets are then transmitted, in order, and reassembled by the destination computer.

The fundamental elements that make up the Internet are as follows:

1. The computers locally and globally that are connected to the network.
2. The various programs which enable information to be processed in the system.
3. The people who use the computers, e.g. for business or to 'surf the Net'. In March 2005, it was estimated that 300 million people worldwide used the Internet to communicate electronically.
4. The data provided by the people worldwide who use the system.

Who uses the Internet?

It is widely used by business and individuals. It is used by business for many reasons, for example:

1. Video-conferencing.
2. Accessing information published on the Internet (the Net) by Government Departments.
3. Business transactions, e.g. electronic fund transfer with the bank.
4. Advertising products/services worldwide.
5. Banking: Internet banking is becoming increasingly popular.

A personal digital assistant (PDA) allows you to store information digitally and connect to the Internet.

Challenges and Problems the Internet poses for Business

1. Capital expenditure costs to purchase and update hardware and software must be met.
2. It will be necessary to train staff in IT skills and continually update those skills.
3. There can be uncertainty in relation to the legality of an electronic sale. Consumers' rights may not be the same as when products are purchased in the traditional way in shops.
4. Potential problems can arise if a firm advertises inaccurate information on the Net and a consumer suffers as a result.
5. Firms who do not realise the importance of advertising on the Net could see a big decline in their business to competitors who embrace this method of promotion.
6. There can be problems in relation to intellectual property rights and data security.

There is a one-off fee for businesses connecting to the Internet and obtaining a unique address. These addresses are known as domain names, e.g. www.aerlingus.ie. These addresses are managed by the provider of the connection to the Internet, known as Internet Service Providers (ISP's). Some people register names, which they know will be needed by a business, e.g. someone registers McDonalds.com. In order for the McDonalds business to use the name they must pay the person to buy the address. This is known as 'cyber squatting' and has been made illegal in the US.

> **→ Definition of Intranet**
>
> *Intranet is the internet service operating within a business. It provides internal e-mail and internal services which can only be accessed by company employees.*

Electronic Mail

E-mail is one of the services on the Internet. It is a popular and cost-effective way to transmit data within a firm and between firms or individuals. Using e-mail, management and staff can communicate with each other through the firm's computer network. Anyone who has access to the Internet on their computer can avail of the e-mail service by using their e-mail address, e.g. joe.maguire@folens.ie.

Benefits of E-Mail for a Business

The benefits include the following:

1. Many people can be sent the same message in one transaction.
2. Once the e-mail message is sent, it will remain in the electronic mailbox until it is accessed by the receiver.
3. It is possible for the sender to check that the message has been received and read.
4. It is a fast and cost-effective way of sending information, with big savings on time, postage, phone calls, stationery, etc.
5. It enables management to telework from home.

Information Superhighway (IS)

Information superhighway is a global conglomeration of computer networks that offers access to huge amounts of information through the WWW. The combination of the following methods of receiving and sending data is called the Information Superhighway:

1.	Computer	4.	Telecommunication
2.	Fax	5.	Video-conferencing
3.	E-Mail	6.	WWW

A businesswoman works from home using a laptop.

● E-Business and Shopping Online

Electronic business (E-Business) is business through technology. E-Business refers to business transacted over the Internet. It is a way of conducting business in an efficient and cost-effective manner, using high-speed electronic media. It offers huge advantages to consumers and presents enormous challenges to suppliers. Through the Internet, Cable TV and the telephone line it will lead to big changes in how consumers spend their money and leisure hours. Ease of access will mean a greater use of the Internet in the home. The increased number of users will pressurise more firms to go online, i.e. supply and demand will drive each other forward. Business must realise the growing importance of the implications and benefits of the Internet. Many people who use the Net cannot pay online so they use it to research the range of goods available.

> E-Business is a buzz-word in the business world. Fast becoming part of day-to-day language, it relates to the use of electronic networks to make transactions between firms or direct to customers.

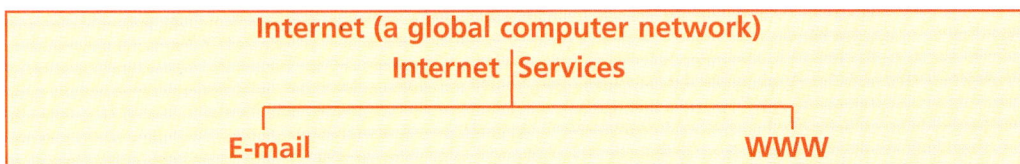

Internet (a global computer network)	
Internet	Services
E-mail	WWW

Features of E-Business

1. There are no restrictions in terms of industry sector and location of the business. Financial services, software, travel and books are some of the more popular sales on the Net. Already, many people are booking concerts, buying books, arranging holidays etc. from their own computers at home.

2. It eliminates geographical boundaries in relation to marketing and sales. An Irish business can compete with a Japanese business on the Net, without anyone having to travel abroad.

3. It makes it possible for business to develop both a local and global market for its products or services.

4. It is restructuring the way that business is carried out between the manufacturer and customer, between the manufacturer and retailer, and business to business.

5. It will enable business in developing countries to emerge and compete with industry worldwide.

6. It facilitates the selling of goods and services online 24 hours a day, 7 days a week, through a website that lists products and allows for secure credit card payments.

> E-Business is a continuation of normal business practice. It is a new medium for reaching customers.

> In March 2005, there were 600,000 Irish customers shopping online.

> E-Business enables business to:
> • improve customer service
> • reach new markets
> • source new suppliers

Benefits of E-Business to Business

1. The seller doesn't have to incur the high costs of storage, employing sales representatives, etc.
2. Payment is facilitated through the use of credit card transactions, so no bad debts are incurred.
3. Firms can market their products worldwide from a remote location, so sales and profits will increase. The local business can now become a global business.

World Wide Web (WWW) and Websites

This is one of the services on the Internet. Multimedia components make up the WWW, i.e. picture, text, graphics, video and sound. The growth in the use of the WWW has hugely increased the popularity of the Internet. There are tens of millions of websites containing a huge amount of information. Every website has an address, so it is easy to locate. The website address is called a URL (uniform resource locater), e.g. www.folens.ie.

How does Business benefit from the WWW?

The benefits include the following:

1. Advertising on the WWW, i.e. global advertising is a low-cost way to reach a worldwide market.
2. A business can develop a global market through the WWW.
3. Cheaper sources of raw materials and goods can be sourced by surfing the net.
4. It is possible to find out what competitors are promoting.
5. Firms can provide an online support service for customers, e.g. responding to queries or complaints.

Exercises

1. (a) Why is information technology important for business?
   (b) Explain what is meant by Electronic Data Interchange (EDI).

2. (a) What do the letters ISDN stand for? (b) Discuss the various uses of ISDN.

3. (a) What is the Internet?
   (b) Indicate the various elements that make up the Internet.

4. (a) Outline the challenges that face business from the Internet.
   (b) Explain what is meant by an e-mail. State the benefits to businesses that use e-mail.

5. (a) What is meant by E-Business? Discuss the features of E-Business.
   (b) What are the benefits of E-Business to modern business?

Applied Business Questions
for Units 1, 2, 3
Leaving Certificate 2004 and 2009

Applied Business Question

Units 1, 2 and 3 for Leaving Certificate 2004/2009

This ABQ is taken from the Leaving Certificate 1999 Sample Paper.

CHAMISE LTD.

Patricia Clarke established her shirt-making business, 'Chamise Ltd', ten years ago after graduating from college. The business has developed well since then, mainly because of her desire and drive to succeed. Recently, the competition from foreign manufacturers has become intense. If the business is to survive, Patricia knows that new production technology must be installed in the factory and the staff trained quickly in its use. The employees have to accept work changes if the business is to meet market demands.

Patricia is a good listener. Her management style has always been to get wide-ranging views from customers, employees and other interested parties and only then make decisions. She has always chosen managers who are good communicators and comfortable working in teams. She feels that her wide business experience and that of her managers will successfully meet the present challenges.

Already, three large customers in Dublin have complained about the seemingly better quality shirts available, at the same price, from a competing business. Patricia is asking herself why quality standards have slipped recently. Customers have been returning imperfect units to retailers. Some retail outlets have treated the customers shabbily, simply blaming 'Chamise Ltd' for the problems and not addressing the customers' complaints adequately.

(A)   Explain the enterprising characteristics that you recognise in Patricia from the
       above information.   (20 marks)

(B)   Describe two conflicts that are present above. Outline a legislative method
       that would be used to solve each one.   (20 marks)

(C)   Analyse the contribution to the business that would result from an improvement
       in Patricia's management activities.   (40 marks)

(Total = 80 marks)

Applied Business Question
Based on units 1, 2 and 3 for Leaving Certificate 2004/2009
This ABQ is taken from the Leaving Certificate 1999 Paper.

B AND M SOLUTIONS LTD

Barry and Marian had long thought about setting up their own business. Both were ambitious, were well educated and had worked successfully for large computer companies. They were aware of the challenges to be met, but felt that they had lots of fresh ideas that they were not afraid to try out. They made the decision to set up 'B and M Solutions', providing small businesses with specially designed computer systems and training of personnel. They planned things out well at the start, organised the tasks between them and sought help from State agencies when needed.

The business has grown quickly. It placed advertisements for its services in trade magazines which proved worthwhile, but sometimes left out important information so that it would get the contracts. Some of B and M's customers were not happy with what they see as a lack of after-sales service, as promised in the advertisements.

Both owners work hard but seem to be always rushing. Marian complains of B and M having no vision for the business in the future. Their employees are generally excellent but, at present, there is constant pressure on staff to meet deadlines by working long hours. The business does not seem to be able to keep good staff for long. Barry has taken to issuing orders to employees recently. He even dismissed one staff member because she requested a day off from work to attend the doctor with her pregnancy. Marian feels his behaviour is not good for the business.

(A)　Outline the enterprise skills employed by Barry and Marian in the above situation.　(20 marks)

(B)　Draft a short report for the Board of Directors explaining the legislative methods that could be used to solve the conflicts in the business.　(20 marks)

(C)　Evaluate how the couple might succeed better in the business if they improved their management skills. Support your answer with reference to the above text.　(40 marks)

(Total = 80 marks)

Applied Business Question

Based on units 1, 2 and 3 for Leaving Certificate 2004/2009

BARGAIN BOUTIQUE LTD

Having worked as the manager of a boutique business for five years, Deirdre Kelly decided to leave and set up her own business. Using savings and a loan from the bank, she established her own business Bargain Boutique Ltd in October, 1999. Deirdre was hard-working, had always wanted to and now enjoyed being the boss, made the business decisions and enjoyed talking to customers. She had a good working relationship with the staff and listened to their viewpoints before making decisions. Her business built up a reputation for selling good quality products at competitive prices.

As business expanded, her husband joined the company as Financial and Human Resource Manager. Within two months, he was involved in conflict with the staff over working conditions, changing the working hours and reducing the Christmas bonus by 25%. His attitude is that unhappy employees can seek employment elsewhere and he has told them so. Deirdre realised that morale was low and that the management–staff relationship was deteriorating. She wanted to resolve issues before they got too big.

Recently Deirdre Kelly received complaints from customers over the selling prices of items advertised in the 'January Sales'. One customer, Mary O'Brien, complained that she purchased a coat for €400 when the advertisement highlighted it was reduced in price from €600 to €400 for the 'January Sales'. In fact, the coats had been on sale in the boutique at €500 for two weeks before the 'January Sales' began. Mary O'Brien complained that Bargain Boutique was using misleading advertising and made an official complaint to the appropriate authority on this matter.

(A)   Outline the enterprise characteristics you associate with Deirdre Kelly from the above information.   (20 marks)

(B)   Identify possible conflicts that exist in Bargain Boutique Ltd. Illustrate one non-legislative and one legislative approach to solving them.   (30 marks)

(C)   In your opinion, is Deirdre Kelly or her husband Peter Kelly the better manager? Support your opinion with reference to the management skills you feel are required in the business.   (30 marks)

(Total = 80 marks)

Applied Business Question
Based on units 1, 2 and 3 for Leaving Certificate 2004/2009

B AND D FINANCIAL AND IT SERVICES LTD

Brendan and Deirdre want to set up their own business. After graduating from college with business qualifications, they both obtained employment with a Global Finance and IT company in London. Both were ambitious and hard-working and within six months, were making suggestions to management on how to improve and expand the range of services to the customers. Some of their recommendations were implemented and within two years both of them were promoted. They were seen as successful intrapreneurs. After five years working in London, they returned to Ireland and established B and D Financial and IT Services Ltd. From the beginning, they recognised the importance of planning as a management activity, especially tactical planning.

The business expanded and within two years it had 10 employees and 300 customers. Most of the growth was in the IT area as many of its customers lacked knowledge in this area. In recent months, some of the customers have complained at the lack of after-sales service as advertised in the company's brochures. One customer has instigated legal proceedings due to losses incurred by the failure of B and D Financial and IT Services Ltd to install a new computer on time.

As the business expands, problems are surfacing and there is disagreement between the shareholders. There is a skilled staff but they are under constant pressure to meet deadlines, even having to work overtime. One employee refused to work overtime and he was dismissed by Brendan. This person is suing for wrongful dismissal. Unknown to Brendan, Deirdre had told that employee that she disagreed with Brendan on this issue and that she was concerned about the growing list of conflicts. The bank has requested an urgent meeting with Brendan and Deirdre due to the ongoing failure of the business to operate within the agreed overdraft limit.

(A) Outline the enterprise skills employed by Brendan and Deirdre in the above situation. (20 marks)

(B) Have all the management skills been effectively used in this business?
Refer where relevant to the above text. (20 marks)

(C) Draft a report for the Board of Directors, outlining the conflicts that exist and explaining the legislative and non-legislative methods that could be used to solve the conflicts in the business. (40 marks)

(Total = 80 marks)

Applied Business Question

Based on units 1, 2 and 3 for Leaving Certificate 2004/2009
This ABQ is taken from the Leaving Certificate 2004 Paper.

PETER PALMOR

Peter Palmor arrived in Ireland from Eastern Europe in 1991 with little spoken English and no money to speak of. He had a university degree in engineering, however, and quickly secured a job with an established property developer in Dublin. His fresh ideas and ability in tackling problems impressed his employer. The Managing Director of the firm had confidence in Peter's ability to appreciate opportunities and to learn quickly.

Peter was ambitious and worked successfully for the business, but felt he needed more. His employer helped him to set up a structural engineering and consultancy firm and gave him his first contract. The building boom in Ireland ensured that the business grew quickly and contracts came from other firms, who recognised Peter's technical skills and 'can do' attitude.

Peter is now experiencing challenges in managing his business, especially in dealings with his employees, investors and suppliers. Peter seems to be constantly under stress and he is fearful that he may begin to make serious mistakes. He finds that he is working too many hours per day and taking work home at weekends. He wishes to improve his lifestyle.

Over both the short and the long term, he wishes to make better use of his time and find effective solutions to his problems. Peter's personal commitment to the business is excellent and he is open to suggestions that will improve the management of his business into the future.

(A)   Explain with illustrations from the above information, four
      enterprising skills and/or characteristics shown by Peter.   (20 marks)

(B)   You are Peter's business advisor. Draft a short report for Peter
      identifying remedies for the challenges he is encountering.   (30 marks)

(C)   Evaluate Peter's management skills with a view to his improving his business
      and lifestyle. Support your answer with reference to the above text.

                                                                           (30 marks)

                                                                  (Total = 80 marks)

9 Household and Business Manager

Objectives

The following topics from **Unit 4** of the syllabus are covered in this chapter:

- Household and Business Manager
- Sources of Income and Finance
- Cash Flow Forecast for a Business and Household
- Loans
- Sources of Finance
- Insurance
- Taxation

The person that runs a business must be a good manager, otherwise the business will not be efficient. Likewise, the person running the household must be a good manager. In both the business and household, there is income and payments (expenditure). In both cases, plans must be prepared and decisions made.

Examples:

1. In business – can the business afford an extension to the factory building at a cost of €300,000?

2. In the household – can the household afford an extension to the house at a cost of €60,000.

In both cases, decisions have to be made.

Both households and businesses should manage their finances carefully for the following reasons:

1. To keep a proper account of all income and expenses.

2. To prepare financial budgets with the final results.

3. To compare the budgets with the final results.

4. To show that financial planning exists when applying for a bank overdraft or term loan from a bank.

Sources of Income for a Household and a Business

The following are the main sources of income for a household and a business:

Household Income		Business Income	
1.	Wages and Salaries	1.	Income from Sales
2.	Child Benefit Allowances	2.	Interest on Investments, e.g dividends
3.	Social Welfare Payments	3.	Grants/Subsidies Received
4.	Interest on Investments, e.g. interest on a savings account	4.	Sale of a Fixed Asset, e.g. sale of machinery
		5.	Money invested by the owners

117

Sources of Finance for a Household and a Business

The following are the main sources of finance for a household and a business:

Household	Business
Short-Term (One Year)	Short-Term (One Year)
1. Creditors	1. Creditors
2. Bank Overdraft	2. Bank Overdraft
3. Loan from a Credit Union	3. Factoring
Medium-Term (1–5 Years)	Medium-Term (1–5 Years)
1. Leasing	1. Leasing
2. Hire Purchase	2. Hire Purchase
	3. Term Loan
Long-Term (Over 5 Years)	Long-Term (Over 5 Years)
1. Savings	1. Debenture (long-term loan)
2. Mortgage	2. Retained Earnings
	3. Ordinary Share Capital (Equity Capital)

Cash Flow Forecast

Cash is the most liquid asset – it is available for immediate spending on household or business goods or services. Have you ever run out of cash to pay a bill or buy something you saw advertised? Did you ever borrow money from a friend or from your parents? If the answer is 'yes' to any of the above questions then you have had a cash flow problem.

In business or household terms, cash flow refers to the flow of money into and out of the business or household over a specified period of time.

Cash Flow into a Business

The main inflows of cash to a business are as follows:

- Cash sales of goods to customers.

- Cash received from debtors, i.e. from customers to whom goods were sold on credit.

- Government grant towards the cost of a project, i.e. new machinery.

- Borrowing money from a financial institution – this causes an immediate cash inflow to the business.

- Additional money invested in the business by its shareholders.

- Investment income, e.g. rental income and interest on a deposit account.

Cash Flow Payments out of a Business

The main outflows of cash from a business are as follows:

- Cash purchases of goods for resale.

- Paying normal business expenses, e.g. wages and advertising.

- Cash payment for capital expenditure items, e.g. machinery and computers.

- Payments to creditors for goods previously purchased on credit.

- Payment of taxes and dividends.

- Repayment of interest and loans to financial institutions.

The Cash Flow Cycle

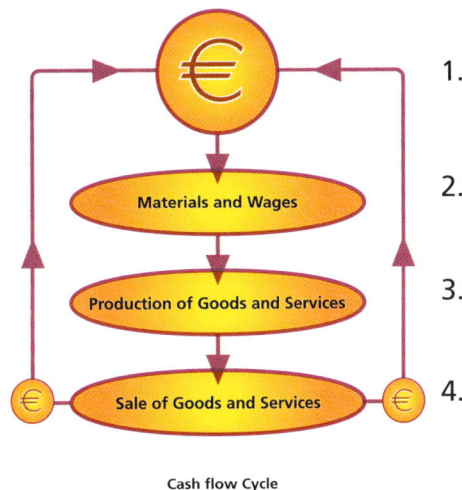

Cash flow Cycle

The cash flow cycle shows the different stages involved in making cash payments for wages, goods etc. and receiving the cash from sales. There are five stages involved in the cash flow cycle:

1. Cash is required by a business.

2. Cash payments are made to purchase raw materials and pay normal expenses, e.g. wages.

3. A manufacturing firm has to produce the goods for the market.

4. The goods are sold – some for cash, the majority usually on credit.

5. The firm receives cash from both cash sales and debtors. This money is then used to purchase raw materials, pay bills etc.

The cash flow cycle highlights the importance of financial planning in a business, for example:

- What would the business do if it couldn't afford to purchase essential raw materials? Sales and profits would be reduced.

- If a business insisted, because of a cash shortage, that its customers pay for their purchases by cash rather than giving them credit, business might be lost to competitors.

- If a business were so short of cash that it couldn't pay its trade creditors, then it would have a liquidity problem.

Cash Flow Forecast for a Business

A business cash flow forecast can be used for different reasons, for example:

1. To project when cash is due into the business.

2. To highlight how much cash is available on a regular basis to pay bills, repay loans etc.

3. To show evidence to the bank manager that the business is properly managed.

4. To highlight when an overdraft facility will be required.

5. To highlight if the business has surplus cash, which could be invested in a deposit account where interest can be earned.

The cash flow forecast will show the cash position and cash requirements of a business.

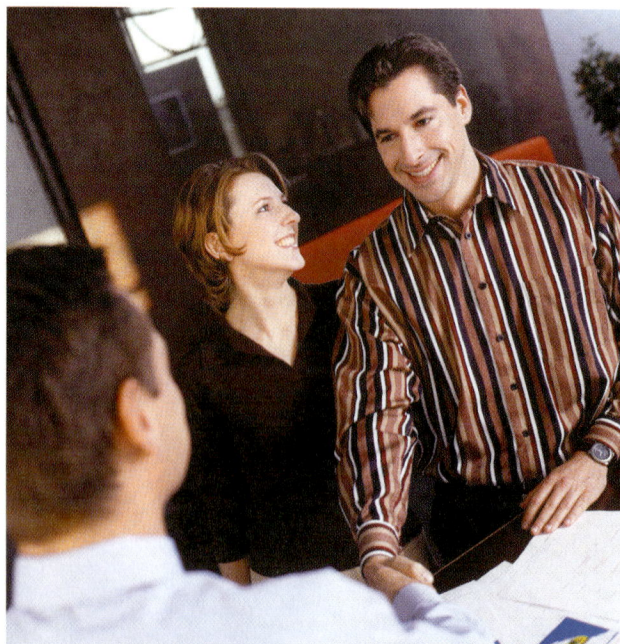

When applying for a bank loan, it's important to show that cash flow has been managed properly.

EXAMPLE

What information is highlighted in the cash flow forecast for Iron Works Ltd?

Example of a Business Cash Flow Forecast for Iron Works Ltd				
	Oct	Nov	Dec	Total
Receipts (Inflows)				
Cash Sales	60,000	80,000	30,000	170,000
Receipts from Debtors	30,000	70,000	20,000	120,000
Loan from Bank	0	0	40,000	40,000
Share Capital	50,000	0	0	50,000
VAT Refund	0	0	10,000	10,000
Total (A)	140,000	150,000	100,000	390,000
Payments (Outflows)				
Cash Purchases	35,000	60,000	40,000	135,000
Payments to Creditors	65,000	70,000	30,000	165,000
Taxes	0	30,000	0	30,000
Sundry Business Expenses	10,000	20,000	20,000	50,000
Total (B)	110,000	180,000	90,000	380,000
Net Cash (A–B) = (C)	30,000	(30,000)	10,000	10,000
Opening Cash = D	15,000	45,000	15,000	15,000
Closing Cash = E (C + D)	45,000	15,000	25,000	25,000

The cash flow forecast reveals the following:

* In October, the business will receive €30,000 more than it will spend.
* In November, the business will spend €30,000 more than it will receive.
* In December, the business will receive €10,000 more than it will spend. If the bank loan of €40,000 had not been received, there would have been a revenue shortfall of €30,000 for the second month in a row.
* Overall, there is a cash surplus during the three months.

Cash Flow Forecast for a Household

Before preparing a household cash flow forecast (often called a household budget), it is necessary to examine the three types of household expenditure (payments):

1.	Regular Expenditure
2.	Irregular Expenditure
3.	Discretionary Expenditure

1. Regular Expenditure

This refers to known bills which have to be paid on a regular basis, usually monthly, e.g. mortgage repayments or yearly car insurance.

2. Irregular Expenditure

This refers to known bills which vary in amount but have to be paid when received, e.g. phone, grocery and ESB bills.

3. Discretionary Expenditure

This refers to non-essential spending, where expenditure can be reduced if there is a cash shortfall, e.g. holidays or new clothes.

A household cash flow forecast can be used for different reasons, for example:

(a) To project the family income on a monthly basis.

(b) To highlight how much money is available on a regular basis to meet the regular, irregular and discretionary expenditure.

(c) To show evidence to a bank manager that the household finances are planned and monitored.

(d) To highlight when an overdraft may be required.

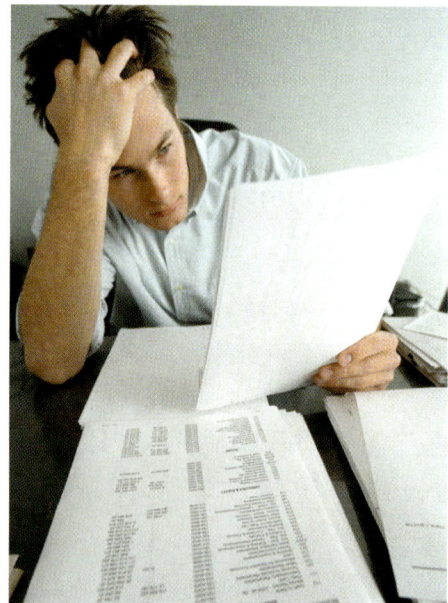

A cash flow problem may mean that debts go unpaid.

EXAMPLE

Household Cash Flow Forecast (Budget for Mr & Mrs Collins)							
	April	**May**	**June**	**July**	**Aug**	**Sept**	**Total**
Income							
Wages of Mr & Mrs Collins	900	900	900	900	1,000	1,000	5,600
Child benefit	40	40	40	40	40	40	240
Deposit interest	0	50	0	0	0	0	50
Loan from Credit Union	0	0	0	0	0	400	400
Total income (A)	940	990	940	940	1,040	1,440	6,290
Expenditure							
Regular							
Mortgage	400	400	400	400	300	300	2,200
Car insurance	0	0	0	0	0	400	400
Irregular							
Phone bill	90	0	70	0	80	0	240
ESB bill	0	70	0	40	0	80	190
Supermarket bill	450	480	460	400	410	520	2,720
Discretionary							
Holidays	0	0	0	800	0	0	800
Clothes	0	250	0	200	0	400	850
Entertainment	50	50	100	150	200	0	550
Total Expenditure (B)	990	1,250	1,030	1,990	990	1,700	7,950
Net cash (A–B) = C	(50)	(260)	(90)	(1,050)	50	(260)	(1,660)
Opening cash (D)	1,000	950	690	600	(450)	(400)	1,000
Closing cash (E) = C + D	950	690	600	(450)	(400)	(660)	(660)

What information is highlighted in the cash flow forecast for the household budget of Mr & Mrs Collins?

The cash flow forecast reveals the following:

- During five of the six months, the monthly expenditure is greater than the monthly income.
- The opening cash balance of €1,000 is all spent by June.
- If the July holiday was cancelled, there would be a positive cash balance of €350 at the end of July.
- An overdraft of about €550 is required for July if the holiday is to be taken.
- August is the only month when they live within their means.
- The loan of €400 from the Credit Union in September is obviously to pay for the car insurance. Perhaps a bigger loan of €1,000 should be requested.
- Overall, they have not lived within their means. Their biggest problem area is the discretionary expenditure of €2,200 during the six-month period. There may also be some scope to reduce the size of the phone bills.

Sources of Finance

Short-Term (1 year)	Medium-Term (1–5 years)	Long-Term (over 5 years)
Trade creditors	Leasing	Share capital
Bank overdraft	Term loan	Debenture
Accrued expenses	Hire purchase	Retained earnings
Factoring		Venture capital
		Grants

Which Sources of Finance should be used?

Different sources of finance are available for different periods of time. The following are some factors to consider before deciding which source of finance to use:

1. The **cost** of raising the finance, e.g. bank overdraft at an 8 per cent interest rate. Different financial institutions charge different interest rates, so it pays to shop around. By law, all financial institutions must publicise their APR (Annual Percentage Rate). This is the true cost of the loan with no extra charges. By checking APR, customers can compare the cost of credit available from different financial institutions.

> **Which sources to use:**
> - cost
> - security
> - control

2. The **value** of the asset which has to be given as security, e.g. deeds of business premises for a business loan.

3. The **reason** the money is required. A long-term investment, e.g. machinery, should be financed by a long-term source of finance. This is called the 'matching principle' of borrowing.

4. Would a new share issue be **successful?** If yes, then this is a low-cost, long-term source of finance for a business.

Short-term Sources of Finance

1. Trade Creditors

This is a regular source of short-term business finance, e.g. suppliers giving a firm 60 days' credit. Using this source of finance is regarded as 'leaning on the trade'. This is a vital source of finance for large and small firms alike. Big stores, e.g. Tesco Ireland, buy with an average of 60 days' credit from their suppliers. These stores operate on a cash sale system of 'big turnover, small unit profits'. They then earn more profit by saving money on deposit for almost 60 days and earning interest.

Benefits of Creditors as a Source of Finance

    (a) No security has to be provided to obtain the goods on credit from suppliers.

    (b) It is a cheap source of finance as there are no interest repayments.

    (c) It keeps the pressure on management to operate a good cash management service. This enables the firm to always pay debts on time and thus avail of agreed discounts.

2. Bank Overdraft

This is a very common source of finance and easy to obtain for current account customers. It has to be negotiated with the bank manager. An overdraft takes the form of permission to overdraw up to an agreed limit, e.g. €10,000. Interest is only charged on a daily basis on the amount of the overdraft used, e.g. if the customer only overdraws the current account (cheque book account) up to €5,000, then interest is only charged on that €5,000. If a person exceeds the agreed overdraft limit, the bank will charge an extra interest called a surcharge. Overdrafts are generally used by business to buy stock and pay creditors and by householders to pay bills.

3. Accrued Expenses

This is regarded as a small source of finance used by both householders and business for a short period of time. Services have to be provided before the bills are sent. Therefore, expenses are incurred and unpaid until the suppliers send the bills, e.g. ESB, telephone etc.

PAYE, PRSI and VAT are examples of tax collected by business. These do not have to be paid over to the Revenue Commissioners immediately. In fact, a firm could have the use of this 'tax' money for a few weeks before it has to be paid.

4. Factoring

This involves selling trade debts to a factoring firm, i.e. a finance company. (Some banks now offer this service.) The debts are sold for less than their full value. A firm with debtors of €80,000 may sell them to a factor for €70,000. The initial cost is €10,000 but there are also benefits. The factor proceeds to collect the full debts, i.e. €80,000.

Benefits of Factoring

    (a) It releases cash which was tied up in debtors.

    (b) The working capital requirements of the firm are reduced, so extra borrowing is avoided.

> *Factoring is a costly source of short-term finance that is only available to business. It is not available to households.*

Medium-term Sources of Finance

1. Leasing

Leasing an asset (e.g. machinery) gives a firm the opportunity to use it without owning it. The business does not purchase the asset, it rents it from the leasing company (the lessor). It involves three parties: the buyer, the seller and the leasing firm.

Features of Leasing

(a) The leasing company purchases the asset required by the business and leases it to the business (customer).

(b) The lease is for a specific number of years and requires regular payments to the lessor by the lessee.

(c) The customer (lessee) does not own the asset but has the use of it without having to borrow. This is good for the cash flow of the lessee.

(d) A business can always have the most up-to-date equipment. If an asset which is being leased becomes obsolete during the period of the lease, the lessee has the option to trade it in for more modern equipment. The lease payments will be increased to facilitate this situation.

(e) The lessee is responsible for all insurance and maintenance costs of the asset being leased.

(f) One hundred per cent of the cost of the asset is financed by the lessor, so the working capital of the business remains intact.

(g) The leasing payments are regular and known, so it is possible for a business to plan its expenditure when preparing its cash budget for the year.

Leasing Periods

There are two leasing periods, primary and secondary. The **primary** period is fixed – usually three to five years. During this period there are regular fixed payments. The total payment over the life of the primary lease equals the net cost of the asset plus a service charge and interest rate. When the primary lease is up, the leasing firm may renew the lease at a lower lease payment, i.e. the **secondary** period.

   Many firms use leasing to finance assets such as machinery, computers, vehicles etc. It is available to householders but is not a popular source of finance among them.

2. Term Loan

A medium-term loan is granted for a stated reason. Repayments are agreed stated amounts to be paid for a period of one to five years. It is a suitable source of finance to purchase assets such as computers, equipment, vehicles etc. In order to obtain a term loan from the bank, the customer must be able to show an ability to repay the loan. The interest on the term loan is a tax allowable business expense.

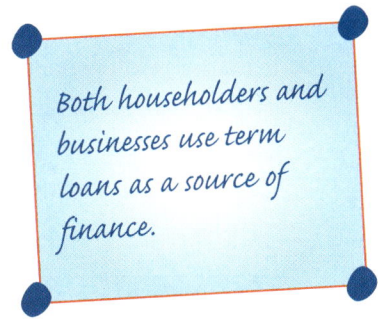

Both householders and businesses use term loans as a source of finance.

3. Hire Purchase (Buy Now – Pay Later)

Hire purchase is a popular form of instalment buying. It is a suitable way to purchase durable goods such as a car, TV, video, washing machine etc. The ability to buy items on HP allows the customer to purchase now and pay for it out of future earnings. The asset will be owned when the final HP instalment is paid. Similar to leasing, it involves three parties: the buyer, the seller and the finance (HP) firm.

How does a HP Transaction happen?

(a) A business requires new machinery which will cost €60,000 and arranges to purchase it from a supplier.

(b) A deposit (e.g. 20 per cent – €12,000) is paid to secure the deal and an arrangement is made for a HP firm to pay the balance (i.e. €48,000) to the supplier.

(c) A contract is agreed between the business and the HP firm to reap the €48,000 by instalments over an agreed period of time not exceeding five years.

(d) The business does not own the machinery until the final instalment is paid to the HP firm.

Benefits of HP to the Customer

(a) The customer has possession and use of the product immediately. Payments are spread over time and will be taken from future earnings.

(b) No security has to be provided to avail of this source of finance.

(c) It increases the standard of living of customers who purchase necessities (e.g. furniture) using this system of payment.

(d) If the customer falls behind with agreed payments, but has already paid more than one-third of the value of the asset, the HP company cannot take back the asset without the permission of the courts.

Is Hire Purchase Expensive?

It is more expensive to purchase using HP than by paying cash or using a bank loan. The interest is based on the initial sum borrowed, not on the amount due at any one time. The true cost of interest can be calculated using the following formula:

> *Hire Purchase is a costly source of finance that is used more by households than by business.*

$$\frac{\text{Quoted \% PA x 2 x Number of Instalments}}{\text{Number of Instalments + 1}}$$

EXAMPLE

Gerry Dolan Motors Ltd advertised the following offer to the public:

> ## NEW CAR €15,000
> ## Payment Terms Deposit €1,000
>
> Balance of €14,000 to be financed by Good Value HP Finance Company to be paid at 11% over 60 months.

The bank loan interest is 12.5%.

Which offer should a customer take?

Apply the formula above to calculate the time rate of interest charged by the HP company:

i.e. $\dfrac{11\% \times 2 \times 60}{61} = \dfrac{1320}{61} = 21.6\%$

It is much cheaper for a customer to finance the purchase of the car by bank loan than by HP.

Long-term Sources of Finance

1. Share Capital (Ordinary Share Capital/Equity Capital)

The holders of ordinary shares are the main risk-takers in a company. They invest their money with no guarantee of dividends. Ordinary shares are the equity share capital of a company. The holders of the ordinary shares are entitled to the equity or balance of profits when the company is being wound up. Every ordinary shareholder has a vote, i.e. one vote per share. A shareholder who owns 51 per cent of the ordinary shares can control and run the company. Such a situation is common in private companies but very rare in public ones.

Many people invest in public companies for two reasons:

(a) To receive a dividend from the profit.

(b) To sell the shares in the future at a profit.

Benefits to the Company from Equity Capital

(a) It provides the business with a cheap source of long-term finance. This money does not have to be repaid to the shareholders unless the company is dissolved.

(b) There are no interest repayments on the capital (unlike a bank loan).

(c) No security has to be provided to raise the finance.

(d) Every ordinary shareholder has a vote at the AGM. If they are not satisfied with how the business is doing, they can attend the AGM and voice their concerns. It is the shareholders who appoint the directors. The shareholders can also replace the directors, i.e. the shareholders have the power to make decisions.

2. Debentures

A debenture is a long-term loan from a bank. It carries a fixed rate of interest and has a specified repayment date (maturity date), e.g. '€200,000 15 per cent debenture 2009.'

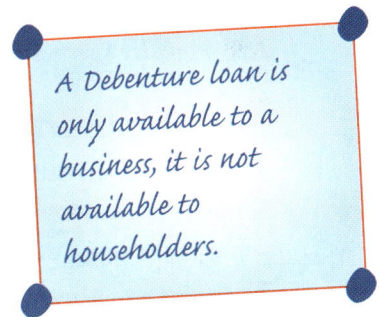

A Debenture loan is only available to a business, it is not available to householders.

Features of a debenture loan include the following:

(a) They are long-term loans from a bank but the debenture holders have no votes.

(b) Interest on the debenture is paid before dividends are paid to shareholders.

(c) Debenture interest is a tax-allowable business expense.

(d) The company will usually have to provide security (collateral) in order to obtain a debenture loan, e.g. deeds of business premises.

3. Retained Earnings ('Ploughing Back' Profits)

This is a free source of long-term finance and does not create any financial debts. At the end of a financial year, profits can be paid as dividends to shareholders or re-invested in the business.

Benefits of using Retained Earnings

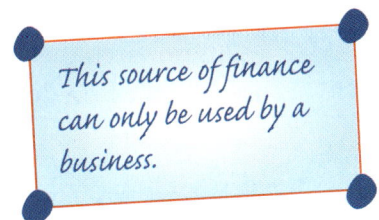

This source of finance can only be used by a business.

(a) The control of the firm is not affected.

(b) There are no interest repayments and the money is available for immediate use.

(c) No security has to be given.

4. Venture Capital

Venture capital is defined as investing by means of equity participation in companies where the risk is high but the potential profit is good if the venture succeeds.

It is a long-term source of finance, whereby companies are prepared to sell some of their shares to a venture capital company (risk investor) in return for an agreed cash investment. The venture capital company shares in the profits of the venture in which they have an unsecured risk investment.

Venture capital is a suitable source of long-term finance in the following cases:

(a) Starting up a new business – seed capital is required to finance the new project.

(b) Financing growth in an existing business – development capital is required as there is less risk involved than in seed capital, so it is easier to attract finance.

> *This source of finance can only be used by a business.*

(c) Management buy-out – finance is required so that existing management can buy the firm as a going concern from its owners.

AIB Venture Capital is the largest venture capital company in Ireland.

5. Government Grants

A grant is an amount of money given by a State agency to an enterprise (business) or some organisation (e.g. club).

Different types of grants are available:

(a) Capital expenditure grants (available from IDA Ireland) finance the purchase of machinery and buildings.

(b) Feasibility study grants (available from Enterprise Ireland) finance market research into export potential.

IDA IRELAND

(c) Training grants (available from FÁS) are provided to teach workers the skills required by enterprise.

(d) Business enterprise grants (available from County Enterprise Boards or CEBs) are intended to support and develop small local business enterprises.

> *This source of finance can only be used by a business.*

Most grants are non-repayable, e.g. training grants. Some grants however, that are linked to job targets, may have to be repaid if the firm does not reach the agreed target.

Banking For Business and Household
Current Account

Current account holders lodge money to the account in the bank (or credit union). This kind of account is also called a cheque book account. Withdrawals are made by cheque, ATM card (automated teller machine), direct debit, Laser card etc.

Features of a Current Account

1. Payments are usually made by cheque or direct debit.

2. Once a cheque has been 'cleared' by the bank, there is proof of payment of a debt.

3. The holder of the current account can obtain overdraft facilities from the bank. This allows for the withdrawal of an amount of money in excess of the amount in the account.

4. Account holders receive regular bank statements, which give details of money lodged and withdrawn, bank charges and overdraft interest charges on a daily basis.

Bank Statement					
Date	Details	Cheque No.	Debit	Credit	Balance
01-04-05					1000
10-04-05	Lodgement			5000	6000
15-04-05	Cheque	00354X	1400		4600
28-04-05	ATM		200		4400

Business Loans and Personal Loans

There are two parties to every loan, i.e. the borrower (customer) and the bank (financial institution). Banks are in business to make profits. Interest charged on loans to customers is an important source of revenue for banks. Banks are happy to give loans when there is no risk involved.

Business Loan

The following factors should be considered by a bank manager when assessing a request for a loan from a customer:

1. The Size and Reason for the Loan
How big is the loan required and is it for a productive reason, e.g. buying machinery, or is it for a risky venture, e.g. buying shares?

2. The Credit Rating of the Customer
What is this customer's credit rating in the bank? Were previous loans repaid on time?

3. The Nature of the Business
What does the business sell? Is it a growth industry, e.g. information technology, or a declining industry, e.g. textiles?

4. Security
Is there adequate security for the loan, e.g. deeds of business premises or directors acting as personal guarantors?

5. Ability to Pay
Can the business afford to repay the loans? It is necessary for the borrower to submit a business plan showing cash flow projections etc.

6. Duration of the Loan
For how long is the loan required, i.e. short-term, medium-term or long-term? The longer the time period, the greater the risk to the lender, so the reason for the loan must be solid.

7. Legal Constraints

A company may have a clause in its Memorandum of Association which restricts the level of borrowing. A bank manager must inspect the Memorandum of Association for such clauses.

8. Is the Firm Profitable?

The trend of the firm's profits in recent years will be examined in order to project future earnings.

Personal Loan

The following information is required when considering a request for a personal loan:

Important factors to consider when assessing a loan application:
• size of loan
• credit rating
• type of business
• security
• ability to repay
• length of loan
• what is it for?

1. Name of the customer.

2. Occupation.

3. Size of loan required.

4. Salary/wages.

5. Reason for the loan.

6. Length of time for which the loan is required.

7. Were previous loans repaid as per agreement?

8. Age of the applicant.

9. Is the applicant in full-time or part-time employment?

Household and Business Management Compared

There is a big overlap between managing a household and managing a business, e.g. making decisions and spending money.

The similarities and differences include the following:

1. Taxation

(a) PAYE/PRSI are common to both.

(b) Businesses pay additional taxes, i.e. VAT and corporation tax.

(c) A business can reclaim VAT, whereas a household cannot.

2. Business Forms

(a) Some forms must be completed by both households and businesses, e.g. income tax forms, insurance forms and loan application forms.

(b) Businesses have to complete additional forms regarding VAT and corporation tax.

3. Raising Finance

(a) Raising finance is relevant to both, but the size of the finance required will differ.

(b) The household will borrow for house improvements, educational reasons, family holidays etc., and is therefore more likely to use a short-term or medium-term source of finance.

(c) The business is more likely to borrow for working capital or capital expenditure requirements. Capital expenditure requirements, e.g. machinery, are more likely to be financed by using a medium-term or long-term source of finance.

4. Decision Making

Both business and households have to make decisions on an ongoing basis:

(a) Household decisions include deciding who does certain tasks in the house, what new furniture to buy and how to raise finance for holidays.

(b) Business decisions include deciding how much to spend on new projects, who to appoint as a new manager and when to have a special board meeting to discuss specific issues.

5. Management Activities

Both households and businesses are involved in planning, organising and controlling in order to achieve objectives.

Household and Business Contrasted

There are some issues which are related to both a business and household but are significantly different for the following reasons:

1. Size

In comparison to a household, a business is bigger in size, has more people involved and has to deal with more people.

2. Legislation

Everyone is subject to the laws of the country. A business formed as a limited company is subject to the Companies Acts 1963–1990.

3. Management

Managers with appropriate skills are employed to run a business, e.g. accountant, sales manager etc. In business, cash flow statements are prepared and monitored by management because of their importance. In a household, the householders alone are responsible for managing household accounts, which do not require the same level of expertise. A business has more resources and personnel than a household to carry out tasks.

Similarities and Differences of Household and Business:
- taxation
- business forms
- finance
- decisions
- planning
- organising
- controlling

Risk Management

The main objective of business is profit. Every business wants to keep its losses to a minimum. Risk management is an organised approach to assessing and managing all the potential risks that a business or individual can face. In business, a **risk manager** is appointed by management to be in charge of this area.

A **risk manager** has the following tasks:

1. To assess all the risks, e.g. risk of fire, theft etc. and decide if insurance cover is necessary.

2. To decide the likelihood of some risk occurring, e.g. if the premises are situated on high ground, there is no need to take out insurance against a flood.

3. Find out the costs involved in insuring against the various risks.

Risk Reduction

The following are measures that can be taken to prevent or greatly reduce risks that threaten businesses or households:

1. Motorists can greatly reduce the risk of injury by wearing seat belts (compulsory in law but not always worn) and also by regular car maintenance.

2. Have a good security system in operation – security staff, burglar alarm etc. This will help to reduce the risk of theft.

3. Fire risks can be reduced by banning smoking on the premises, installing a sprinkler system and by having a smoke alarm.

4. Organise regular and unexpected inspections of the premises, e.g. security patrols.

5. Provide adequate training courses to ensure that everyone is aware of the risks which exist in each area. In a factory, machine operators should be

aware of all the risks associated with operating machinery. In a household, all occupants should be aware of the risk connected with electrical goods.

6. Reduce the stock levels in business, i.e. have a policy of minimum stock levels rather than maximum stock levels. This will reduce the likelihood of theft, so the risk is reduced, as is the premium to be paid to the insurer.

7. Transfer the risk of suffering a loss to an insurer and pay a premium for this service, e.g. fire insurance.

Insurance

Insurance is a protection against possible loss, i.e. against a loss you hope will not happen. Risk is the basis of the insurance contract. Risk is the chance or possibility of danger, loss, injury or other adverse conditions. In the area of insurance, there are three types of risk:

The 2004 flood in Fermoy at its height.

1. **Pure risk**, e.g. insuring a house against fire. If there is a fire, a claim will be made. If there is never a fire, then no claim will be made.

2. **Speculative risk**, e.g. investing in shares. The value of the share investment may rise or fall. You cannot insure against this risk.

3. **Fundamental risk**, e.g. losses incurred by an act of God or by war. Such risks are uninsurable. Damage to property caused by floods is not insurable. Such losses are usually borne by the taxpayer.

The insurance company is called the **insurer.** The person seeking insurance is called the **insured.** The fee charged by the insurer is called the **premium.**

Insurers in Ireland include the following:

1.	Hibernian	3.	AXA
2.	Allianz	4.	Quinn Direct

Basic Legal Principles of Insurance

1.	**Insurable Interest**
2.	**Indemnity**
3.	***Uberrimae Fidei* (Utmost Good Faith)**
4.	**Subrogation**
5.	**Contribution**

1. Insurable Interest

A person or business must have an insurable interest in what is to be insured. The insured must benefit by its existence and show that they would suffer from its loss. The insured item (e.g. a house) must have a monetary value.

2. Indemnity

The principal of indemnity means that the insurer will compensate the insured for any loss suffered, but will not allow the insured to make a profit from the loss. A risk is insured for the cost of replacing it if a loss is suffered, e.g. a house which cost €100,000 should be insured for €115,000 at the outset. In theory the house is over-insured. In practice, however, it will cost more than the original cost to replace the house if it is totally destroyed by fire. Life assurance and personal accident insurance are exceptions to the principal of indemnity.

3. *Uberrimae Fidei* (Utmost Good Faith)

All insurance contracts are contracts of good faith. This means that the insured must make full disclosure of all material facts to the insurer. A material fact is one which could influence the insurer either to accept or reject the risk involved or charge a higher premium. The insured provides the information on the proposal form. It is on the basis of the information supplied that the insurer decides the premium to charge. The greater the risk, the higher the premium. The person who calculates the premium is called the actuary.

4. Subrogation

The insured is entitled to compensation from the insurer for any loss suffered which was properly insured. The insurer has the legal right to claim against a third party who caused the damage, e.g. if A's house valued at €90,000 was deliberately burned down by B, A is entitled to compensation from the insurer, who can then sue B for the damage to A's house.

> Subrogation and Contribution are corollaries of Indemnity.

EXAMPLE

Peter Jones has stock insured against theft with Guardian Royal Insurance for €20,000 and with PMPA for €10,000. Following a break-in at his premises, €6,000 worth of stock was stolen.

QUESTION: How much insurance compensation is Peter Jones entitled to?
ANSWER: €6,000

QUESTION: How much compensation will each insurer pay?
ANSWER: This will be calculated as follows:

Amount insured with one insurer x loss suffered
  Total amount insured with different insurers

Guardian Royal will pay $\dfrac{€20,000 \times €6,000}{30,000} = €4,000$

PMPA will pay $\dfrac{€10,000 \times €6,000}{30,000} = €2,000$

5. Contribution

If there is over-insurance due to a risk being insured with two insurers, then the principal of indemnity applies. In such a case the insured is not allowed to make two full claims against the two insurers. In the event of one insurer paying out in full, that insurer is entitled to recover a certain proportion of the amount paid from the other insurer. The objective of contribution goes to the very heart of insurance. The insured should not profit from a loss. If a risk is insured with two insurers, in the event of a claim each insurer will pay compensation in proportion to the risk insured by them.

Average Clause

The principal of indemnity endeavours to restore the insured person's risk to the same position as it was before any loss was suffered.

   Average loss applies when a **partial loss occurs** and the risk is **under-insured**. If, when the loss occurs, the market value of the loss suffered is greater than the amount for which it was insured, the insured will suffer from a partial loss. The insurer will not pay the full value of the loss suffered by the insured. Every business should always have adequate insurance cover.

EXAMPLE

Paul Cavanagh owns a house which was partially destroyed by fire on 3 March 2005. The house was valued at €120,000 on the date of the fire. It was only insured for €90,000. The fire caused €20,000 worth of damage.

QUESTION:

How much compensation is Paul Cavanagh entitled to receive from the insurer?

ANSWER:

- The house is insured for €90,000.
- The value of the house is €120,000.
- The house is only $3/4$ insured.
- The insurer has to pay $3/4$ of the loss suffered.
- Damage caused = €20,000.
- Compensation to be paid by the insurer = €20,000 x 3/4 = €15,000.

The following formula is used when applying the Average Clause rule:

$$\frac{\text{Amount Insured}}{\text{Value of risk on date of loss}} \times \text{Amount of damage caused}$$

$$= \frac{€90,000}{€120,000} \times €20,000 = €15,000$$

Paul Cavanagh will receive €15,000 from the insurer, so he suffers a personal loss of €5,000.

Proximate Cause

An event which causes a loss is called a peril. In the area of insurance, there are two types of peril:

1. Insurable perils, e.g. insurance against fire, theft etc. Theft is the insured risk under a theft policy.

2. Uninsurable perils, e.g. damage caused by war – you cannot insure against this.

Insurance exists to indemnify the insured against financial loss. When the insured makes a claim on a claim form for a loss suffered, the loss must be shown to have been caused by the insured peril.

EXAMPLE

Maureen Hogan insured her jewellery for €5,000 against theft. Sometime later her jewellery was stolen and so she made a claim against the insurer.

QUESTION:

Is she entitled to compensation from the insurer?

ANSWER:

Yes. The proximate cause of the loss was the theft of her jewellery – theft is the risk she had insured against.

The Risk and the Premium

The greater the risk of the insured event happening, the higher the premium quoted and charged. Insurance works when insurers can collect together a large number of identical exposure units. An exposure unit is the object which is exposed to the possibility of damage or loss. The owner of a house takes out a fire insurance policy – the house is the exposure unit.

Motor insurers quote higher premiums for drivers under 25 years of age. Why? The answer is that insurers know from their own statistics that more claims are made by drivers under 25 years of age. Each applicant for insurance fills in a Proposal Form. All questions on this form must be answered truthfully *(uberrimae fidei)*. A policy is given for a fixed time period, usually one year, and is only renewable by the consent of both parties. Based on the information in the proposal form, the insurer can assess the risk and decide the premium to charge. The premium is the amount of money the insured has to pay the insurer on the insurance policy. The person who calculates the premium is called the actuary.

The greater the risk, the higher the premium.

Why are Premiums so High?

The premium is calculated by the actuary. The premium must be enough to cover the risk involved for the insurer, expenses (e.g. salaries and advertising) and profit for the owners. Premiums are set at a high level when the risk to be insured is high, e.g. car insurance for an eighteen-year-old person.

Types of Insurance for a Business

The following are the different insurance policies that a firm should have:

1.	Fire	Insurance against stock and premises being destroyed by fire. This policy should also cover losses caused by water damage, consequential loss and loss of profits due to the fire.
2.	Theft	Insurance against stock and money being stolen.
3.	Fidelity guarantee	Insurance against embezzlement of revenue by employees.
4.	Employees' liability	Protection against injury on the premises to employees.
5.	Public liability	Protection against injury on the premises to members of the public.
6.	Motor	Insurance against the consequences of a motor accident. This is compulsory under the Road Traffic Act 1933. Policies include: • Third party insurance. • Third party, fire and theft. • Fully comprehensive insurance. This is the costliest form of motor insurance because it provides complete indemnity to all the people and vehicles involved in an accident.
7.	Cash in transit	Insurance against the risk of money being stolen while on its way to be lodged in the bank.
8.	Plate Glass Window	Insurance against window breakage. This is very important for shop owners.

Types of Insurance for a Household

Similar to a business, a household should have insurance in the following areas:

1.	Fire	The house and its contents should be covered by insurance.
2.	Theft	Insurance against theft of the house contents.
3.	Motor	If the householder owns a car, then at least third party insurance should be taken out.
4.	Mortgage Protection	This is now compulsory for people getting a mortgage from any financial institution. This policy provides for the full repayment of the balance due on the mortgage in the event of the death of the mortgage holder.
5.	Health	Householders are advised to take out health insurance cover with the VHI or BUPA.
6.	Life Assurance	Life assurance is the exception to the principle of indemnity. The main purpose of life assurance is to provide: (a) Financial protection for the family in the event of an untimely death. (b) Savings for any special purpose, e.g. retirement.

Insurance and Assurance

The major difference between insurance and assurance is that with insurance there is a guarantee. If no loss is suffered, then no compensation has to be paid by the insurer. In an assurance policy, the insurer must pay money on the occurrence of some event which definitely will happen, e.g. death or reaching a specified age. Insurance is taken out against events which might happen and is, therefore, short-term, i.e. it has to be renewed yearly by the insured. Assurance is taken out against an event which will definitely happen and is a long-term arrangement.

Types of Life Assurance

1. Whole Life Assurance

The insured (assured) pays the premium for the rest of his/her life. The insurer then pays the sum assured to the dependants of the assured person when he/she dies. This type of policy is ideal for any person who wishes to provide for dependants in the future.

2. Endowment Assurance

The total sum assured is payable in the event of death or in the event of the assured reaching a specified age, whichever comes first. This is a very popular policy and it is often used when a person is buying a house or obtaining a loan from a bank. This policy is usually taken out for a 20-year period but it may be for a shorter or longer period. As a form of saving, endowment assurance is both effective and attractive.

Business and Household Insurance Compared

There are many similarities between businesses and households in relation to insurance. They both have to do the following:

1. Take out appropriate and adequate insurance cover, i.e. insure their property, contents, vehicles etc.
2. Complete insurance proposal forms and answer all questions accurately.
3. Take appropriate steps to reduce risks in order to minimise the premiums charged by the insurers.

Business and Household Insurance Contrasted

There are some differences between households and business in relation to insurance, for example:

1. A business has a wider range of risks to identify and insure against than a household.
2. The premiums charged to a business are bigger than those charged to households.
3. A business can write off the insurance premiums as an expense against profits, thus reducing its tax bill. A household has no tax credit claim for insurance premiums paid.

Taxation

Taxation is an instrument of economic regulation which can be used for different reasons, for example:

- To influence consumption
- To encourage saving

A tax is a compulsory payment to the Exchequer to meet the expenses of the Government. The taxes are paid to the Revenue Commissioners, who are responsible for collecting this money for the State. Taxes are paid by individuals and businesses. The following is a summary of the different taxes paid:

Taxes paid by Households/Individuals		Taxes paid by Businesses	
1.	PAYE (Pay As You Earn)	1.	Corporation Tax and PAYE
2.	VAT (Value Added Tax)	2.	VAT
3.	DIRT (Deposit Interest Retention Tax)	3.	DIRT
4.	CGT (Capital Gains Tax)	4.	CGT
5.	SAIT (Self-Assessment Income Tax)	5.	SAIT
6.	Motor Vehicle Tax	6.	Motor Vehicle Tax
		7.	Customs Duties
		8.	Commercial Rates on Property

Taxes can be direct or indirect. Direct tax is deducted from income, e.g. income tax and corporation tax, whereas indirect tax is not deducted from income but is borne by consumers and businesses through different kinds of taxes, e.g. Value Added Tax (VAT) is collected by adding the tax to the price of goods and services.

Direct Tax

Direct tax is a tax paid by the taxpayer and includes income tax and corporation tax.

Income Tax

Income tax is a direct tax taken out of a person's salary before they are paid. The income tax year is 1 January to 31 December. Income tax consists of PAYE and PRSI.

PAYE (Pay As You Earn)

PAYE is a tax collected by the employer by deducting the correct amount from salary when paying each employee. The standard rate cut-off point is the amount of income that is taxed at the standard rate of 20 per cent. An individual's standard rate cut-off point is determined by their personal circumstances, e.g. single, married. Any income above your standard rate cut-off point is taxed at 42 per cent. (These rates are subject to change in the annual budget.)

STANDARD RATE TAX BANDS FROM JANUARY 1 2005		FUTURE CHANGES	
Personal Circumstances			
Single taxpayer	29,400 @ 20%; Balance @ 42%		
Married couple (one	38,400 @ 20%; Balance @ 42%		
Married couple (both spouses with income)	58,800 @ 20%; Balance @ 42%		

So for example, a single taxpayer's salary is currently taxed at 20 per cent on the first €29,400 (subject to change in the annual budget). Any income in excess of the standard rate cut-off point is taxed at 42 per cent (subject to change). **Gross pay** (gross salary plus overtime and benefit-in-kind) is taxed to find '**gross tax**'.

Benefit-in-kind (BIK) is a benefit which is in a form that cannot be converted into money, but which benefits an employee, e.g. company car, accommodation provided for an employee, personal loan provided on favourable terms. The value of the BIK is calculated and added to gross salary. Tax is calculated on this total.

EXAMPLE

Single employee
Gross salary   €20,000
Add Benefit-in-Kind   €10,000
Gross pay   €30,000
Income Tax Calculation
29,400 @ 20%   €5880
   600 @ 42%   €252

Gross tax before deduction of Tax Credits: €6,132

Tax Credits

Under the PAYE Tax Credit System, every employee receives an annual tax certificate called Notification of Determination of Tax Credits and standard rate cut-off point.

  Tax credits are the part of your income on which you are not liable for tax. Tax credits are worked out according to your personal circumstances and can depend on whether you are single, married or widowed and whether you are a PAYE employee. Tax credits are deducted from gross tax to find **tax payable**.

TAX CREDITS ON 1 JANUARY 2005		FUTURE CHANGES
Personal Circumstances		
Single	€1,580	
Married	€3,160	
Widowed (without dependent children)	€1,980	
Employee (PAYE)	€1,270	
Incapacitated child	€1,000	

EXAMPLE

Single PAYE employee
Gross tax before deduction of Tax Credits: €6,132
Less tax credits
Single   €1,580
PAYE   €1,270   €2,850
Income Tax payable: €3,282

PRSI (Pay-Related Social Insurance)

Both employers and employees contribute to this tax scheme which raises money for the Social Insurance Fund, which is used to pay pensions and social insurance payments by the State, e.g. unemployment benefits (dole money). An employee's social insurance contributions are deducted by the employer and collected by the Revenue Commissioners. The employer will also pay social insurance on behalf of the employee.

As well as paying into the Social Insurance Fund, employees pay what is called the Health Contribution, which is charged at 2 per cent on all income. The Health Contribution is used to fund health services in Ireland. PRSI is calculated on gross income (i.e. including benefit-in-kind).

PRSI RATES		FUTURE CHANGES
Private sector employee:	4% of gross pay up to a ceiling of €44,180	
Public sector employee:	0.9% of gross pay up to a ceiling of €44,180	
Health Contribution Levy	2% on all income	

EXAMPLE

Private sector employee
Gross pay: €30,000
Less PRSI rates
4% on €30,000   €1,200
2% on €30,000   €600
PRSI and levy payable   €1,800

Personal Public Service Number (PPS)

In order to check your social insurance record, you will need your PPS (Personal Public Service Number). Every taxpayer receives a PPS number and this is included on all tax forms. This number is a unique identification number that you will need when dealing with State agencies.

WORKED EXAMPLE

Calculate the net yearly take-home pay of Deirdre Burke, a financial controller employed by Global Services Ltd.

Gross Salary	€70,000		
Benefit-in-Kind	€10,000		
Tax Credits	→ Single Personal Credit	€1,580	
	→ PAYE Credit	€1,270	
Tax Rates	→ 20% on the first	€29,400	
	→ 42% on the balance over €29,400		
PRSI Rates	→ 4% up to	€44,180	
	→ 2% Health Contribution on all income		

SOLUTION

Gross Salary		€70,000
Add Benefit-in-Kind		€10,000
		€80,000

Income Tax Calculation

Income Tax

29,400 x 20% =	€5,880	
50,600 x 42%	€21,252	
Gross tax before deduction of Tax Credit		€27,132
Less Tax Credits		
Single Personal Credit	€1,580	
PAYE Credit	€1,270	€2,850
Income Tax Payable		€24,282
PRSI Calculation		
4% on €44,180	€1,767	
2% on €80,000	€1,600	
PRSI payable		€3,367

Gross Salary		€70,000
Less Income Tax	€24,282	
Less PRSI	€3,367	€27,649
Net yearly take-home pay		€42,351

N.B. (a) BIK is added to Gross Salary for income tax purposes.

(b) PRSI rates are calculated on gross salary including BIK.

Deirdre Burke's net yearly take-home pay is:	€42,351		
Her net monthly take-home pay is:	€42,351		
	12	=	€3,529
Her net weekly take-home pay is:	€42,351		
	52	=	€814

Corporation Tax

- This is tax on company profits.
- The rate of corporation profits tax is 12.5 per cent.

● Indirect Tax

Indirect tax is a tax that is not deducted from income; it is paid and collected through different taxes like capital gains tax and VAT.

1. Capital Gains Tax (CGT)

- This is a tax on the profit made on the sale of certain assets, e.g. land, property or investments in shares.
- The rate of capital gains tax is 20 per cent but is subject to change in the yearly Budget.
- Profits on life assurance, lottery, prize bonds and from the sale of your principal private residence are exempt from this tax. The first €1,270 is exempt from CGT.

2. Value Added Tax (VAT)

- This is a tax on goods and services and is paid by the consumer in the form of higher prices.
- VAT is chargeable when VAT taxable goods or services are sold to consumers. The current high rate of VAT is 21 per cent but this is subject to change.
- Every business must register for VAT if its annual sales exceed the following:

  (a) €51,000 a year for traders selling goods only.

  (b) €25,500 a year for traders supplying services only.

3. Customs Duties

- These are taxes imposed on imports from non-EU countries.

4. Commercial Rates

- This is a tax on the value of property owned by a business.
- The rates are levied and collected by the local authorities and are a local tax on business.

Self-Assessment

- This system applies to people who do not pay all their tax under PAYE, i.e. the self-employed.

- Tax payments are based on a person's tax return or calculation of tax liability.

- The Preliminary Tax is the taxpayer's estimate of the income tax and PRSI payable for the year and must be paid by 31 October each year.

- In due course, the tax inspector will issue an assessment of the total tax due. Credit is allowed for the preliminary tax paid and any balance due must be paid.

Business and Household Compared

There are a number of similarities and differences between how businesses and households must manage taxation.

Similarities

1. They both have to register with the tax office.

2. They both have to pay their taxes on time at the appropriate rates.

3. They both pay VAT.

4. Both can be liable for capital gains tax.

5. They both have to fill in tax forms and maintain proper records of their income for tax purposes.

Differences

1. Employers (businesses) have to collect the tax under the PAYE system and send it to the Revenue Commissioner.

2. Most businesses have to register for VAT purposes and can claim a VAT refund. Householders cannot register for VAT, so they cannot claim a VAT refund.

3. Businesses pay corporation tax on profits, whereas householders pay their direct tax through either the PAYE or self-assessment system.

Tax Forms

Form 12

This form is filled in by an employee in order to obtain a Tax Credit Certificate (TCC) from the tax office. This form has to be completed if requested by the Revenue Commissioners or if there is a change in the taxpayer's personal circumstances. It is in fact the taxpayer's tax return for the year. On receipt of a completed Form 12 tax form, the tax office will inform the taxpayer of the amount of tax credits to which he/she is entitled. Failure by the taxpayer to submit this form may result in the employer deducting too much tax when paying wages to the employee.

Form P45 (Cessation Certificate)

An employee who resigns/leaves employment during the tax year must receive a special form called a P45 (Cessation Certificate) from the employer. This form shows the following information:

1. The gross income paid to an employee in respect of the tax year in which they are leaving, i.e. from the date of commencement to the date of leaving in the year they are leaving.

2. The amount of tax deducted by the employer from the employee's gross earnings.

> **Four important tax forms:**
> - Form 12
> - P45
> - P60
> - P21

The P45 and TCC forms must be given by the employee to the new employer who will then know how much tax to deduct from the new employee's wages.

Form P60

This form is issued by the employer to the employee at the end of each tax year. It contains the following information:

1. Gross wages paid to the taxpayer.

2. Total amount of tax and PRSI deducted during the year and thus the amount of net pay received by the taxpayer.

This form is proof for both the employee and the Revenue Commissioner of how much tax was deducted by the employer and paid to the tax office. This form can be used by the employee as proof of income when seeking a bank loan, certain medical services or an education grant for a member of the family.

Form P21 (PAYE Balancing Statement)

This form is called a balancing statement. It is issued by the Revenue Commissioners to the taxpayer on request. It contains details of the taxpayer's annual total income, tax credits and PAYE tax paid at the different rates for the year. If too much tax was paid, the taxpayer will receive a refund. If too little tax was paid, the taxpayer will receive details of how the underpayment is to be collected – usually through a reduction of tax credits for the next year.

FORM P45

CERTIFICATE NO. V300064

INCOME TAX - PAY AS YOU EARN - CESSATION CERTIFICATE
Particulars of Employee Leaving

PLEASE COMPLETE

Surname

First Name(s)

Unit Number

PPS Number

Date of Leaving   Deceased

○ Weekly   ○ Monthly (Please

Weekly/Monthly   Week/M
Tax Credit   Numbe

(a) **TOTAL PAY & TAX** deducted from 1 January la

Total Pay

(b) If Employment

P60

CERTIFICATE OF PAY, TAX AND
PAY RELATED SOCIAL INSURANCE
YEAR ENDED 31st DEC

K CAPITALS

PAYE - PRSI

To be given to each employee who was in your employment on
31st December, whether or not tax was deducted.

Name of
Employee:

Address:

Personal Public
Service No.
(PPS No.)

Enter 'W' if week 1 / month 1 applied.

(A) PAY.

1. Total pay (i.e. gross pay less any superannuation contributions
   allowable for income tax purposes) in above year including
   pay in respect of previous employment(s), if any.

2. Pay in respect of previous employment(s), if any, in above year.

(B)

Tax Credit €

'1' indicates that temporary basis applied
'2' indicates that emergency basis applied } at 31st December.

Enter 'X' if there were 53 pay days in the year.

Enter 'D' if employee was a director.

**Standard Rate
Cut Off €
Point**

E9

F9

(C) PRSI in this employment   €

1. EMPLOYEE'S PRSI.

2. TOTAL (employer + employe

3.

Form P21c   INCOME

S o u r c e

INCOME TAX - PAY AS YOU EARN
ALLOCATION OF TAX CREDITS AND STANDARD RATE CUT-OFF POINT
FOR THE YEAR 1ST JAN 2005 TO 31 DECEMBER 2005 AND FOLLOWING YEARS

PPS Number:

Unit Number:

Employer's Name:

Employer's Number:

A Certificate of Tax Credits and Standard Rate Cut-Off Point has been issued to your employer (quoted above)
showing:-

	Euro €
Total Tax Credits	
Monthly Tax Credit	4881
Weekly Tax Credit	406.75
	93.87
Standard Rate of Tax	
	20%

Standard Rate Cut-Off Point	Euro €
Monthly Cut-Off Point	38400
Weekly Cut-Off Point	3200.00
	738.47
Higher Rate of Tax	
	42%

For your own information, the details of the Total Tax Credits
allocated to you are as follows:-

PAYE   TAX   CREDIT
MISC   CREDITS

1270
3611

Issued by

SEAMUS O'CATHASAIGH
INSPECTOR OF TAXES
CITY CENTRE REVENUE DISTRICT
14/15 UPPER O'CONNELL STREET
DUBLIN 1
PHONE 1890 33 34 25

Issue date   14 JAN 05

P2N - Employee Notification

GENERAL NOTES

If any of the details quoted on this certificate are incorrect you can contact the tax office at the 1890 LoCall number
shown above.

Please make sure you have both your PPS No. and Employers No. (both shown above), to hand, when you phone us.

How is my tax calculated?

This example shows how tax would be calculated on a weekly basis - if you are paid fortnightly or monthly the same
principles will apply.

Tax is calculated at Standard Rate 20% on income up to the level of your Standard Rate Cut Off Point   €   738.47
If your Standard Rate Cut Off Point is Zero then tax is calculated on all of your income at the higher rate   42%.
Tax is calculated at 42% on all income over and above the level of the Standard Rate Cut Off Point.
The tax calculated at 20% and 42% are added together to give the gross tax due.
The gross tax due figure is then reduced by the amount of your Tax Credits, €   93.87   to arrive at the amount of
actual tax that you pay in that week.

Exercises

1. Business Cash Flow Forecast for Engineering Supplies Ltd.

	Jan	Feb	March	Total
Receipts (Inflows)				
Cash Sales	20,000	60,000	80,000	160,000
Receipts from Debtors	40,000	30,000	50,000	120,000
Loan from bank (secured)	0	0	40,000	40,000
VAT Refund	0	10,000	0	10,000
Share Capital	0	50,000	0	50,000
Total inflows (A)	60,000	150,000	170,000	380,000
Payments (Outflows)				
Cash Purchases	15,000	30,000	55,000	100,000
Payments to Creditors	40,000	80,000	70,000	190,000
Taxes	10,000	0	15,000	25,000
Sundry Business Expenses	25,000	30,000	40,000	95,000
Total outflows (B)	90,000	140,000	180,000	410,000
Net Cash (A–B) = C	(30,000)	10,000	(10,000)	(30,000)
Opening Cash = D	15,000	(15,000)	(5,000)	15,000
Closing Cash = (C + D) = E	(15,000)	(5,000)	(15,000)	(15,000)

(a) Engineering Supplies Ltd is the name of the company. What is the significance of the word Ltd?

(b) During March, a €40,000 secured loan was received, what does this mean?

(c) Why should Engineering Supplies Ltd prepare a cash flow forecast?

(d) Is this business trading within its means?

(e) Explain what is meant by a VAT refund.

(f) Why do you think that the €50,000 from shareholders was raised during February? Give two reasons for your choice.

(g) February is the only month that the firm has a positive net cash balance. What suggestions can you make to enable the firm to have a positive net cash position in March?

(h) What source of finance could this firm use to improve its liquidity problem?

2. (a) What is a cash flow forecast?

(b) Indicate the main business cash inflows and outflows.

(c) Explain what is meant by the cash flow cycle.

3. 'A wide range of short-term, medium-term and long-term sources of finance are available.'

   (a) What factors should be considered before deciding which source(s) of finance to use?

   (b) State three short-term sources of finance regularly used by both a household and a business.

   (c) Which source of finance do you think would be suitable for a household to use in the following circumstances?

   (i) To purchase a dishwasher   (iii) To build an extension to a house

   (ii) To purchase a television   (iv) To pay for goods in a supermarket

---

4. (a) State and discuss three medium-term sources of finance used by businesses. Give one example of what each source of finance could be used for.

   (b) What is a long-term source of finance?

---

5. (a) Why would a business use a long-term source of finance rather than a medium-term source of finance?

   (b) State and discuss three long-term sources of finance used by a business. Give one example of what each source of finance could be used for.

---

6. (a) Outline the features of a bank current account.

   (b) What factors should be considered by a bank manager when assessing a request for a three-year term loan of €25,000 from Boutique Ltd, one of the bank's customers?

---

7. Discuss the similarities and differences between managing a household and managing a business.

---

8. (a) Discuss the importance of risk management for a business.

   (b) In relation to insurance, explain each of the following terms:

   (i) Pure risk (ii) Premium (iii) Insurer (iv) Uninsurable Risk

---

9. (a) State and explain the basic legal principles of insurance.

   (b) Discuss the concept of the average clause.

---

10. 'It would be very risky for a household not to have adequate insurance cover.'

    (a) Outline the different types of insurance cover a household should have.

    (b) Discuss the role of the actuary in insurance.

---

11. Explain, with an example, each of the following:

    (a) Direct tax   (c) PAYE

    (b) Indirect tax   (d) Self-Assessment

---

12. (a) What similarities exist between a household and a business in relation to paying tax?

    (b) State two examples of business taxes which are not paid by a household.

---

13. (a) Discuss the following tax forms:

    (i) Form 12   (ii) P45   (iii) P60   (iv) P21

    (b) Explain the following taxes:

    (i) Corporation Tax   (ii) Value Added Tax   (iii) Capital Gains Tax

---

PAYE Tax Credit Exercises

The following information on Tax Credits, Tax Rates and PRSI Rates are the same for each of the following questions:

Tax Credits	→	Single Personal Credit	€1,580
	→	PAYE Credit	€1,270
Tax Rates	→	20% on the first	€29,400
	→	42% on the balance over	€29,400
PRSI Rates	→	4% up to €44,180	
	→	2% Health Contribution on all income	

14. Calculate the net yearly take-home pay of Kevin Daly, a HR manager in Slaney Services Ltd.

Gross Salary: €75,000

He has a company car, which has a BIK value of €15,000.

15. Calculate the net monthly take-home pay of Sheila Boland, who is employed as a Bank Manager in Limerick.

Gross Salary: €80,000.

She has a preferential loan from the bank, which has a BIK value of €10,000.

16. Calculate the net weekly take-home pay of Mary Kelly, who is employed as an accountant for Financial Advisers Ltd.

Gross Salary: €90,000

She has a company car which has a BIK value of €14,000. She has a preferential loan from the firm, which has a BIK value of €9,000.

17. Read the information supplied and answer the questions which follow.

Mary and Catherine run a thriving coffee shop, 'The Stopover', in a busy town in Co. Kildare. They employ two full-time staff and one part-time person at the weekends. They lodge the cash takings, which amount to €500 per day on average, on a daily basis. The replacement value of the premises is €50,000 and it is insured for €40,000.

Two months ago, they had a fire in the kitchen, which caused extensive smoke damage. They sent in a claim for the cost of repairing the damage amounting to €10,000. Last week, they received a cheque for €8,000 from the insurance company.

(a) Name the insurance clause that results in €8,000 instead of €10,000 being paid out on the insurance claim.

(b) Explain three principles of insurance.

(c) Describe the types of insurance you would advise Mary and Catherine to take out in order to cover all the risks to their business.

(d) What is the relationship between risks and cost of insurance?

(e) Distinguish between insurance and assurance.

18. High Tech Ltd is based in Cork. A fire in the factory caused €300,000 worth of damages. The building originally cost €500,000 but had a current value of €800,000 due to extensions and improvements, etc. It was discovered that the premises were insured by two insurers, both at the original cost of €500,000.

From your knowledge of insurance, calculate the amount of compensation the insured can expect to receive from the insurers. Explain the answer clearly.

10 Human Resource Management

Objectives

The following topics from **Unit 4** of the syllabus are covered in this chapter:

- What is Human Resource Management?
- Functions of Human Resource Management
- Employing Staff
- How can Management motivate employees?
- Training and Development of Staff
- Trade Unions

What is Human Resource Management?

Human Resource Management (HRM) involves managing personnel requirements and dealing with the concerns of staff in the workplace. To ensure that a proper system of communication exists in the important area of worker–management relations, larger firms have a human resource department. The person in charge of this department is called the human resource manager.

Functions of Human Resource Management

The main functions include the following:

1.	Manpower planning
2.	Employing staff
3.	Motivating Employees
4.	Training and development of staff
5.	Industrial relations matters
6.	Performance appraisal
7.	Employee services and welfare facilities
8.	Teamwork
9.	Emloyer and Employee Relationships

1. Manpower Planning

This involves liaising with the manager of each department to forecast the number of employees and skills required for the business.

The Characteristics (Features) of Manpower Planning

These characteristics include the following:

(a) Assessing the future personnel needs of the business. Some departments may have more IT requirements than others (e.g. accounts department). This involves liaising with each department manager.

(b) Providing ongoing training to upgrade the skills of existing employees. This investment in existing staff will increase their loyalty and commitment to the firm.

(c) Planning future personnel requirements. This is necessary as the human resource manager should know when employees are due to retire. This ensures that new employees are recruited in time.

(d) Having a company policy of filling vacancies. If the staff are aware that some vacancies can be filled from within, this will encourage employees to avail of training courses being provided by the firm.

(e) The human resource manager should update employees' files when they have reached the required skills level to be considered for vacancies that arise.

(f) Keeping up to date with employment trends, national wage levels and employee legislation.

2. Employing Staff

This involves employing people who have both the ability and skill to carry out the tasks as outlined in the job specification. The following factors should be considered before employing a new person in a firm:

(a) Whether there is a definite need for a new employee and if so what wages will have to be paid.

(b) The skills and experience required of the new employee, e.g. computer skills.

(c) Whether the vacancy is to be filled on a permanent or temporary basis.

Every employee is entitled to a contract of employment.

(d) Whether an exact job description is available for use in the interview.

(e) How the vacancy will be advertised, i.e. in the newspapers, with an employment agency, or on the Internet.

The following action must be taken when a candidate has been selected to fill a vacancy:

(a) References should be checked when interviews are completed.

(b) Terms for the written contract of employment should be decided. This contract is given to the successful candidate and must be signed by both the employee and employer.

The contract of employment should contain the following:

- Name of employer and employee
- A date when the position commences
- Job Title
- Hours of work
- Place of work

- Wages
- Holiday entitlement
- Length of notice required for terminating the contract
- The firm's disciplinary rules and procedures
- Pension scheme arrangement

Job Description

→ **Definition of a Job Description**

A job description is a statement of the purpose, scope, duties and responsibilities attached to the job being advertised.

A job description is essential before any vacancy can be properly filled. The content of the job description forms the basis of the contract of employment for the successful applicant. It is prepared by the human resource manager before a vacancy is advertised. A copy of the job description is sent to all applicants.

The job description should include the following:

(a)	The job title (e.g. sales manager).	(f)	Number of people (if any) that the job-holder will have to manage.
(b)	The duties of the successful candidate.	(g)	Working conditions.
(c)	The department where the employee will work.	(h)	Performance standards required.
(d)	Details of specific qualifications required, e.g. experience, diploma or degree.	(i)	Salary and Bonus.
(e)	The person to whom the employee will report.		

Benefits of a Job Description

(a) The employer benefits because the human resource manager has to consider how to attract the most suitable applicants for the job.

(b) The suitability of applicants can be assessed more easily because of the existence of the standard job specification.

(c) It reduces the chance of unsuitable applicants applying for the job.

(d) Each applicant knows exactly what the job entails.

Filling a Vacancy from Within (Internal Recruitment)

Some firms have a policy of promoting or filling a vacancy from within the ranks of their own employees, e.g. if a bank manager retires, the bank does not advertise the vacancy in the newspapers. Instead, an assistant bank manager in some branch will usually be promoted to the rank of manager to fill the vacancy.

Filling a vacancy from within is quick and easy to do – but is it the right thing to do?

Benefits

The potential benefits of filling a vacancy by internal recruitment include the following:

(a) Staff morale is good as employees are motivated to work hard in the knowledge that this will be taken into consideration when vacancies arise.

(b) Top employees are happy to remain with the firm as they know that prospects for career development and promotion are good.

(c) It is quicker, cheaper and easier to fill a vacancy from within as this person will be familiar with all aspects of the firm. No costs are incurred in advertising the job.

Disadvantages

The negative features associated with internal recruitment include the following:

(a) It may be difficult to implement major changes if an internal person is promoted. It might be easier for an outsider to implement such changes.

(b) The management skills required may not be available within the firm.

(c) If the internal vacancy is not filled on a seniority basis, there may be resentment and a lack of co-operation from some former colleagues.

(d) No new creative ideas or experience are introduced into the business.

Filling a Vacancy by External Recruitment

The majority of jobs are filled by external recruitment. The jobs are usually advertised in newspapers, trade magazines or with employment agencies.

Filling the vacancy from outside:
- Outsider may have more experience.
- Can be more objective.
- Can have new ideas.

Benefits

(a) A suitable person with appropriate skills can be employed, e.g. a computer specialist.

(b) Employing the best person is good for the firm. If the best candidate for the job is an outsider, then this person should be appointed to fill the vacancy.

(c) It is easier for an outsider to introduce changes in the operation of the business.

Criteria for Assessing Applicants for Jobs

Interviews are held in order to appoint the best person to fill the vacancy. The following criteria could be used when assessing an applicant after the interview:

(a) Experience – is their experience relevant to the job as per the job spec?

(b) Educational qualifications – second/third level courses taken etc.

(c) Self-confidence – a nervous person might be unsuitable in a crisis situation.

(d) Level of pay – how does the pay compare to the applicant's current or previous jobs?

(e) Location – where is the applicant's home address in relation to the place of work?

(f) Information received from references – it is advisable to check in confidence with the referee.

(g) Contribution – what can this person contribute to the firm?

Remuneration for Employees

People work for different reasons, for example:

(a) To earn money to pay their bills.

(b) For job security.

(c) For job satisfaction.

Management should motivate their employees; this will have the impact of increasing output and reducing absenteeism. Money alone will not always guarantee that employees are fully motivated.

3. Motivating Employees

The issues that can motivate employees, whether they are working in customer service or on the factory floor, are as follows:

A.	Monetary rewards	B.	Non-monetary rewards

The combination of both is referred to as a remuneration package.

It is used by some firms for the following reasons:

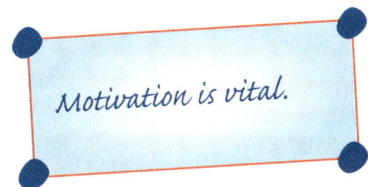

Motivation is vital.

(a) To attract a top person to fill an important vacancy in a firm, e.g. an export sales manager.

(b) To encourage key employees to remain with the firm and not move elsewhere.

(c) To reward increased productivity.

(d) To reward employees who give long service to a firm.

A. Monetary Rewards
(i) Wages

Wages are paid weekly or monthly, usually by cheque or credit transfer into an employee's bank account. Wages can be paid on the basis of Time Rate or Piece Rate.

Time Rate

This is a fixed hourly rate, e.g. €10 per hour for a 37-hour week. This equals a gross wage of €370. This form of payment is easy to calculate by the employer. The number of hours worked are usually recorded by a clock-in clock-out system in the firm. Firms will use this system of payment if the rate of output is difficult to measure or speed up. A criticism of this system is that both the efficient and inefficient workers can be paid the same wage. Examples of jobs where a time rate system is used include:

- bus driver
- business receptionist.

Piece Rate

This is where the wages paid to employees are related to the output level, i.e. the number of units produced. A basic wage, e.g. €120 is usually paid and an extra wage related to an employee's measured output is added to this – the more they produce, the more they are paid. This system of payment is usually applied in the following situations:

- Where the output is constant and can be measured.
- Where workers can be encouraged to increase output by being rewarded with an automatic increase in wages.

The big advantage of this system is that workers require less supervision, are rewarded for becoming more efficient and increasing output.

A risk for the firm with this system is that some workers may try to increase output at the expense of quality. A good quality control system should exist to ensure that faulty goods are not produced.

(ii) Commission

This is an additional payment to sales staff. They are usually paid a basic weekly salary, e.g. €250. Additional payment will be related to sales targets.

This form of payment is a good way to motivate sales people. They have an incentive to work hard to reach sales targets.

> **EXAMPLE**
> Helen Doyle earns a basic weekly salary of €250. She is also entitled to a sales commission of 5 per cent of sales. Her sales for the first week in April added up to €5,000.
>
> **Question**: How much did she earn for the first week in April?
> **ANSWER:**
> | | | |
> |---|---|---|
> | Commission = 5% of €5,000 | = | €250 |
> | Salary | = | €250 |
> | Total wages for the week | = | €500 |

(iii) Bonus

This is an additional lump sum gross payment to employees for achieving an agreed target, e.g. increasing output by 10 per cent. It is usually paid at the end of the year.

(iv) Profit-Sharing

This occurs when an agreed percentage of the profits are paid to employees in addition to their basic wages. This system helps to control costs and improve efficiency levels in a business. This system helps to motivate employees because they share in the increased profits of the business. This approach is fine when profits are high and rising. If profits fall, the workers may feel that they are not responsible and might seek a bigger share of the reduced profit.

In 2004, 18.2% of management and 13% of clerical staff were employed by firms who operated a profit-sharing scheme.

(v) Performance-Related Pay

Sometimes it is difficult to measure output, e.g. how do you measure the output of a graphic designer in a publishing firm? In order to recognise the contribution of certain employees, it is necessary to have a performance appraisal. A manager or supervisor performs the appraisal by talking to the employee. Discussing the efficiency of the work being done will enable management to decide how much extra (if any) to pay the employee.

B. Non-monetary Rewards

In addition to the monetary reward (wages), some firms pay non-monetary rewards to some employees, for example:

(i) Fringe Benefits (also called Benefit-in-Kind or 'Perks')

These are given in addition to salaries paid, e.g. company car, lunch vouchers, VHI payment and goods at a special staff discount. Such payments are good for staff morale, and can improve job status and help to attract new employees to the firm.

(ii) Employee Share Ownership

This system exists when an agreed number of shares are given to employees instead of a cash bonus. Tax must be deducted from a cash bonus, so the share system is good for staff morale and encourages employees to stay with the firm. If profits increase, then so does the value of their shares. Owners of the shares also receive dividends from profits.

(iii) Holidays

Some firms give employees additional holidays linked to years of service, e.g. an additional week's holidays for employees with more than 20 years service.

4. Training and Development of Staff

Training is very important in modern business. It is a form of investment in human resources rather than in capital expenditure (e.g. machinery).

> **→ Definition of Training**
>
> *Training is the planned acquisition of knowledge, skills and ability required to enable employees to perform their tasks effectively.*

Types of Training

The following are the different types of training:

(a) On-the-Job or Off-the-Job

Training is both a cost and an investment and can be carried out in-house (on-the-job training) or outside the firm (off-the-job training). Most firms prefer in-house training as workers can learn from the experience of colleagues, who can immediately clarify problems that may arise. With off-the-job training, employees attend courses, lectures and seminars at another location, i.e. the training is done by specialists. These courses may be very costly but must be seen by management as a necessary investment.

(b) Induction Training

New employees will know very little about the firm they have joined. They may need special training, e.g. training on new software. Induction training involves the following:

(i) Introducing new employees to their superiors and colleagues.

(ii) Explaining the rules, regulations and working conditions of the firm.

> **Induction Training**
>
> *The training that is necessary for new employees.*
> *It helps them get off to a good start. (Induction training applies to new employees only.)*

(iii) Instructing/training them on how to carry out the tasks assigned to them as per the job description.

Reasons for Training

(a) Industry requires highly-skilled operatives, engineers and managers. Existing employees may have to be retrained to improve their knowledge and upgrade their skills, so that they can continue to play an important role for their employers.

(b) Many tasks are now done by automated machinery, so it is necessary to train the workforce to be multi-skilled.

Training for Different Employees

(a) Shop-Floor Training
New employees on the shop-floor can be trained by the shop-floor manager or supervisor.

(b) Administrative Training
Training will be necessary if a new computer system is installed in a firm.

> Training is necessary:
> - for existing employees
> - for new employees

(c) Technical Training
This form of training is for apprentices and technicians. They may be involved in ongoing, on-the-job training, as well as attending college on a part-time basis before being fully qualified, e.g. printers.

How do Firms benefit from Training and Development?
There are many benefits to firms who invest in training and development. They include the following:

(a) At shop-floor level, the skilled employees are able to increase output, improve quality, reduce wastage and reach targets.

(b) Customers will receive a better service, so the image of the firm is improved.

(c) Employees will be happy that they are being trained properly to carry out their duties. This is good for staff morale which leads to the operations of the firm becoming more efficient.

(d) The labour turnover in a firm will be down and this is good for the firm.

(e) The business becomes more competitive and can give a better service to customers.

5. Industrial Relations

What is a Trade Union?

> ➡ **Definition of a Trade Union**
>
> *A trade union is an association of workers (members) whose main objective is to regulate the working relationship between employer and employee.*

Employees in Ireland have a right set down in the Constitution to join a trade union. One of a trade union's aims is achieved by replacing individual bargaining with collective bargaining.

In 2004, there were 61 trade unions in Ireland with about 750,000 members.

A trade union can provide an important source of information and protection in relation to employment matters. It can negotiate with employers for better pay and conditions for its members.

A trade union is funded by a levy on its members, who pay at the rate of 0.5% to 1% of gross salary each year. This levy is deducted from the wages by the employer and sent to the trade union.

Shop Steward

The shop steward is appointed by the union members.

Functions of a Shop Steward

The functions of a shop steward include the following:

(a) Representing members in discussions with union officials and management.
(b) Ensuring that agreements between the union and the firm are adhered to by both sides.
(c) Recruiting new members to the union.
(d) Ensuring that union dues are paid by the members.
(e) Informing the members of any information received from head office.

It is important for both management and the workers to have an efficient shop steward. Management benefits because the shop steward will try to solve problems that may arise. The workers benefit because they are represented by a person that they appointed. This person will understand their problems and accurately reflect their views in discussions with management.

Collective Bargaining

Collective bargaining involves the negotiation of wages, hours and working conditions between employers and employees represented by unions. The negotiations are called collective bargaining and take place on a voluntary basis. When both sides agree on the conditions of employment, a collective agreement is drawn up. A collective agreement is not legally binding and this voluntary aspect is a big weakness to this kind of approach.

The merits of collective agreements include the following:

(a) Negotiations take place between management and unions without any third party presence, i.e. direct negotiations without the presence of a conciliator or an arbitrator. Both sides are now responsible for ensuring that the agreement is adhered to.

(b) The voluntary nature of discussions is important and agreement is reached without legally binding conditions being included.

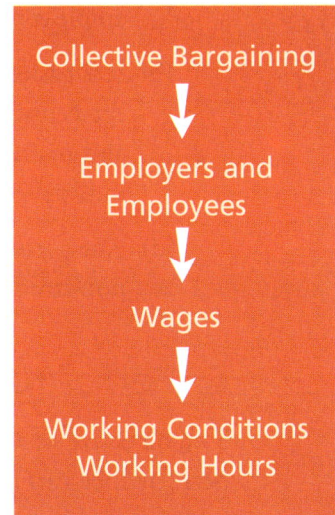

> **Collective Bargaining**
> ↓
> **Employers and Employees**
> ↓
> **Wages**
> ↓
> **Working Conditions Working Hours**

Centralised Wage Agreements

The major stakeholders in the Irish economy are party to the Centralised Wage Agreements (e.g. Sustaining Progress 2003/06).

These stakeholders, known as the social partners, are as follows:

- The Government
- Irish Congress of Trade Unions (ICTU)
- Irish Business and Employers Confederation (IBEC)
- The Construction Industry Federation (CIF)
- The Irish Farmers' Association (IFA)

> *The existence of centralised wage agreements has helped the industrial relations climate.*

The following areas of agreement are included in a Centralised Wage Agreement:

- Wage increases.
- Development of small business – important for job creation.
- Agri-industry, food, forestry and rural development.
- Tax reform.
- Public sector services, e.g. health and education.

Merits of Centralised Wage Agreements

(a) Management face less uncertainty because wage levels over the life of the agreement are agreed by all sides.

(b) Industrial problems are reduced and this is good for employers, employees, unions and the economy.

(c) It is easier for the Government to plan the running of the economy, control inflation, attract foreign industry and maintain the competitive position of Irish industry.

(d) The agreements always keep in mind the low paid and non-union workers in the economy.

> **Performance Appraisal**
> - Feedback
> - Determines a possible bonus or wage increase
> - Good for the business
> - Good for the employee

6. Performance Appraisal

The objective of a performance appraisal is to identify areas where an employee's performance can improve. The appraisal may be done by the human resource manager or by the department manager, who meets the employees at agreed intervals (e.g. once yearly).

Many firms have a policy of performance appraisals for the following reasons:

(a) An appraisal is necessary if an employee is on a fixed-term contract, e.g. a six-month contract. It would be carried out before a decision is made on extending the contract or making the position permanent.

(b) The performance of employees who are being considered for promotion must be assessed – this is a form of manpower planning.

(c) Appraisals assist in determining whether improvements can be made by some employees in how they perform their duties, e.g. some training may be necessary.

(d) A person's salary may be fixed, but the bonus is related to that person's performance during the year. A good performance may be rewarded with a big bonus, a poor performance may result in no bonus being paid to the employee.

7. Employee Services and Welfare Facilities

It is important that proper employee services and welfare facilities exist. Here are some examples of how this can be done:

(a) Ensuring that proper health and safety regulations exist.

(b) Providing proper canteen facilities.

(c) Setting up a social club in large firms to improve staff morale.

8. Teamwork

An important requirement of many jobs is the ability of employees to work as members of a team. In business a team has been defined as 'a group of employees working together to achieve the same goal'. The team's goal is of greater importance than those of any member of the team.

Characteristics of Teamwork

(a) All team members agree with the common goal to be achieved.

(b) All team members contribute to discussions and problem solving.

(c) All team members accept and share the responsibility for any failures or successes.

(d) Any bonus payments from management are equally shared by the team members, e.g. a sales bonus of €10,000 for achieving an agreed target would be shared amongst all members of the sales team.

Basic Stages in the Team-building Process

There are five basic stages in the process of encouraging a group of employees to develop a teamwork approach:

Stage 1 →	Forming
Stage 2 →	Storming
Stage 3 →	Norming
Stage 4 →	Performing
Stage 5 →	Transforming

Stage 1: Forming (The Team)

This is when the team is formed and the team members get to know each other. They discuss issues to be tackled and appoint a team leader.

Stage 2: Storming

This is where conflict occurs as team members openly disagree on how the common goal should be achieved. During this stage, the team members get to know each other and understand the reasons for their different viewpoints.

Stage 3: Norming

During this stage, the working relationship amongst the team members improves. Different opinions are considered rather than ignored and the trust between the members improves.

Stage 4: Performing

The team becomes task orientated as they realise the stated goal has to be achieved. Conflicts have been resolved and the team works as a unit to reach the agreed target, i.e. the team performs.

Stage 5: Transforming
When the team has achieved its goal, it should be reorganised to take on some new task or be disbanded.

Benefits of Teamwork

(a) The team is made up of people with a mix of talents, abilities and experiences. Different team members can contribute to discussions.

(b) Within a team, different members can be given tasks related to their strengths. This is called specialisation.

(c) Within a team some members can be trained to carry out different tasks. This means that the progress of the team is not dependent on any one member. This is called flexible working.

(d) Team members are more motivated because they work as a team; problems can be shared and the best outcome achieved. Success is celebrated by the team. In some firms, the bonus is paid based on team performance rather than individual performance.

9. Employer and Employee Relationships

Both employers and employees are members of the stakeholders team. A good working relationship between both sides is essential for the smooth working of every firm and for the existence of a good industrial relations climate. The human resource manager has an important role to play in ensuring that both employers and employees trust and respect each other.

How is a Trusting and Co-operative Relationship Achieved in Business?
This important relationship is achieved by the existence of the following in business:

(a) Open communication between employers and employees. This can be achieved by regular meetings between management and staff. Both sides should openly explain their problems or relevant issues. Such meetings will eliminate rumours that could be damaging to the business, e.g. rumours of impending job cuts, etc.

(b) The existence of a company policy regarding induction and ongoing training for employees. Improving employees' skills will show them that they are appreciated by management.

(c) The existence of agreed procedures for resolving conflict between both sides. Conflicts can arise over issues such as redundancy, promotion, bonus, etc. The existence of agreed appeal procedures is good for both sides.

(d) Having a recruitment policy that ensures that suitable employees are employed to fill vacancies that arise.

(e) Valuing employees by treating them with dignity and respect and by accommodating their needs where possible. This can be achieved by:

    (i) Introducing flexi-time, which allows staff discretion regarding the time they start and finish work daily. This would help to reduce any friction over employees being late for work. This arrangement will assist the human resource manager to recruit skilled new staff and retain existing employees.

    (ii) Introducing a policy of job-sharing where two employees share the one job. This is very popular in the Civil Service.

(f) Ensuring the existence of a pleasant work environment and sourcing activities which in turn improve the team spirit in a firm. This is particularly important in big firms with large numbers of employees.

Exercises

1. (a) Explain what is meant by human resource management.

    (b) Discuss the functions of human resource management in a large firm.

2. Explain each of the following terms:

    (a) Industrial Relations   (b) Benefit-in-Kind   (c) Time Rates

    (d) Performance Appraisal   (e) Manpower Planning   (f) Profit-sharing

3. 'Some jobs can be filled from amongst the staff, other jobs have to be advertised externally.'

    (a) Why does management sometimes fill a vacancy from within the firm? Give an example.

    (b) Why is it sometimes necessary to fill a vacancy by advertising it externally? Give two examples.

    (c) What factors should be considered when assessing a person's suitability to fill a vacancy in a firm?

4. (a) Outline the different forms of remuneration for employees.

    (b) Which form of remuneration do you think employees would prefer? Give two reasons for your answer.

5. (a) What is a trade union?

    (b) Discuss the functions of a shop steward.

6. Explain each of the following:

    (a) Collective Bargaining

    (b) Centralised Wage Agreement

    (c) Induction Training

7. A vacancy for a computer operator exists in a firm.

    (a) Using a fictitious name and address, draft a letter to the human resource manager of the firm, indicating four characteristics to be looked for when interviewing candidates for the position.

    (b) Under what circumstances might it be suitable to fill the vacancy from within the firm?

8. A vacancy for an export sales manager exists in Global Products Ltd.

    (a) Explain with reasons where this vacancy might be advertised.

    (b) How would you assess the suitability of a potential candidate for the position?

    (c) The managing director is of the opinion that it may be necessary to fill the vacancy by head hunting. Explain what this means and why might it be necessary to adopt this approach.

9. (a) Explain what is meant by performance appraisal.

    (b) Why do some firms have a policy of performance appraisal?

    (c) What steps can be taken to enable an employee's performance to improve?

11 Changing Role of Management

Changing Role of Management

Objectives

The following topics from **Unit 4** of the syllabus are covered in this chapter:
- Changing Role in Management
- Empowerment of Workers
- Total Quality Management
- Making Changes in Business
- Impact of Technology on Business

For a business to compete it must be managed efficiently. There are many factors putting increased pressure on business in today's world, for example:

- The Single European Market
- Growth of competition
- Consumer demands
- Requirements of investors

It follows that in a changing business environment, the role and attitude of management has to change with the times. Management must respond to new situations and react swiftly.

Reasons for the Changing Role of Management

The reasons for the changing role of management include the following:

1. The speed of technological developments has forced businesses to mechanise many services in order to compete with larger firms. Management can now install high-tech computer facilities at home, so they can 'link up' with the business and keep up to date. This enables them to respond in time to important matters, rather than when business has been lost to competitors.

> For a business to compete, it must be managed. For a business to survive, it must change.

2. Global competition has become easier due to the existence of the Single European Market (SEM) and the emergence of the World Trade Organisation (WTO), which has helped in eliminating trade barriers and has forced management in Irish industry to respond by improving the quality and range of goods for consumers.

3. Through mergers and takeovers, firms have become bigger, management structures have changed and there is more delegation than previously.

4. Industrial democracy, which ensures that workers have representatives on the board of directors, has forced management to respond to workers' issues and recognise their contribution to business.

5. Both consumers and employees are better educated. Product life cycles are shorter due to a more demanding consumer.

6. Employees work mainly in teams and require less supervision.

Changing Role of a Manager from Controller to Facilitator

A business must modernise in order to survive and remain profitable. The role of management must change from controlling all aspects of the business to facilitating the changes that have to take place. Unions and staff may resist management changes due to fear of job losses or worsening of working conditions or wages/bonuses. A good manager will be able to facilitate the introduction of change by ensuring the following:

> *Change is good for business. Change leads to improvement. No change – no future for some firms.*

1. The manager must have people skills, e.g. they need to be understanding, experienced and imaginative. These skills will allow the manager to help employees achieve self direction at work. If employees are assisting to plan the direction of their jobs, then they are more responsible for problems that arise in their areas. This lessens the need for employees to be responsible to higher management.

2. The manager must create a climate of trust in the workplace, otherwise some employees will fear being blamed for problems that may arise. If that fear exists they may cover up problems.

The existence of people skills and the creation of the climate of trust will enable the manager to ensure that employees contribute to changes required in the business.

Managing Change in Business *(Higher Level Only)*

Once management have decided to introduce changes in the business, it is important to have the support and goodwill of the workers. The factors required to implement change include:

1. Management must be fully committed to the changes.

2. Management should consult with the trade unions and employees about the need for change: when and how it will take place and what effect (if any) it will have on employees (e.g. job security is guaranteed).

> *Consultation between management and staff is necessary for change to be understood, accepted and supported.*

3. Where new technology is part of the change, it is essential to guarantee employees that proper training will be provided. This will give them the confidence to support the changes being introduced. Improving the high-tech skills of workers improves their status and makes them more employable.

4. There must be proper and ongoing communication between both sides in order to clarify situations and ensure a smooth implementation of the change.

5. Where a change involves an increase in productivity or some economic gain for the business, the workers should be promised some gain also, e.g. a bonus or wage increase.

6. If the staff are in full agreement with the changes, they should be asked for their suggestions on the matter.

7. Do not criticise those employees who resist change. Encourage them to give it a chance because it is good for the firm and for their own job security, i.e. both sides benefit.

8. Adequate finance should be provided to fund all the changes.

9. There should be an ongoing review process, so that problems can be highlighted and resolved.

10. An agreed time frame should exist to implement the changes.

Empowerment of Workers

Employees are a very important 'asset' for every firm. Many employees are in the 'front line', dealing with customers, whereas management are usually in the background. It is important that employees are trained, not only to deal with customers, but also with other issues that may arise.

The empowerment of workers means placing decision-making responsibility in the hands of those employees who are closest to the customer. Decisions are more effective since those making them are closer to the problems in question.

Empowered employees are more capable when it comes to solving customers' problems

Empowerment is not just a form of delegation – it is a good way of getting employees to realise their full potential in the job.

Benefits of Empowerment of Workers to a Business

The benefits of empowerment include the following:

1. There is an improved service to customers, which is good for business, so sales and profits should increase.

2. Workers are committed to the job, so wastage is reduced, costs are controlled and profits should increase.

3. Staff morale and loyalty is improved as the workers are involved in decision making and are not dictated to by supervisors or management. This leads to the production of better quality goods.

4. Where empowerment exists, workers are more open to new ideas and so it is easier for management to get support from workers for change.

5. Work has become more challenging and enjoyable for employees.

Implementing Empowerment

A good management–staff relationship must exist for a business to implement a policy of empowerment. Before such a policy can be implemented, management must be confident that the workers in question have the necessary skills to recognise problems and react with solutions. The manager should empower the workers to carry out tasks which are part of their normal day's work. To introduce the policy of empowerment the manager must do the following:

> *Empowerment can only work if the workers have the skills to realise there is a problem and the ability and skill to solve that problem.*

1. Inform the employees about problems facing the business in the marketplace and the reasons why changes in work practice are required.

2. Assure the workers that adequate training will be provided to enable them to adopt the changes. Workers will now feel that they are an important part of the change, so they will now co-operate with management.

3. Outline to the workers the additional wages/bonus that can be earned from 'savings' which would be guaranteed following the introduction of empowerment.

4. Clarify each worker's role and responsibility and the steps to take if they are unable to solve a problem.

5. Assure all employees that the top management in the business fully support the changes in order to ensure the future of the business.

Management Skills Required to Facilitate Empowerment

Unless the workers are fully clear on their new role and responsibilities, the concept of empowerment will not work. Changes will be resisted by workers if they are not convinced that the changes are for the better, both for the business and for themselves. The following managerial skills are necessary to support the policy of empowerment:

1. Enabling

Employees must be provided with all the financial and training resources required to give them the necessary skills to carry out the tasks.

> *Total co-operation between management and workers must exist for TQM and empowerment to be successful.*

2. Facilitating

All obstacles that would prevent empowerment from being effective should be removed, e.g. unnecessary bureaucracy.

3. Consulting

Regular contact between management and staff raises issues from both sides. Management should consider the suggestions of the employees when implementing empowerment.

4. Mentoring

An experienced manager will influence, advise and encourage workers as they carry out their tasks.

5. Collaborating

The employees should be seen as equal stakeholders in the process of change taking place in the business. This helps to improve the motivaton levels of the staff.

Total Quality Management (TQM)

To prevent errors in production, Japanese companies introduced methods known as Total Quality Management (TQM). These quality methods are now practised worldwide and have proved very effective. TQM is a process of continuous improvement, which aims to prevent rather than detect defects.

The main aim of TQM is to focus businesses on the requirements of their customers and the relationship between suppliers and customers. It requires the existence of control procedures to check the quality of goods at each stage in the process of production. Faults are spotted and corrective action taken before production is completed. Employees are given the responsibility to ensure that faults are spotted and only quality goods are produced – this is empowerment in practice.

TQM Principles

The principles which relate to the process of TQM are as follows:

1. To satisfy the requirements of consumers on product, service and value (price).

2. To have a policy of ongoing improvements in production methods and control procedures. This ensures sustained efficiency and controls unit costs.

3. To have teamwork throughout the organisation, i.e. total commitment to satisfying the consumer.

4. There is an emphasis on zero defects.

5. There must be commitment and support from top management.

> The vital principle of TQM is that the customer is vital for the success of business.

TQM and Empowerment

Total Quality Management TQM does not just involve management; it cannot be achieved without the full co-operation of workers. It follows that empowerment must exist for TQM to be achieved. TQM can be achieved as follows:

1. Giving the workers the authority to make decisions that affect their work.

2. Setting up quality standard teams, so that workers can seek assistance from colleagues on the team. If necessary, the quality team could meet to try to solve the problem.

3. Not penalising workers who make a genuine error. It is important, however, that errors be recognised and steps taken to ensure they are not repeated.

4. Sharing all relevant information amongst the workers. New ideas for change and improvement should be shared.

5. Assessing the training needs of the workers on an ongoing basis. Additional training to improve skills should be provided.

6. Ensuring a level of trust exists between management and staff. Staff must feel that the management can be trusted to perform their own functions effectively. If this is the case, employees will learn by example and react positively. At the same time, management must illustrate that they trust their workers with the responsibility. Management must treat the staff as if they were customers. Without customers, a business could not survive. Without efficient staff, a business would not exist.

Importance of TQM to Business *(Higher Level Only)*

The main aim of TQM is to focus businesses on the requirements of their customers. The benefits of TQM to a business include the following:

1. The quality of the goods produced will increase. This is important for the firm's reputation in the marketplace.

2. There will be a reduction in the quantity of faulty goods produced. This in turn reduces the number of complaints from customers.

3. Costs will be reduced, so sales and profits increase because the requirements of the customer are met.

4. It ensures that a business is not in breach of the Sale of Goods and Supply of Services Act 1980, which requires that goods on sale are of merchantable quality.

5. Staff morale is improved because they see that management are committed to running the business in an efficient manner.

Successful Implementation of TQM in a Business
(Higher Level Only)

A firm can successfully implement its policy of TQM in the following way:

1. Management should inform employees of the importance of implementing a new policy of TQM.

2. The aim is to have zero defects, so control procedures must be put in place to prevent errors occurring.

3. TQM must be seen by both management and staff as a new culture, where the emphasis is on satisfying the consumer.

> **To make a satisfied customer:**
> • zero defects
> • consumer surveys
> • ongoing monitoring
> • benchmark standards
> • teamwork

4. Management should conduct ongoing consumer surveys to gauge consumer reaction to existing products and services.

5. Products should be manufactured to consumer specifications.

6. The production process should be designed so that the goods are produced and delivered on time to the customer.

7. Monitoring and testing samples of the product should take place at each stage of the production process.

8. The standards set up by competitors should be the benchmark standards for the firm. Any improvements over the competitors' standards will improve the competitiveness of the firm.

9. Ensuring that teamwork exists, i.e. people working together as part of a team rather than as individuals. This involves sharing information and helping and encouraging colleagues, e.g. sales team.

Impact of Technology on Business

Technology is in a constant state of change with new advances being made all the time. Businesses must progress with technology if they are to survive. Modern developments in technology have brought many positive changes for business and consumers, for example:

1. New products – video recorders, CDs, DVDs and computer chips.
2. New services – automated banking, satellite link-up, video-conferencing and E-commerce.
3. New skills – computers.
4. New approaches – video-conferencing (very helpful for the management of global firms).

The growth of technology has improved the accuracy and reliability of information, which enables management to make fast and accurate decisions.

Impact of Technology on Personnel

The growth of technology has impacted on jobs in many ways:

1. It has reduced the number of employees required in both manufacturing and service firms.

2. High-tech jobs in computers, research and development and consultancy work have been created.

3. Modern management require high-tech skills, so that accurate information can be accessed speedily when required.

4. Technology enables the management of global businesses to use video-conferencing in order to link up with their companies in different countries. Group management can make global decisions quickly.

5. Technology has enabled firms to hire employees who work from home through teleworking (telecommunicating). In March 2005, 58 per cent of Irish households had computers (PCs etc.).

Video-conferencing is a substitute for face-to-face meetings with the same advantages of direct visual and voice access.

Impact of Technology on Business Costs

Despite the many advantages, the growth of technology in business has many costs. Some of these costs include the following:

1. Purchasing and installing computers involves a high capital cost. These computers then have to be maintained.

2. Industrial relations problems often incur costs, e.g. when unions resist the introduction of change and redundancies are an issue.

3. Redundancy payments may have to be paid before new technology can be installed.

4. Training costs are necessary to ensure that technology is used effectively.

It costs money:
- to buy a computer
- to maintain/service a computer

Substantial financial savings would also arise if new technology meant a reduction in the number of employees and managers required.

Benefits of Technology to Business

The benefits include the following:

1. The use of technology in manufacturing allows for the streamlining of production through the standardisation of products. This enables mass production to take place, thus reducing unit costs. Firms can become more efficient and competitive.

2. Through the use of e-mail and video-conferencing, management are able to link up with foreign-based companies for decision-making and management discussions. This also greatly reduces travel costs.

3. The substitution of capital for labour greatly reduces the wage costs in business. The use of bar codes in shops means that sales are recorded accurately with less staff required.

> **Benefits of technology to business:**
> - production is streamlined
> - high-tech link-up is possible
> - wage costs reduced
> - there is a greater span of control for management

4. The management span of control is greater because high-tech facilities can be effectively used to control the activities of subordinates.

5. The growth of teleworking has led to a reduction in the levels of supervision. This is because teleworkers' salaries are usually related to agreed performance levels.

6. Firms which have developed their own websites can market their products worldwide. This has the potential to provide a large increase in sales and profits.

7. The use of high-tech products like mobile phones, portable computers etc. has dramatically improved communication within business and between business and the marketplace.

8. The use of technology enables firms to increase productivity, reduce costs, resist global and local competition and increase profits.

```
┌──────────────────────────────────────────────────────────────────┐
│ ⊝ ⊙ ⊛                    Video Conference                    ⬭     │
├──────────────────────────────────────────────────────────────────┤
│  🚫      ↰       ↰       ↱       🖨                                 │
│ Delete  Reply  Reply All Forward Print                             │
├──────────────────────────────────────────────────────────────────┤
│  From:  Frieda Donohoe                                             │
│ Subject: Video Conference                                          │
│  Date:  17 February 2005 11:06:48 GMT                             │
│   To:   Gary Dermody                                               │
│                                                                    │
│ Dear Gary,                                                         │
│                                                                    │
│ I would like to confirm our availability to participate in a video │
│ conference on Tuesday 15 February at 2.30 pm GMT. Both Geraldine   │
│ Kenny, our marketing manager, and Peter O'Driscoll, our sales      │
│ manager, will be sitting in on the meeting.                        │
│                                                                    │
│ I look forward to this opportunity to discuss a potential strategic│
│ alliance with your firm.                                           │
│                                                                    │
│ Kind Regards,                                                      │
│ Frieda Donohoe                                                     │
│ Folens Publishers                                                  │
│                                                                    │
│ Hibernian Industrial Estate,                                       │
│                                                                    │
│ Greenhills Road,                                                   │
│                                                                    │
│ Tallaght,                                                          │
│                                                                    │
│ Dublin 24.                                                         │
│                                                                    │
│ Phone: 01 413 7226  Fax: 01 413 7276                              │
│                                                                    │
│ Email: frieda.donohoe@folens.ie                                   │
└──────────────────────────────────────────────────────────────────┘
```

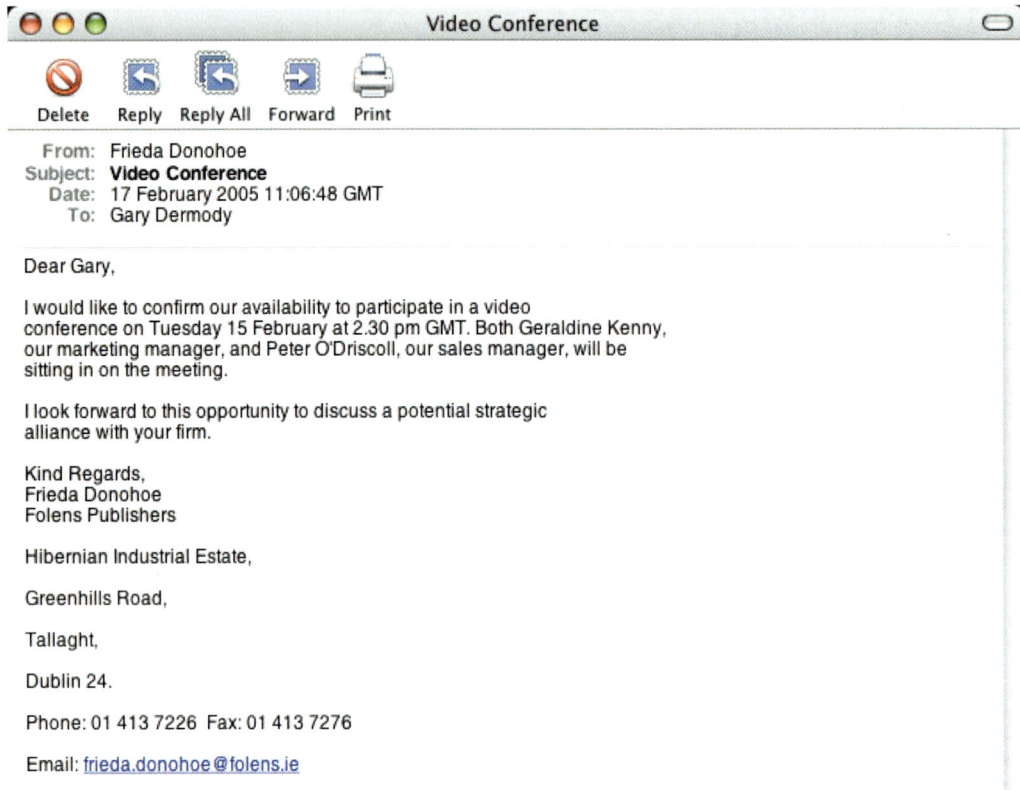

E-mail allows people to communicate in a fast and efficient manner.

Impact of Technology on Business Oppurtunities for Irish Industry

Information technology has enabled many firms to avail of business opportunities, both at home and abroad, for example:

1. Some major high-tech companies, e.g. Intel, have set up plants in Ireland to supply their products to both the Irish and foreign markets.

2. Indigenous software companies export their products because there is an export market available.

3. The existence of the Internet enables worldwide promotion of products and services. New services have been developed through the use of the Internet, e.g. airline booking can now be arranged online by paying with a credit card via the Internet, without even speaking to a salesperson.

4. Communication between Irish businesses and their export customers has improved through IT developments, e.g. e-mail and video-conferencing. This can lead to increased export sales and profits.

5. The growth in the use of production technology has led to the standardisation of many products, e.g. video recorders, DVDs, etc. In turn, these products are mass produced and unit costs of production are reduced, so consumers benefit from lower selling prices.

Exercises

1. (a) Why was it necessary for the role of management to change?

   (b) What is a global business?

2. (a) Explain what is meant by empowerment of workers.

   (b) Is the concept of empowerment of workers good for business?

3. (a) What is meant by Total Quality Management (TQM)?

   (b) Why is TQM important for business?

4. 'Unless changes are made, the business will not survive.'

   (a) Why would it be necessary for management to change the way a business is run?

   (b) Why do staff sometimes resist the introduction of changes?

5. (a) Outline the many benefits of technology to business.

   (b) Explain the following terms and show how they are of benefit to modern business:

   (i) E-mail

   (ii) Video-conferencing

6. Outline the benefits of empowerment of employees to the business and the employer.

7. (a) What are the principles of TQM?

   (b) Analyse the benefits of TQM to a manufacturing business.

Monitoring the Business

Objectives

The following topics from **Unit 4** of the syllabus are covered in this chapter:

- Why Monitor the Business?
- Who is interested in the Financial Position of an Enterprise?
- How important is Financial Information to a Business?
- The Final Accounts
- Ratio Analysis
- Accounting Ratios

Why monitor the Business?

Just because a business is making profit, it doesn't mean that it is doing well. A corner shop selling newspapers, cigarettes, sweets etc., making a yearly profit for its sole trader owner of €15,000, might be seen as doing well. A big enterprise with sales of €10 billion and 150 employees, making a profit of €50,000 would not be seen as doing well. Profit has to be assessed in the light of a firm's sales, number of employees, market potential, capital invested etc.

The bigger the business, the more important it is for financial controls to be in place.

Financial Controller

The financial controller in a business is responsible for ensuring that proper financial controls and procedures are in place. This person also prepares the final accounts and balance sheet of the business.

The final accounts are known as the trading, profit and loss accounts or income statements and balance sheet.

1.	Trading Account
2.	Profit and Loss Account
3.	Balance Sheet

> Not every profitable business is doing well.

> Proper financial controls and procedures should exist in business.

1. Trading Account

This account records the sales less the cost of sales to show the firm's gross profit for a trading year:

> sales – cost of sales = gross profit

2. Profit and Loss Account

In the profit and loss account, the business expenses are deducted from the gross profit to show the firm's net profit for the year:

> gross profit – expenses = net profit

3. Balance Sheet

This is a financial statement that shows the value of a firm's assets and liabilities on a specified date.

Who is Interested in The Financial Position of an Enterprise?

The following stakeholders are interested in how a business is performing:

1. The Board of Directors

Appointed by the shareholders to run the business, the directors will want to assess the performance and compare it with the budgets. If sales and profits are below budget, the board of directors will require an explanation from the managing director.

Who is interested?
- Board of Directors
- Shareholders
- Creditors
- Banks
- Employees
- Unions
- Competitors
- Revenue Commissioners

2. Shareholders

Shareholders are interested in the profits made for the year and the size of the dividends they will receive. In a PLC, the share price will rise if profits are good. This enables shareholders to sell their shares at a profit.

3. Trade Creditors

Trade creditors are those who supply goods on credit to the business. They will want to be confident of the firm's ability to pay its bills when they are due. The liquidity position of the firm will therefore interest them.

4. Financial Institutions

If a business requires a loan from the bank, it will be necessary to submit a copy of its accounts with the loan application. The bank manager will have the same approach as trade creditors in relation to interest and loan repayment. The liquidity position will be examined, as well as the existence of prior charges, e.g. a loan from a different bank.

5. Employees and Unions

Employees and unions are interested in the size of profits made by a firm. If profits are very high, it strengthens the union's position when negotiating a wage increase. Some firms now have a profit-sharing scheme in operation. Such a system gives employees a bigger interest in the firm.

6. Competitors

Obviously competitors will be very interested in how other firms in the same industry are doing. It is possible to compare sales, profits and market share with a competitor. This information can influence future decision making.

7. Potential Takeover Bidder

If the accounts are published (e.g. with a PLC), it is possible for a potential takeover bidder to know the exact net asset value of the business, before deciding how much to offer.

8. Government Agencies

(a) The Revenue Commissioners will be interested in the accounts in order to ensure that the correct amount of tax is paid.

(b) If the business unit is a company (Ltd or PLC), the Companies Office will be interested because certain information must be filed.

9. Consultants/Advisers

Those who provide professional services to the business, e.g. auditors, will be interested in the accounts. It is on the basis of the accounts that auditors are able to offer professional advice.

Importance of Financial Information to Business

Financial information is important because it has an impact on decision making by management. This is useful in the following areas:

1. Liquidity and Cash Flow

The liquidity of a firm is an indication of its ability to pay debts when they are due. If possible, a firm should try to avoid using an overdraft facility because of the interest charges. This can be achieved by timing the receipts from debtors before payments are made to creditors.

2. Control of Debt

The level of debtors and the age of some of the debts will indicate if any 'risky' debts exist. It may now be necessary for management to review its credit policy with some customers.

3. Size of Creditors

Relevant information can assist management in deciding how long payment to creditors can be deferred without loss of any discount.

4. Profitability and Profit Portfolio

(a) The actual profit figure is known and this can be compared to the figure from the previous year and to the budget. Appropriate action can be taken if profits are unsatisfactory.

(b) It may be possible to examine the product range and isolate any products which are losing money for the business. Appropriate action can be taken, e.g. increase selling prices, withdraw such products etc.

5. Value of the Net Assets of the Business

The net value of the business would interest management if future borrowings were required or if a management buy-out was being considered.

6. Filing the Accounts

If the business is a company (Ltd or PLC), certain information from its accounts must be filed with the Companies Registration Office.

7. Future Planning

Future plans will depend on the profitability and liquidity position of the business. Management will consider future decisions in the light of what the business can afford.

The Final Accounts
1. The Trading Account

The reason for preparing a trading account is to calculate the gross profit for the year.

Sales	20,000
Less	
Cost of Sales	8,000
Gross Profit	12,000

sales – cost of sales = gross profit

EXAMPLE

Business Services Ltd, Galway

Trading, Profit & Loss Account for the years ended 30 April 2004 and 2005

	30-4-2005		30-4-2004	
Sales		500,000		400,000
Less Cost of Sales				
Opening stock of goods	15,000		20,000	
Purchases	120,000		90,000	
Carriage inwards	10,000		5,000	
Cost of goods available for sale	145,000		115,000	
Less closing stock	25,000	120,000	15,000	100,000
Gross profit (gross margin)		380,000		300,000
Less Expenses				
Advertising	12,000		8,000	
Wages	72,000		56,000	
Insurance	9,000		7,000	
Telephone	900		1,400	
Legal expenses	3,600		2,100	
Auditor fees	5,000		4,000	
Bank charges	940		800	
Motor expenses	7,800		5,900	
Postage	900		600	
Rent & rates	7,000		6,000	
Total expenses		119,140		91,800
Net profit (operating profit)		260,860		208,200
Add opening balance		15,000		10,000
		275,860		218,200
Less dividends		160,000		100,000
Balance = retained earnings		115,860		118,200

2. The Profit and Loss Account (P & L a/c)

The reason for preparing the profit and loss account is to calculate the net profit (before tax) for the year:

gross profit – expenses = net profit before tax

It is normal to classify expenses into categories:

- **Establishment expenses:** rent, rates, insurance, light/heat.

- **Financial expenses:** legal fees, bank charges, bad debts.

- **Selling expenses:** advertising, motor, sales commission.

Gross Profit	12,000
Less	
Expenses	7,000
Net Profit	5,000

What happens to Net Profit before Tax?

This amount of money can be distributed as follows:

(a) Tax on profits is paid to the Revenue Commissioners.

(b) Dividends are paid to the shareholders.

(c) The balance is held by the business to finance future projects, i.e. retained earnings – a long-term source of finance.

Benefits of the Profit and Loss Account to the Financial Management of a Business

(a) It enables management to calculate the net profit for the year and see how it compares to the previous year and what was budgeted for.

(b) It shows all the expenses and highlights where any increases have occurred.

(c) It highlights for management the efficiency of the business in operating within the agreed budget. Doing so is a sign of good financial management.

(d) It confirms the existence of control procedures to stop the business getting into debt.

3. Balance Sheet

The balance sheet of a business is a financial statement that shows the value of the assets and liabilities (including capital) on a certain date.

> assets = liabilities (including capital)

Fixed Assets

These assets are part of the permanent infrastructure of a business, e.g. premises, machinery and furniture. Purchase of these items is referred to as capital expenditure. These assets are bought for long-term use, not for immediate resale. Because of wear and tear, a firm is able to write off some of their value each year, this is called depreciation. Some firms use long-term finance, e.g. a share issue, to raise the finance for capital expenditure. This finance is called fixed capital, therefore we say that fixed capital finances fixed assets.

Vehicles used for transporting goods are fixed assets.

Current Assets

These are the short-term assets of a business, e.g. stocks, debtors and cash. These assets are always changing in value, e.g. stock is bought and sold, debtors pay their bills, cash is lodged, etc. These assets are usually held for less than one financial year, i.e. short-term or current assets.

Current Liabilities

These are short-term debts which the business expects to pay within one financial year, for example:

Stock in the warehouse is classified as a current asset. The forklift truck in the picture is a fixed asset.

- Creditors – a firm may have received 45 days' credit from a supplier.
- Bank overdraft – a short-term facility received from the bank.
- Unpaid bills – ESB, phone bills, taxes due.

Capital Employed

The capital (money) invested in a business can come from different sources:

- Equity share capital – from the shareholders.
- Debt capital – debenture, long-term loan.

The relationship between debt capital and equity capital is called the **capital gearing** of the business.

Authorised Share Capital

This is the maximum amount of share capital a company can raise. This amount is stated in a company's Memorandum of Association, e.g. 200,000 €1 ordinary shares.

Issued Share Capital

This is the actual amount of long-term finance raised from a share issue, e.g. 100,000 €1 ordinary shares.

Revenue Reserves

These are the profits which were reinvested by the shareholders rather than paid out as dividends. This money is 'saved' to finance future plans of expansion,

How does the Balance Sheet benefit the Financial Management of a Business?

(a) It confirms which assets the business owns, e.g. premises.

(b) It confirms if the business is overtrading. This would be the case if current liabilities were greater than current assets.

(c) It shows the capital structure of the business and if additional shares can be issued to raise finance.

The Independent Printers, City West Business Park, Dublin

EXAMPLE			Paula Byrne Ltd			
		Balance Sheet as at 30 April 2004 and 2005				
			30-04-2005		30-04-2004	
Fixed Assets			€			€
Buildings			100,000			80,000
Land			70,000			50,000
Machinery			30,000			20,000
Vehicles			90,000			70,000
			290,000			220,000
Current Assets						
Debtors	16,000			10,000		
Stocks	4,000			15,000		
Insurance prepaid	4,000			3,000		
Bank	2,000			7,000		
Cash	3,000			5,000		
		29,000			40,000	
Less Liabilities due within one year						
Trade creditors	18,000			21,000		
Taxes due	8,000			9,000		
Unpaid expenses	5,000	31,000		5,000	35,000	
Working capital			(2,000)			5,000
Net assets			288,000			225,000
Financed by		Authorised	Issued		Authorised	Issued
Ordinary shares		200,000	132,000		200,000	86,000
Reserves						
Retained earnings			115,860			118,200
Liabilities due after one year						
Long-term loan (secured)			40,140			20,800
			288,000			225,000

Ratio Analysis

→ Ratio Analysis

Ratio Analysis involves examining the relationships between financial figures in the accounts and expressing them as ratios or percentages.

Prepare Accounts
↓
Analyse Accounts
↓
Understand Accounts

For legal reasons, a firm must prepare annual accounts. It is important to analyse the accounts. An effective way of doing this is by ratio analysis. Information presented as a ratio is clearer and more useful to a manager than a long list of financial figures, e.g. net profit is 25 per cent of sales. This statement is simpler than giving the figures for sales, expenses and profits.

Ratios are not an end in themselves, but they are effective in understanding a situation and deciding what action to take. The interested parties in ratio analysis include directors, creditors, shareholders and banks.

Benefits of Ratio Analysis

Ratio analysis is important for the following reasons:

1. Comparisons can be made with results from the previous year, as well as with the financial budgets for the year and with competitors.

2. Relationships can be made between relevant areas, e.g. profits to sales, profit to capital etc.

3. It highlights the existence of a pattern, e.g. profit percentage was 30 per cent in 2004 and 18 per cent in 2005 – the trend is clear – a decline.

> **Benefits of ratios:**
> - comparisons can be made
> - relationships can be made
> - patterns emerge
> - efficiency is measured

4. The efficiency of management can be measured, e.g. if management predicted a profit percentage of 20 per cent but the final accounts show the figure at 26 per cent, this is a sign of management inefficiency.

5. Results can be measured against firms in different industries. This information can be used when deciding future investment strategies.

Limitations of Ratio Analysis

1. The accounting methods used by the different auditors can vary, making comparisons with other firms ineffective, e.g there might be different policies on depreciation rates.

2. The financial year of a firm may end at a different time to its competitor, e.g. firm X's financial year ends on 30 September but firm Y's financial year ends on 30 December. The existence of a three-month time difference makes it difficult to make direct comparisons.

3. Ratios do not paint the complete picture of a business. Issues such as the level of staff morale are also very important to a firm.

4. Economic issues such as loans and interest rates can make it difficult to make comparisons with competitors.

5. Unless the competitor's product portfolio is identical, it is not possible to make accurate comparisons.

6. Ratios are based on past results and do not indicate what steps have been taken by management to improve a situation.

Ratios

The following ratios are important:

1.	Profitability ratios	These show if a business is making a reasonable profit for its size.
2.	Liquidity ratios	These show the ability of a firm to pay debts as they fall due.
3.	Debt capital/Equity capital ratio	This shows the gearing position in the business.

1. Profitability Ratios

(a) Gross Profit Percentage (Margin)

(b) Net (Operating) Profit Percentage (Net Margin)

(c) Return on Investment (ROI)

A. Gross Profit Percentage (Margin)

gross profit percentage (margin) = $\frac{\text{gross profit}}{\text{sales}} \times \frac{100}{1}$

This means that the gross profit is expressed as a percentage of sales.

> **EXAMPLE**
>
> The following information relates to the accounts of N. Martin Ltd, a boutique owner in Galway:
>
> 2005 Sales €550,000   Gross profit €110,000
> 2004 Sales €700,000   Gross profit €210,000
>
> | | | | 2005 | 2004 |
> |---|---|---|---|---|
> | gross profit % = | $\frac{\text{gross profit}}{\text{sales}}$ | $\times \frac{100}{1}$ | $\frac{110,00 \times 100}{550,000 \times 1}$ | $\frac{210,000 \times 100}{700,000 \times 1}$ |
> | | | | = 20% | = 30% |
>
> The gross profit percentage has fallen from 30 per cent to 20 per cent. Why?

Reasons for a Decline in the Gross Profit Percentage

    (i) A change in the sales mix, where there was an increase in the sale of less profitable items.

    (ii) Losses due to stolen goods.

    (iii) Reduction in selling prices due to new competition.

B. Net (Operating) Profit Percentage (Net Margin)

This means that the net profit is expressed as a percentage of sales. It is called the net profit margin and it highlights the operational efficiency of a business. This ratio is better than the gross profit percentage because the expenses have been deducted from gross profit.

$$\text{net profit percentage} = \frac{\text{net profit before tax}}{\text{sales}} \times \frac{100}{1}$$

EXAMPLE

The following information relates to the accounts of N. Martin Ltd, a boutique owner in Galway:

2005 Sales €550,000   Net profit €82,500

2004 Sales €700,000   Net profit €140,000

	2005	2004
Net profit % = $\frac{\text{net profit}}{\text{sales}} \times \frac{100}{1}$	$\frac{82,500}{550,000} \times \frac{100}{1}$	$\frac{140,000}{700,000} \times \frac{100}{1}$
	= 15%	= 20%

The net profit percentage has fallen from 20 per cent to 15 per cent. Why?

Reasons for a Decline in the Net Profit Percentage

    (i) A decline in the gross profit percentage.

    (ii) An increase in expenses, e.g. rates, insurance.

    (iii) Not paying bills on time may have caused the firm to lose discounts.

What Steps can a Firm take to improve its Profitability?

The following steps could be taken:

    (i) Change the product mix to sell more of the highly profitable items.

    (ii) Consider bulk buying popular products in order to avail of bigger discounts.

    (iii) Increase the advertising budget and use the Internet as a means for advertising.

C. Return on Investment (ROI)

> return on investment (return on capital employed) =
> net profit (before tax) x 100
> capital employed

This expresses the net profit made by the firm as a percentage of the amount of money invested in the firm by its owners.

EXAMPLE
From the accounts of N. Martin Ltd, Galway:

| 2005 Net Profit | €82,500 | Capital Employed €440,000 |
| 2004 Net Profit | €140,000 | Capital Employed €500,000 |

	2005	**2004**
ROI = net profit (before tax) x 100	82,500 x 100	140,000 x 100
capital employed	440,000 x 1	500,000
	= 18.75%	= 28%

The ROI (also called the Primary Ratio) is a very good measure of how efficiently the management are running the business. It relates the profit before tax to the capital invested in the business. It is now important to compare the ROI with the rate of interest that could be made from a bank deposit account or dividends from investments in shares. It is important that the ROI is bigger than alternative investment returns: otherwise why stay in a risky business?

2. Liquidity Ratios

There are two important ratios:

A.	Working Capital Ratio (Current Ratio)
B.	Acid Test Ratio (Quick Asset Ratio)

A. Working Capital Ratio

> Working Capital Ratio = current assets : current liabilities

Working capital (also called circulating capital) is the finance required to operate a business on a daily basis. It is a firm's current assets minus current liabilities.

> *Working Capital = CA – CL*
> *Working Capital Ratio = CA : CL*

- Examples of current assets – stock, debtors, cash, bank.

- Examples of current liabilities – creditors, taxes due, bank overdraft.

- If current assets are greater than current liabilities, it means that a firm can pay its debts as they fall due, i.e. the firm does not have a liquidity problem.

EXAMPLE

Current Assets	=	€200,000
Current Liabilities	=	€100,000

Working Capital Ratio	=	Current Assets	:	Current Liabilities
	=	€200,000	:	€100,000
	=	2	:	1

An ideal working capital ratio is 2:1 – this is the type of ratio that a bank or major supplier would like a firm to have. In practice, many firms have a ratio lower than 2:1, e.g. 1.5:1. This is satisfactory as the firm does not have a liquidity problem. A sudden adverse change in a ratio could be a cause for concern, e.g. if a ratio changed from 1.5:1 to 0.5:1, it would mean that current liabilities were twice as big as current assets. Management would have to take action to improve the liquidity position of the firm.

Overtrading (Inadequate Working Capital)

If current liabilities are greater than current assets, it means that the firm would not be able to pay all its debts in full if payment were due or demanded, i.e. it has a liquidity problem. Such a situation is called overtrading, i.e. trading in excess of the current financial resources of the business.

Causes of Overtrading

(i) Mismatching the source of financing capital expenditure, e.g. using a bank overdraft (short-term source) to pay for new machinery (a long-term source, e.g. share capital, should be used).

> *Overtrading should be avoided if possible.*

(ii) Too much leaning on the trade, i.e. owing large amounts of money to creditors, banks and the Revenue Commissioners.

(iii) Incurring bad debts because of a poor credit control department.

Steps to Improve an Overtrading Situation in Business

(i)   Request that creditors extend the length of credit to take the pressure off the firm to pay the debts. This may damage its future credit rating with suppliers.

(ii) Arrange for earlier payments by debtors to improve the bank balance.

(iii) Raise long-term finance, preferably from a share issue. This will really improve the liquidity position and could eliminate the overtrading.

(iv) Reduce the selling price or increase the discount on slow selling stock. This will have the effect of increasing sales and will also generate cash which can be lodged in the firm's bank account.

Working Capital Management

Working capital management involves managing the finance necessary for the day-to-day running of the business. It involves:

(i) Ensuring there is adequate finance to pay bills and purchase stock.

(ii) Operating an efficient system of collecting debts.

Factors that affect Working Capital Management

(i)   Lodging money on a daily basis: if the firm is overtrading, the lodgements will reduce the overdraft and interest charges.

(ii) Slow-paying debtors affect a firm's liquidity because they cause a costly interest-payment financial mismatch.

(iii) An aged debtors and creditors analysis is important, i.e. examining the age of all the debts due to and owed by the firm. An ideal situation is for a firm to buy on 60 days' credit and sell on 30 days' credit. This is called the **operating cycle** of the business, i.e. the time between receiving payments from debtors and making payments to creditors for stock purchased on credit.

(iv) A poor stock control policy.

(v)   Mismatching funds, i.e. where short-term finance is used for long-term purposes, e.g. using an overdraft to purchase machinery.

B. Acid Test Ratio (Liquidity Ratio) or Quick Asset Ratio

current assets – closing stock : current liabilities

This ratio shows if a firm has the ability to pay its current liabilities (debts) quickly from cash or bank balances and thus avoid any loss of discounts resulting from late payment of debts.

The Acid Test Ratio is an example of a Liquidity Ratio.

An ideal Acid Test Ratio is 1:1.

EXAMPLE

Current Assets	=	€200,000		
Stock	=	50,000		
Current Liabilities	=	€100,000		
Acid Test Ratio	=	Current Assets – Stock	:	Current Liabilities
	=	€200,000 – €50,000	:	€100,000
	=	€150,000	:	€100,000
	=	1.5	:	1

---

3. Debt Capital/Equity Capital Ratio

Debt Capital : Equity Capital (Share Capital + Reserves)

Debt capital is a long-term debt which has to be repaid, e.g. a debenture. This is a long-term source of finance on which a fixed rate of interest has to be paid.

Example: €150,000 14 per cent debenture 2012.

The debt/equity ratio shows the relationship that exists between the debt capital and the equity capital (ordinary share capital). The ratio by which the capital of a company is split between debt capital and equity capital is called the gearing of a business (gearing is also called leverage).

A company that has more borrowed funds (external debt) than shareholders' funds is highly geared.

High Gearing

A company is said to be highly geared if the ratio of debt capital to equity capital is high. This means that the business is financed more from borrowed money than from the shareholders' money.

If more than 50% of the capital employed is Debt Capital, the gearing is high.

EXAMPLE

€150,000 14 per cent debenture 2009
Ordinary Share Capital €75,000

Debt/Equity Ratio	=	Debt Capital	:	Equity Capital
	=	€150,000	:	€75,000
	=	2	:	1

This firm is highly geared.

Low Gearing

A company is said to be lowly geared if the ratio of debt capital to equity capital is low.

If less than 50% of the capital employed is Debt Capital, the gearing is low.

EXAMPLE

Company Y Ltd

Ordinary Share Capital   =   €400,000

15 per cent debenture 2005   =   €100,000

Debt/Equity Ratio   =   Debt Capital : Equity Capital

                                  =   €100,000   :   €400,000

                                  =   1   :   4

                                  =   Low Gearing

How does a Firm benefit from Low Gearing?

The benefits are as follows:

(a) If profits are high, the level of dividends paid to the shareholders should be high.

(b) The company can raise finance for expansion from a bank because of the low level of debt capital.

(c) The company is more attractive to shareholders for investment.

Spreadsheets

The spreadsheet package is a very important piece of computer software, which is mainly used in the finance and marketing department. It can perform difficult calculations and present the answers in graphical form. It is used for recording, storing and monitoring financial and marketing data, e.g. sales.

On the computer screen the spreadsheet looks like a sheet of squared graph paper. Each square is known as a cell. Financial data, e.g. selling price and quantity of units sold, can be recorded in the cells and automatic calculations are made on the data recorded. This enables management to prepare 'What if' questions, e.g. if the selling price increased by 10 per cent, what impact would this have on sales volume and profit?

Uses and Benefits of Spreadsheets

1. Spreadsheets are used for financial budgeting and statistical analysis.

2. They automatically process information and can also present the outcome in the form of graphs, barcharts, pie charts etc.

3. They are used for recording, storing, accessing and monitoring financial data.

4. All calculations can be done in a fast and accurate manner.

5. It is easy for the user to make changes to the data in the cells because the impact of the changes will be automatically calculated throughout the sheet. The results are visible on screen.

Revision of Important Terms	
• Financial Controller	• Capital Employed
• Trading Account	• Ratio Analysis
• Profit and Loss Account	• Profitability Ratios
• Balance Sheet	• Liquidity Ratios
• Creditors	• Return on Investment
• Fixed Assets	• Overtrading
• Current Assets	• High Gearing
• Current Liabilities	

Exercises

1. (a) Why does a business prepare a trading account?

   (b) Why is a profit and loss account prepared?

   (c) What is a balance sheet?

2. (a) Name the various stakeholders who are interested in the financial position of a business.

   (b) In relation to any three stakeholders, outline the issues that interest them.

3. 'Financial information is important because it influences decision making by management.' Discuss.

4. Explain each of the following business terms:

    (a) Final Accounts   (b) Stakeholders   (c) Balance Sheet

    (d) Capital Employed   (e) Authorised Share Capital   (f) Financial Controller

5. (a) Outline reasons for the importance of ratio analysis.

    (b) Indicate four possible limitations of ratio analysis.

6. (a) State three profitability ratios that can be used in business.

    (b) Distinguish between gross profit and net profit.

    (c) Why might the gross profit percentage decrease?

7. (a) Explain what is meant by the net profit margin.

    (b) Why might the net profit margin decrease?

    (c) What steps could be taken to stop the decrease in the net profit margin?

8. (a) What is working capital?

    (b) Explain what is meant by the working capital ratio.

    (c) What is the acid test ratio? What is its relevance to business?

9. The following is from the final accounts of Multi-Services Ltd, Nenagh, Co. Tipperary:

	2005	2004
Sales	€400,000	€300,000
Gross profit	€160,000	€120,000
Net profit	€240,000	€190,000

    (a) Calculate the gross margin for 2005 and 2004.

    (b) Calculate the net margin for 2005 and 2004.

    (c) Do you think the management of the business are happy with the trend in the accounts? Why?

10. (a) From the following information, calculate the return on investment for the shareholders in Hotel Supplies Ltd, Ballina, Co. Mayo:

	2005	2004
Profit	€150,000	€200,000
Capital employed	€75,000	€80,000

   (b) Give possible reasons for the trend in the business.

11. The following information was obtained from the accounts of Video Supplies Ltd:

	2005	2004
Current assets	€30,000	€40,000
Capital employed	€18,000	€20,000
Closing stock	€15,000	€10,000

   (a) Calculate the working capital ratio for both years.

   (b) Calculate the acid test ratio for both years.

   (c) Comment on the trend in the ratios.

12. (a) Calculate the debt equity ratio from the following information in the books of Photo Services Ltd:

	2005	2004
Ordinary share capital	€100,000	€100,000
Retained earnings	€25,000	€20,000
Long-term debt	€25,000	€10,000

   (b) Do you think the management will be happy or concerned with the trend of the debt equity ratio? Give reasons for your answer.

13. (a) Explain the importance of good financial information (e.g. financial ratios) to the management team of a business. Use examples to illustrate your answer.

   (b) Examine the following figures from Western Carpet Manufacturers Ltd:

	2005	2004
Current assets	€90,000	€80,000
Current liabilities	€60,000	€40,000
Closing stock	€45,000	€40,000
Equity share capital	€250,000	€250,000
Long-term debt	€250,000	€120,000
Retained earnings	€20,000	€15,000

   (i) Calculate for 2005 and 2004:
   • working capital ratios • acid test ratios • debt equity ratios

   (ii) Applying your knowledge, comment on two trends that you notice developing in the business. Suggest what you would do about them.

14. Study the information supplied and answer the questions which follow:

Film Services Ltd			
Balance Sheet as at 30 April 2005			
Fixed Assets			
Premises			150,000
Plant & Machinery			100,000
Office equipment			20,000
			270,000
Current Assets			
Stock	80,000		
Debtors	50,000		
Bank & Cash	20,000		
		150,000	
Current Liabilities			
Creditors	85,000		
Bank overdraft	0		
Dividends due	20,000		
		105,000	
Working Capital			45,000
			315,000
Financed by	*Authorised*		*Issued*
Ordinary €1 shares	300,000		200,000
Reserves			
Retained earnings			40,000
Liabilities due after one year			
Term Loan			75,000
			315,000

(a) Define a balance sheet.

(b) Based on the balance sheet of the firm, calculate the following ratios for the year ended 30 April 2005:

    (i) Working capital ratio

    (ii) Acid test ratio

    (iii) Debt equity ratio

(c) State three long-term sources of finance which Film Services have used.

(d) Identify the limits of using ratio analysis.

(e) Is the firm overtrading? Explain your answer.

15. (a) How is the debt/equity ratio of benefit to a financial controller in monitoring the financial performance of a business?

    (b) Analyse the profitability and liquidity trends in Timber Supplies Ltd from the following figures in their final accounts for the years ending March 2004 and 2005:

	30 March 2004	30 March 2005
Current assets	€25,000	€35,000
Equity share capital	€90,000	€90,000
Gross profit	€15,000	€28,000
Current liabilities	€15,000	€21,000
Closing stock	€10,000	€20,000
Retained earnings	€25,000	€30,000
Sales	€85,000	€110,000
Net profit	€5,000	€10,000

    (c) Considering that there was an increase in sales of €25,000, do you think the profit increase of €7,000 is reasonable? Why?

16. (a) Analyse the working capital, acid test, and debt equity positions of XYZ Ltd from the following information:

	2004	2005
Equity share capital	€300,000	€300,000
Current assets	€95,500	€82,450
Long-term debt	€200,000	€70,000
Retained earnings	€31,000	€22,000
Closing stock	€50,410	€41,359
Current liabilities	€45,000	€36,000

    (b) Discuss the importance of financial ratios in general for the efficient management of a business.

Applied Business Questions
for Units 2, 3, 4
Leaving Certificate 2005 and 2010

Applied Business Question
Based on units 2, 3 and 4 for Leaving Certificate 2005/2010

STONE PRODUCTS LTD (LEAVING CERTIFICATE 2000)

Paddy Murphy was very proud of himself for having set up a successful business. Ever since he left school and trained with his father as a stone mason, he had wanted to own a quarry and building business of his own. He worked hard at everything he did – at school, as an apprentice and now in his own business. He always concentrated on the future and because of this he tried to make the best decisions in the interest of the business.

Over the past 20 years, the stone and concrete business had changed a lot, especially in the areas of quality, customer service and in stock and financial management. The changes caused some difficulties in the business but Paddy's approach was to collaborate with the staff to tackle the challenges. He liked to train his own employees in general but also, when necessary, to recruit people from outside.

Stone Products' customers were mainly in the construction industry and they returned to trade with the company on a regular basis. Customers were happy with the way Paddy did business. Success resulted from finding out as much as possible before making a decision and having as many of the employees as possible organised into teams and involved in making the decisions. He liked people with initiative to work for him, especially those who would stick with jobs, spot challenges early and find solutions quickly. He allowed his staff to deal with customers directly, paid them well but expected targets to be met.

(A) Illustrate, from the above information, the enterprising characteristics
shown by Paddy. (20 marks)

(B) Analyse the management activities used by Paddy in the running of his
successful business. Refer to the above text in your answer. (20 marks)

(C) Paddy often said that good human resource management was the key to
his success. Would you agree with his view? Using the information
available about Stone Products Ltd, explain your answer fully. (40 marks)

(Total = 80 marks)

Applied Business Question

Based on units 2, 3 and 4 for Leaving Certificate 2005/2010

AN INDEPENDENT PRODUCTION

Hilary Kennedy had mixed feelings the day she left work after finishing her last day as a television producer with STV. Hilary was made redundant after ten years working on various programmes and gaining vast experience in all aspects of television programme production. While sad at leaving, Hilary took with her a wealth of experience, a generous redundancy package and greatly enhanced enthusiasm for her work. She now looked forward to putting into action the plan which had been at the back of her mind for the last three years – to set up her own independent production company and produce programmes which she could then sell to television companies both at home and overseas.

One of the first actions Hilary took before embarking on her new business venture was to carry out a S.W.O.T. analysis. Among the factors she considered relevant was her vast experience in TV programme production, her determination to succeed, her lack of knowledge and experience in financial matters and other matters relevant to the setting up and operation of a small business and her tendency to spend money as soon as she got it, resulting in an absence of any real personal capital. Hilary was also concerned about the number of firms already operating in this sector, as well as the increasing popularity among the viewing public of US productions over home-produced material. However, she did note that there were Government plans to license two further independent television stations, which she hoped would result in an increased demand for programmes.

Hilary discussed her plans with her sister Louise who had some financial experience from her years working in the accounts department of a Software company. Louise had resigned her job six years earlier to concentrate on managing her busy household, but was now looking forward to taking up a managerial position with her sister's new venture. She was confident that the skills she had acquired from managing the finances of both a business and a household would be very helpful in her new role.

(A) Outline from the above information the main characteristics of
     enterprising people like Hilary Kennedy.   (20 marks)

(B) What is meant by a S.W.O.T. analysis? With reference to the above passage,
     outline the points which could make up Hilary's S.W.O.T. analysis.
     Include two points under each heading.   (20 marks)

(C) Outline four similarities and four differences between managing the finances
     of a business and a household.   (40 marks)

                                                                (Total = 80 marks)

Applied Business Question
Based on units 2, 3 and 4 for Leaving Certificate 2005/2010

BUILDERS LTD

James Hogan joined Builders Ltd in 2002 as Human Resource Manager, having spent the previous four years in a similar position with a smaller company in the private sector. David had a business degree from university and a Master's degree in Human Resource Management.

Since starting, James has always had great admiration for the staff of Builders Ltd, who have been loyal and hard-working despite little recognition from a management viewed by them as aloof. James believes that the staff and the business would benefit greatly if the employees were encouraged to get more involved in the business as a whole, rather than being confined to their own small area. He has already discussed with senior management the concept of empowerment of staff and has now begun to meet the staff in small groups to discuss how they can become more involved in the running of the business. This, James feels, will improve the standard of the firm's output, as workers become more productive and more concerned about the overall quality of their work. Their increased satisfaction and the additional skills they acquire will, he hopes, further their productivity and increase the profits of the business.

James firmly believes that the workforce at Builders Ltd will favour his plan. However, he is concerned that the necessary changes required for empowerment to take place will not find favour with the more senior management team. The answer to this question will become known after he makes his presentation at the next board meeting.

(A) Outline the main functions of James Hogan, the Human Resource Manager in Builders Ltd. (20 marks)

(B) Explain how an employee involvement scheme may help a firm. Support your answer with reference to the above text. (20 marks)

(C) Draft a memo to the Board of Directors outlining the various requirements of management in order to facilitate empowerment of workers. (40 marks)

(Total = 80 marks)

13 Identifying Business Opportunities

Objectives

The following topics from **Unit 5** of the syllabus are covered in this chapter:

- Sources of Opportunities
- Development Process of a New Product
- The Importance of Researching New Ideas
- Identifying Opportunities
- Market Research

Why start a Business?

The idea to start up a business can come about for a variety of reasons:

1. Anyone working for an employer who goes on to start up their own business obviously has a preference for self-employment.

2. Some people see opportunities in the business they are in and start an enterprise in order to introduce new products or improve existing ones.

3. On some occasions, a new business is developed by a person who was made redundant. This person may use their redundancy money as the capital for the new business.

Development Process of a New Product/Service

There are seven stages involved in the development of a new product/service. These are as follows:

1.	Idea Generation
2.	Product/Service Screening
3.	Concept Development
4.	Feasibility Study
5.	Prototype Development
6.	Test-marketing
7.	Launch the Product

1. Idea Generation

This is a systematic approach to generating ideas that will find new ways to service the market and win over new customers. Special management meetings may be held to consider new ideas. Such meetings are referred to as **brainstorming** sessions. These meetings discuss wide-ranging ideas – if just one of them is good, the business will benefit.

2. Product Screening

This involves analysing different products and identifying the ones which have the best potential for sales. A screening committee is set up to carry out this function.

3. Concept Development

This involves developing good ideas into a reality. The resulting product should fulfil a consumer need in relation to price, quality, etc.

4. Feasibility Study

This entails researching the market to test consumer reaction to the proposed new product. It also involves assessing the profits from potential sales. If production costs are too high, the product might not be profitable.

Seven development stages for a new product:
- Idea generation
- Product screening
- Concept development
- Feasibility Study
- Prototype
- Test marketing
- Launch on the market

5. Prototype Development

This requires the production of one unit of the new product to enable it to be test marketed. It can be a lengthy and expensive phase, during which all the characteristics of the product become clear, i.e production problems, costings and the selling price required to make it profitable.

6. Test-marketing

This is necessary in order to determine the reaction of potential customers and reduce the costly risk of consumer rejection of the product. As a result of the test marketing, a firm may decide to change the marketing mix of the product or delay the launch onto the market until a later date.

7. Launch the Product

This involves making the consumers aware that the product is available through advertising and sales promotion.

The Importance of Researching New Ideas

1. Test marketing can save the business a lot of money. Doing research will provide unbiased information that will guide a firm in making the right decision. If the research shows that an idea is unlikely to succeed, then no investment will be made in premises, machinery, training etc.

2. By understanding consumer demand, a firm will have an advantage over its competitors.

3. Undertaking and carrying out market research into a business idea may also provide information on the strengths and weaknesses of competitors.

Identifying Opportunities

The source of a business idea can be internal or external.

Internal Sources

Internal sources include the following:

1. From the Employees

Some firms have suggestion boxes and pay a bonus to the employee whose idea is used.

2. Brainstorming Meetings

Discussion sessions involving management and staff.

3. Research and Development

Many big enterprises have a research and development department where highly-skilled people are employed. This department is expected to identify new opportunities for the business.

4. Feedback from Customers

Comments from customers, e.g. complaints, can force management to consider new options in order to rectify the problem and ensure that the customers are satisfied.

5. Sales Personnel

Sales people 'know the market' so they are in a good position to make suggestions, either at sales meetings or in their regular reports to the sales manager.

6. SWOT Analysis

A firm that carries out a SWOT analysis should get some ideas which will help to eliminate any weaknesses that are highlighted.

External Sources

External sources include the following:

1. Competitors

It is important for a firm to be aware of the areas where customers believe competitors to be better, e.g price, quality of products, after sales service, etc.

2. Customer Requirements

It may become necessary to modify the design, packaging or price of the product to avoid losing potential customers.

3. Research Agencies

Specialist agencies in market research may make suggestions for change.

4. Government Agencies

State agencies, e.g. Enterprise Ireland, may advise the firm in relation to potential exports.

ENTERPRISE IRELAND

5. Foreign Travel

Ideas may come from observations made at foreign trade fairs and exhibitions.

6. Franchising

Seeing how franchising works may encourage some entrepreneurs to sell franchised products.

7. Public Procurement

A firm may get the idea to tender for Government contracts because of the existence of the EU policy on public procurement.

> **➡ Public Procurement**
>
> *The right of firms to tender for Government contracts, which must be put to tender.*

Market Research

> **➡ Market Research**
>
> *Market research is very important for every business. It is defined as the gathering, recording and analysing of all the facts and data concerned with the transfer of goods from the producer to the consumer.*

Reasons for Market Research

A business is likely to use market research for the following reasons:

1. Descriptive Reasons

A firm may wish to find out what is happening in the market, i.e. who its customers are, what market share its competitors have and why.

2. Predictive Reasons

A firm may wish to predict what changes its customers will require in the future. **Example**: A travel agency will want to know what changes in holiday arrangements its customers will require. They will then plan and promote holiday packages to satisfy their customers.

3. Explanatory Reasons

A firm may want to explain, to the public, issues relating to its marketing. **Example**: A private bus hire company might want to research why there has been a 20 per cent reduction in the number of passengers in certain areas.

4. Exploratory Reasons

A firm may want to check out the size of the market for a new product. This involves finding out the number of potential customers, their age and spending patterns.

Stages in a Market Research Programme

The different stages involved in market research include the following:

1. Deciding the objective of the market research. For example, is the aim of the research one of the following:
   (a) to discover the size of the potential market for the product?
   (b) to determine why competitors are successful?

2. Determining how the information is be obtained, i.e. questionnaires, competitors' brochures and catalogues, interviews with retailers etc.

3. Deciding who is to carry out the research for the firm, i.e. the company could appoint a market research manager or employ the services of a market research agency.

4. Deciding the size of the sample and then how much time is to be given to carrying out the market research, i.e. ten days.

5. Carrying out the research and finding the answers to specific questions:
   (a) What competitors exist and what is their market share?
   (b) How do the firm's products (new or existing) compare to the competitors' in important areas such as quality, price and after-sales service?

(c) Is the size of the market rising, static or in decline?

(d) What is consumer reaction to the firm's existing products and after-sales service? If the image is poor, this may colour consumer reaction to new products.

6. Arranging the collection of the results.

7. Evaluating the results of the research and confirming the accuracy of the information obtained.

8. Presenting a market research report to management.

Compiling Information from Market Research

The different approaches to gathering the information are:

1.	Desk Research (Secondary Research)
2.	Field Studies (Primary Research)

1. Desk Research

Desk research involves the use of secondary data, i.e. analysing all the internal and external information that is available.

Internal Sources of Information (also called Qualitative Information)

- Some information may be in the records and files of the business, e.g. market research reports.
- Sales manager should have information on previous sales to the target market.
- The finance department may have information on production costs etc.

External Sources of Information (also called Quantitative Information)

These are sources of information which are in the public domain, for example:

- Statistics published by the Government and the EU, e.g. trade statistics on imports and exports.
- Reports published in various magazines and newspapers.
- The household Budget Survey, which publishes the spending patterns of Irish consumers on different kinds of goods.
- The Population Census published by the Central Statistics Office (CSO). This report gives detailed information about the population in every town and village etc. This information will enable firms to estimate the size of a national consumer market.
- Information available on the Internet.

2. Field Studies (also called Primary Research)

Field studies involve market research which is done by contacting people in the target market to obtain new information called primary data.

The following field study methods for market research are available:

(a)	Survey	(e)	Estimating
(b)	Questionnaire	(f)	Feasibility Study
(c)	Sampling	(g)	Prototype
(d)	Observing	(h)	Test-marketing

(a) Survey

The main reason for undertaking a survey is to ascertain from consumer responses the potential of a new or existing product. If a decision is to be made on the basis of the results of a survey, then the size of the survey must ensure the reliability of its findings, i.e. the sample group must be sufficiently large to reflect the opinions of the total target market. Mail surveys and telephone surveys are used to obtain information. In a mail survey, questionnaires are sent by post to people, who are then requested to complete and return them.

Usually some incentive is offered to return the questionnaire, e.g. names will be included in a special draw. This is not an expensive form of research, but its reliability will depend on the number of people who give accurate answers and return the questionnaire.

In a telephone survey the person's answers are usually recorded by the interviewer. Generally, the response rate is higher than for mail surveys and the answers are more accurate.

(b) Questionnaire

A questionnaire has to be carefully designed. Since every person receiving the questionnaire is asked the same questions, it is important that the questions are designed to ensure that the answers are accurate. A poorly worded questionnaire often provides useless information to the firm. The questionnaire can be used to seek consumers' opinions on products, quality, usage, interest in using the products etc. Every question must be simple, short, clear and easy to answer. If you want to know the age of the person filling in the questionnaire, you should give a choice e.g. 25–30, 30–40. You should avoid open-ended questions unless opinions are required.

Market Research Questionnaire

Open-ended Question

What is your opinion of the Visa Card?   ....

....

Dichotomous Question

Do you have a Visa Card?   Yes....................

No....................

Multiple Choice Question

Which age group are you in?

Answer with an X:

Under 25	
25–29	
30–40	
41–50	

(c) Sampling

If a decision is to be made based on the results of a sample, then the sample must be reliable.

(i)   Random Sampling – people are chosen at random, so each member of the population has an equal chance of being chosen. The accuracy and reliability of this form of sampling will depend on the size of the sample in relation to the size of the market.

(ii) Cluster Sampling – a cluster of samples is selected at random, e.g. a random selection of people in new housing estates where there is a widely-dispersed population. This method is often used for opinion polls.

(d) Observing

Information is gathered by watching people's reactions in certain situations. This is an accurate way to see how people react, but it doesn't indicate the reason for their reaction. This method is often used by management in supermarkets.

(e) Estimating

The estimated size of the market is vital information for a business. Once the size of the market is known, the next step is for the firm to estimate how much of the market share it will get, e.g. 20 per cent or 50 per cent. Information on potential market share can be obtained from many sources, for example:

(i)   Wholesalers and retailers.

(ii)   The firm's marketing people.

(iii) The firm's own internal records, e.g. sales records, and external information, e.g. published reports and telephone surveys.

215

(f) Feasibility Studies

This is an investigation of a proposal in order to assess its technical and financial viability. The results of this study will determine whether a firm will proceed with its plan to produce a new product or not.

A feasibility study will try to provide the following information to a business:

     (i)   The estimated sales of the product.

     (ii) The costs of production.

     (iii) The impact on profits if the product is produced and marketed.

A feasibility study is a reliable way of getting accurate information. It provides the firm with factual information so as to reduce the risk of losing money on the new product.

(g) Prototype

This involves producing one unit (or maybe a few units) of the product and seeing what problems arise in manufacturing, costing, selling price and unexpected costs. The prototype can be test-marketed and the decision on whether to proceed or not can be made by management.

(h) Test-marketing

This determines the reaction of potential customers to the prototype. Based on consumer reaction, it may be necessary to modify aspects of the product before mass or batch production quantities are made available, e.g. it may be necessary to improve the design, change the size, reduce the price etc. Test-marketing definitely reduces the risk of failure of the product.

   Secondary research is a cheaper way of obtaining information than primary research. This is because the research has been carried out by other people and is now publicly available.

Revision of Important Terms	
• Idea generation	• Target markets
• Prototype	• Questionnaires
• Test-marketing	• Sampling
• Brainstorming	• Feasibility study

Exercises

1. (a) Discuss three internal and three external sources of business ideas.

   (b) Why is it important to research new business ideas?

2. (a) What is market research?

   (b) Why is market research important to a business?
   Outline the different stages in a market research programme.

3. (a) How could a firm estimate the size of the target market?

   (b) How does information obtained from market research benefit a firm?

4. (a) State the various types of field study methods of market research that a firm could undertake.

   (b) Which three methods included in your answer to (a), do you think are most important? Give two reasons for your answer in each case.

5. (a) State the various stages involved in the development of a new product.

   (b) Explain any three of the stages.

6. Explain each of the following terms:

   (a) Public Procurement   (b) Market Research   (c) Feasibility Studies

7.
   > Patricia and John Bergin are planning to set up a clothes shop. Before doing so, they have decided to accept the advice of friends and do some market research. A recent publication from the local Chamber of Commerce revealed the following:
   >
   > • The local population has increased by 28 per cent in the last four years.
   > • Unemployment in the area is down by 15 per cent.

   (a) Is the information published by the Chamber of Commerce primary or secondary data? Explain your answer.

   (b) What other sources of information could be used to enable them to estimate the size of the potential market?

14 Marketing

Objectives

The following topics from **Unit 5** of the syllabus are covered in this chapter:

- What is Marketing?
- Marketing Management
- The Marketing Strategy
- Market Segmentation
- The Marketing Mix
- Product
- Price
- Promotion
- Place
- Evaluation of the Marketing Mix
- Break-even Analysis

What is Marketing?

Marketing lies at the heart of every successful business.

> ➡ **Definition of Marketing**
>
> *Marketing is the management process responsible for identifying, anticipating and satisfying customer requirements profitably.*

1. It begins with market research to find out what the customers want.

2. The next stage is product development, i.e. to produce a product that will be profitable for the firm and also satisfy consumer requirements.

3. The final stage is to develop a marketing strategy that will get the product to the market at a competitive and profitable price. This involves advertising, selling and distribution procedures.

Marketing Process

> ➡ **Definition of Marketing Process**
>
> *This is the process that takes the product through the different stages, from the potential customer to the satisfied customer.*

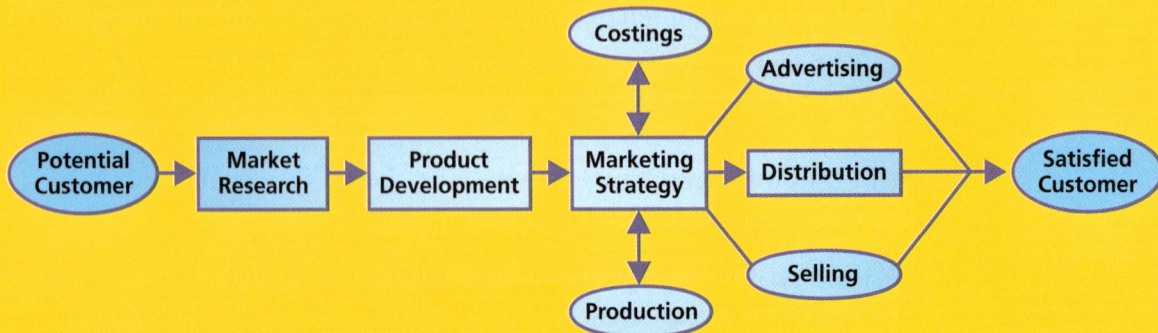

The Marketing Concept

The marketing concept is defined as a managerial outlook that accepts the following as important tasks of the firm:

1. Finding out what customers want.

2. Producing and delivering such requirements profitably and more effectively than competitors.

> **Marketing involves:**
> - market research
> - selling
> - product development
> - advertising
> - distribution

Marketing Management

This relates to all the activities that are involved in satisfying customer requirements. The marketing manager is responsible for controlling the marketing of the firm's products.

Functions of the Marketing Manager

1. To carry out **market research** to learn the exact requirements of consumers and submit a report to management.

2. To prepare **sales forecasts**, i.e. sales budgets for the board of directors.

3. To identify the different **markets** for the firm's products.

4. To decide on the **selling price** of new products.

5. To ensure that goods are **attractively packaged** for shop display.

6. To **plan the marketing campaign** for both new and existing products. This involves liaising with wholesalers/retailers to inform or update on new products, marketing plans etc.

The Marketing Strategy

The marketing strategy is a marketing plan which outlines how the policies relating to product, price, promotion and place are carried out in order to achieve the business sales and profit targets. It is a carefully worked out medium- to long-term plan that will ensure that the business is aware of consumer demands. It also shows how a business is responding to a changing market.

Developing a Marketing Strategy

1. Assess the market to see if any new business opportunities can be identified.

2. Select the target market for a new product, e.g. third level student market with a product with a low selling price.

3. Undertake market research into the needs of the selected target market.

4. Prepare a marketing plan.

The Marketing Plan

A marketing plan will help determine future decision making in relation to trading, financial requirements and the direction the business should take, e.g. whether to develop an export market.

Important Stages in the Marketing Plan

Before reviewing future needs, an effective marketing plan will carry out a detailed SWOT analysis of the existing marketing area. The following should be considered:

Without a marketing plan, a firm is unlikely to succeed in maximising sales and profits.

1. The range of products currently being sold – are any of them losing money for the business?

2. How old are some of the products, i.e. at what stage are they in the product life cycle?

3. The customer prospect mix, i.e. whether the business has a large number of regular customers or is mainly dealing with 'temporary customers'.

4. Recent trends in the sales of each item in the product portfolio of the business.

5. The competitors' share of the market – is it rising or in decline?

6. Steps that are necessary for the firm to increase its market share.

7. The costs of implementing a new plan (changes) in relation to projected sales, expenses and profits.

Benefits of a Marketing Plan

Since marketing is all about the future, a good marketing plan will have many benefits for a firm.

1. A good plan can only exist after management have undertaken the SWOT analysis. This enables management to establish priorities and make better decisions.

2. A good plan means that the firm is well organised, aware of its targets and able to cope with any deviation that might occur.

3. The existence of a marketing plan will impress potential investors and/or a bank if additional finance is required for expansion.

4. A marketing plan integrates the efforts of the firm in relation to its products, price, promotion and place, i.e. the marketing mix.

5. Creating a marketing plan stimulates management to think of new strategies and better ways of doing things in the future.

6. From the viewpoint of the staff, a plan encourages co-operation both within and between the different departments.

Market Segmentation

The concept of market segmentation is based upon three assumptions:

1. That consumers have varying profiles, e.g. male, female, young and old.

2. Differences in consumers are related to differences in market demand, e.g. income levels are different.

3. Within each market, further divisions of customers (known as segments) can be identified. Isolating these different segments enables the marketing manager to target them with different offers to suit their different needs, disposable income etc. In relation to market segmentation, a firm's marketing policy must be clear on the following:

   (a) Is the firm aware of the segments of the market that will not buy its products (e.g. a minority share who can't afford the product)?

   (b) Does the firm accept that it is not cost-effective to sell to all segments of the market and is therefore better to concentrate on the segment from which it gets the larger share? For example, if a small number of reliable customers make up a big proportion of the sales, they are the market segment on which to concentrate. To go after the other segments would involve Split Marketing and may not be cost-effective.

   (c) Is the firm aware that marketing to a small market is not profitable? If so, then the firm should concentrate its marketing on the main market.

Niche Markets

A niche market is a small segment of a bigger market. It is a specialist market with only a few suppliers who supply new or poorly served market sectors. It involves aiming to serve a target market with a specialised product or service which meets the needs of consumers of that niche. Niche markets are identified using market segmentation methods. The product, price, promotion and place is specifically targeted in a concentrated effort to reach all the niche customers. Firms selling into niche markets charge high prices because the size of the market is small. Rolls Royce sells its cars to those on very high incomes. They have successfully identified and targeted this niche market. The niche market is the opposite of the the mass market.

The Green Consumer

Success of the economy at any cost is not an acceptable idea to the general public. For example, a chemical manufacturing company would have to take public opinion into account when considering the location of a new plant. It would have to be located away from highly populated areas due to the dangers to health and the environment associated with fumes, pollution etc.

Some consumers take concern for the environment a step further and will only buy products that minimise damage to the environment. These are known as 'green' consumers. The marketing manager must be aware of the requirements of the 'green' customer when targeting that segment of the market. Green (environmentally friendly) products are designed to reduce the impact on the environment of their production and eventual disposal.

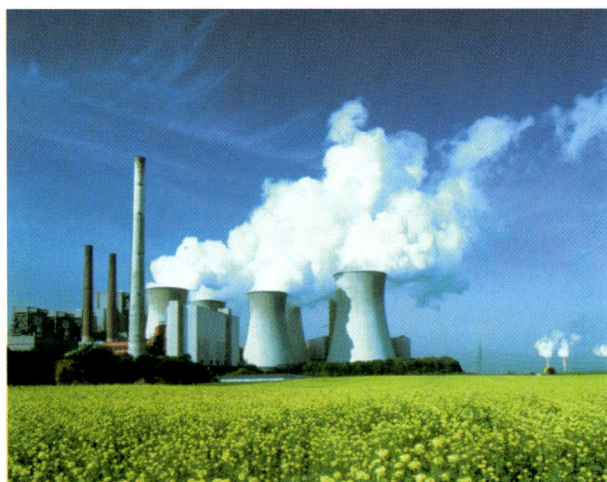

Disposable products such as razors and fast food, which come with a lot of wasteful packaging, would not be purchased by the green consumer. An EU directive requires all member states to have a policy of recycling all waste packaging.

The Marketing Mix

Marketing is a business attitude that puts the customer first. The marketing mix is made up of the following components:

1.	Product	3.	Promotion
2.	Price	4.	Place

> ➜ **The 4 Ps of Marketing**
>
> *Product*
> ↓
> *Price*
> ↓
> *Promotion*
> ↓
> *Place*

The mix represents the interplay of all the activities which are required to enable a firm to sell its goods profitably to its potential customers. A product will not be sold unless it is supported by various activities, e.g. advertising.

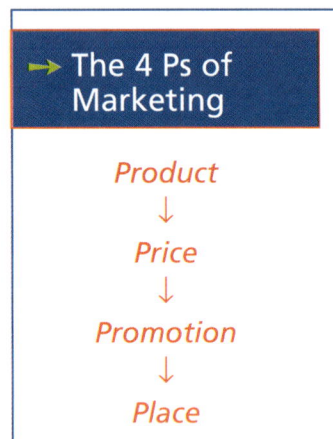

1.	The Product	This relates to factors concerning the product, including quality, packaging, after-sales service, design, size, brand and any unique selling point (USP).
2.	The Price	The relevant issues here include the actual selling price, discounts, credit terms, market demand and competitors' prices.
3.	The Promotion	This involves informing consumers by advertising, sales promotion, merchandising, personal selling etc.
4.	The Place	This concerns the role of wholesalers and retailers, location of sales outlets etc. This is called the sales operation.

The correct combination of the four components of the marketing mix is essential for sales and profits to be achieved. A good quality product that is overpriced may not achieve projected sales, even with an extensive advertising campaign. Any mis-match of the ingredients in the mix will cause selling problems for a firm and reduce profits. For example, a costly cosmetic product would have to be wrapped in expensive packaging and only sold in suitable places such as a high-class shopping outlet.

1. Product

Products are the goods produced by the manufacturer and sold to consumers. There are different types of goods, i.e. consumer goods and producer goods.

A. Consumer Goods

These are goods which are purchased and consumed or used, e.g. food, washing powder.

B. Producer Goods

These are products that are produced and used by businesses and individuals, e.g. computers, machinery, vehicles, etc.

What makes a Successful Product?

Every business wants to produce and sell a successful product. The following are the requirements of a successful product:

(a) It must satisfy consumer requirements.

(b) It must meet the quality standards required by consumers.

(c) It must have a competitive selling price.

(d) Design must be attractive.

(e) If relevant, an after-sales service must be provided.

(f) The image of the manufacturer is very important.

Brand Names (Branding)

Branded goods carry a copyright name registered with the Controller of Patents, Designs and Trade Marks. The brand name enhances the value of the product and the firm that owns it. The business which has a registered branded product is automatically protected because no competitor can use that brand name. Branded goods clearly distinguish one manufacturer's goods from similar products produced by competitors. Trade marks are also recognised as brand names because they identify products. The brand leader is the brand which has the biggest market share. Famous brand names include Coca-Cola and McDonalds.

Own Brand Goods

Large retailers who buy in bulk from manufacturers sometimes insist on their own brand names on the products, e.g. St Bernard is the brand name used by Dunnes Stores. This brand name becomes exclusively associated with a retailer. The fact that a big retailer would insist on using its own brand name is clear proof that branding is a form of advertising that helps to increase sales.

> In April 2005, Coca-Cola valued their brand name at $62m.

Benefits of Branding

(a) Branding helps to remind consumers about a product.

(b) Branded goods are more likely to be accepted by consumers than non-branded ones.

(c) Branded goods are easily identified on display stands, so selection is made easy for customers, e.g. Macleans toothpaste.

(d) Manufacturers promoting branded goods find it easier to introduce new products into the range, e.g. Levis now have a wide range of casual clothes (jeans, jackets etc.).

Product Life Cycle

Very few products last forever. Advances in technology, changes in fashion, new products etc. all affect the choice consumers have when buying goods. Some consumers just want to change because they are fed up using a product. Consumers are becoming more and more demanding, so the product life cycle is getting shorter.

The product life cycle describes the various stages that a product will go through, from its introduction to a market, through a period of growth, until it is firmly established. Eventually it declines as consumers switch to new products. Some products have a short life cycle, e.g. fashion goods, monthly magazines.

Stages in a Product Life Cycle

There are five stages in a product life cycle:

(a) The product is developed after the market research is completed.

(b) The product is introduced (launched) into the market and there are some initial sales.

(c) If successful, the new product enjoys a period of increasing sales (growth), due to advertising and sales promotion campaigns.

(d) The rate of growth levels off. The sales may have peaked but the product is firmly established as a mature product. If the market is saturated, there will be some drop in sales.

(e) Competitors react with new products with different features, consumers like to change, so sales of the old product decline.

Product Life Cycle

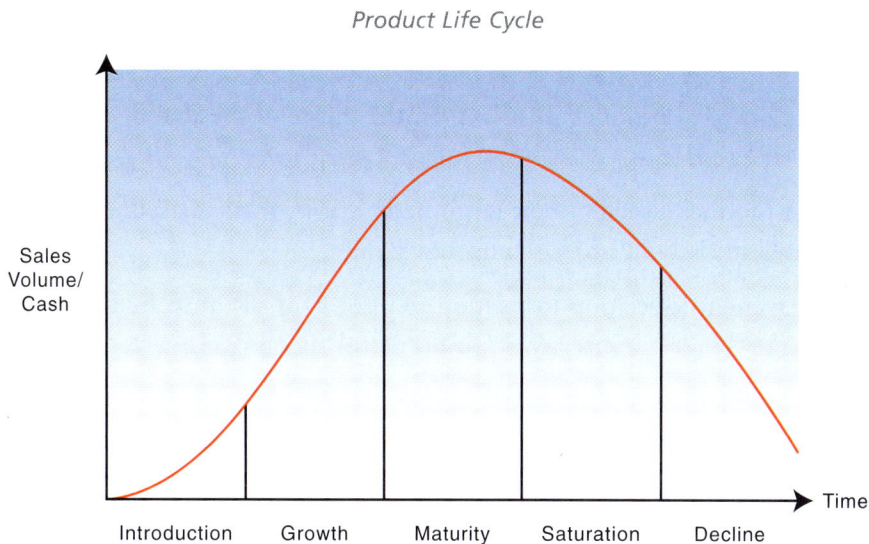

The manufacturer may eventually withdraw the obsolete product and replace it with a new one, or the product could keep going by receiving periodic overhauls.

Patents

A patent for an invention is the granting by the State of exclusive rights to the inventor for a maximum of 20 years. An inventor normally goes to a patent agent to have the patent legalised by the Official Government Patent Office. The official fee for filing a patent application (20-year term) is €127. There are other fees involved in maintaining a patent. A patent protects the inventor of a new product and stops competitors from copying it. A firm which has the patent on some product may allow other firms to use the same product name for an agreed fee called Patent Royalties.

2. Price

The selling price is a very important part of the marketing strategy of a business. If the selling price is too high, sales will be lost to competitors. Price is the most flexible element of the marketing mix.

What Factors determine the Selling Price?

The following factors should be considered by the sales manager before deciding on the selling price of a product:

(a) The selling price of the competitors' products. If the products are similar (e.g. shampoo), then the selling price should be slightly lower in order to have some marketing advantage, e.g. advertising can highlight savings which consumers can enjoy by purchasing the new product.

(b) The production and distribution costs. These must be recovered during the life of the product, otherwise the product will lose money for the business.

(c) The target market for the product. For example, are the consumers in the target market high income or low income earners? This will determine the price.

(d) How much money will be spent on an advertising campaign to promote the sale of the product?

(e) Is it a branded product? If it is, then the image of the brand will influence the selling price.

(f) Is the product aimed at new customers? If it is, then the selling price may be lowered initially in order to encourage sales.

(g) Government legislation in relation to price controls must be taken into account. There are price controls on petrol, alcohol, cigarettes etc.

(h) The product's current position in the product life cycle.

Pricing Strategies

(a) Cost Plus Pricing

The total costs in relation to the product are calculated and a profit is added to calculate the selling price. **This is called the mark-up**.

> ➡ COST PLUS PRICING
>
> *This is the cost of producing goods plus a profit mark-up.*

(b) Penetration Pricing

This strategy is used when launching a new product. It involves undercutting the selling price of competitors in order to gain a market share. It may involve selling at a very small profit. BIC adopts this strategy with new Biro pens.

(c) 'Skimming' Pricing

This can relate to both new or existing products/services. It is where a firm can charge a high price for a new product which is in big demand, e.g. a new computer game. It can also apply to an existing service where demand exceeds supply, e.g. some hotels in Dublin increase accommodation prices by up to 50 per cent when major sporting events take place.

> ➡ SKIMMING PRICE
>
> *This is where a firm charges a high price in the short term.*

(d) Going Rate or Market Pricing (also called Competitive Pricing)

This involves matching the competitors' selling prices, e.g. if a competitor reduces selling prices by 10 per cent, your firm must do the same in order to close off the pricing advantages. It is very common in the airline, telephone and supermarket businesses.

(e) Premium Pricing or Prestige Pricing

This is associated with high-quality items, e.g. jewellery and fashion clothes. In fact, consumers expect to pay high prices for such products. This is kept in mind when deciding on the selling prices of such products. It is called premium pricing or premium mark-up.

(f) Seasonal Pricing

Some products and services enjoy seasonal peaks, e.g. Christmas toys and holiday packages in the summer. But what do hotels do during the winter? Some hotels offer special weekend bargain holidays in order to generate sales to cover low season costs.

(g) Sales Pricing (also called Promotional Pricing)

'Special offer' sales in a wide range of consumer products take place after Christmas. These 'sales' take place in order to enable retailers to clear their stocks of slow-moving products and to make room for the new season's lines. This pricing only lasts for a short time period, e.g. four weeks.

(h) Loss Leader Pricing

This is a marketing strategy used by retail stores whereby certain products (e.g. bread in a supermarket) are sold at cost price. It is a pricing policy used to attract customers into the store. Once inside, the store managers are confident that these customers will also buy other items which are sold at a profit. In some cases, customers may buy items they hadn't intended purchasing. This is referred to as impulse buying.

3. Promotion

This involves communicating with customers through advertising, sales promotions, public relations and personal selling.

Promotion is covered in detail in the next chapter.

4. Place

This refers to the various ways used by manufacturers to sell and distribute products to their customers, i.e. the target market. Manufacturers have a choice in deciding which channel of distribution to use to get their products to the customers, for example:

(a) Some manufacturers sell to wholesalers, who in turn sell to retailers, who then sell to consumers, e.g. Jacobs sell biscuits to wholesalers, who then sell them to retail shops, who sell them to consumers.

(b) Some manufacturers bypass the wholesaler and sell direct to retailers, e.g. newspapers.

(c) Some manufacturers sell direct to consumers (customers) and bypass both the wholesaler and retailer, e.g. a manufacturer of industrial machinery would sell direct to the customer. Dell and Gateway sell computers direct to customers.

Most manufacturers use more than one channel to distribute goods to their customers. The different channels are referred to as the Distribution Mix.

Channels of Distribution

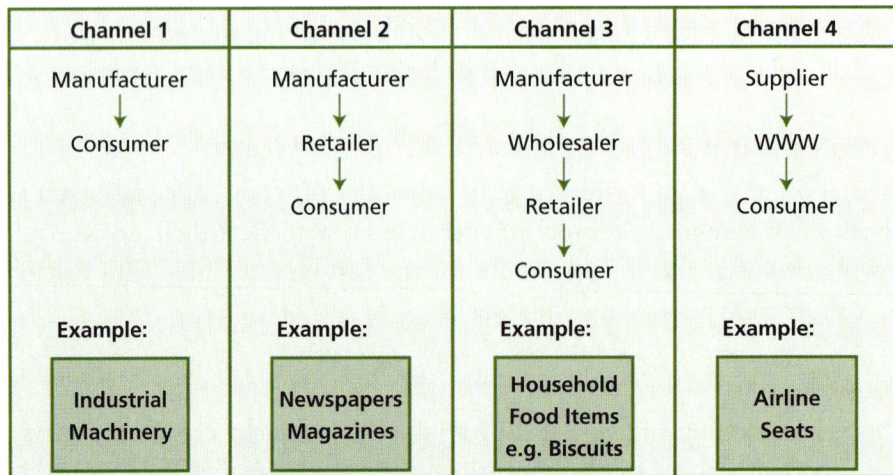

Channel 1	Channel 2	Channel 3	Channel 4
Manufacturer ↓ Consumer	Manufacturer ↓ Retailer ↓ Consumer	Manufacturer ↓ Wholesaler ↓ Retailer ↓ Consumer	Supplier ↓ WWW ↓ Consumer
Example:	**Example:**	**Example:**	**Example:**
Industrial Machinery	**Newspapers Magazines**	**Household Food Items e.g. Biscuits**	**Airline Seats**

Which Channel of Distribution should be used?

The following factors influence the choice of distribution method:

(a) The Kind of Goods Involved

Are they bulky, fragile, perishable, expensive etc.? If the product is expensive, e.g. jewellery, then security is vital, so it is likely that the manufacturer will deal directly with the retail jeweller.

(b) The Size of the Market

If the target market is large, then it may be wiser and more cost-efficient for the manufacturer to distribute through a number of nationwide wholesalers than directly to retailers.

(c) Transport Costs

A firm may use its own delivery vehicles or subcontract this job to outside hauliers.

(d) Speed

The speed of the various modes of transport available. This is important if the goods are urgently required.

(e) Security

How safe are the goods in the different modes of transport? If a consignment of jewellery had to be sent to a customer, then security would be vital because of the value of the goods.

> The manufacturer should always use the method of distribution that will effectively reach the target market, minimise costs and maximise sales.

(f) Distance

What distance is involved between the sender and the receiver of the goods? It is more difficult to have goods delivered to an export customer in New York than to a local customer in Cork.

(g) Costs

What are the costs of the different suitable forms of transport available? For example, if air transport costs €2,500 and sea transport costs €700 and the goods are not urgently required, the seller will use sea transport to deliver the goods.

Links in Distribution Channels

(a) The Wholesaler

(i) The wholesaler is the link between the manufacturer and the retailer in the chain of distribution.

(ii) The wholesaler buys bulk quantities from the manufacturer and sells in smaller quantities to retailers.

(iii) The wholesaler is closer to the target market than the manufacturer and can update the manufacturer on changing trends in the market. It is then up to the manufacturer to respond in order to maintain market share.

Channels of Distribution

Manufacturer
↓
Wholesaler
↓
Retailer
↓
Consumer

(b) The Retailer

The retailer is the third link in the chain of distribution. The retailer buys from the manufacturer or wholesaler and sells directly to the customer, e.g. a grocery shop. Retailers are located nationwide and sell a wide range of goods.

(c) Direct Selling

This is where the products are sold directly by the manufacturer to the consumer/user. Examples include machinery and computers. Mail order firms are also involved in direct selling by post to consumers.

(d) Agents

Agents are appointed by manufacturers to stock and sell a specified range of products, e.g. a local car dealer may be an agent for the Ford range of cars.

Evaluation of the Marketing Mix *(Higher Level Only)*

The marketing mix of product, price, promotion and place are based on the customers' needs. A firm must have the right marketing mix in order to maximise sales and profits. The marketing department should combine all ideas together and produce a Marketing Plan. They choose a specified product or service and decide how each of the four Ps will be adapted to meet the requirements of the target market. The Marketing Plan is an evaluation of the four Ps for each product or service. A successful plan results in sales and profit targets being achieved.

EXAMPLE 1 – Marketing Plan Evaluation of a Product

Product – BMW Motor Car
1. This relates to the product manufactured and sold to customers.
2. A range of BMW cars are available for sale.
3. Safety features include a driver's airbag and the anti-locking brake device.
4. It is batch produced for the world market and the unit cost of production is high.
5. This product is imported into Ireland from Germany.

Price of the BMW Motor Car
1. The selling price is an important part of the marketing strategy of a business.
2. This range of cars has a high selling price, e.g €60,000.
3. The target market is high income earners.
4. The selling price includes a guaranteed free break-down service for three years.
5. It has a high resale value.

Promotion of the BMW Motor Car
1. This involves informing the target market about the range of BMW cars available for sale. Promotion is used to support advertising in order to encourage new or existing BMW car users to buy a new one.
2. The advertising budget should be high because of the brand image of quality, reliability and high price.
3. It should be advertised in business magazines, in motor supplements, in newspapers and at motor trade fairs.
4. Gimmick special offers used in supermarkets are not appropriate.

Place – To buy the BMW
1. The BMW must be available for sale where and when the customers want to buy, i.e. through motor dealers, direct selling, agents, etc.
2. BMW car distributors exist in the big cities and large towns nationwide.
3. The limited range of outlets selling this car is an indication of the high quality of the product.
4. Because its selling price is so high, it can only be sold by people who can provide the required back-up after-sales service.

EXAMPLE 2 – Marketing Plan Evaluation of a Service

Service – Local Taxi Service

1. This relates to the taxi service offered to people within a 30 km radius.
2. This is normally a competitive service to offer.

Price of the Local Taxi Service

1. The cost of the taxi service is controlled by legislation so there is no competitive price advantage in this area.
2. The selling price is not as important as the reliability of the service.

Promotion of the Local Taxi Service

1. This involves informing the local target market about the availability of the service.
2. Only a small advertising budget is required.
3. Advertising in the local newspapers, on local radio and giving business cards to customers should be adequate.

Place – Where to Avail of the Local Taxi Service

1. This service should be available at known taxi ranks.
2. Customers should know if it is possible to book this service in advance by ringing the taxi owner.

Break-even Analysis

Fixed and Variable Costs

When calculating the costs of running a business, management must realise the difference between 'fixed costs' and 'variable' costs. **Fixed costs** do not vary with the number of units produced or sold. These costs are incurred and must be paid whether the business is open or not, e.g. rent and insurance. **Variable costs** vary with the number of units produced or sold. They are also called 'direct' costs as they can be linked to a particular product, e.g. raw materials (such as paper for books) and electricity.

> **Total Costs = Fixed Costs + Variable Costs**

Break-even Chart

A break-even chart shows the level of output required for the business to break even. This occurs when revenue equals costs, i.e. no profit is earned or loss incurred. Until the break-even point is reached, the firm is not making profit. A break-even chart also shows how costs and revenue change as sales increase or decrease.
In order to draw a break-even chart, it is necessary to have information about the fixed costs, variable costs and revenue of the business.

EXAMPLE 1
The following information relates to Academic Book Publishers Ltd.
Fixed Costs   €20,000   Selling Price   €20
Variable Costs   €12 per book   No. of books that can be printed 4,000

Question: You are requested to show this information on a break-even chart
and calculate the profit at full capacity, i.e. when all the 4,000 books
produced are sold.

Solution: Number of books sold   4,000
Selling Price   €20
Gross Revenue (4,000 x 20)   €80,000
Less Costs
Fixed Costs   €20,000
Variable Costs (4,000 x 12)   €48,000   €68,000
Profit   €12,000

Before drawing a break-even chart, let us complete a simple table as follows:

Number of units sold	Selling Price	Variable Costs	Fixed Costs	Total Costs	Revenue	Profit
0	20	0	20,000	20,000	0	0
4,000	20	48,000	20,000	68,000	80,000	12,000

Question:
How many books have to be published for the business to break even?
Answer:
1.   Calculate the contribution towards the fixed costs from each book
sold.
i.e. Selling Price – Variable Cost = Contribution
i.e.   €20 –   €12   =   €8

2.   Divide the contribution of each book into the total fixed costs, this
gives you the break-even point.
Break-even point = _____Total fixed costs_____
Contribution per unit
= €20,000 = 2,500
€8

Sale = 2,500 books @ €20 each = €50,000
Fixed Costs   = €20,000   Break-even Point
Variable Costs = 2,500 x 12   = €30,000
€50,000

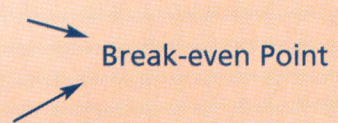

Preparing a Break-even Chart

1. Calculate the break-even figure, i.e. $\dfrac{\text{Fixed Costs}}{\text{Contribution}}$

2. Calculate the total sales revenue, i.e. number of units sold multiplied by the selling price.

3. On the horizontal line (x) record the sales quantity in units.

4. On the vertical line (y) record the following:
   (a) sales (b) costs.

5. Record the fixed costs on a horizontal line parallel to the x axis.

6. Record the total costs (FC + VC) at the relevant point on the vertical axis (y), i.e. from where the fixed costs line meets the vertical axis.

7. Plot the revenue line and locate the break-even point. You then show the following:

   (a) profit areas   (b) loss areas   (c) margin of safety

> Break-even equals
> $\dfrac{\text{Fixed Costs}}{\text{Contribution}}$

> Contribution equals
> Sales Price – Variable Costs

Break-even Chart for Academic Publishers Ltd

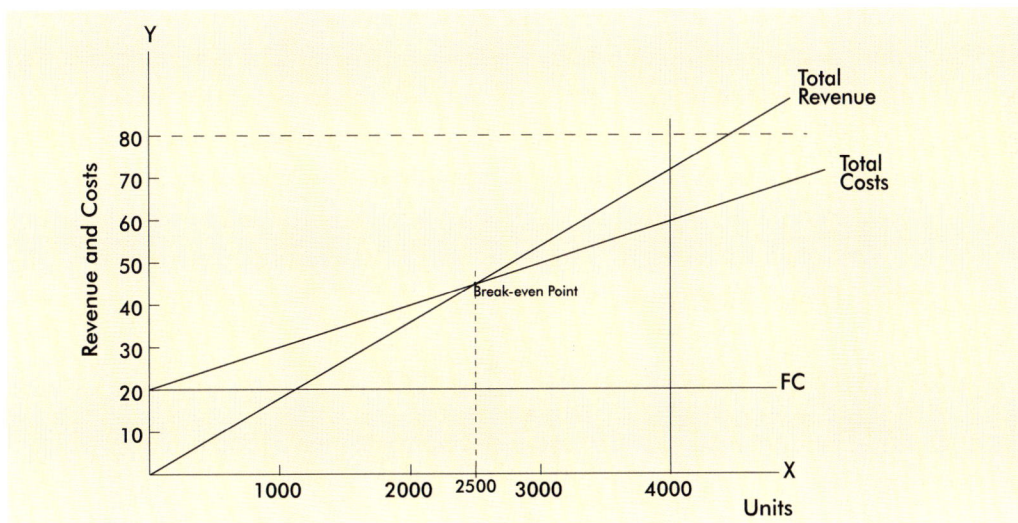

Information Available from Break-even Charts

1. They show the level of output where total revenue from sales equals the total costs incurred. In the example, the break-even output level was 2,500 units.

2. They provide management with information regarding the sales quantity required to break even.

The chart on the previous page gives us the following information about Academic Book Publishers Ltd:

1. The firm is losing money on sales less than 2,500 units.

2. The firm will make profit on all sales over 2,500 units.

3. If the firm sells the 4,000 books available, it will make a maximum profit of €120,000.

What are Break-even Charts used for?

Break-even charts provide management with important information, for example:

1. If the selling price is increased, the amended break-even chart will show management what new sales/output level in units is required for the firm to break even. Obviously, when the selling price is increased, the break-even level is reduced.

2. If variable costs (e.g. raw materials) increase, the break-even point will be adversely affected. This information will interest management, who may decide to try to source the raw materials more cheaply. In a manufacturing firm, management might decide to close down a department and buy in the product rather than continue to produce it.

3. If fixed costs increase, it will be necessary for management to calculate the new break-even point in order to recover the additional costs.

4. The break-even chart illustrates the impact decisions to increase or reduce selling prices have on profits. In a monopoly situation, a firm might decide to increase selling prices. On the other hand, in a competitive market, (e.g. selling televisions) a firm may decide to reduce selling prices in order to increase sales. In this situation, the break-even chart will show the new break-even point required to justify such a decision. Management can use this information in determining whether the marketing decision to reduce selling prices is justified.

Limitations of Break-even Charts

Even though they have many uses, break-even charts also have limitations of which management must be aware, for example:

1. They are drawn up on the assumption that all the goods will be sold – this does not always happen.

2. Fixed costs only remain fixed if the scale of production does not increase, e.g. in order to expand output a firm may have to invest in new machinery causing a rise in fixed costs.

3. They assume no other stocks are available for sale.

Calculating Break-even

In practice, many firms do not draw break-even charts as they are mainly interested in calculating the actual break-even figure and making decisions from there.

EXAMPLE

Crystal Ltd manufacture a range of low-price, hand-cut crystal and are able to sell all of the crystal produced. The following information is available:

Selling price of each hand-cut glass	=	€50
Variable Costs	=	€20
Fixed Costs	=	€6,000

Question: How many hand-cut crystal glasses must be produced and sold for the firm to break even?

Answer: Selling Price – Variable Cost = Contribution per unit

= €50 – €20 = €30

This means that each glass is making a contribution of €30 towards the fixed costs of €6,000.

$$\text{Break Even} = \frac{\text{Total Fixed Costs}}{\text{Contribution per unit}} = \frac{€6,000}{€30} = 200 \text{ units}$$

Answer: The break-even point is 200 crystal glasses.

Margin of Safety

The 'margin of safety' is the excess of the projected or budgeted sales volume over the firm's break-even point. It is the amount by which a firm's sales can fall before the break-even point is reached. It is the difference between a firm's sales and its break-even point. It may be stated in units or in euro.

EXAMPLE

Sales of mobile phones in April	=	10,000 units
Break-even quantity of sales required	=	6,000 units
Margin of Safety	=	4,000 units
Selling Price	=	€50
Revenue Margin of Safety	=	€200,000

In the above example, the number of mobile phones sold in April could fall by 4,000 before any loss is made. The higher the margin of safety, the less likely it is that the firm will lose money.

Revision of Important Terms	
• Marketing	• Marketing Plan
• Marketing Concept	• Market Segmentation
• Marketing Management	• Niche Market
• Marketing Manager	• Green Consumer
• Marketing Mix	• Brand Name
• Mark-up	• Product Life Cycle
• Skimming Pricing	• Loss Leader
• Wholesaler	

Exercises

1. (a) What is marketing?

   (b) Explain what is meant by the marketing concept.

   (c) Outline the work of the marketing manager in a business.

   (d) Why is the work of the marketing manager so important for a business?

2. (a) Explain what is meant by the marketing strategy in a business.

   (b) What is a marketing plan?

   (c) Outline the benefits to a business of a marketing plan.

3. Explain each of the following terms:

   (a) Marketing   (c) Niche Market   (e) Market Segmentation

   (b) Marketing Plan   (d) Marketing Strategy

4. (a) Explain what is meant by market segmentation.

   (b) 'A business should be aware of the viewpoints of green consumers.' Discuss.

5. (a) What is meant by the marketing mix?

   (b) How does the marketing concept differ from the marketing mix?

6. Explain each of the following terms:

    (a) Patents   (c) Product Life Cycle

    (b) Brand Name   (d) Marketing Concept

---

7. (a) Show by means of a diagram the product life cycle for a motor car of your choice.

    (b) Why is the marketing manager interested in a firm's product life cycle?

---

8. 'The higher the selling price, the bigger the profits.'

    (a) What factors should a sales manager consider when deciding the selling price of a new television?

    (b) Explain each of the following:

        (i) Cost Plus Pricing (ii) Skimming Pricing (iii) Premium Pricing

---

9. (a) Outline the factors to consider when considering which methods of distribution to use for a manufacturing business.

    (b) Show by means of a diagram the 'Channels of Distribution'.

    (c) Discuss the role and importance of the wholesaler in the channel of distribution.

---

10. A local auctioneer has advertised a house for sale at €140,000. Evaluate the marketing mix for this house.

---

11. (a) Show by means of a diagram the various channels of distribution available to manufacturers for getting their products to their customers.

    (b) Give two examples of a product suitable for each channel of distribution.

---

12. A business only makes profits when revenue exceeds costs.

Illustrate the following figures by means of a break-even chart:

Fixed Costs	=	€20,000 p.a.
Variable Costs	=	€5 per unit
Selling Price	=	€10 per unit

13. (a) Illustrate the following figures by means of a break-even chart:

Fixed Costs	=	€10,000 p.a.
Variable Costs	=	€4 per unit
Estimated Sales	=	2000 units
Selling Price	=	€10

(b) Using this break-even chart show the following:

   (i) Break-even point

   (ii) Maximum profit when all units are sold

   (iii) The margin of safety

14. Paula and John Byrne own a restaurant. On average, each of their customers spends €20 on a meal. The owners know that variable costs per customer are €8 and that weekly fixed costs are €5,040. They have, on average, 500 customers per week.

   (a) How many customers are required for the business to break even each week?

   (b) How much profit will the business make in a normal week?

   (c) Using the information available, prepare a break-even chart for the business for a typical week.

15. (a) A business will not survive unless it meets all its costs. Illustrate the following information by means of a break-even chart:

Fixed Costs	=	€10,000 p.a.
Variable Costs	=	€50 per unit
Selling Price	=	€80 per unit
Forecasted Sales	=	80,000 units

(b) Using this break-even chart show the following:

   (i) Break-even point

   (ii) Profit at full capacity

   (iii) Margin of safety

15 Promotion

Objectives

The following topics from **Unit 5** of the syllabus are covered in this chapter:

- What is Promotion?
- Advertising
- Sales Promotion
- Public Relations
- Personal Selling

What is Promotion?

Promotion involves communicating with customers about products or services to encourage them to buy. There are four important methods of promotion:

1.	Advertising	3.	Public Relations
2.	Sales Promotion	4.	Personal Selling

The combination of these four methods is called the Promotion Mix or the Communication Mix.

Most goods and services require advertising and promotion.

Promotional methods must be used for the following reasons:

1. To inform customers about the availability of a product, its price and where it is available for sale. This is called **informative promotion**.

2. To encourage and persuade consumers to buy the product, which means that a firm's sales and profits should rise. This is called **persuasive promotion**.

3. To remind consumers that a long-established product is and will continue to be available. This is called **reminder** or **reassuring promotion**.

4. To extend the shelf-life of a product and stop its decline in the product life cycle. If successful, the sales and profits should rise and the seller doesn't have to invest in a new consumer product.

Promotion should be:
- informative
- persuasive
- reassuring

1. Advertising

It is important for firms to advertise or they will lose sales to competitors.

➥ Definition of Advertising

Advertising is the paid form of publication of information regarding a firm's goods or services through newspapers, magazines, radio and TV which is designed to inform customers and persuade them to buy the advertised item.

In 2004, €967m was spent on advertising in Ireland. This figure can be broken up into the various forms of media:

Television	Radio	Newspapers/Magazines
€335m	€198m	€434m

239

Objectives of Advertising

The objectives of advertising are as follows:

(a) To **inform** both existing and potential customers in the target market about the availability of products or services, price, special features and where they can be purchased.

(b) To **persuade** customers in the target market to purchase the advertised item.

(c) To **remind** customers about a product or service by regular advertising. This encourages customers to have confidence in the product.

(d) To **increase** sales and profits.

> Aims of Advertising:
> • inform
> • persuade
> • remind
> • increase sales

Who Advertises?

Most advertising is carried out by manufacturers and big retailers.

(a) Manufacturers advertise their products to inform the public of their existence and to encourage them to buy their products when next shopping.

(b) Big stores continually advertise in order to persuade customers to shop in their stores rather than elsewhere.

(b) The combination of the above two forms of advertising is called **consumer advertising**. Non-profit businesses also advertise, e.g. charities.

The Effective Advertising Campaign

Advertisers have different advertising media to choose from. Which one should be used? Can an advertiser afford to advertise on TV?

The following factors should be considered when assessing the most effective advertising medium to use:

(a) The objective of the advertising: a clear objective must be set and later evaluated to see how successful the campaign has been.

(b) The **target** market: low income or high income consumers.

> *Half of the money spent on advertising is wasted. Which half is it?*

(c) The **type** of product. Certain types of specialist and expensive products, such as computers, require selective advertising in business magazines.

(d) The **size** of the advertising budget. The bigger the budget, the more elaborate the campaign, hence the greater the chance of success.

(e) The **reason** for the advertising campaign. Is it to launch a new product or to give a specific message to the target market?

Main Advertising Media
(a) Television Advertising

(i) This is a very effective method of advertising and demonstrating the product nationwide and worldwide.

(ii) Once the target market is known, it is possible to 'time' the advertisement for when such customers are likely to be watching.

(iii) It is a costly method of advertising, e.g. €2,000 for 20 seconds during peak viewing. Due to the high cost, the message to the consumer must be catchy, clear and precise.

> *The fact that €335m was spent on TV advertising in Ireland in 2004 is evidence that it is a cost-effective and successful means of advertising.*

(b) Newspaper Advertising

(i) National newspapers, e.g. *Irish Independent* and *The Examiner,* have a nationwide readership and so are suitable for advertising when the target market is nationwide.

(ii) Circulation of local newspapers is confined to a local geographical area, e.g. *The Nenagh Guardian.* The majority of advertising in local newspapers is for the local target market.

(iii) It is cheaper (by about 60%) to advertise in a local newspaper than a national one.

(iv) Newspapers are quickly disposed of, so advertisements have to be well designed and displayed if they are to be effective.

> **Examples of provincial newspapers:**
> - Midland Tribune
> - Connacht Champion
> - Nenagh Guardian
> - Longford Leader
> - Donegal Democrat
> - Kerryman

(c) Magazine Advertising

(i) Magazines are usually published weekly (e.g. *Business and Finance*) or monthly (e.g. *VIP*). They have a longer life than newspapers.

(ii) Magazines are aimed at a special target market, e.g. business people, sports people, teenagers etc.

(iii) A lot of advertisements in magazines are in colour and are generally more catchy, more effective and very costly, e.g. a full-page A4 size advertisement in *Hello!* magazine costs in the region of €10,000.

> *Advertising in newspapers and magazines is referred to as advertising in the print media.*

(d) Radio Advertising

(i) This can be an effective method of advertising a product nationwide.

(ii) Local radio stations, which are cheaper than national media, can be effectively used to advertise to a local target market.

(iii) Radio advertising is much cheaper than TV advertising.

(e) Outdoor Advertising

(i) Billboard advertising is common in cities and large towns.

(ii) It involves prominent positioning of the posters to catch the attention of the 'moving' consumers, e.g. on a busy road or beside an airport.

(iii) The advertisements are big and well designed in order to be seen and understood.

(f) The Internet

This is a new channel of distribution for promoting goods. It is becoming more widely available both nationwide and worldwide. Credit cards are used as a means of payment. E-commerce via the Internet is a vital part of business.

How is Advertising Regulated in Ireland?

The following bodies exist to regulate the advertising industry and protect the public from being misled:

(a)	The Advertising Standards Authority for Ireland (ASAI)
(b)	The Office of the Director of Consumer Affairs
(c)	The Broadcasting Complaints Commission
(d)	The Independent Radio and Television Commission

(a) The Advertising Standards Authority for Ireland (ASAI)

This is a self-regulating body which insists on the highest standards of advertising. Its code of practice is known as The Code of Advertising Standards in Ireland. It states the following:

(i) All advertising should avoid any form of illegality or dishonesty, i.e. they should be legal, decent, honest and truthful.

(ii) Advertisements should in no way unfairly criticise competitors' products.

The ASAI has no statutory powers. It is the industry's supervisor and its recommendations are usually accepted by advertisers. You cannot sue the ASAI. If you lose money due to misleading advertising, contact the Director of Consumer Affairs.

(b) The Office of the Director of Consumer Affairs

Under the Consumer Information Act 1978, the Director of Consumer Affairs can instigate legal proceedings against advertisers involved in misleading advertising.

2. Sales Promotion

> **➡ Definition of Sales Promotion**
>
> *Sales promotion has been defined as the marketing techniques used on a temporary basis to make goods more attractive to consumers by providing some extra benefit, e.g. a free gift.*

Sales promotion activities are undertaken to support advertising. They concentrate on offering some bonus or incentive to consumers, e.g. coupons, rather than emphasising the quality of the product. Sales promotion can be used to target consumers and retailers in order to increase sales.

Examples of Sales Promotion Methods

(a) Getting customers to collect tokens or trading stamps. These can be used to get a free gift, e.g. a customer who collects 200 Esso tokens can receive a free camera.

(b) Offering 'Two for the price of one'. This is a short-term offer for products such as soaps, toothpaste, tea etc.

(c) Giving a price reduction for a short period (25 per cent off). This encourages consumers to buy certain products.

(d) Providing vouchers with certain products. These may be used to obtain a discount when buying the products.

(e) Offering free trial offers on new products, e.g. shampoo.

(f) Giving a free gift with a product. For example, a free CD might be included in a computer or music magazine.

(g) Branded packs, e.g. a free toothbrush with every box of toothpaste.

Sales promotion is a form of advertising and the marketing manager is responsible for implementing it and checking its effectiveness.

Sales promotions are now actively used by firms. In the competitive business world, firms feel that they should be making special offers to customers. Sales promotion techniques bring the customers closer to the product in the short term. If customers are satisfied with the product, then ongoing sales will bring long-term benefits to the business.

Benefits of Sales Promotion to a Business

(a) It helps to generate sales during times of the year when sales are usually low, e.g. after Christmas.

(b) It attracts new customers to certain products.

(c) It encourages existing customers to purchase the 'regular product' at a better price.

(d) It enables firms to clear surplus stocks.

Mail Order

It is easy to assess the effectiveness of a sales promotion campaign in a mail order firm. In this form of selling, the business advertises in newspapers and magazines and also sends catalogues to customers. Mail order is now more popular due to the convenience of shopping on the Internet.

Merchandising

Merchandising is an extension of the selling process. The manufacturer provides 'point of sale' material to ensure that products are sold as quickly and as profitably as possible by the retailer. Advice and assistance is given to the retailer by:

- recommending the best location for the product.
- providing display stands at impulse location points (e.g. display stands for books in a book shop).
- providing posters and leaflets for the shops.

The objective of all the back-up or support services provided by the manufacturer to the retailer is to increase the sales of the manufacturer's products – not all products.

Merchandising certainly leads to impulse buying by consumers. In 1998, research findings in the US showed that 9 per cent of sales in large stores were linked to impulse buying by its customers. This figure had increased to 13 per cent by March 2005.

Direct Marketing

Direct marketing involves making direct contact with customers. It identifies the exact target market, so the seller knows the requirements of the potential customer. Direct contact can be made in the following ways:

(a) Telemarketing (Telesales)

The potential customers are contacted by telephone. This form of marketing is increasing in popularity. It is mainly carried out by banks, travel agents etc, which are service firms. Research has shown that some consumers do not like this form of 'aggressive marketing'.

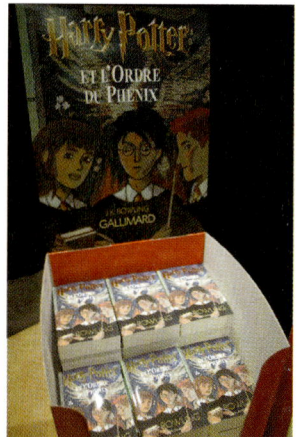

(b) Direct Mail

This involves sending catalogues, brochures, leaflets etc. by post to the potential consumer. This is referred to as untargeted marketing and is not very effective. It is known to many receivers as junk mail.

(c) Direct Response Mail

This is where potential consumers request the advertiser to send them promotional material. Inserts in magazines are used with this method.

Importance of Direct Marketing to Promoters

Direct marketing has the following benefits to promoters who use this approach to selling:

- It is possible to accurately contact the 'target markets', e.g. IT managers.
- It is possible to quantify the results of the marketing campaign, e.g. sales, customers sending in business reply cards etc.
- It is much cheaper than advertising on radio or on TV and it can be more effective. In 1999, 7 per cent of advertising expenditure went on direct marketing.
- It is easy to check if it is cost effective by comparing the sales and profits generated with the actual costs incurred.

3. Public Relations (PR)

> **➡ Definition of Public Relations**
>
> *Public Relations is the planned and sustained effort to establish and maintain goodwill and mutual understanding between a business and the public.*

The public relations (PR) function involves creating and maintaining a positive and beneficial image of the firm's policies and products to both its customers and the general public. Using various methods, public relations aims to promote the public understanding and acceptance of a firm, its products, services and policy. It is not a form of direct selling as there is no direct campaign to sell a product. The aims of public relations include the following:

(a) To promote the good name and image of a firm.

(b) To generate goodwill from the public for the firm.

(c) To ensure that the public are aware of the existence of the firm, its products, its size and what gives it a competitive advantage over competitors.

Duties of the Public Relations Officer (PRO)

(a) Relationship with the Media

The PRO issues press releases and handles queries from the media in relation to the firm's activities. For example, a news conference would be organised by the PRO.

(b) Relationship with Customers

Complaints from customers or the general public should be dealt with and not ignored – 'The customer is always right'. The PRO must have a positive attitude towards customers.

(c) Relationship with Employees

Employees are an important asset of every business. Treating the employees well is a form of internal goodwill, which has both internal and external benefits. It is important to inform the employees on major issues affecting the business and to listen to their views.

(d) Relationship with the Local Community

Supporting local clubs and organisations and co-operating with the local Chamber of Commerce and the local authorities is good for gaining local goodwill. It is also important to be a good neighbour, e.g. minimising noise and pollution.

(e) Sponsorship

Sponsorship involves the provision of financial support by a business to another party involved in the organising or performance of some special event. In return, the business gains a publicity opportunity with a commercial purpose.

It is generally associated with fund-raising for charitable, sporting or educational purposes. A firm's name would be associated with the sponsored event and would be tied to any publicity about the event, e.g. Murphy's sponsor the Irish Open and GPA sponsors the Young Musician of the Year.

Sponsorship has become important because it is now possible to reach a target audience through a huge range of TV channels. In sponsorship, it is important for the sponsor to be associated with achievement.

4. Personal Selling

➡ Definition of Personal Selling

Personal selling occurs when the seller, or salesperson, tries to verbally persuade the customer to buy a product.

This form of selling is associated with capital expenditure on industrial products, e.g. computers, machinery etc. It is unlikely that a firm would purchase new machinery costing €100,000 on the basis of an advertisement in a catalogue. It is the most expensive and most persuasive element of the promotion mix. Due to the opportunities provided by technology, some personal selling is done by phone and e-mail.

Attributes of a Salesperson

(a) Familiarity with the product so as to convince the customer when answering queries.

(b) A friendly manner when meeting the customer. This is essential in order to hold the customer's attention.

(c) The ability to convince the customer to buy the product. and finalise the sale.

Exercises

1. (a) State the different methods of sales promotion available to business.

   (b) Why are promotional methods used in business?

2. (a) Outline the reasons for advertising by firms.

   (b) Why would a business choose to advertise its products on TV rather than on radio?

3. (a) What is meant by sales promotion? How does it differ from advertising?

   (b) Explain what is meant by merchandising.

4. Discuss each of the following:

   (a) The aim of public relations.   (b) The duties of a PRO.

5. Describe a suitable medium for advertising fashion shoes. Give reasons for your choice.

6. A car manufacturer intends to launch a new motor vehicle on the market. Describe a suitable promotion mix for the launch of the car.

7. (a) How does personal selling differ from other promotion activities?

   (b) Discuss sales promotion in the context of the promotion mix.

   (c) Using an example, describe how corporate sponsorship can enhance brand awareness.

8. A new hotel has opened on the outskirts of the town and has attracted business from many of your customers. What steps can the management of your hotel take to 'win back' the customers?

16 Getting Started in Business

Objectives

The following topics from **Unit 5** of the syllabus are covered in this chapter:

- Development Cycle of a Business
- Considerations Before Starting up a Business
- Sources of Finance for New Business Enterprises
- Working Capital
- Cash Flow
- Which Business Organisation Options to Adopt
- Production Option for Manufacturing Business
- The Business Plan

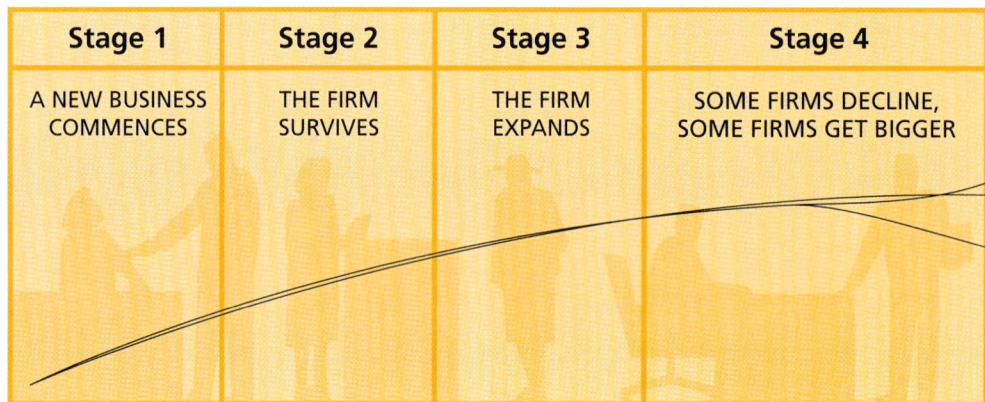

Development Cycle of a Business

Every business passes through different stages of growth, each one involving different problems and solutions. Some firms close down, others survive and expand and, in some cases, become very big.

Stage 1	Stage 2	Stage 3	Stage 4
A NEW BUSINESS COMMENCES	THE FIRM SURVIVES	THE FIRM EXPANDS	SOME FIRMS DECLINE, SOME FIRMS GET BIGGER

Development Cycle of a Business

The four stages in the development cycle of a business are as follows:

1.	Commencing
2.	Surviving
3.	Growth
4.	The Future

Stage 1 – Commencing

(a) This is the start-up stage, i.e. the firm commences business.

(b) The firm requires management, finance, products, customers, sales and profits.

(c) Management take a short-term view and want to at least break even and then make profits. Some of the profits may be used to finance expansion.

Stage 2 – Surviving

(a) The firm survives and some see this as a sign of success. The firm has overcome the initial problems, but now some additional ones surface, for example:

- organisational problems
- low profit levels
- lack of finance for growth
- cost of employing new staff

(b) For many firms that manage to survive, it is often the case that the owner is the manager and performs a wide range of managerial tasks.

(c) Management are planning for the future, so they are happy to reinvest profits to help finance growth.

Stage 3 – Growth

(a) The firm expands and it can afford to take some commercial risks, e.g. a wider range of goods, more credit etc.

(b) A proper management team is in place, the firm is well organised and profits are good and steady.

(c) The owners are now reaping the rewards of their initial investment and hard work.

(d) Additional finance is required in order to fund the growth.

Stage 4 – The Future

(a) For some firms there is further growth, which may be in the form of diversification or acquisitions. Such firms have benefited from top management.

(b) Some firms will be happy at their existing size, with no ambition for further growth. In this case, opportunities will be lost.

(c) Some firms will decline, sell out and close down – the harsh reality of commercial life.

(d) Some companies engage in a management buy-out or bring in new management to develop the business further.

249

Considerations Before Starting a Business

Starting up your own business is often referred to as a 'green field venture'. Obviously there are many concerns and risks involved such as:

- investing money
- targeting the market
- producing and selling the product
- having to work long hours

Benefits of Setting Up a Business and being Self-Employed

1. The entrepreneur is independent and flexible.
2. If the business venture succeeds, the investor will be satisfied with the profitable return on the investment.
3. A successful business person will enjoy a good image and high status in the community.
4. The business will provide employment for the owner and his/her family.
5. Being self-employed makes you your own boss and means that you don't have to rely on others to make decisions and do certain work.

Qualities Necessary to Start Up a Successful Business

In order to start up a successful business a person must be:

1. **Ambitious** and want to achieve and be seen as successful (self-actualisation).

2. **Flexible** and prepared to compromise. The new business not only requires a plan, it also needs a vision against which everything is compared. Being flexible allows you to take advantage of opportunities to achieve that vision. A flexible person is not afraid of changing direction, while maintaining their vision.

> Six qualities to succeed in business:
> - Ambitious
> - Flexible
> - Resilient
> - Attentive to advice
> - Creative
> - Able to work in a team

3. **Resilient** and determined to overcome setbacks and perhaps turn such problems into opportunities.

4. Prepared to seek and **take advice**. Being able to make decisions is important, but there may be occasions when it is advisable to seek advice before making decisions.

5. **Creative** with new ideas and suggestions on how to improve matters.

6. Able to recognise the **importance of teamwork**, meet deadlines, accept responsibility for decision making and satisfy the requirements of customers.

Sources of Finance for New Business Enterprises

Finance may be required in the short-term, medium-term or long-term.

> A short-term source of finance is due to be repaid within one year.

> A medium-term source of finance is due for repayment between one and five years.

> A long-term source of finance is available to a firm for longer than five years before it is due to be repaid.

The following table shows the various sources of finance suitable for a new business. They are discussed in Chapter 9.

Short-Term	Medium-Term	Long-Term
1. Trade creditors	1. Leasing	1. Ordinary share capital
2. Bank overdraft	2. Term loan	2. Grants
3. Accrued expenses	3. Hire purchase	3. Venture capital
		4. Long-term loan/Debenture

Cash Flow

Cash is a liquid asset of a business. It is available for immediate spending on goods or services. An efficient control of money in and out of a firm is essential for its survival. It is essential for management to know when payments are due from debtors and when payments have to be paid to suppliers. The cash flow cycle shows the various stages involved, from paying bills to receiving cash from sales.

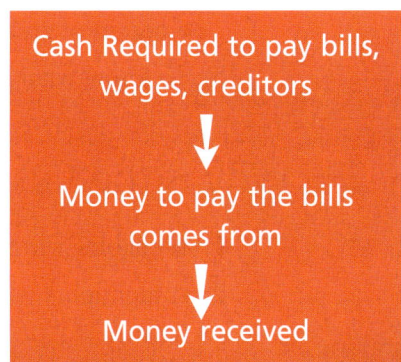

Cash Required to pay bills, wages, creditors
↓
Money to pay the bills comes from
↓
Money received

Steps a Firm can take to Improve its Cash Flow

1. Make sure that there is no delay in sending out invoices to debtors. Contact debtors if they do not pay on time. If necessary, fax a copy of the original invoice as a reminder.

2. Avoid as much as possible operating in an overdraft situation with the bank. Where possible, delay paying creditors until money is received from debtors and lodged.

3. Offer an attractive cash discount to encourage an early settlement of accounts by debtors. If this succeeds, it has the effect of reducing debtors, reducing the risk of bad debts, improving the bank balance and helping the working capital position.

4. Ensure that the firm has a good credit control system. Where necessary, withdraw credit from some customers and operate on a cash basis. This eliminates the risk of bad debts with such customers.

5. Have a good stock control system and, where possible, operate a Just-In-Time (JIT) system of ordering from suppliers.

6. Certain assets such as machinery, computers etc. can be leased rather than purchased. This would spread the payment (outflow) over a long period. It stops a large payment when the asset is acquired.

7. Invoice discounting can be used to convert debts into cash so that the cash flow into the business is quickened.

What is a Cash Flow Forecast? (CFF)

A Cash Flow Forecast (CFF) is an estimate of future movements of cash into and out of a business, as a result of receipts from customers and payments to suppliers. A business should prepare a cash flow forecast for the following reasons:

1. To check when money is due to be received and when payments are due to be made.

2. To check if the business can pay its creditors when payment is due.

3. To check whether there will be a shortfall or surplus and if so, when.

4. To highlight if areas of weak financial management exist, i.e. giving too long a period of credit to customers.

5. To know what level of overdraft may be required and when.

Why is the Cash Flow Forecast (CFF) Important?

1. It enables a firm to predict its potential bank balance at any given time.

2. It highlights when payments have to be made and their impact on the bank balance.

3. It shows how payments can be streamlined to be cost-effective for the firm, e.g. the firm may delay paying some of its bill payments for one week. Meanwhile the lodgements of payments the firm's bank account receives from its debtors may cover the delayed payments and thus avoid the firm entering an overdraft situation.

4. The opportunity cost can be maximised, e.g. if payment can be deferred,

the money can be left in a deposit account, earning interest. Over a 12-month period, the potential interest to be earned might be €10,000 for a large firm. If this potential gain is lost, then so is the opportunity of using that money for market research etc.

> ### → Definition of Opportunity Cost
>
> *The opportunity cost is defined as the cost of not being able to do something else with the sum of money in question.*
> *For example, a person has to choose between buying a motor car priced at €20,000 or speculating in shares for the same amount. If they choose to buy the car, then the opportunity to invest in the shares is lost, this is the opporutnity cost of the decision.*

Cash Flow Projections, i.e. Cash Inflows and Cash Outflows

1. Cash Inflows
Cash inflows are amounts of money being received by a business:
- Cash sales.
- Receipts from debtors (e.g. credit sales made some weeks ago).
- Loan received from a bank (term loan).
- Loan received, e.g. from the Government.
- Money received from an issue of shares to shareholders.
- A VAT refund from the Revenue Commissioners.

2. Cash Outflows
Cash outflows are payments being made by a business:
- Cash purchases.
- Payments to creditors (for goods purchased some weeks ago).
- Wages.
- Insurance, light and heat, telephone.
- Advertising.
- Loan repayments.
- PAYE.
- Capital expenditure (e.g. purchase of machinery).

What Are Cash Flow Forecasts used for?
Cash flow forecasts are used in the following situations:
- As a guide for the owners of a new business, who use them to prepare cash projections.
- In order to keep the bank manager informed of the financial position of the firm.
- To ensure that income and expenditure budgets are being adhered to in an existing business.

EXAMPLE OF CASH FLOW FORECAST

The following is a Cash Flow Forecast of Brendan Jones Ltd, a boutique business in Co. Mayo.

Cash Flow Forecast

	January	February	March	Total
Receipts €	60,000	70,000	60,000	190,000
Payments €	48,000	80,000	75,000	203,000
Net Cash €	12,000	(10,000)	(15,000)	(13,000)
Opening Cash €	2,000	14,000	4,000	2,000
Closing Cash €	14,000	4,000	(11,000)	(11,000)

The following information is available from an examination of the above cash flow forecast:

1. In January, the receipts are greater than the payments by €12,000. At the end of this month, the business has €14,000 in cash.
2. In February, the payments are greater than the receipts by €10,000. At the end of the month, the cash flow was only €4,000, i.e. €10,000 less than the end of January.
3. In March, the payments are greater than the receipts by €15,000. The closing balance is (€11,000).
4. At the end of the three months, the amount of money spent was €13,000 greater than the amount of money received.

Summary of The Information from the Cash Flow forecast:

1. January will be a good month for the business.
2. In February, the business will decline as the receipts were less than the expenditure. The cash balance from January enabled the firm pay its debts in February.
3. March will be a poor month for the business. The payments are €15,000 greater than the revenue, leaving a shortfall of €15,000. Since the opening cash balance was only €4,000, it means that the business has a shortfall of €11,000 at the end of March.

What Steps Can The Business Take to Solve the Problems?

1. Analyse the various expenses to see if some of them can be reduced or deferred.
2. Advertise in order to increase sales and revenue for the business.
3. Arrange an overdraft facility with the bank.
4. Invest more capital in the business, e.g. an injection of €15,000 share capital from the shareholders would eliminate the negative cash balances.

Which Business Organisation Option to Adopt?

The owners of a new business have three options when setting up the business:

| 1. | Sole Trader | 2. | Partnership | 3. | Private Limited Company |

1. Sole Trader – Opportunities and Challenges

> **➡ Definition of a Sole Trader**
>
> *This is where one person owns and runs a business. In law, the sole trader and the Business are the same, e.g. Martina Hogan's Hair Stylist.*

The sole trader is responsible for all the business debts. If the business fails, the sole trader may have to sell private assets (e.g. house) to pay the business debts.

The opportunities for the sole trader include the following:

(a) It is quick and easy to form this type of business.

(b) Quick decision making is possible without consultation with others.

(c) The sole trader can keep all the profits.

The challenges of being a sole trader include the following:

(a) The sole trader has unlimited liability – a foolish risk to take.

(b) One person is responsible for managing the business – problems will arise if the person doesn't have all the managerial skills necessary.

(c) There may not be enough capital for the business to expand.

2. Partnership – Opportunities and Challenges

> **➡ Definition of a Partnership**
>
> *A partnership is the relation which exists between at least two and not more than 20 persons carrying on a business, with a view to making profit. The business is jointly owned by all the partners.*

The opportunities for those in partnership include the following:

(a) There is more capital available as each partner invests money.

(b) Better decision making is possible because problems can be discussed.

(c) Losses can be shared, so the risk is reduced.

The challenges for those in partnership include the following:

(a) Disagreement amongst the partners may cause poor decision making.

(b) Profits have to be shared.

(c) There is unlimited liability if the business goes bankrupt.

In 1999, there were 161,000 private limited companies in Ireland.

3. Private Limited Company

> ➡ **Definition of a Private Company**
>
> *A private limited company is a business that is set up under the Companies Act 1963–1999 and is owned by a minimum of 1 and a maximum of 50 shareholders. All the shareholders have limited liability and the share price is not quoted on the Stock Exchange.*

The majority of businesses in Ireland operate as private limited companies. The opportunities for a private limited company include the following:

In a private company the shareholders have limited liability.

(a) All the shareholders have limited liability, so that if the business goes bankrupt, they do not lose any private assets. In such a situation, they only lose the money invested in the company. This is one of the main reasons why it is easier to raise finance from shareholders.

(b) The existence of a proper management structure means the firm can be run efficiently. It also allows for expansion to take place.

(c) There is continuity of existence after the death of any shareholder, i.e. the business continues.

(d) Corporation tax rates (12.5%) are lower than PAYE tax rates.

The challenges for a private limited company include the following:

(a) Annual audited accounts have to be submitted to the Registrar of Companies. In some cases they are published.

(b) There are legal issues involved and registration expenses are incurred when forming the company.

(c) Directors acting *ultra vires* (outside their authority) may lose their limited liability.

(d) Relationships with suppliers and customers are not as personal as with other business units.

(e) Finance cannot be raised by selling shares to the public.

Production Options for a Manufacturing Business

Production involves changing raw materials into finished goods. The following are the different types of production options to be considered:

1.	Job Production
2.	Batch Production
3.	Mass Production

1. Job Production

This involves producing a single product to specific requirements. Each operation is a unique job which might not be required again. The product is not produced for stock, it is produced to order, e.g. building a bridge or a ship, making a suit to measure or assembling an aeroplane.

The main features of job production are as follows:

A ship being built at Harland and Wolff in Belfast.

    (a) There is a single product, produced to specific requirements.

    (b) The order is received and an advance downpayment is made before production starts.

    (c) It involves the use of highly-skilled labour.

    (d) The product to be produced is expensive due to the need for high-quality raw materials, original designs and highly-skilled and high cost labour. As these are special one-off products, the purchaser must pay dearly for them, i.e. the selling price is high.

2. Batch Production

This relates to the majority of industrial firms of medium size producing a range of products, e.g. baking bread and cakes of different sizes, making fashion shoes/clothes of different designs and sizes, printing books for the home market or printing local newspapers.

The main features of batch production are as follows:

    (a) The goods are produced for stock in anticipation of their being sold in the normal course of events.

(b) Production must be carefully planned since there is a need for constant stopping and restarting of the machine to produce the different batches required. This leads to downtime, when there is no output as the machinery is being set up for the next job. This lost production time must be kept to a minimum due to the costs involved.

(c) The labour required does not have to be as skilled as in job production. In many causes semi-skilled workers will be suitable. Their wage costs are less than for job production.

(d) It is the most widely practised form of production of average quality products.

Bread is an example of a batch produced product.

3. Mass Production (also called Flow Production)

Mass production involves producing large quantities of the same product – thus achieving savings in production. This helps to greatly reduce the unit cost of production. A successful marketing campaign must exist because with mass production there must also be mass sales. Most manufacturing is automated due to the use of computer aided manufacturing (CAM), e.g. Biro pens, golf balls, children's toys, calculators, soap powders, baby foods and cigarettes.

The main features of mass production are as follows:

(a) A reasonably low-priced product.

(b) Standardised goods are produced in huge quantities in anticipation of huge sales. No downtime costs are incurred.

(c) You do not associate high quality with some mass produced goods. Consumers do not expect a high quality Biro pen for €1.

CDs are mass produced.

(d) Specialised, costly machinery is used and this is geared towards producing identical products only.

(e) The majority of the staff are unskilled assembly line workers performing work of a repetitive nature.

Should a Firm Mass Produce?

The following factors should be considered by a firm before deciding to mass produce its products:

(a) Is there a large existing market for the product?

(b) Is there an ongoing demand for the product, e.g. biro pens, or weekly magazines?

(c) Can the firm afford to mass produce?

(d) Does the firm have large enough storage facilities and an efficient distribution system?

The Business Plan

A Business Plan is a document that sets out how a business will operate and succeed.

Functions of a Business Plan

1. To enable the management to think carefully about every aspect of the business. It is then easier to explain why decisions were made.

2. By planning ahead, management are able to foresee difficulties and take steps to deal with problems that may rise.

3. To impress upon the bank and other potential investors that you are well organised and fully understand the business and its market.

4. To provide a basis for assessing the actual performance of the business, i.e. to compare results with what was expected.

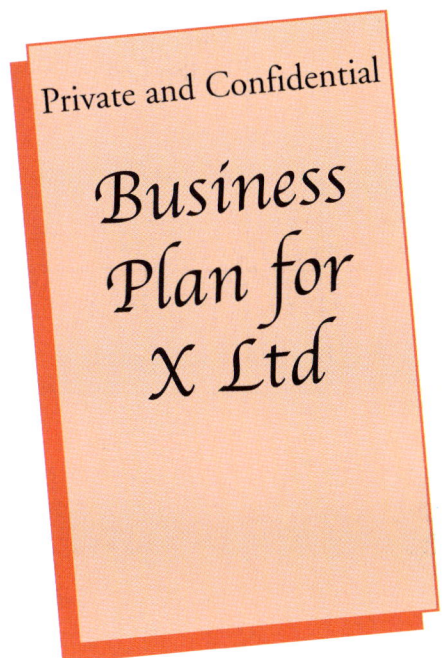

Private and Confidential

Business Plan for X Ltd

Outline of a Business Plan

A good business plan should include the following:

1.	Introduction	The current situation in the business and the prospects for the future.
2.	Management	The key people involved on the management team and their experience.
3.	Product	The product (or service) to be sold.
4.	The Market	Information on existing customers, the level of sales and the potential for growth.
5.	Pricing Policies	Prices necessary to succeed in the target market. Information on competitors' prices should also be included.
6.	Legal Issues	The legal structure of the business, e.g. sole trader or a private limited company.
7.	Location	Location of the premises and its proximity to the firm's markets.
8.	Financial Information	Financial information on the following should be included: • Cash flow forecast. • Sales and profits forecast. • Financial requirements, i.e. short-term, medium-term or long-term. • Reasons why additional capital is required.
9.	Conclusion	A summary of the main features of the business and an outline of a proposed timescale for implementing the plan.

Contents of a Business Plan

1.	Executive Summary	
2.	Promoters and Company background information.	
3.	Outline of proposed business venture	– Overview of proposed business venture – Business history – Expected sales increase – Objectives and strategy – Industry analysis – Profit level increase – Return on investment
4.	Market Research and Analysis	– Target market selection and customer profile – Primary and secondary research – Market positioning, size and share – Nature of competition
5.	Marketing Plan	– Sales plan – Distribution and promotion strategy – Pricing strategy
6.	Production	– Required capacity and Quality issues – Level of capital expenditure required – Production plan and costings – Labour force and training requirements – Suppliers and sourcing of materials
7.	Venture Team	– Outline of prospective shareholders – The management team – Nature of responsibilities and organisation structure – List of external bodies used, such as accountants, solicitors, consultants, state agencies etc.
8.	Financial Plan	– Sources of funding – Profit and loss and balance sheet projections – Sales and Cash flow projections
9.	Schedule of events to be undertaken	
10.	Appendices	

Example of a Business Plan

Deirdre Doyle is a 30-year-old business graduate, who has five years' experience working as a financial controller for a firm. She is confident that she can succeed in her own business as a financial consultant. She has set up a business called Financial Consultants Ltd. She prepared the following business plan:

Business Plan for Financial Consultants Ltd

Company Name:	Financial Consultants Ltd
Owners:	Deirdre Doyle, Colm Doyle
Registered Office:	28 Main Street, Navan, Co. Meath
Solicitors:	Ryan & Co., Navan, Co. Meath
Accountants:	Jones Accountants, Navan, Co. Meath
Bankers:	AIB, Navan, Co. Meath
Managing Director:	Deirdre Doyle, 30 years old, 5 years' experience as a financial controller
Date:	March 2005

Service Offered	• Financial adviser to existing firms
	• Financial advice to people considering starting up a business
	• Negotiating bank loans on behalf of clients
Marketing	• Direct contact with 30 firms personally known to Deirdre Doyle
	• There is a potential target market of 200 firms – ongoing advertising will attract some of these to contact for discussion, advice etc.
Pricing Policy	• 25 per cent below normal competitive rates for the first year

Financing

• Six-year lease of unit in new office block	€20,000	
• Equipment, furniture	€10,000	
• Working capital	€10,000	€40,000
• Finance invested by shareholders	€24,000	
• Additional funding required from potential investors, bank etc.	€16,000	€40,000

• Financial Projection		
	Year 1 profits	€12,000
	Year 2 profits	€19,000
	Year 3 profits	€35,000

Signed: *Deirdre Doyle*

Exercises

1. (a) Show by means of a diagram the development cycle of a business.

   (b) Some people prefer to be self-employed, i.e. own their own business – give four reasons why.

2. (a) State three short-term, three medium-term and three long-term sources of finance that can be used in business.

   (b) Explain what is meant by working capital. How is it calculated?

3. Explain each of the following terms:

   (a) Working Capital   (c) Creditors

   (b) Working Capital Management   (d) Cash Flow Forecast

4. (a) State four cash inflows and four cash outflows in a manufacturing business.

   (b) What steps can a firm take to improve its cash flow position?

5. Hilda and James Collins have decided to give up their jobs and set up a restaurant business.

   (a) List the different types of business organisation they could establish.

   (b) Recommend one of the options and give three reasons for your answer.

6. (a) Indicate which type of production is relevant to the following:

   (i) A tailor making a suit to measure   (iv) Hand-cut crystal

   (ii) Daily newspaper printing   (v)   Local bakery producing bread

   (iii) Manufacturing cigarettes   (vi) Ship-building

   (b) Indicate the main features of each of the following:

   (i) Job Production   (ii) Batch Production   (iii) Mass Production

7. (a) How does a firm benefit by preparing a business plan?

   (b) Outline the important points to be included in a business plan.

8. Michael Hickey is a sales manager with High Tech Supplies Ltd, based in Kilkenny. The firm is ten years in business with branches in Wexford and Ballina. He would like the business to open a new branch in Galway city. Draft the business plan he should prepare for the board of directors regarding his proposal for the business to open a new branch. You can make your own assumptions.

9. The following is a cash flow forecast for Car Rental Ltd:

	April	May	June	Total
Receipts €	80,000	100,000	110,000	290,000
Payments €	76,000	106,000	115,000	297,000
Net Cash €	4,000	(6,000)	(5,000)	(7,000)
Opening Cash €	5,000	9,000	3,000	5,000
Closing Cash €	9,000	3,000	(2,000)	(2,000)

(a) Why did Car Rental Ltd prepare a cash flow forecast?

(b) Why was April a good month for the business?

(c) The business had problems in May and June. What were the problems? State possible reasons for these problems.

(d) What steps can the business take to help solve the problems?

10. The following is an extract from the cash flow forecast for Euro Skills Ltd:

	October	November	December	Total
Receipts €	70,000	80,000	50,000	200,000
Payments €	55,000	70,000	75,000	200,000
Net Cash €				
Opening Cash €	10,000			10,000
Closing Cash €				

Answer the following questions in your exercise copy:

(a) Give two reasons why Euro Skills Ltd prepared a cash flow forecast.

(b) Which month was best for the business? Why?

(c) What problem did the business have in December?

(d) How would it benefit the business if a bank term loan of €40,000 was obtained in December?

11. The following is a Cash Flow Forecast for Castlebar Repair Services Ltd:

	July	August	September	Total
Receipts	€	€	€	
Cash Sales	40,000	45,000	30,000	
Receipts from debtors	10,000	18,000	10,000	
Deposit interest	0	3,000	0	
Bank loan received	8,000	0	0	
Share capital invested	0	0	10,000	
Total Receipts (A)	58,000	66,000	50,000	
Payments	€	€	€	
Cash purchases	18,000	14,000	24,000	
Payments to creditors	21,000	20,000	26,000	
Business expenses	9,000	10,000	18,000	
Motor vehicles	0	0	15,000	
Computer	12,000	0	0	
Taxation	5,000	0	9,000	
Total Payments (B)	65,000	44,000	92,000	
Net Cash (A–B) = (C)	(7,000)	22,000	(42,000)	
Opening cash (D)	5,000	(2,000)	20,000	
Closing cash (C + D)	(2,000)	20,000	(22,000)	

(a) In your answer book complete the total column.

(b) Why did the management instruct the financial controller to prepare a cash flow forecast for discussion at a board meeting?

(c) What impact did the bank loan received in July have on the net cash situation for that month?

(d) Would it have been better for the firm if the finance had been raised from the shareholders in July rather than in September?

(e) How would the firm have benefited if the motor vehicle had been leased rather than purchased?

17 Expansion

Objectives

The following topics from **Unit 5** of the syllabus are covered in this chapter:

- What is Expansion?
- Reasons for Expansion
- Source of Finance and Expansion
- The Implications of Expansion on a Business
- Methods of Expansion/Growth for an Enterprise
- Exporting

What is Expansion?

The main objective of business is profit. No matter how profitable they are, some business owners want to make more profit. This can be achieved by expansion. Expansion can be achieved by either Organic or Inorganic Growth.

- Organic growth (internal growth) involves increasing the size of the existing business by increasing sales and reinvesting the profits. This form of growth may take time, but it provides a strong base for future development.

- Inorganic growth (external growth) involves increasing the size of the business by merging with or taking over another business, either in the same or different type of business.

Challenges of Expansion

The following are some of the major challenges facing management during periods of expansion:

1. Having to change from operational management to business management. Many of the daily tasks must be delegated to allow the management to consider the future of the firm.

2. Ensuring that management and staff work as a team.

3. Realising how fast the business world is changing and understanding the importance of making changes to be part of the future. This is especially true in relation to changes in technology and its impact on business.

Reasons for Expansion

The small business (sole trader, partnership or a small private limited company) will want to expand for the following reasons:

1. To try out new products which have the potential to be very profitable.

2. To enjoy the personal satisfaction of watching the small firm expand.

3. To benefit from economies of scale by operating a bigger firm.

4. To reduce the risk of continuing to operate on a small scale.

Why Established Firms wish to Expand

1. Economies of Scale

In a larger firm the business functions can be rationalised, which results in savings on premises, staff numbers, purchasing, marketing, technical etc. The cost benefits and savings which arise from doing things on a bigger scale rather than on a smaller scale are called economies of scale.

2. Synergy

This is the idea that 2 + 2 = 5, i.e. the combined effect of two firms merging will give a greater overall benefit than if the two firms remained separate. After the merger, surplus assets can be sold and competing products can be discontinued.

3. Security

Being a big business in the market will enable the firm to survive new competition or a recession.

4. Diversification

Growth through diversification into different lines of business enables the firm to spread the risk as they are not overdependent on any one area.

5. Supply

If a firm is dependent on stocks of essential raw material, there is commercial logic in merging with or acquiring the major supplier of that raw material. This will ensure future supplies of raw materials for production.

6. Markets

A firm wants to be less dependent on the small home market. Growth can be achieved by merging with or acquiring a firm which has established itself on the foreign market.

7. Profits

Increased sales and profits can be achieved by expanding.

8. Growth in the Agri-Industry

In order to survive and compete in the large European market, many co-ops became public limited companies (PLCs) in the early 1990s. Examples include Kerry Group PLC, Waterford Foods PLC, Avonmore Foods PLC and Golden Vale PLC. Co-ops expanded when they became PLCs for the following reasons:

(a) Huge amounts of additional long-term finance was raised from share issues to the public. Such finance was necessary to pay off debts and allow for expansion.

> **Seven reasons why firms want to be bigger:**
> - Economies of scale
> - Synergy
> - Security
> - Diversification
> - Supply
> - Increased profits
> - Less dependent on one market

(b) As PLCs, co-ops could compete more effectively in the highly competitive Euro agri-markets.

(c) The co-ops could afford to attract top management to run the business if they were PLCs.

(d) Farmers could buy shares in the co-op PLCs and so would have a greater commitment to the company.

Sources of Finance for Expansion

The following sources of finance may be used to finance expansion:

1.	Issue new shares, i.e. ordinary share capital (equity share capital). This is only possible for a private or public company.
2.	Ploughing back profits, i.e. retained earnings.
3.	A bank term loan.
4.	Investment from venture capital companies.
5.	State grants, e.g. from Enterprise Ireland, the aim of which are to give financial support to Irish firms in all sectors.
6.	Hire purchase and leasing can be used to finance capital expenditurerequirements, e.g. machinery.

1. Ordinary Share Capital (Equity Capital)

Features of ordinary share capital:

(a) Those who purchase ordinary shares are the initial risk-takers in the company – there are no guaranteed dividends.

(b) Ordinary shares are the equity share capital (owners' share capital). The holders of these shares are entitled to the equity or balance of profits on the winding up of the company.

(c) The shareholders appoint the directors and the company auditors.

Funding Expansion by Ordinary Share Capital
Benefits

(a) It provides the company with a cheap source of long-term finance. No repayments have to be made to the shareholders unless the company is being dissolved.

(b) There is no interest repayment on the share capital. Compare this situation with a bank term loan, where both interest and the loan must be repaid.

(c) The company does not have to provide security to raise the finance. Compare this situation with a bank term loan where the bank may require security (e.g. deeds of business premises) before granting the loan.

Drawbacks

(a) If profits are low in a PLC, many shareholders may decide to sell their shares. This will bring down the share price so the company may become a target for a cheap takeover bid.

(b) There are legal formalities and high costs involved in selling shares to the public.

(c) In order to be listed on the stock exchange, a company has to meet very costly and demanding requirements.

2. Ploughing Back Profits – Retained Earnings

Funding Expansion by Ploughing back Profits

Benefits

(a) It is a free source of long-term finance, i.e. no repayments of interest or money.

(b) It does not create any external debt.

(c) No security has to be provided.

(d) No control of the firm is lost.

Drawbacks

(a) The profits must first be earned before this source of finance can be used. This restricts management from planning very far in advance.

(b) Shareholders in a PLC who disagree with the decision to use this source of finance may sell their shares. This may adversely affect the share price on the stock exchange.

3. Long-Term Loan (Debt Capital)

A long-term loan is granted for a stated reason. Repayment of the loan is by agreed stated amounts, during a period of time up to seven years. To obtain this type of loan, the borrower must be able to show an ability to meet the repayment provisions, as outlined in the loan agreement.

Funding Expansion by Borrowing

Benefits

(a) It is a quick and easy form of finance to source, i.e. from the bank.

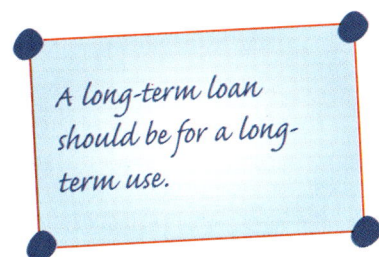

A long-term loan should be for a long-term use.

(b) Repayments of interest and the loan are structured to suit the borrower.

(c) Interest on the loan is a tax allowable expense, thus reducing the amount of tax the company has to pay.

(d) Since it is a long-term source of finance, there is no pressure on the business for immediate repayment of the loan.

Drawbacks

(a) Both the interest and the amount borrowed must be repaid. Problems may arise if the business starts to decline and repayments cannot be made as per agreement.

(b) Using a loan as a source of finance may cause the capital structure of the company to become highly geared. A highly-geared PLC is generally not in the interests of the ordinary shareholders as it may have difficulty raising additional finance from a share issue.

(c) The existence of debt capital may affect the credit rating of a company with some suppliers.

The Implications of Expansion on a Business

When a business is small, the owner can do most of the work. When the enterprise expands, it is essential to expand the managerial team and delegate many tasks. The implications of expanding the business include the following:

1. Management Structure

A proper management structure has to be put in place, e.g. managers have to be appointed to different departments: marketing, finance, distribution etc.

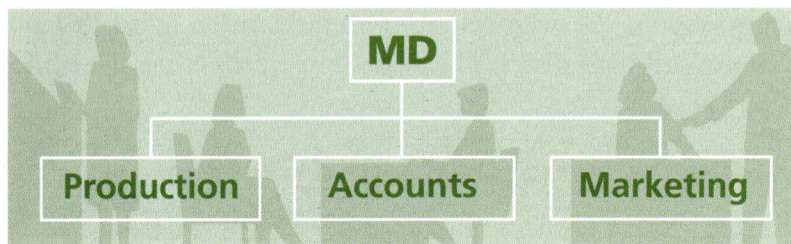

2. Funding

Additional finance is required to fund different requirements, e.g. capital expenditure projects: machinery, computers, research and development of new products etc. If this finance is obtained by share issues, it stops the company's capital structure becoming highly geared.

3. Financial Structure and Control

The firm must ensure that financial budgets are monitored in order to avoid a cash flow problem and an overtrading situation. Cash flow forecasts must be prepared and monitored.

4. Human Resources

With a large increase in the number of employees, it is important to appoint a human resource manager. This is necessary if industrial relations problems are to be avoided. Employees are an important resource of an expanding business. Their contribution must be recognised in order to keep them motivated.

5. Research and Development (R&D)

Ongoing planning and research and development are necessary for the firm to sustain its success. The product mix must be widened to meet the requirements of a larger number of potential customers.

6. Planning

Ongoing strategic planning (long-term planning) is necessary. It is important to be up to date with competitors. A SWOT analysis should be undertaken once a year. Expansion should be embraced within the planning process.

7. Profits and Dividends

There will be a large increase in profits, so it is possible to pay a satisfactory dividend to the shareholders. It is sensible to have a policy of building up a reserve fund to finance additional growth and to avail of future opportunities without borrowing.

Methods of Expansion/Growth for an Enterprise

The following methods can be considered:

1.	Growth (organic growth)
2.	Purchasing an existing business
3.	Management buy-out (MBO) and management buy-in (MBI)
4.	Diversification
5.	Developing a new business
6.	Business acquisition/takeover
7.	Strategic alliances and joint ventures
8.	Licensing

1. Growth (Organic Growth)

This form of expansion involves increasing the size of the existing business. This can be achieved in the following ways:

(a) widening the product range

(b) selling into new target markets, e.g. export markets

(c) employing more sales people

(d) re-investing profits

The above changes should lead to increased sales and profits for the expanding business.

> ➡ **Organic Growth**
>
> *This form of internal growth is usually financed by retained earnings.*

2. Purchasing an Existing Business

This is a fast way to become involved in business, i.e. buying an existing business. This involves acquiring an existing market share plus staff, machinery and maybe a brand name.

The following factors should be considered before purchasing a business:

(a) Exactly what is being purchased? Are the premises freehold or leasehold?

(b) How much will it cost? Is the price high or low? How will the deal be financed?

(c) What is the location of the business and the population size and trend in that area, i.e. what are the future growth prospects?

(d) Is the business being purchased as a going concern? Is it in decline or has it got growth potential?

(e) Are there any liabilities being purchased, e.g. creditors or unpaid taxes?

(f) How will the staff react to a new owner? Will there be union problems?

(g) How much would it cost to start up a new business? This option is called the Greenfield approach.

3. Management Buy-out (MBO) and Management Buy-in (MBI)

An MBO arises when a trading firm is sold by its owners to its directors, managers, employees or a combination of the three parties. The firm is sold as a going concern.

Reasons for an MBO

(a) A parent company may decide to sell off a subsidiary as a going concern to its management.

(b) Due to financial problems, the parent company may require cash. One way to raise the finance is to sell off a subsidiary company to its management. It is often done to reduce the balance sheet debt of a group.

(c) The owners of a business may be close to retirement and there may be no family successors.

(d) The owners may be unhappy with the level of profits and so may decide to sell the business. Selling to the existing management may be the quickest and easiest way of selling the business.

If the deal is financed by heavy borrowing, it is referred to as a **leveraged buy-out**.

An MBI arises where managers with financial resources and business experience, who are unhappy in their current positions but have the ambition and resolve to run a business, identify a suitable target and buy their way into it. The MBO is not an option because the owners of the business where they work will not sell.

4. Diversification

Growth by diversification involves merging or acquiring another business involved in a similar or different product.

The reasons for diversification include the following:

(a) To spread the risk by not having to rely on one business or product range.

(b) To produce and distribute additional products which are more profitable than the existing range.

(c) To make the maximum use of all a firm's resources, e.g. machinery and premises.

Diversification may be horizontal or vertical:

- Horizontal diversification is where two firms producing similar products merge, e.g. a merger of two computer manufacturers.

- Vertical diversification is where two firms involved in different types of business merge, e.g. a hotel merging with a supermarket.

5. Developing a New Business

Growth can be achieved by establishing a new business which has a 'link-up' to the existing business. The new venture would be a separate legal entity but would be a commercial benefit to the first business, e.g. a publishing company sets up its own printing company. It is obviously going to be cheaper for the publisher to have its publications printed by its own printer than giving the contract to an outside printer, who will only do the job at a commercial profit.

6. Business Acquisition/Takeover

In the short term, this is the costliest form of growth. A takeover arises when one company purchases the majority or all of the voting shares of another company. This can be 'friendly', i.e. when the current board of directors agree, In March 2005, the Cavan based building materials group Kingspan acquired the Monaghan based Century Homes – a major house manufacturer – for €98m. This deal will enable Kingspan to increase the scale and breadth of its product range to the construction industry.

7. Strategic Alliances and Joint Ventures

An alliance is an agreement between different firms to actively promote business interests which are of benefit to both sides.
Examples include:

- distribution alliances – very common with exporters
- joint ventures and marketing alliances

Firms involved in strategic alliances want to succeed in the global market. They could not succeed on their own due to the massive financial costs involved. Each firm in the alliance retains its own separate legal entity, but agrees to the deal because both parties benefit from it. For example, RTÉ and BBC formed an alliance to co-produce certain documentaries for global TV markets.

Benefits of Forming Alliances

(a) It is a voluntary agreement, so the legal formalities are kept to a minimum.

(b) Each party remains a separate legal entity.

(c) Both parties benefit from the alliance – skills are shared, e.g. technology transfer.

(d) The alliance can be terminated, so it is more suitable and cheaper than a merger.

(e) It increases the range of services offered, thus giving each party a competitive advantage.

(f) It enables the parties to share technology and have access to wider markets.

(g) It is easier to succeed in global markets.

Problems of Alliances

(a) One partner may dominate another.

(b) Trade secrets have to be shared.

(c) One partner may be interested in a short-term gain, e.g. one of eircom's partners sold at a big profit shortly after the share issue.

Joint Ventures

A joint venture is a form of partnership set up to carry out some specified commercial operations. It is important in global business, where one firm with local knowledge can obtain financial backing from a foreign firm. They agree to a joint venture with profits being shared as per agreement. It is often used by firms wishing to develop into foreign markets.

8. Licensing

Licensing is where the owner of a patent allows a firm to use this patent for a fee called patent royalties. In a way it is similar to franchising.

Exporting

Because of the limited size of the home market, some firms see exports as the way to achieve growth in sales and profits. This is a form of organic growth.

Reasons for Developing an Export Market

1. Sales and profit which would not be possible on the home market can be achieved through exporting.

2. A firm becomes less dependent on the home market, i.e. the business risk is spread.

3. A manufacturer should be able to benefit from economies of scale due to the production and sale of larger quantities. This enables the firm to become more competitive on both the domestic and foreign markets.

> **Benefits from Exporting:**
> - Increased sales
> - Increased profits
> - Less dependent
> - Economies of scale

4. If a firm has an exportable product (e.g. CDs), there may be no reason to restrict its sales to the home market.

Direct and Indirect Exporting

A manufacturer should not assume that selling and distribution methods used on the home market will be suitable in the foreign market.

Direct Exporting

Direct exporting involves the following:

1. Selling through a distributor that is established in the foreign market and sells similar products. The distributor will have storage and distribution facilities. The distributor buys from the exporter and resells the goods at a profit. This is an ideal method of exporting for the Irish manufacturer, who then doesn't have to worry about an export sales team, warehousing or distribution.

2. Selling through an export agent who promotes the products and passes the orders back to the exporter. The exporter has to process the order, arrange delivery to the foreign customer and obtain the payment. The agent receives a commission on sales from the exporter.

3. Selling directly to export customers. Orders can be received as a result of advertising in catalogues or promotion at trade fairs and exhibitions.

4. Selling through a wholly-owned foreign company. For example, Folens Publishers in Ireland sell school books in England through a wholly-owned UK company called Folens UK Ltd.

Indirect Exporting

Indirect exporting involves selling to a foreign based trading company, who purchases the products from the Irish exporter and sells them on to their customers, e.g. Irish Media Books in Chicago purchases books from Irish publishers and sells them to a select range of bookshops in America.

The Role of the State in helping Firms expand Abroad

Enterprise Ireland assists firms involved in developing an export market. It focuses on the export marketplace. It provides information for firms, which can help them to identify export market opportunities and improve their competitive edge. It undertakes export market research and feasibility studies on behalf of Irish firms.

The Role of the State in controlling Expansion

One of the reasons for the Competition Act 1991 was to prevent large firms from abusing a monopoly position. If, as a result of a proposed merger or takeover, a firm has more than 50 per cent of the market, this proposal must be referred to the Competition Authority appointed under the Act. The Competition Authority has the authority to prevent a merger or takeover from proceeding.

Revision of Important Terms	
• Expansion	• Equity Capital
• Diversification	• Retained Earnings
• Economies of Scale	• Debt Capital
• Synergy	• Organic Growth
• Agri-Industry	• MBO and MBI

Exercises

1. (a) Show by means of a diagram the life cycle of a business.

   (b) Why do some firms expand and become more successful?

2. (a) What challenges do management face when expanding their business?

   (b) Why do established businesses want to expand?

3. (a) State four sources of finance that may be used to finance growth.

   (b) Outline the benefits and drawbacks of two of the sources of finance you mention.

4. 'Unless expansion is planned it is unlikely to succeed.' Discuss the implications of expansion for a business.

5. (a) State five different methods of expansion that a firm may choose.

   (b) Discuss the benefits of any two of the methods you mention.

6. Explain each of the following terms:

   (a) Economies of Scale

   (b) Diversification

   (c) Alliance

   (d) Synergy

   (e) Competition Authority

7. (a) 'Exporting is an obvious form of expansion.' Do you agree?

      Give four reasons for your answer.

   (b) Distinguish between direct and indirect exporting.

Applied Business Questions
for Units 3, 4, 5
Leaving Certificate 2006 and 2011

Applied Business Question
Based on units 3, 4 and 5 for Leaving Certificate 2006/2011

AORA LTD (LC 2001)

Aileen O'Rourke established her ladies' fashion business and label, 'AORA' almost three years ago. Aileen had studied design at college and had graduated with distinction, coming among the top 10 per cent in her class. Because of her desire and drive to succeed in anything she undertakes, the business has developed well. She had the flair and creativity necessary for the enterprise to thrive. Over the past few years, however, competition from European designers and manufacturers has been growing. She is beginning to notice delays and shortages that were not a feature of the business in the past. A family friend, who is experienced in business management, has indicated to her that the controls in her business are not as tight as he would have expected and that changes in these areas are essential.

Aileen has a democratic management style. This has worked well up to now, but she is having doubts about whether the changes needed in the business can be achieved with such a management style. While her advisor has indicated that changes are needed quickly to raise standards and retain customers, he has not pointed out to her how she might go about achieving these changes.
The business also needs an injection of capital. It needs to expand and acquire the technology to produce the high quality products for the niche market that the 'AORA' label is aiming at. From her meeting with her advisor, Aileen knows that a credible business plan to guide the future of the business and for presentation to the financial institutions is an immediate requirement.

(A) Illustrate two areas of control that you would recommend be put in
place immediately in the business. Outline one reason in each case
and refer to the above text in your response.   (30 marks)

(B) Discuss strategies that Aileen could use to successfully manage the change
process in the business. Explain your answer fully.   (30 marks)

(C) Using appropriate business headings to guide your thinking, describe how you
see the future of the enterprise. Make relevant assumptions that you feel may
be necessary given the above details.   (20 marks)

(**Total = 80 marks**)

Applied Business Question
Based on units 3, 4 and 5 for Leaving Certificate 2006/2011

COMPUTER SERVICES LTD

Dermot Jones graduated with a Masters Degree in technology. He wanted to be his own boss. In 1997, with financial assistance from his parents, he set up his own company Computer Services Ltd, specialising in advice and back-up service for industrial computer users. Within two years, his business expanded and he employed four 'high tech' graduates to service his expanding list of customers. He believed in a policy of empowerment, so that his staff could give an immediate and better service to the customers. This policy ensures more effective decision making, which is what customers require. It is also good for staff morale as workers are committed, costs are controlled and so profits should increase.

By modern criteria, Dermot Jones would be regarded as a good leader. He is decisive, has plenty of initiative and is a good communicator. He consults with his staff at monthly meetings. He introduced a management system of job titles, performance appraisal and promotion because he said that he disagreed with McGregor's Theory X, which claims that employees just do the job, take the wages and accept no responsibility, that they are basically lazy and lack ambition.

By July 2000 sales were €2.5m, with profits of €500,000. Business was booming and life was comfortable but Dermot Jones was anxious to expand his business into the huge Euro market. Having researched the market, he decided to 'go for it'. He had an excellent relationship with his bank and was confident of raising the necessary finance, i.e. €1 million. He approached his bank manager with a request for a 6-year term loan of €1 million. The bank manager requested a copy of his Business Plan before deciding on the request.

(A) Explain what is meant by empowerment. With reference to the above passage, outline the benefits of empowerment of employees to
Computer Services Ltd.   (20 marks)

(B) With reference to the above passage, state the management skills required by business and shown by Dermot Jones. Indicate the non-financial methods which he introduced to motivate his staff. How does McGregor's Theory Y differ from his Theory X as outlined in the above passage?   (20 marks)

(C) With reference (where relevant) to the above passage, you are required to prepare a business plan which Dermot Jones could submit to his bank manager. You can make appropriate assumptions.   (40 marks)

(Total = 80 marks)

Applied Business Question

Based on units 3, 4 and 5 for Leaving Certificate 2006/2011

MAGAZINES LTD

Caroline Dempsey graduated in 1993 with a Marketing Degree. She spent four years working for a publishing firm in London. In 1997 she returned to Ireland to set up her own publishing firm, Magazines Ltd. This firm published monthly magazines in the areas of fashion and finance. By June 1999, due to her leadership and motivational skills, her firm employed 15 people and had a yearly turnover of €500k, with a net profit of €50k. Having attended a conference on Global Marketing, Caroline decided to research a new monthly magazine that could attract an international audience. She was confident that substantial advertising revenue could be generated, as she would be selling the magazine on the World Wide Web, thus reaching a worldwide market. Selling online would be a very cost-effective way to market her magazine worldwide. Customers ordering online would have to pay in advance, so no bad debts or credit control problems would arise.

The new monthly magazine, entitled *World Business Dot.Com* was first published in November 1999, but by June 2000 its sales were already showing a steady decline, plunging from an early high of €100k to just €30k. Not only was it losing money, but management was distracted from its core business, so the sales of the other magazines also declined. By July 2000 the firm was now <u>overtrading</u> and had a <u>liquidity problem</u>. The Acid Test Ratio was 1:2 and creditors (mainly printers) were objecting to the ongoing late payments, i.e. the firm was leaning on the trade and bad debts were being incurred. Competitors' 'global magazines' were deemed to be of superior quality and more up to date on 'high tech' developments in modern business. Caroline employed a business consultant, Peter Dillon, to analyse all aspects of the business. His report to the board of directors revealed the following:

1. The business was unclear on its marketing concept and marketing strategy.
2. The business had an inadequate marketing plan.

(A) With reference to the passage, evaluate how Magazines Ltd would benefit from online marketing. (20 marks)

(B) (i) What evidence is there to show that Caroline has used her management skills in managing the business?

   (ii) Explain the underlined words and outline reasons why the Acid Test Ratio is unsatisfactory. Use the information in the passage where relevant. (30 marks)

(C) (i) Explain what is meant by the marketing concept and marketing strategy. Refer to the above passage where relevant.

   (ii) What evidence exists to show that the firm's marketing concept has failed?

   (iii) Outline the benefits of a marketing plan and indicate which element of the marketing mix must change. (30 marks)

(Total = 80 marks)

281

Categories of Industry

Objectives

The following topics from **Unit 6** of the syllabus are covered in this chapter:

- What is Industry?
- Primary Industries
- Secondary Industries
- Tertiary Industries, service industries
- Changing Trends in Business

What is Industry?

For goods to be available for sale there has to be a highly organised and developed economy. This economy is made up of different industries.

> Industry is made up of the different firms which produce all the output of a product or service.
>
> **EXAMPLE:** The Construction Industry is made up of all producers of products required and used in the building trade, e.g. builders, builders providers, etc.

There are three categories of industry:

1.	Primary Industries (also called Extractive Industries)
2.	Secondary Industries (also called the Construction/Manufacturing Industries)
3.	Tertiary Industries (also called Service Industries)

1. Primary Industries (also called Extractive Industries)

Primary industries are based on supplying or obtaining the country's natural resources and include:

(a)	agriculture	(c)	fishing
(b)	forestry	(d)	mining

Primary or extractive industries 'extract' wealth from the land or sea. Some of the goods produced by these industries are the essential raw materials required by manufacturing industries, e.g. sand and gravel, coal etc. Natural gas fields exist around the Irish coast and a nationwide gas pipeline network has been developed. This source of home-produced energy is good for industry, home users and the economy.

A. Agriculture and Agri-Business

The term agri-business is used to describe agriculture plus the other industries which use agricultural output as a source of raw materials. Agriculture is an important industry for many reasons.

For example:

- It provides essential raw materials for industry, e.g. milk, poultry.

- In 2004, 11 per cent of the total workforce were employed in agriculture.

- It makes an important contribution to both the balance of trade and balance of payments.

Agriculture is the most important of the primary industries. Agri-business is a dominant industry and is a major exporter and job provider.

Why has Agriculture declined?

Since 1970, the number of people employed in agriculture in Ireland has declined for many reasons. For example:

(i) Free trade forced many farmers to cease trading because they could not compete.

(ii) The industry became mechanised, so fewer employees were required.

(iii) Farm workers were attracted to higher paid jobs and better working conditions in other industries located in cities and towns.

(iv) Euro-Agri-Pensions were available to older farmers, who retired and passed on their farms to their families.

The manufacture of agricultural raw materials.

(v) The Agri-Industry is subject to the CAP policy of the EU. This policy demanded:

- increased productivity

- free trade between member countries

- reasonable prices for consumers

- minimum prices for farmers

> **→ AGRI-BUSINESS**
>
> *This term is used to describe the business of agriculture plus related industries.*

(vi) Due to overproduction leading to surplus stocks, the EU in 2005 introduced a new system for paying farmers. Farmers will now be paid a single form payment which is based on their average output in 2000, 2001 and 2002, no matter how much each farmer produced in a year. This policy, which 'decoupled' payment from production, will lead to a reduced payment to those farmers whose previous surplus stock was bought by the EU. The price paid for that surplus stock was called the Intervention Price. This no longer exists.

B. Forestry

The State agency Coillte was established in 1989 with the objective of ensuring that the State had a proper commercial attitude to forestry. The forestry industry in Ireland is now run almost exclusively by Coillte, but some private firms also grow timber to avail of attractive grants and tax incentives offered by the State.

In 2004 Ireland imported €1.6m worth of timber. Ireland is a net importer of wood.

C. Fishing

The fishing industry is small when compared with the manufacturing industry. In 2004, this industry provided employment for about 1,500 people (down from 3,200 in 1980).

Some leading Irish ports for the loading of fish include:

- Killybegs

- Howth

- Dingle

- Castletownbere

The fishing industry is subject to the Common Fisheries Policy (CFP) of the EU. Competition from foreign trawlers, e.g. Russian factory ships, makes it very difficult for the Irish to compete. Irish fishing trawlers need to be modernised or more jobs will be lost and imports will increase. Under the CFP, there is an agreement to prevent overfishing in Irish waters, which is designed to guarantee a livelihood for those working in the domestic fishing industry.

Fishermen mending nets in Dingle, Co. Kerry.

2. Secondary Industries

This sector is made up of the construction and manufacturing industries. The construction industry is involved in the construction of roads, schools and hospitals – all part of the infrastructure of the State, i.e. for everyone's benefit. The industry is also concerned with house-building and factory-building. The raw materials for this industry are obtained from the extractive industry.

The Construction Industry

The construction industry is important for the following reasons:

    (a) In March 2005, 110,000 people were employed in this industry.

    (b) Some of the large firms have in excess of 1,500 employees.

    (c) Output in 2004 was in excess of €7bn.

    (d) It is a good barometer of the state of the economy.

Manufacturing Industries

Manufacturing industries are involved in changing raw materials into finished products required by consumers, e.g. textiles, footwear, food-processing and books.

  In March 2005, 14 per cent of the workforce were employed in manufacturing firms nationwide. Such firms are involved in food-processing, pharmaceuticals, electronics etc. There is now a greater emphasis on high-tech industries, rather than labour intensive ones.

The Importance of the Secondary Industries

The combination of the construction and manufacturing industries is important for the Irish economy. Secondary industries benefit the economy in many ways, for example:

Robots welding on a production line in a car factory.

    (a) A few hundred thousand people are directly employed in these industries.

    (b) The construction industry has played an important role in modernising the country's infrastructure – roads, office blocks, apartments, hospitals.

    (c) The manufacturing industry has successfully modernised its manufacturing processes in order to be competitive in both the home and foreign markets. The ongoing surplus in the balance of trade in Ireland – where visible exports exceed visible imports – is proof that consumers are buying the products being produced.

    (d) The manufacturing industry has enabled import substitution to take place. This has led to a reduction in visible imports. In turn, this helps the balance of trade and job creation.

(e) Through direct tax (PAYE) and indirect tax (VAT), revenue is generated for the Exchequer.

3. Tertiary Industries, i.e. Service Industries

There are many people whose occupations are not classified as extractive, constructive or manufacturing. They do not produce goods, but play an important role in the commercial life of a country. Service industries and the service sector employ most people in the economy.

Examples of service industries include:

(a)	Financial services	→	banks, building societies
(b)	Professional services	→	accountants, solicitors, auctioneers
(c)	Medical services	→	hospitals, doctors, dentists, nurses
(d)	Stock-holding services	→	wholesalers, retailers
(e)	Transport services	→	trains, buses, air transport
(f)	Communication services	→	phone, fax, e-mail
(g)	Catering services	→	hotels, cafés
(h)	Government services	→	education, justice, training

The service sector has the fastest growing industries in Ireland. In March 2000, 85 per cent of small firms in Ireland were in the service area. Only 15 per cent were involved in manufacturing/construction. In March 2005, almost 64 per cent of all employees in Ireland were employed in services.

The International Financial Services Centre (IFSC) in Dublin has boosted the financial services sector in Ireland.

Intel Ireland opened its plant in Leixlip creating thousands of jobs for the area.

Reasons for the Growth in Tertiary Industries

(a) Increased prosperity in the economy.

(b) Higher wages have greatly improved living standards. Consumers have more disposable income to spend on services, e.g. travel and entertainment.

(c) The boom in the Irish economy since the mid-1990s has greatly reduced the level of real unemployment. Many foreign multinationals have located in Ireland and have created jobs.

(d) The growth in the economy has resulted in an increased demand for teachers, doctors, nurses etc.

(e) More entrepreneurs are prepared to take the risk of starting up new businesses.

(f) The Government, through a State agency, Enterprise Ireland (formerly Forbairt), has promoted the development of internationally traded services; this has made a big contribution to enterprise and growth. Enterprise Ireland set out goals to develop the following areas:

   (i) Technological services

   (ii) Science and innovation services

   (iii) Investment policy

   (iv) Consultancy services

ENTERPRISE IRELAND

(g) Social and demographic changes have also had an effect on the growth of service industries. Such changes include the following:

(i) A drop in the size of the population. By 2006, there will be 25 per cent fewer children in Ireland than in 1996.

(ii) A large increase in the number of people involved in education, e.g. part-time courses, evening courses, degrees etc.

(iii) An increase in the number of women in full- and part-time employment.

(iv) A longer life expectancy due to improved medical facilities and living standards.

(v) An increase in the number of people taking early retirement.

(h) People have more time for leisure and entertainment. The market for TVs, radios, CDs and home computers has boomed.

(i) Research has shown that people have become more health conscious and are reducing their spending on cigarettes, tobacco and 'non-green' products. They are spending more on education and leisure activities.

> Social and demographic changes have implications for business:
> * Population down
>   ↓
> * Sales down
>   ↓
> * Impact on Profits?

Benefit to the Economy from the Tertiary Industries

The tertiary industries make a bigger contribution to the economy than either the primary or secondary industries for the following reasons:

(a) Almost 64 per cent of the labour force are employed in this sector.

(b) Almost 85 per cent of small indigenous businesses are involved in the service industry. Many of the owners of those firms are self-employed.

(c) These industries contribute large amounts of tax to the Exchequer, i.e. PAYE, PRSI, VAT, corporation tax etc.

(d) Tourism is an important service industry which employs a large number of people and makes a big contribution to the balance of payments.

(e) Tertiary industries include telecommunications, e.g. e-mail, Internet and software development, which play a significant role in developing the 'high-tech' modern economy. This is very important when attracting foreign industry to establish businesses in Ireland.

Changing Trends in Business

Each industry makes an important contribution to the growth and development of the economy. Since 1980, there has been a decline in both agriculture and manufacturing industries. Higher wages attracted many workers to the tertiary industries where jobs are seen as more secure because of the involvement of multinationals.

> *Each industry is important but the tertiary industry makes the best contribution.*

Exercises

1. Industry is made up of firms that produce goods or supply services.

   (a) What categories of industry exist in the Irish economy?

   (b) Discuss the importance of any one of them.

2. (a) 'Agri-business is so important for Ireland's economy.'

   Do you agree with the above statement? Give four reasons for your answer.

   (b) Explain what is meant by agri-business.

3. Discuss the importance of each of the following to enterprise in Ireland:

   (a) Forestry   (c) Construction

   (b) Fishing   (d) Manufacturing

4. Using appropriate examples, explain reasons for the expansion in Ireland of service industries.

Business Organisations

Business Organisations

Since 1985, almost one in every four new businesses in Ireland has failed. This means that almost 75 per cent of new ventures have succeeded. Many people prefer to own their own business. The sole trader and the private limited company are the most common forms of business unit. Very few partnership businesses are set up, but a small number of local co-op ventures are established. Traditionally in Ireland, the majority of businesses operated as sole traders. Problems due to unlimited liability, whereby the owners could be held personally liable for the debts of the business, caused many sole traders to change the legal status of the business to a private limited company.

Which Type of Business Unit should be set up?

Entrepreneurs have a choice of setting up as a sole trader, a partnership or a private limited company.

The following factors will determine the type and size of business unit to establish:

1. The amount and availability of capital required.

2. The degree of personal interest the entrepreneur has in controlling all aspects of the business. A person who wants to be the sole owner, make all the decisions and keep all the profits will likely opt for a sole trader business.

3. The amount of investment risk involved. If the risk is great, then the investors may insist on having limited liability – hence, a private limited company should be formed.

Sole Trader

The sole trader is a very common form of business unit. The title 'sole trader' clearly means that there is only one owner, i.e. a self-employed person. This type of business is easy to form and this gives it an advantage over other forms of business, e.g. a company. If a sole trader (e.g. Joan Jones), trades under her own name, she may commence business immediately. If she decides to trade under any other name, e.g. JJ Computer Services, then

she must register the trading name under the Registration of Business Names Act 1963. Examples of sole traders include the following:

1. Retailers in villages and towns selling to the general public, e.g. grocers or butchers or those offering services, e.g. hairdressers.

2. Personal services offered by painters, plumbers, mechanics etc.

Benefits of being a Sole Trader

1. The sole trader business is easy to form as there are few legal formalities involved. The legal issues only relate to registering for VAT and registering the business name if relevant.

2. The sole trader is the boss, supervises the operations, can make speedy decisions and keeps all the profit.

3. The sole trader is able to keep in touch with all the customers and employees.

4. Business affairs are kept confidential because the accounts of the business do not have to be published.

Disadvantages of being a Sole Trader

1. A sole trader has unlimited liability, i.e. if the business gets into financial difficulties, the sole trader is personally liable for all its debts, even to the extent of losing private property. For this reason it is unwise for a person to operate a business as a sole trader.

2. The sole trader may not have all the necessary managerial skills to properly run the business. He/she may be overworked in trying to do too many jobs, e.g. purchasing stock, checking the stock, selling the goods, keeping proper VAT records, paying suppliers, lodging money etc.

3. The sole trader has to have the capital to start the business. The capital available may be insufficient to enable the business to expand and reach its potential.

4. The sole trader has to make all the decisions – a bad decision may be very costly for the business.

5. There may be no continuity of existence as there may be no-one to take over if he/she dies.

6. From a taxation viewpoint, the sole trader is at a big disadvantage – being self-employed, the sole trader has to pay income tax on profits at a higher rate than corporation tax.

Partnership

→ Definition of Partnership

This is where at least two and not more than twenty people carry on a business with a view to making a profit. The business is jointly owned by all the partners.

Deed of Partnership

B & B Designs

Capital Investment
€50,000 each

Profit Share: 50/50
Salaries: €30k each

A business partnership may exist because one party has the managerial skill and technique to run the business and the other has the capital to finance it. Since there is more than one person involved, it is important that partners have a written agreement so as to avoid conflict in the future. The written agreement is called the Deed of Partnership. The following are some of the clauses that should be included in the Deed of Partnership:

1. How much capital each partner is to invest in the business.

2. How the profits are to be shared between the partners.

3. Salaries to be paid to each partner.

Benefits of Partnership

1. A number of people can contribute more money to the business than in a sole trader situation.

2. Different partners have various talents and expertise, which can all be used to make the business efficient and successful.

3. There may be up to 20 partners in the business, who can consult with each other at special meetings if any major problems arise. Better decisions should be made from this form of consultation.

4. Any losses suffered by the partnership are shared between all the partners – no one partner has to carry the loss.

5. The accounts of a partnership do not have to be published.

Disadvantages of Partnership

1. A partnership has unlimited liability, i.e. if a partnership business gets into financial difficulties, the partners are all personally liable for the debts of the business.

2. Profits must be shared between all the partners, as per the agreement in the Deed of Partnership.

3. The partners may disagree with each other to the extent of diminishing the efficiency of the business.

The main examples of partnership are solicitors, accountants and architects.

Because of the negative implications regarding unlimited liability, it is not advisable to operate a business unit as a partnership. It is not a popular form of business unit today.

Company

> **→ Definition of a Company**

A company is a separate legal entity formed under the Companies Acts 1963–1999 for the purpose of carrying out business activity. It is owned by shareholders, who contribute money to a common fund called share capital. Profits are distributed to shareholders in the form of dividends.

The company is run by a board of directors appointed by the shareholders, who all have limited liability. This means that they are not personally liable for the debts of the company. They can only lose the amount of money they invested in the company. Since every company is a separate legal entity, this means it can sue and be sued in law. There are different types of companies, i.e. private companies and public companies.

Limited Liability

Limited liability was introduced to promote trade. It encourages people to invest in companies as shareholders in the knowledge that, if the business went bankrupt, their only loss would be the amount invested. They have no personal liability for any business debts. There are, however, some circumstances under which a company director can lose the protection of limited liability. For example:

1. If a director is willingly involved in carrying on business with the intention of defrauding creditors. Such a director is known as a reckless director.

2. If a director is aware that the company is acting *ultra vires* (outside its authority).

Private Limited Company

Features of a Private Limited Company (Under the Companies Acts 1963–1999)

1. The company must have a share capital and all shareholders have limited liability.

2. There must be a minimum of one and a maximum of 50 shareholders.

3. The last word of the name of the company must be 'limited' (or Teoranta), e.g. Financial Services Ltd.

> The process of forming a company is called Incorporation.

4. Shares cannot be issued to the general public or sold on the stock exchange.

5. Business cannot legally commence until the company receives a Certificate of Incorporation from the Companies Registration Office.

6. Under a 1980 EU directive, private companies of a certain size must publish their accounts. Small- and medium-sized companies only have to publish a limited amount of information from their accounts. Large companies have to publish their audited accounts in full.

The majority of companies in Ireland are private (174,000 in 2004). The reasons for this include the following:

1. There are a large number of 'family business' firms nationwide operating with limited liability – this type of business is not suited to becoming a public company.

2. Many private companies are very profitable and do not require additional finance from shareholders, i.e. no need to go public.

3. Many private companies would not meet the criteria required to become a public limited company so they must remain private.

4. There is a greater chance for the owners to retain control of the business.

> The Memorandum of Association and Articles of Association are called the Constitution of the Company.

Formation of a Private Limited Company

1. Legally required documents must be prepared and submitted to the Registrar of Companies.

   (a) The Memorandum of Association – this sets out the relationship that exists between the company and the general public.

   (b) The Articles of Association – this sets out the internal rules for running the company.

2. **Form A1** must be completed by providing the following information:

   (a) A statement of the amount of the authorised and issued share capital.

> The authorised share capital is the maximum number of shares the company can legally issue. Stamp duty is payable on this amount.
>
> EXAMPLE: The Authorised Share Capital is 100,000 €1 Ordinary Shares. The Issued Share Capital is the actual number of shares issued by the company to the shareholders. The Issued Share Capital is 70,000 €1 Ordinary Shares.

    (b) The list of those who have agreed to become directors of the company.

    (c) The written consent of each director to become a director.

    (d) A signed declaration of compliance with the requirements of the Companies Act 1963–1999.

3. All the documents plus fees have to be submitted to the Registrar of Companies in Dublin.

4. If all the documents are in order, then the Registrar of Companies will issue a Certificate of Incorporation (this is the birth certificate of a private limited company).

5. The private limited company must hold a Statutory Meeting (first company meeting) for the following reasons:

    (a) To present the Memorandum of Association and Articles of Association to each shareholder.

    (b) To give the share certificates to each shareholder.

    (c) To formally appoint the directors of the company.

    (d) To appoint auditors.

    (e) To authorise opening a company bank account.

6. The Private Limited Company is now incorporated, which means:

    (a) It can start trading.

    (b) Its shareholders have limited liability.

    (c) It is a separate legal entity which can be sued in its own name.

Memorandum of Association

The Memorandum of Association sets out the relationship that exists between the company and the general public. This document clearly defines the powers of the company. It contains the following statutory clauses:

1. Every company must end its name with the letters Ltd (limited) for a private company and PLC (public limited company) for a public company.

2. The objects of the company must be specified. The objects would not only include the immediate aims of the company, but also related activities in

which the company might engage in the future. The company cannot legally carry out any activity not included in the Memorandum of Association. If it does, it is acting *ultra vires*, i.e. outside its authority. In such a situation, the directors will not have their protection of limited liability.

> A company is acting ultra vires if it carries out an act which is not covered by its objects, as stated in the Memorandum of Association.

3. A statement that the company is limited in liability must be included, i.e. that the shareholders are limited in their total liability for company debts.

4. It must state the amount of the authorised share capital.

5. It must be signed by each subscriber who has agreed to form the company and they must confirm that they agree to take the number of shares specified opposite their names.

> Memorandum of
> Association
> of
>
> Waterford
> Financial
> Services Ltd

6. The location of the registered office of the company must be included. This is where all legal documents are to be sent.

To be valid, the Memorandum of Association must be printed, stamped, signed and witnessed.

Articles of Association

The articles of association set out the internal rules for the running of the company. It is not compulsory for a company to prepare its own articles of association because it can adopt the model articles of association (known as Table A), which are set out in the Companies Acts.

Contents of the Articles of Association

1. A statement of the authorised share capital of the company and its division into different classes of shares, i.e. ordinary shares and preference shares.

2. The voting rights attached to the different classes of shares.

3. The procedure for calling meetings of shareholders.

4. The procedure for electing or replacing directors. (There must always be at least two directors.)

5. The procedure for issuing and transferring shares.

6. The procedure for winding up the company.

Benefits of being a Private Company

1. Limited liability is very important when encouraging people to invest in the company.

2. Continuity of existence is assured because the company does not close down as a result of the death of a shareholder.

3. The company is a separate legal entity which can sue and be sued. Individual shareholders cannot be sued.

4. The directors are protected by limited liability as long as they always carry out their duties within the terms of the Memorandum of Association and the Companies Act. Directors acting with authority are acting *intra vires.*

> **Benefits of a Private Company:**
> • Limited Liability
> • Continuity
> • Separate legal entity
> • Issue shares to raise finance
> • Management Structure

5. As a general rule, a company has a better credit rating with the bank than a sole trader.

6. Finance can be raised by issuing shares to the shareholders.

7. The original shareholders are able to maintain control by owning and holding on to the majority of the issued shares.

8. There is a formal organised management structure. The shareholders elect a board of directors, who then appoint a managing director. The business is therefore properly run.

In April 2005, there were about 150,000 private limited companies in Ireland.

Disadvantages of being a Private Company

1. There are more legal formalities involved in forming a private company than a partnership or sole trader business.

2. The formalities are costlier than for a partnership or sole trader.

3. Profits must be shared between all the shareholders.

4. Activities are restricted to the objectives specified in the Memorandum of Association.

5. The accounts must be audited and presented to the shareholders at an AGM. Financial returns of some nature must also be made to the Registrar of Companies.

6. There is reduced access to capital as shares cannot be issued to the general public.

Public Limited Company (PLC)

Some profitable private limited companies decide to expand further as they are confident that they can become 'big players' in the marketplace. Additional finance is required and one way to raise this finance is to go public. This involves having the company's shares quoted on the Stock Exchange and becoming a public limited company (PLC).

A PLC is registered under the Companies Acts 1963–1999. The characteristics of a PLC include the following:

Examples of PLCs in Ireland:
- AIB PLC
- Kerry Group PLC
- Greencore PLC

1. It must have a minimum of seven shareholders (no maximum) before it can apply for registration.

2. Finance can be raised by an issue of shares to the general public (a public share issue).

3. The shares are quoted on the Stock Exchange and the company has no control over who buys or sells them.

4. A Trading Certificate must be received from the Registrar of Companies before business can commence.

5. Each year a copy of the audited accounts must be sent to the Registrar of Companies and published.

6. Under the terms of an EU Directive, every public company must end its name with the letters PLC (public limited company).

In April 2005, there were 78 PLCs with an Irish Stock Exchange quotation, compared to 113 in 2000.

Benefits (Advantages) of being a Public Limited Company (PLC)

1. There is the ability to raise large amounts of capital through share issues.

2. All shareholders have limited liability and this encourages investment through share issues.

3. Continuity of existence: when a shareholder dies, the shares of the deceased are sold.

4. The PLC form of business unit enables people who have no business knowledge to invest their money profitably.

5. Accounts must be published annually; this helps both existing and potential shareholders in their investment decisions.

6. Having the share price of the company listed (quoted) on the Stock Exchange is good for the image of the business.

7. The issued share capital cannot be withdrawn by any shareholder. This means that the finance raised from issuing shares remains as the permanent capital of the company.

Disadvantages of being a Public Limited Company (PLC)

These include the following:

1. The costs of forming a PLC are very high (e.g. minimum cost is €150,000).

2. The costs of running a PLC are very high because of Stock Exchange regulations.

3. Final accounts must be published. This can be bad for the business if profits are declining. It also provides valuable information to the competitors.

4. Profits are shared between all the shareholders.

5. Activities are restricted to the objectives specified in the Memorandum of Association.

6. The company's share price is quoted daily on the Stock Exchange. This makes it easy for a potential takeover bid, as it is easy to calculate the value of the company.

EXAMPLE:	Stock Exchange Price	€2
	No. of Issued Shares	450,000
	Takeover Bid Value	€900,000

➡ Enforcement

The main function of the Director of Corporate Enforcement is to encourage compliance with Company Law and to take appropriate action where suspected breaches of the Companies Acts take place.

Managing Director (MD)

The managing director is appointed by the board of directors to carry out the following functions:

1. To organise and run the business on a daily basis.

2. To make sure that company policy is implemented.

3. To inform and update the directors on matters relating to the performance of the business.

4. To appoint managers to the different departments and to motivate all employees so that the firm is efficiently run.

5. To keep up to date with developments that may affect the company, e.g. new competition.

The managing director submits regular reports to the board of directors on issues such as sales, profits, market information etc.

Business Alliance

A business alliance is a business agreement between two non-competing firms to promote business interests which will be profitable to both.

Franchising

There are two parties to every franchise agreement – the franchisor and the franchisee.

Franchisor: This is the person or business that sells a licence to replicate their system.

Franchisee: This is the person or business who buys a licence to replicate a business system.

> Be your own Boss
> ↓
> Be Wise – Franchise

➡ Definition of Franchising

Franchising is a method of marketing goods/services via a proven business formula, licensed by the franchisor to the franchisee to copy within an agreed geographical area.

> *Franchising is a popular, simple and effective partnership for growth.*

EXAMPLE:
John and Deirdre Doyle wish to open a new bookshop. They can call it Book Supply or arrange a Franchise Agreement with Easons. In this case, Easons become the franchisor and John and Deirdre Doyle become the franchisee.

Benefits of Franchising
Both the franchisor and franchisee benefit from franchising.

Benefits to the Franchisor
1. It enables them to expand their business into areas where they have no market share.

2. The amount of capital invested is less than if they set up business in an area.

3. It increases their profits as they receive an agreed financial return from each franchisee.

Benefits to the Franchisee

1. The business name (e.g. Easons) is well known, so it is easier to attract customers.

2. There is reduced business risk to the franchisee as the established business is more likely to succeed than a new venture.

3. There are economies of scale (savings) in areas such as advertising and sales promotion and centralised stock purchasing.

4. The franchisee has a guarantee that there will be no competition using the same name in a specified area.

Disadvantages to the Franchisee

1. An initial payment for the licence, plus a percentage of sales (a royalty) must be paid to the franchisor. The royalty payment is usually in the region of 5 per cent of sales.

2. There is a loss of control. The franchisor imposes restrictions to protect their name, product or service. Minimum quality standards will have to be guaranteed and the range of products sold will be specified by the franchisor.

3. The franchisee will be unable to sell the business without the agreement of the franchisor.

4. Franchising has grown in importance in Ireland, for example Bewley's of Dublin has franchised outlets in Cork and Limerick.

In 2004, Easons opened its first franchised bookshop in Monaghan. Fastway Couriers was founded in New Zealand in 1983. It now has 30 franchised operations in Ireland.

Co-operatives

The co-operative movement began in the small cotton town of Rochdale in Lancashire. The Rochdale pioneers drew up a set of rules called the Rochdale Principles. These are the guidelines or principles that govern the conduct of co-operatives; they are as follows:

1. Open membership – anyone can join.

2. Democratic control – every member has only one vote. Each co-operative is controlled by a management committee elected at the AGM.

3. Limited (small) return on capital invested.

4. Any surplus or profit is to be distributed to members in proportion to their trade with the co-op.

5. There should be co-operation between co-ops at local and national level in order to serve the interest of the members and the communities where they operate.

6. There should be ongoing education for the co-op members and employees as well as the general public.

Examples of co-ops: Avonmore, Kerry and Golden Vale are all agricultural and dairy co-ops who have changed their status to PLCs.

Worker Co-operatives

A worker co-operative is a business that is owned by the workers. The workers make all the decisions on how to run the business, they also work in the firm. They receive a salary for their work and a share of the profits.

EXAMPLE: When the workers in Irish Shoe Supplies in Belmullet, Co. Mayo were told that the factory was closing down, they decided to pool their redundancy payments and form a worker co-operative. It was an example of a worker buy-out as distinct from a management buy-out.

Features of a Worker Co-operative

1. There must be at least eight workers all over 18 years of age.

2. The business should be commercially viable.

3. The workers must enjoy the protection of limited liability.

4. It is suitable for starting up a new business or taking over an existing one that is going to close down.

5. The business is owned by the workers who provide the capital.

6. Every worker has an equal say in decision making.

Benefits of a Worker Co-operative

1. The workers tend to be more productive because they are working for themselves.

2. Demarcation problems and absenteeism do not arise.

3. Workers (owners) are more willing to accept short-term sacrifices, i.e. lower wages, flexible working hours etc.

4. The workers receive all the profits made by the business.

In March 2005, there were 134 worker co-operatives operating in Ireland and engaged in computer services, shoe-making, furniture manufacturing etc.

The Legal Position of a Worker Co-operative

In order to have limited liability, a worker co-operative must register as a private limited company under the Companies Acts 1963–1999 or as an industrial and provident society under the Industrial and Provident Society Act 1978.

Community Co-operatives

These are usually set up to provide an important local service for people in the area, e.g. to provide social and community services for those in need.

Credit Unions

A Credit Union is a financial co-operative owned and run by its members. It is not run for profit but to give the best possible value to members. It offers the following services:

1. Savings accounts where members can save and earn interest.
2. Giving loans to members at a reasonable rate of interest. Only members can obtain loans which are given for many purposes, e.g. buying furniture.

In Ireland, Credit Unions are the leading source of social finance to individuals and community projects, for example:

(a) a local creche which employs six people in Co. Wicklow

(b) a community centre in Co. Monaghan

Other characteristics include the following:

- The Credit Union is operated by a board of directors who are elected by the members.
- The profits of a Credit Union are divided between the members in proportion to their shareholding and deposits.

In March 2005, there were 531 Credit Unions in Ireland affiliated with the Irish League of Credit Unions.

Transnational or Multinational Company

A transnational company is a firm that has its headquarters in one country, but owns and operates businesses in many countries. The transnational company is usually a holding company that owns the majority of shares in a number of other firms located in different countries. It is not just an exporter, it has business operations in different countries.

Transnational companies are large firms, selling millions of euro worth of goods in the electronics, pharmaceutical, health care and software sectors. They are often referred to as Business Giants.

The Coca-Cola bottling factory in Los Angeles.

Why does Ireland want Multinational Companies (MNCs) to locate Here?

The Irish Government actively encourages these firms to locate here for the following reasons and benefits:

1. An inflow of foreign investment is good for the economy and jobs are created for the construction industry. When a plant opens, there are further jobs created as management and staff must be employed. In March 2005, almost 125,000 people were employed in MNCs in Ireland.

2. Imports of certain products are reduced and exports increase, both of which have a positive effect on the balance of trade and balance of payments.

3. Business knowledge, skills and technology are brought with the new company; this is good for the economy.

4. Such companies are very profitable and so pay substantial taxes to the Revenue Commissioners, which boosts Government funds.

5. Multinationals have a huge impact on the commercial life of the area where they locate, e.g. on housing, schools, roads, shopping centres and hotels.

6. Such large profitable companies are better able to resist a downturn in the economy and are unlikely to go bankrupt.

7. From the viewpoint of the Government, they will find it easier to attract more foreign investment, once they can highlight the existence of multinational firms operating successfully in Ireland.

> *In 2004, MNCs accounted for 71% of Ireland's industrial exports.*

> *In 2004, there were 39 American MNCs operating in Ireland.*

Examples of MNCs in Ireland:
- Shell
- Intel Ireland
- Coca-Cola
- Ford
- Nestlé

Dangers Associated with Multinational Companies

1. Once established, they may abuse their power by demanding State incentives such as grants, tax concessions etc.

2. If they close down, there are serious social implications, e.g. huge unemployment. Can you imagine the impact on the social and commercial life of an area if a firm with 1,000 employees closed down? There would be problems for employees with mortgage repayments etc.

3. As a result of cheaper labour costs in developing countries, they may relocate their operations. The threat of closure may be used to ensure that there are no industrial relations problems.

LOCAL MULTINATIONAL TO CLOSE — 1000 JOBS LOST

4. They repatriate their profits and so do not always reinvest and will switch their production from countries with high taxes to countries with low taxes.

5. If they import finished products, there is an adverse effect on the balance of trade.

The State in Business

Some of the biggest businesses in Ireland are owned by the Government. These firms are called semi-state bodies or statutory public corporations. They are managed by directors appointed by the Government. Each statutory firm is responsible to and controlled by a Government minister, who is in turn answerable to the Dáil, e.g. CIÉ, Aer Rianta and ESB.

Why should the State be involved in Business Enterprise?

1. The State provides many vital services to areas of the country which require much investment and generate little or no profit. Such services, e.g. transport (CIÉ) and electricity (ESB), would not be provided by a commercial enterprise, as profit is not guaranteed in every area of supply. Can you imagine what it would be like for those in some remote areas of the country if they had no electricity?

2. The State may, for security and economic reasons, wish to control certain key industries, e.g. ESB. Electricity is an important part of the infrastructure of the State as it is essential for economic development.

3. The financial requirements for some essential services may be too great for private enterprise, so this vital service must be provided by the State, e.g. rail transport.

4. To protect and create employment. There are about 40,000 people directly employed in various State firms.

5. The rationalisation of competitive services eliminates duplication, thus leading to economies of scale (savings) and an efficient service to customers, e.g. it would not be viable to have four electricity firms in competition in a small market.

6. Economic and industrial development can be promoted through State agencies, e.g. Fáilte Ireland promotes tourism. Private enterprise would not invest in such a promotional service. Forfás is a State agency that promotes the development of industry and technology in Ireland.

7. To develop natural resources, e.g. Bord na Móna and Bord Gáis.

Financing of State Firms

1. Some State firms are profitable and self-financing, so State loans or subsidies are not required, e.g. in 2004 ESB profits were €15m.

2. Some State firms charge for their services and losses incurred are paid for by the State with subsidies from tax revenue. For example, CIÉ and Bus Éireann charge customers for bus, train and catering services but are also semi-financed by the State in the form of a yearly subsidy. In 2004, the CIÉ group received a subsidy from the State of €257m (€252m in 2003).

3. Because of their high credit rating, State firms can borrow from the banks at preferential low interest rates.

4. International borrowing is an area open to such firms as loans are guaranteed by the State, e.g. the ESB has obtained loans from the World Bank.

Examples of State Firms

Production	Transport	Finance	Marketing	Services	Training
Bord na Móna Bord Gáis ESB	Aer Rianta Dublin Bus	IDA Ireland SFADCO Udarás na Gaeltachta	Fáilte Ireland Enterprise Ireland Bord Iascaigh Mhara	An Post VHI	FÁS

Indigenous Firms

Indigenous firms are Irish-owned firms, i.e. they are established and operating in Ireland. It is Government policy to support indigenous firms. In 2004, almost 80,000 jobs were created in Ireland by indigenous firms, some of whom are involved in the high-tech software industry. These new firms have replaced some of the long-established traditional industries that have declined, e.g. textile, footwear. Such firms lost out to free trade as they could not compete on costs and selling price.

Development of Large Firms

The following factors have changed the trend in the ownership and organisational structure of firms and resulted in the development of large firms:

1. The concept of limited liability enables large amounts of finance to be raised through share issues. The importance of having limited liability is the reason firms (especially family businesses) now operate as private limited companies rather than sole traders.

2. If a large amount of finance is required for expansion, it may be advisable for the business to change its status from a co-op or a private limited company to a public limited company. The finance can now be raised by a public share issue. For example, in 1986 Kerry Co-op became a public limited company: Kerry Group PLC.

3. It may be easier for a firm to expand by forming an alliance or entering into a franchise arrangement. Such options were actively under consideration by State firms in April 2005, e.g. Aer Lingus, An Post.

4. The change in structure from sole trader to private limited company will enable a firm to expand by bringing in new investors. This will allow the firm to employ specialists in production, marketing and distribution.

5. The State may change its policy of involvement in business and decide to 'sell off' its investment. This involves changing the status of the State-owned firm to a PLC. It is then possible to sell the company shares to the public – this is called privatisation.

In July 1999, the State-owned firm Telecom Éireann became a PLC and was then privatised by the Government. Shares were issued to the public at £3.07 (€3.90) each – they were valued at €4.80 in April 2000. The Government received €3.4 billion from the privatisation of Telecom Éireann which is now called eircom PLC.

Examples of firms that changed structure and ownership:

1. State Firms

(a) Irish Life, a State-owned life assurance company, was privatised and operated for a time as Irish Life PLC. Irish Life then merged with Irish Permanent to become Irish Life and Permanent PLC.

(b) The Irish Sugar Company, another State-owned enterprise that has been privatised, is now called Greencore PLC and is a very profitable business in the area of food production and distribution. Its profits increased by €15m the year after it was privatised.

(c) Telecom Éireann was privatised in 1999 and is now called eircom PLC.

2. Producer Co-operatives

Producer co-operatives are mainly found in the agri-industry. With the creation of the single European market, it was necessary for co-ops to change in order to survive the hectic competition.

(a) In 1986 the Kerry Group PLC was incorporated and acquired all the subsidiaries of Kerry Co-op. It is now one of the top 20 companies in Ireland.

(b) Golden Vale Co-op became Golden Vale PLC.

(c) Waterford Co-op became Waterford Foods PLC.

(d) Avonmore Co-op became Avonmore PLC.

(e) Avonmore PLC and Waterford Foods PLC merged to become Glanbia PLC.

How do Co-ops benefit by Changing their Status to a PLC?

(a) Large amounts of long-term finance can be raised by share issues to the public.

(b) Top management from the business sector can be employed.

(c) Shares can be used as part payment in a takeover.

(d) It enables them to compete and be very profitable.

Revision of Important Terms	
• Sole Trader	• Entrepreneurs
• Service Provider	• Franchising
• Articles of Association	• *Ultra Vires*
• Memorandum of Association	• CAP
• Secondary Industry	• CFP

Exercises

1. (a) State the advantages of operating a business as a sole trader.

   (b) Indicate some of the disadvantages of running a business as a sole trader.

2. (a) What are the benefits of being in business as a partnership rather than as a sole trader?

   (b) Explain the following statement: 'Both sole traders and those in partnership have a problem due to unlimited liability.'

3. (a) How does a private limited company differ from a partnership?

   (b) Outline how a private limited company is formed.

4. (a) Distinguish between a Memorandum of Association and Articles of Association.

   (b) Indicate the benefits of operating a business as a private limited company.

5. (a) How does a private limited company differ from a public limited company?

   (b) Explain what is meant by the term *ultra vires*.

6. (a) Outline the work done by a managing director.

   (b) Why is it more appropriate for a business to exist as a PLC rather than as a private limited company?

7. (a) Explain what is meant by franchising. Give an example.

   (b) Outline the benefits of franchising to an entrepreneur.

8. (a) State the rules associated with a co-op.

   (b) Discuss the role of a worker co-op in a local area.

9. (a) What is a transnational company? Give two examples.

   (b) Why does the Irish Government encourage transnational companies to set up business in Ireland?

10. (a) Why is the State involved in business in Ireland?

    (b) Name a State firm involved in the following areas:

       (i) Production   (ii) Marketing   (iii) Training   (iv) Services

11. (a) What are indigenous firms? Why are they important to Ireland's economy?

    (b) 'We are living in the age of big business.' Do you think that the above statement is true?

20 Community Development

Objectives

The following topics from **Unit 6** of the syllabus are covered in this chapter:

- What is Community Development?

- Benefits of Business Enterprise to a Local Community

- Community Development Organisations:

  – LEADER Plus

  – CEBs

  – FÁS

  – APCs

What is Community Development?

Community Development involves helping people to set up local businesses that will create jobs as well as provide products or services for the local people. The main reason for community development is to promote the economic development of an area, i.e. to tackle unemployment, to develop enterprise and improve the local infrastructure.

Benefits of Business Enterprise to a Local Community

The following are the main benefits to a local community of setting up business enterprises:

1. Jobs are created and so unemployment is reduced. In some cases, emigration from the area is also reduced.

2. There is an improvement in the commercial life of the area, e.g. more business for banks, hotels, shops etc.

3. Employees have more disposable income (money to spend), which in turn increases their standard of living.

4. A developing area will have a greater demand for housing; this boosts the construction industry in the local area.

5. The success of new local firms will encourage more local entrepreneurs to set up their own businesses.

The Government encourages the promotion of local economic development through the Local Development Programme. The thrust of this programme is to incorporate local involvement in the promotion of enterprise in each area. If this is successful, employees' skills will improve from training, unemployment will be reduced and the local economy can improve.

Community Development Organisations

There are a number of organisations which were established to assist local business enterprise. Examples include:

1.	**LEADER Plus**
2.	**County Enterprise Boards (CEBs)**
3.	**FÁS**
4.	**Community Partnerships**

1. LEADER Plus

This is an EU initiative for promoting rural development in Ireland. It replaced the Leader 2 initiative in 2001.

Leader Plus is aimed at encouraging and supporting high quality and ambitious integrated strategies for local rural development. It puts a strong emphasis on co-operation and networking between rural areas.

All rural areas of the EU are eligible under Leader Plus.

Thirty-five Leader Plus groups exist in Ireland. Funding is available on a 70:30 ratio by the EU and the Irish Government for investment in the following areas:

- Rural tourism development.

- Training and recruiting employees.

- Small firms, craft enterprises and local services.

- Local exploitation and marketing of agricultural, forest and fishery products.

- Technical support for rural development.

- Improving environment conditions.

2. City and County Enterprise Boards (CEBs)

City and County Enterprise Boards were established in 1993. Between 1986 and 1992, over 50 per cent of new small local firms failed. This prompted the Government to set up a new initiative to support small firms. In 1992, almost 20 per cent of the private sector workforce were employed in firms that had fewer than 10 employees.

The aim of CEBs is to help small and start-up enterprises locally, i.e. to encourage local initiative in order to stimulate economic activity at local level. This is done by providing financial support, advice and training for the development of enterprises which have fewer than 10 employees.

There are 35 Enterprise Boards in Ireland; each one is a separate company, limited by guarantee. Board members are drawn from elected local authority members, State Agencies, ICTU, IBEC, IFA and the County Manager. Each CEB has a special Evaluation Committee which is responsible for making recommendations on how much financial aid to give for an enterprise project.

Each CEB will provide a mentor for a new business. The mentor is an experienced person who, on a temporary basis, advises the owner/manager of the new business in areas such as finance, marketing and planning.

Each Enterprise Board has access to enterprise funds to assist local projects. Only projects which require grant aid of less than €50,000 are considered. The following range of grants are available:

- A maximum of 50 per cent, up to a maximum figure of €50,000 of the cost of capital and investment required.
- A maximum of 75 per cent, subject to a limit of €5,000 towards the cost of preparing a feasibility study.
- A maximum grant of €5,000 for each new full-time job created.

Benefits of CEBs to a Local Area

Benefits include the following:

(a) Local entrepreneurs with a viable project can be grant-aided to help the idea become a reality, i.e. to establish the business.

(b) Every new project creates at least ten jobs. This reduces the level of unemployment in an area.

(c) The commercial life of an area is improved by the creation of new enterprises and jobs. More money is in circulation with spin-off benefits to a wide range of local firms, e.g. shops, cafés, hotels and boutiques.

3. FÁS

FÁS (Foras Áiseanna Saothair – Training and Development Authority) was set up by the Government in 1988. It is responsible for industrial training in Ireland and administers a wide range of training and employment programmes to provide a skilled workforce for enterprise.

FÁS Training Schemes

The following training schemes are available:

(a) FÁS Enterprise Scheme

With this scheme, unemployed people are paid a weekly wage for a certain period of time if they set up their own business.

(b) FÁS Training Programme

Training programmes are available for the long-term unemployed. Apprenticeship training is also provided.

(c) Community Enterprise Programmes

Advice, training and financial aid is given to community-based groups who have a viable business plan that will provide local employment.

4. Community Partnerships

Area Partnership Companies (APCs)

The APCs were set up under the terms of the Government's Programme for Economic and Social Progress (PESP). This programme was subsequently renegotiated and was called Partnership 2000. The board of directors of APCs is made up of representatives from trade unions, State agencies (e.g. FÁS), local employers and farming bodies. The capital (finance) for the APCs is provided both by the Irish Government and the EU.

- The aim of the APCs is to work at local level to generate more jobs.

- The aim is achieved through the promotion of local economic projects and initiatives. This involves promoting job creation for the long-term unemployed, especially in disadvantaged areas.

- Each APC works on a local development plan for its own region.

- Financial support, including non-repayable grants and loans, is available to support the development of business plans.

- Training is available with support from FÁS.

- Similar to Enterprise Boards, a mentoring service is available.

Benefits of Area Partnerships to a Local Area

(a) By generating jobs at local level, they help to improve the commercial life of the area.

(b) It helps to stop the decline of a disadvantaged area.

(c) Improving employees' skills and experience through training and mentoring makes them more employable for the long term and reduces the need for them to emigrate.

Revision of Important Terms	
• Community Development	• Mentor
• Community Development Organisations	• Enterprise Boards
	• FÁS
• LEADER Plus	• APCs

Exercises

1. (a) Why is community development important to an area?

   (b) Outline the benefits to an area of setting up new business enterprises.

2. (a) Discuss the role of LEADER Plus as a community development organisation.

   (b) Indicate the benefits to a local area from the activities of LEADER Plus.

3 (a) What is a County Enterprise Board?

   (b) What services are provided by a CEB?

   (c) Outline the benefits to an area from the activities of a CEB.

4. Discuss the role of each of the following:

   (a) FÁS

   (b) Area Partnership Companies

   (c) LEADER Plus

5. Outline the various supports available to enterprise.

6. Read the information supplied and answer the questions which follow.

   > In many small towns and rural parts of the country the absence of industry makes it difficult to develop the commercial life of an area.

   (a) What work is done by Leader Plus in community development?

   (b) Name one other organisation involved in community development.

   (c) How does a local community benefit from the setting up of new businesses?

21 Business and the Economy

Objectives

The following topics from **Unit 6** of the syllabus are covered in this chapter:

- What is an Economy?
- Types of Economy
- The Factors of Production
- Economic Variables

What is an Economy?

→ **Definition of an Economy**

An economy can be defined as the legal, political and social framework within which business is conducted.

Within an economy, business operates through entrepreneurs, who make use of available machinery, raw materials and employees for the production of goods and services required by consumers in the marketplace.

A Free Market Economy:
- Private ownership of factors of production
- Freedom of choice
- Free market
- Competition

Types of Economies

There are different types of economies, for example:

1.	Free Market Economy	2.	Controlled Economy

1. Free Market Economy

A free market economy occurs when there is private ownership of the factors of production and the means of distributing goods and services to consumers. The consumer decides what is wanted, not the State. These economies are known as market economies, free enterprise economies, *laissez-faire* or capitalist systems. Ireland and America are examples of a free market economy.

Benefits of a Free Market Economy

(a) Everyone in the State is free to participate in business in order to make profit.

(b) The business economy is competitive, so consumers benefit from a higher standard of goods and services for lower prices.

(c) It is consumers who create the demand and producers respond to satisfy this demand profitably.

Mixed Economy:
- Private enterprise provides some goods
- The State provides some goods

2. Controlled Economy

A controlled economy exists when the Government tries to control economic activity by owning all the factors of production. China is an example of a centralised controlled economy.

The Factors of Production *(also called Resources of Production)*

These are the resources which are available to produce goods required by consumers. Our standard of living depends on the amount of these factors which exist and how they are organised.

There are four factors of production:

1.	Land	3.	Capital
2.	Labour	4.	Enterprise

1. Land

(a) Land is fixed in supply as it is provided by nature.

(b) It includes natural resources, e.g. mineral resources.

(c) It is essential for housing, factories, farming etc.

(d) If land is scarce in supply, its value increases. This is one of the main reasons why land for house-building is so expensive in Ireland.

(e) The economic return on land is rent.

2. Labour

(a) This refers to the workers who are available to carry out the work.

(b) There are two kinds of labour – skilled and unskilled.

(c) The size of the labour force depends on the size and age of the population, as well as the amount of work each worker has to do.

(d) Labour is rewarded in the form of wages.

This is the workforce of the business.

3. Capital

(a) There are different types of capital:

 (i) Consumer capital – money for a house, car, TV etc.

 (ii) Social capital – money for infrastructure: roads, schools, hospitals etc.

 (iii) Private capital – money invested in business enterprise.

 (iv) Fixed capital – machinery, factories etc.

 (v) Working capital – raw materials, stocks and money required for daily business operations.

> *Capital refers to the finance, machinery and equipment used in business.*

(b) Capital usually starts off as cash. It is then used in a form that will create wealth. The different types of capital have a value which can be exchanged using money.

(c) Interest is the economic return on capital.

4. Enterprise

> *Without the entrepreneur, there is no enterprise.*

(a) The entrepreneur is the person who decides to risk private money (savings) to finance business ideas, i.e. to start up a new business.

(b) No economy could function without enterprise.

(c) Entrepreneurs are the people who have the ideas, money and ability to see their aims implemented.

(d) Entrepreneurs invest capital, employ labour and buy or rent land in order to develop the business.

(e) The economic return for the successful entrepreneur is profit.

Economic Variables

The following are the characteristics of an economy that is doing well:

1. Business is good and so profits are high.
2. Unemployment levels are low, skilled workers have jobs and are in demand, so wage levels may rise.
3. Inflation and interest rates are low.
4. The balance of payments is in surplus.
5. The Government has a budget surplus.
6. New entrepreneurs set up businesses.

If economic conditions are bad, businesses will be closing down, unemployment will rise, inflation and interest rates will rise and the Government will have a budget deficit and will have to increase its borrowing.

The following economic variables have an effect on the economy:

1.	Interest rates
2.	Inflation
3.	Exchange rates
4.	Taxation
5.	Subsidies and grants
6.	Employment and unemployment

1. Interest Rates

➡ Definition of Interest Rates

The amount of interest charged by a bank or other financial institution for giving a loan is the price that the borrower has to pay for the use of the money.

A customer who saves money in a bank is in fact lending money to the bank. That customer will be paid interest on the savings by the bank, e.g. 4 per cent. The bank will use this money to make profit by lending it to another customer. The bank will charge a higher rate of interest, e.g. 8 per cent, on any loan it grants to a customer. This difference between the two interest rates is known as the margin.

Factors that affect the Rate of Interest

The following factors affect the rate of interest to be charged on loans to borrowers:

(a) The demand for loans – if there is a big demand for loans, then interest rates are usually high. This is not the case if there is hectic competition between the lenders.

(b) How much the borrowers are prepared to pay.

(c) The ratio of interest that has to be paid to savers (i.e. customers lending money to the banks).

(d) The length of time for which the loan is required, e.g. interest charged on a ten-year loan will be higher than on a three-year loan.

(e) The risk involved – the greater the risk (even with security), the higher the rate of interest to be charged.

Impact on Business of an Interest Rate Increase

An increase in interest rates would affect business in the following ways:

(a) Borrowing would become more expensive and this would reduce profits and adversely affect a firm's ability to compete.

(b) Some firms might decide not to borrow because of the high cost of repayments.

(c) High interest rates restrict business expansion and job creation and reduce profits and savings.

(d) High interest rates may cause high inflation; this reduces consumer demand because of the loss in value of disposable income.

2. Inflation

What does it mean when we say that inflation is 6 per cent? It means that prices are 6 per cent higher than last year.

> → **Definition of Inflation**
>
> *Inflation has been defined as a sustained increase in the level of selling prices over a specified period as measured by the Consumer Price Index (CPI).*

Money is not constant in value – as prices increase, the value of your money decreases, i.e. the purchasing power of your money is reduced.

Impact of Inflation on Enterprise and the Economy

High (or rising) inflation is bad for business and the economy for the following reasons:

(a) The higher cost of raw materials causes selling prices to rise. Firms become less competitive when selling against cheaper imports. A decline in home sales and profits may lead to job losses.

(b) Manufacturers may source a cheaper supply of raw materials from abroad. This increase in imports has an adverse effect on the balance of trade and balance of payments. It also affects the sales and profits of the home-based supplier of the raw materials.

(c) Many people may prefer to invest in property rather than business. Reducing the number of entrepreneurs also adversely affects job creation.

(d) Unions will use the high level of inflation to justify wage increases for their members, without any increase in productivity.

(e) A decline in export sales has a negative impact on the balance of trade.

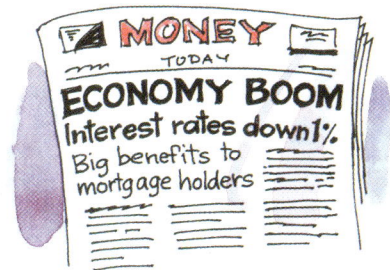

A low rate of inflation is good both for business and the economy for the following reasons:

(a) Firms are prepared to borrow for capital expenditure purposes. This is good for job creation, output and profits.

(b) Manufacturing and wage costs are not increasing. This enables a firm to remain competitive.

(c) The Government does not find it necessary to increase taxes. In fact, the Government may be able to reduce tax levels. This is of benefit to employers when wage negotiations take place.

(d) Entrepreneurs are willing to invest in new business ventures. This is good for job creation and helps to further reduce unemployment.

3. Exchange Rates

Countries have different currencies of varying value. Exporters want to be paid in their own currency – but how much is it in comparison to a different currency?

> ➡ **Definition of Exchange Rates**
>
> *The price of a particular currency when expressed in another currency is its rate of exchange, e.g. €1 = $2*

An Irish importer of goods from America will have to pay for them in US Dollars. This transaction will usually take place in the foreign exchange section of the bank. Since 2002, the euro currency is the single currency in the majority of EU member states. Trading in the single currency will eliminate problems with exchange rates within the member states. Problems can arise when trading with non-EU states, e.g. in America, it will be necessary to exchange euros for dollars.

Fixed Exchange Rates
A fixed exchange rate makes it easier for firms involved in foreign trade to make plans for their business, since they can be confident that no currency losses will be incurred when payments are received or paid.

Floating Exchange Rates
A floating exchange rate means that it is impossible to predict the exchange rate that will exist when payments have to be made.

Impact of Changes in Exchange Rates

(a) A fall in the value of the euro means that other currencies (e.g. US Dollar) become dearer, e.g. €1= $3, becomes €1 = $2. This means that exports become cheaper and imports dearer. This increases the costs for Irish manufacturers who import essential raw materials from America. It benefits exporters as sales and profits should increase.

(b) A rise in the value of the euro means that other currencies (e.g. US Dollar) become cheaper, e.g. €1 = $3, becomes €1 = $4. Exports then become dearer and imports cheaper. Cheaper imports makes it more difficult for Irish enterprises to compete on the home market against foreign competition.

(c) Foreign tourists are very conscious of exchange rates. Tourists want exchange rates to be stable so that they can financially plan their holiday. Receipts from tourists make a significant contribution to Ireland's balance of payments.

4. Taxation

A tax is a compulsory contribution to the Exchequer to meet the expenses of the Government. Taxation is a source of finance for the Exchequer. There are different types of taxes, e.g. PAYE, VAT, corporation tax and capital gains tax. When the economy is booming, there is an increase in the amount of taxes collected by the Government.

Effects of Taxation

(a) Business Enterprises

Taxation reduces the amount of profit available for reinvestment in the business or distribution to the shareholders as dividends.

> **Taxation affects:**
> - Business
> - Consumers
> - Wage earners

(b) Consumers

VAT increases the cost of goods/services to the consumer. This can reduce the demand for certain products.

(c) Wage Earners

PAYE is a direct tax deducted by employers from the wages paid to employees. The amount of tax deducted reduces people's disposable income, so they have less to spend. A high rate of PAYE would be a disincentive for employees to work overtime.

5. Subsidies and Grants

A subsidy is a payment of money by the Government to a firm. It is a form of price support to business, so it is the opposite to taxation, for example:

(a) The State pays a subsidy (or subvention) to CIÉ. This enables CIÉ to continue to provide services which it deems unprofitable, but which the State regards as socially desirable, e.g. providing a bus service in remote areas.

(b) State agencies such as Fáilte Ireland receive financial subsidies to enable them to provide a vital service that benefits the economy. Fáilte Ireland is the State firm that promotes the Irish tourist industry.

A grant is a non-repayable amount of money received by a business from either the Government or the EU to increase its competitiveness. Some grants have to be repaid if specified criteria relating to output, jobs, etc. are not met.

(a) Many firms have been attracted to Ireland as a place to locate because of the large number of grants available from Enterprise Ireland.

(b) Since becoming a member of the European Union, the Irish economy has received huge grants from the following funds:

   (i) European Regional Development Fund

   (ii) European Social Fund

   (ii) European Cohesion Fund

6. Employment and Unemployment

In 1992, there were 217,000 people registered as unemployed in Ireland. By March 2005, this figure had reduced to 160,000. Unemployed people have a reduced amount of disposable income.

One of the reasons for the reduction in unemployment is the success of the Government in attracting multinational companies to set up business in Ireland. A contributing factor to unemployment is the lack of suitable skills for jobs available. High-tech firms want workers with special skills. The State agency FÁS provides training courses to upgrade skills.

Negative Implications of Unemployment

(a) Unemployed people only purchase essentials.

(b) Sales and profits of many firms are less than in times of high employment. This can affect the job security of existing staff.

(c) Taxation levels are high to enable the State to pay unemployment benefits.

(d) Social problems increase in areas of high unemployment.

Reducing Unemployment

The following steps could be considered to reduce the number of people who are unemployed:

(a) Provide training and educational courses to improve skills and make people more employable.

(b) Improve the economy and in turn increase demand, so that additional employees are required.

(c) Provide tax incentives to encourage people to start up their own business, i.e. become self-employed.

(d) Give generous tax-free allowances to encourage the unemployed back to work.

Revision of Important Terms	
• Economy	• Circular Flow of Income
• Free Market Economy	• Interest Rates
• Factors of Production	• Inflation
• Economic Variables	• Taxation
• Enterprise	• Rate of Exchange

Exercises

1. (a) 'Ireland is an example of a free market economy.' What does this mean?

   (b) State and explain the factors of production.

2. (a) Why is enterprise important for the Irish economy?

   (b) Discuss the importance of land as a factor of production.

3. (a) What are the features of a booming economy?

   (b) What impact would an increase in interest rates have on enterprise in Ireland?

4. (a) Why is a low rate of inflation good for enterprise and the economy?

   (b) What impact does high taxation have on business and consumers?

5. (a) State and explain the factors of production.

   (b) Why are the factors of production important for enterprise?

22 Government and Business

Objectives

The following topics from **Unit 6.5 and 6.6** of the syllabus are covered in this chapter:

- 6.5 Government and Business
- Government Role in Encouraging and Regulating Business
- Reasons for Government Intervention
- How the Government Encourages Business
- Role of Government in Business
- Social Responsibilities of Business
- Ethical Business Practice
- Environmental Issues and Business
- Characteristics of Environmental Business

Why does the State Intervene in Business?

Business in Ireland is owned and run by both private enterprise and the State. This combination of ownership is known as an open market economy.

The State intervenes in business for many reasons, for example:

1.	To regulate business
2.	To advise and assist business
3.	To provide business and essential services
4.	To raise taxes for the State

1. To regulate Business

Every business must adhere to the various Acts passed by the Government, for example:

    (a) Consumer Information Act 1978

    (b) Sale of Goods and Supply of Services Act 1980

    (c) Industrial Relations Act 1990

These Acts protect consumers and employees from being exploited by business.

2. To advise and assist Business

Economic development can be promoted through State agencies such as Enterprise Ireland. This agency will advise and may assist firms involved in exporting. Likewise, Fáilte Ireland advises and assists firms involved in tourism, e.g. hotels and guesthouses.

3. To provide Business and Essential Services

    (a) Many vital services are provided by the State to all sections of the economy, in some cases at a loss, e.g. CIÉ and ESB. Private enterprise would only provide such essential services at a profit in every area.

    (b) State firms have been set up to develop the natural resources of the country, e.g. Bord na Móna and Bord Gáis.

4. To raise Taxes for the State

The Government raises taxes from many sources, for example:

   (a) From business – VAT, Corporation Tax.

   (b) From employees – PAYE.

Taxation is a source of revenue for the Government to meet the expenses of running the country.

Fiscal and Monetary Policy of the Government

> ### ➡ Definition of Fiscal Policy
>
> *Fiscal policy relates to Government policy in relation to financial receipts (income) and expenditure, e.g. a 10 per cent increase in the rate of VAT may cause a decline in sales.*

> ### ➡ Definition of Monetary Policy
>
> *Monetary policy relates to Government policy that affects the amount of money in circulation for spending, e.g. an increase in interest rates restricts the amount of money that the financial institutions can lend.*

Effects of a Change in Fiscal Policy by the Government

1. (a) If PAYE taxes are increased, employees have less disposable income. Savings are reduced and business sales and profits fall.

   (b) If PAYE taxes are reduced, employees have more disposable income so business sales and profits increase. The amount of corporation tax paid to the Government also increases.

2. (a) An increase in corporation tax reduces the amount of money that companies have for reinvestment. This can have an adverse effect on job creation.

   (b) A reduction in corporation tax increases the amount of interest-free money that companies have for reinvestment. This enables firms to expand, increase sales and profits and create more jobs. (In 1990, corporation tax in Ireland for non-manufacturing companies was 50 per cent. It is now 12.5 per cent for all companies.)

3. An increase in the rate of VAT, currently 21 per cent, may reduce sales and profits especially on luxury (non-essential) items.

4. Any change that reduces the income of the Government also reduces its expenditure on roads, schools, hospitals etc. This change also affects the number of employees working in construction firms. Expenditure on infrastructural projects helps economic development and job creation.

5. In February 2005, about 32,000 people were directly employed in various State agencies and many thousands in the civil service. The wages earned by State employees have a huge impact on the commercial life of the areas where this money is spent.

Effects of a Change in Monetary Policy by the Government

1. An increase in interest rates restricts the amount of money that financial institutions can lend. (In 1985, building societies were charging 16 per cent for mortgages. This figure had reduced to 4 per cent by February 2005.)

2. If interest rates are reduced, it is cheaper for business and consumers to borrow. This will lead to an increase in investment by firms and spending by consumers. This spending is good for industry and employment.

Privatisation

Privatisation occurs when a State-owned firm is sold to private enterprise by means of a share floatation. The shares are sold to public investors, thus transferring both ownership and control. The State monopoly of the firm would cease, so normal competitive market forces would arise, e.g. in June 1999, the Exchequer received €3.8bn, from the privatisation (sale) of Telecom Éireann (now called eircom PLC). Its shares were floated on the Irish Stock Exchange. In July 1999, the share price was quoted at €3.40. In February 2005, the share price was quoted at €1.90.

Telecom Éireann used to be owned by the State, but was privatised in 1999 and renamed eircom PLC.

The Benefits of Privatisation

The benefits and opportunities afforded by privatisation include the following:

1. The Government receives money from the sale of the State firm, e.g. in 1991 the Government received €483m from the privatisation of Irish Life and Greencore (formerly the Irish Sugar Company).

2. The Government's financial commitments are reduced when an unprofitable State firm is privatised. Less taxpayers' money will be used in unprofitable State firms in the future.

3. The elimination of a monopoly situation usually leads to increased efficiency, improved services and lower prices for consumers.

4. The new owners will have profits as their main objective. They will employ top management and pay them higher wages than State firms would pay. The firm should now be run more efficiently.

> **Many benefits from privatisation for:**
> • **the Government**
> • **new owners**
> • **the consumer**
> • **new investors**

5. The huge revenue received from the sale of the State firm can be used in many ways, for example:

   (a) To reduce taxation.

   (b) To repay Government loans.

   (c) To reduce future borrowing requirements.

   (d) To pay for Government programmes.

6. Privatisation increases share ownership, which encourages greater interest and support for the business. It also encourages and allows for employee share ownership.

7. The privatised entity will have access to wider sources of capital and will be better able to compete in global markets.

Negative Features of Privatisation

The negative features and threats of privatisation include the following:

1. Private enterprise has a profit motive. This is often achieved by raising prices and reducing the number of employees.

2. Private enterprise would not have the same social commitment as the State. It would not provide the product/service in unprofitable areas, e.g. rail transport and postal services to remote areas.

3. Trade unions and workers fear privatisation due to potential job losses.

Effect of Government on the Labour Force

The State is a large provider of employment in secure jobs. The public sector workforce is made up of those working in the public service, e.g. teachers, gardaí and those working in State agencies, such as Enterprise Ireland, ESB and CIÉ.

The Government positively affects the labour force in the following ways:

1. The Government is the single biggest employer in Ireland, e.g. civil service, education, the Army and State firms. In January 2005, there were 196,000 public service employees.

2. The Government, through Enterprise Ireland, attracts foreign firms to Ireland. Grants are paid in return for job creation.

3. The Government provides funding for FÁS to train workers in order to make them more employable.

4. If the Government increases its spending on infrastructure (roads, hospitals etc.), this has the effect of increasing the number of workers employed in the construction industry.

5. The Government has invested heavily in information technology (IT) in education at both second and third level. This greatly improves IT skills, which are required for modern industry and enables people to obtain employment in high-tech firms.

6. Reducing PAYE rates makes it more attractive for some unemployed people to take up employment rather than continue to claim social welfare payments.

How Does the Government Create a Business Climate?

The Government creates a suitable climate for business enterprise in the following ways:

1.	Ongoing spending on education and training leads to a better workforce.
2.	Reducing PAYE rates helps to control wage demands and encourages employees to work overtime.
3.	The policy of privatisation enables private enterprise to invest in former 'no-go' areas.
4.	Engaging in social partnership has led to Centralised Wage Agreements. This has greatly reduced industrial unrest and makes it easier for firms to become competitive. It has also made it easier for the Government to attract foreign enterprise to set up business in Ireland.
5.	The availability of grants encourages new firms to start up – this is good for job creation.
6.	Government policies which result in low inflation, low interest rates and a booming economy greatly encourage industrialists to invest and expand. Such firms will require extra staff.
7.	The 12.5 per cent corporation tax rate has been a big attraction to industrialists.
8.	The good management of public finances reduces Government borrowing requirements. This has led to a reduction in PAYE levels.
9.	Ensuring the existence of procedures for settling industrial problems, e.g. Labour Court, Labour Relations Commission.

Government Departments and Agencies

There are many Government departments and agencies which are directly or indirectly involved with business.

● Government Departments

Examples include:

1. The Department of Finance

This department is responsible for the following:

    (a) Raising money from taxation and borrowing.

    (b) Spending money as agreed in the budget.

    (c) Preparing the Government's budget, i.e. deciding how much money is required to run the country, how it is to be raised and how it will be spent.

> This Department plays a vital role in relation to:
> • Public expenditure
> • Taxation
> • Economic policy
> • Public services
> • The budget

2. The Department of Agriculture and Food

This department is responsible for the following:

    (a) The agri-industry.

    (b) Implementing EU directives in relation to agriculture.

    (c) An Bord Bia.

    (d) Teagasc.

    (e) Managing the LEADER programmes.

> This Department promotes the development of agriculture and horticulture.

3. The Department of Enterprise, Trade and Employment

This department is responsible for the following:

    (a) Promoting trade and enterprise, e.g. County Enterprise Boards (CEBs).

    (b) Industrial relations, industrial legislation and employment rights.

> This Department is responsible for industrial development policy.

4. The Department of the Environment, Heritage and Local Government

This department is responsible for the following:

    (a) Policy and programmes in relation to the environment.

    (b) A wide range of services provided through the local government system, e.g. environmental protection.

Government Agencies

The following Government agencies assist business in a variety of ways:

1. The Central Statistics Office (CSO)

The CSO, based in Cork, provides statistical information on a wide range of issues, e.g. population facts and trends and economic matters such as inflation rates.

Central Statistics Office, Cork.

2. The Labour Court and the Labour Relations Commission

These two bodies provide an important service in industrial relations, e.g. resolving disputes.

3. Enterprise Ireland

Enterprise Ireland was formed in 1998 to create a linkage of some of the functions of Forbairt, FÁS and An Bord Tráchtála (Irish Trade Board). Its aim is to ensure the existence of a good business climate where industry can prosper.

Legislation that Regulates Business

1. Consumer Information Act 1978

The consumer is protected under the Consumer Information Act 1978. Under this Act, the Office of the Director of Consumer Affairs was set up to implement the Act.

2. Data Protection Act 1988

The Data Protection Act 1988 gives people the right of access to personal information which an employer has on computer. Under this Act, the Office of the Data Protection Commissioner was established to monitor the operation of the Act by employers.

Four important Acts:
- Consumer Information Act 1978
- Data Protection Act 1988
- Companies Act 1963–1999
- Competition Act 1991

3. The Revenue Commissioners

The Office of the Revenue Commissioners advises business on taxation matters and takes steps to ensure that the correct amount of tax is paid. The revenue commissioners implement the Finance Acts each year to implement budget changes.

4. The Registrar of Companies and the Companies Acts 1963–1999

Entrepreneurs starting a new company must adhere to the regulations covered in the Companies Acts 1963–1999. The Registrar of Companies is responsible for ensuring that companies are properly set up before a Certificate of Incorporation is issued.

5. The Competition Act 1991

The Competition Act 1991 was passed to curb abuses of dominant or monopoly positions by firms in commercial and professional areas. Anti-competitive practice, e.g. price fixing, is banned under this Act. Firms involved in mergers or takeovers must get approval from the Competition Authority before an agreement can be implemented.

Local Government

In Ireland, a local government system is made up of local authorities, county councils, urban district councils, town commissions, city corporations and boroughs. Money is allocated to the local authority by the Department of the Environment, Heritage and Local Government. This money is spent on local requirements, e.g. roads, housing and fire services. In February 2005, local government in Ireland had 34,300 employees with a budget of €3,400 m.

Benefits of Local Government to Business

The wide-ranging services provided by local government benefit business as follows:

1. Infrastructure
The existence of good roads (ring roads, toll roads etc.) is essential for transport and communication, as well as attracting industry to an area.

2. Water Supply
The existence of a proper water supply and sewerage system is essential for existing and new firms.

3. Planning Permission
Planning permission is necessary for building factories. In some cases planning permission will be refused, e.g. land may be rezoned for agricultural use.

4. Environmental Protection

Some firms, e.g. chemical manufacturers, must be located away from areas of high population because of fumes, pollution etc. A plentiful supply of water is required for such firms.

Economic Planning by the Government

Economic planning by the Government is necessary to encourage industry, reduce unemployment, reduce inflation and ensure that industry is competitive. One of the biggest problems for industry in the 1980s was the huge number of working days lost by strikes. This problem no longer exists because of the existence of Centralised Wage Agreements agreed by the social partners, i.e. the Government, employers and unions. The existence of these agreements has greatly reduced industrial disputes and enabled firms to plan and remain competitive.

The Impact of Economic Planning on Business

1. Wages

Business can plan ahead knowing the wage levels which have been agreed. Management and workers are confident that there will be no disputes over wages.

2. Competitiveness

Economic planning helps to control interest rates and inflation. This is necessary to enable indigenous firms to compete with foreign competition and also to encourage new firms to set up business.

3. Grants

Giving grants to foreign firms to establish business in Ireland is part of Government economic planning. These firms create many jobs, which reduces unemployment levels.

4. Tax

Economic planning helps to reduce tax levels, e.g. corporation tax and VAT. This enables firms to reinvest and expand more. This, in turn, helps to create more jobs and increase sales and profits.

5. Unemployment

Economic planning is necessary to reduce unemployment. High unemployment levels are very bad for business and the economy for many reasons, for example:

  (a) High social welfare payments.

  (b) Low levels of disposable income.

  (c) Business sales and profits are reduced.

The Impact of the Economy on Business

1. Inflation

Low inflation is good for business because prices remain stable and consumers are in a spending mood. This is good for sales and profits. High inflation is bad for business as prices are too high and disposable income is confined to essentials.

2. Interest Rates

Low interest rates are good for business. Money is cheap to borrow, so firms are willing to expand and create more jobs. High interest rates make borrowing too expensive, so firms will be restricted in their ability to expand.

3. Taxation

Low rates of corporation tax are good for business and for attracting foreign firms to Ireland. A reduction in VAT will increase sales and profits for business.

4. Government Grants

These are sums of money which the Government makes available to indigenous and foreign firms to set up business. They have a big impact on job creation and reduce unemployment.

The Impact of Business on the Economy

1. Employment

Firms give jobs to different types of workers, e.g. skilled, unskilled and trainees. Without the existence of business nationwide, there would be massive unemployment in the country.

2. Taxation

Every business pays tax on its profits to the Revenue Commissioners. Employers deduct tax from wages paid to employees and give it to the Revenue Commissioners. The more successful the economy, the more money the Government will have to spend.

3. Investment

Reinvesting profits in business enables firms to expand, create more jobs and increase sales and profits.

4. Living Standards

The impact of business on job creation and the availability of new products helps to greatly improve living standards.

Social and Ethical Responsibilities of Business

Ethical business practice involves preparing and adopting a set of guidelines for management and staff to be honest, fair and reasonable in decision making. Business ethics should be used in dealings with employees, customers, suppliers, shareholders and Government agencies, e.g. The Revenue Commissioners.

Who is Ethics Relevant to?

1. Employees
They are provided with safe working conditions, good facilities and a fair wage.

2. Customers
Top quality goods are available and they are assured that advertising is not misleading.

3. Suppliers
Suppliers must adhere to agreed trading terms and pay bills when they are due.

4. The Revenue Commissioners
The Revenue Commissioners ensure that all taxes that are due are paid.

5. The General Public
Firms take all steps necessary to reduce pollution caused by their products.

Business Ethics

> **➡ Definition of Business Ethics**
>
> *Business Ethics has been defined as a Code of Behaviour of people in business that is accepted as morally correct. It is based on the assertion of what is right, wrong, honest and fair.*

Every business should have its Code of Ethics. This is a set of rules to be applied to all decisions of management when dealing with any of the stakeholders. Controls should exist to monitor the ethical climate and operations of the firm. Strong management is essential to show that the business is leading by example.

Ethical Issues for Business

The following ethical issues should be considered by business:

1. Should the business aim for maximum profits or should it reduce its prices and profits to help those with a low income buy the products?

2. What steps are necessary to avoid pollution caused by the firm's products and means of manufacture?

3. Is the firm totally committed to paying all its taxes or will it avoid paying some?

4. The quality of raw materials to be used in production. Is it ethical to use cheap, low quality raw materials from a Third World country that exploits workers?

5. Does management recognise and accept the workers' right to join a trade union and be paid a fair wage?

6. How are the various stakeholders going to be treated, e.g. shareholders, suppliers and consumers?

7. What is a fair price to charge for a new product? Is it a price that will make it impossible for competitors to compete?

The Social Responsibilities of Business *(Higher Level Only)*

Business has a commitment to the wider community to act ethically when dealing with all stakeholders. A business exists to make profits for the shareholders. Business has social responsibilities to the following:

1. To Shareholders:

   (a) To earn for them a fair return on their investment in the form of dividends.

   (b) To maintain proper financial records

   (c) To act as per the terms of the Memorandum and Articles of Association if the business operates as a company.

2. To Employees:

   (a) To pay them a fair wage and provide them with proper working conditions.

   (b) To ensure that all employees are treated fairly, with no discrimination in matters of promotion.

   (c) To provide them with proper health and safety facilities.

3. To Customers:

    (a) To sell them top quality goods at a fair price.

    (b) To ensure that there is no misleading advertising of quality, price, etc.

    (c) To accept the customers' right to complain about the products they purchase. Each customer's complaint should be checked out.

4. To the Government:

    (a) To pay all taxes due to the Revenue Commissioners, e.g. VAT. corporation tax, PAYE.

    (b) To ensure that all legislation relevant to running a business is adhered to, for example:

        (i) Consumer Information Act 1978

        (ii) Employment Equality Act

5. To Suppliers:

    (a) To pay them on time as per agreement.

    (b) To treat them fairly.

6. To the General Public:

    (a) To ensure that the means of production used do not cause any pollution problems in the area.

    (b) To obtain the appropriate planning permission from the Local Authority where relevant, i.e. building a new factory, etc.

    (c) To support local community groups with sponsorship.

Business and the Environment

Manufacturing firms have responsibilities, not just to their shareholders and customers, but also to the environment. Management must ensure that its manufacturing processes will not cause pollution that could adversely affect the quality of life of employees and the general public. Management should be sensitive, open and honest in all business decisions.

Characteristics of an Environmentally Conscious Business Enterprise *(Higher Level Only)*

1. It must be sensitive to other people's wishes, so air or river pollution should be avoided. A manufacturer should use clean technologies in production in order to avoid environmental issues.

2. It minimises wastage by ensuring that products can be recycled, e.g. 85 per cent of the parts used in car manufacturing can be recycled.

3. It does not exploit raw materials supplied by Third World countries by paying an unfairly low price for the products. They should be paid a fair market price for the goods.

4. It recognises the importance of ensuring safety when designing new products, e.g. airbags in cars.

5. It provides safe working conditions for employees and does not purchase products from firms that exploit labour.

6. It identifies green market segments that have potential.

7. It consults with consumers before producing and launching new products. This process will generate goodwill and reduce conflicts, e.g. problems with GM foods.

8. It should be open and honest in all its dealings on environmental matters.

Cost to Business of Meeting its Social (i.e. Ethical and Enivironmental) Responsibilities *(Higher Level Only)*

1. Better wages and working conditions for the employees will increase costs and reduce profits.

2. Paying a fair market price for raw materials will increase production costs and reduce profits.

3. In order to reduce air/water pollution it may be necessary for manufacturing firms to upgrade their manufacturing process. This will involve capital expenditure to pay for the new machinery. If the firm has to borrow, the loan interest will increase expenses and reduce profits.

4. Moving towards greater use of recycled products will increase costs. The firm will also incur promotional expenditure to encourage and influence customers to switch to the 'new' products.

5. Extra costs will be incurred to ensure the safe dumping of dangerous and toxic substances. Additional costs would be incurred by way of fines if a firm was found to be in breach of the law on environmental issues.

Opportunities (Benefits) for Business in Meeting its Social (i.e. Ethical and Enivironmental) Responsibilities *(Higher Level Only)*

1. The use of the most up-to-date production processes that will reduce or eliminate environmental issues will lead to improved efficiency and lower costs.

2. If the customers are supportive of environmental issues, then these 'green consumers' will support the business and so sales and profits will increase.

3. Providing satisfactory environmental working conditions is good for staff morale. This leads to a reduction in absenteeism and staff turnover.

4. Adverse publicity is avoided; this is always good for business when dealing with customers, suppliers and banks.

Revision of Important Terms	
• Mixed Economy	• Local Government
• Fiscal Policy	• Economic Planning
• Monetary Policy	• Inflation
• Privatisation	• Business Ethics
• Labour Force	• Social Responsibilities of Business
• Government Departments	• The Environment
• Government Agencies	

Exercises

1. How does the Government intervene in business?

2. (a) Explain what is meant by fiscal policy. Give one example.

   (b) What is meant by monetary policy? Give one example.

3. Outline the effects of change in fiscal policy by the Government.

4. Outline the effects of change in monetary policy by the Government.

5. (a) Explain what is meant by privatisation.

   (b) Outline the benefits and negative features of privatisation.

6. (a) Explain what is meant by public sector workforce.

   (b) How does the Government affect the labour force?

7. 'A good business climate is essential for industry.'

   Outline how the Government creates a good business climate.

8. (a) Distinguish between Government departments and Government agencies. Give three examples of each.

   (b) Outline the different ways that business in Ireland is regulated.

9. (a) Why is economic planning important?

    (b) How does economic planning by the Government influence business?

10. (a) What impact does business have on the economy?

    (b) What impact does the economy have on business?

11. (a) Explain what is meant by ethical business practice.

    (b) Discuss the various ethical areas that affect management decisions in business.

12. Outline the social responsibilities of business.

13. Discuss the following characteristics of an environmentally conscious business:

    (a) Sensitivity   (c) Honesty   (e) Consultation

    (b) Openness   (d) Awareness

14. (a) Discuss the costs to business of meeting its ethical and social responsibilities.

    (b) Outline the opportunities for business in meeting its environmental responsibilities.

Applied Business Questions
for Units 4, 5, 6
Leaving Certificate 2007 and 2012

Applied Business Question
Based on units 4, 5 and 6 for Leaving Certificate 2007/2012

INELL LTD (LC 2002)

The Inell brand is well-established and well-regarded in agricultural circles as the brand of quality when it comes to farm machinery. The growth of the business in Ireland had been good in the 20 years since its foundation by the Murphy brothers, Michael and Patrick. They have both surrounded themselves with the best technically qualified and enterprising employees they could find at every stage of the development of the business. They believe in the empowerment of their employees and have given them the chance to prove themselves at every opportunity.

Several suggestions have been put forward at the monthly management meetings over recent times about the expansion of the business. Expansion, not only on the home market but also into European and world markets, with new and adapted older products has been discussed. Michael feels that the risks are too high and that losses may result, but Patrick feels that, for the business to survive into the future, it must grow in the long term.

The technology in two of the three manufacturing plants located in Ireland is getting old and will, in the very near future, be in need of complete modernisation. It is not up to present-day environmental standards. There have been some minor accidents in the plants, resulting in criticism of the company's attitude to the environment being published in newspapers. Both the founding members recognise that they have responsibilities, not only to their shareholders and employees, but also to their customers and to society in general.

(A)   Analyse the importance of good employer/employee relationships in the running of companies such as Inell Ltd. Refer to the central role of the human resource department in the process.   (30 marks)

(B)   Discuss two strategies that Inell Ltd could use to successfully expand the business. Make relevant assumptions that you feel may be necessary, given the details above.   (30 marks)

(C)   Using appropriate headings to guide your thinking, describe how Inell Ltd could become a more socially responsible business. Refer to the above text in your response.   (20 marks)

(Total = 80 marks)

Applied Business Question

Based on units 4, 5 and 6 for Leaving Certificate 2007/2012

ALICE AND KEVIN HYLAND

Alice and Kevin Hyland have been living in a rented apartment in Dublin since they married two years ago, but have recently purchased a new house in Athy, Co. Kildare. The house purchase was financed by a €250,000 mortgage obtained from AIB. It was necessary to take out a Mortgage Protection Policy with the house mortgage. They work in Dublin and have calculated that, with the improvements in the road network, they can commute from their home to their workplace in approximately one hour. Their immediate priorities, however, are to purchase some contents for their new home as well as a new car.

Recently Alice was browsing through a number of websites belonging to the various financial institutions. She was particularly looking for a suitable loan which they might use to finance the purchase of the car. On the website of one major bank, special motor term loans were being offered over five years. As well as guaranteeing 'low interest rates' and 'flexible repayments to suit your needs', they were also offering a free weekend for two people in a choice of top Irish hotels and free entry into a confined competition with attractive prizes to anyone who took out a loan before the end of that month.

Alice and Kevin both work for a large State organisation in the area of broadcasting. Kevin works as an accountant and Alice is an advertising executive. Due to the nature of their jobs, both have seen at first hand how the organisation has been affected by competition, following the issuing of new broadcasting licences in both the television and radio markets, as well as the increase in satellite and digital broadcasting. Both are also concerned at rumours of privatisation and the need to tackle the problems of overstaffing, ineffective management structures, absence of profit motive and under-productivity, if the firm is to survive in the sector.

(A) Outline the main types of insurance which you would recommend that a couple like Alice and Kevin should take out to cover their personal and household needs. Refer to the information in the above passage in your answer.   (20 marks)

(B) (i) Explain what is meant by sales promotion.   (5 marks)

   (ii) List and explain four types of sales promotion techniques which might be used by a financial institution when trying to sell their products and services to potential customers. Refer to the information in the above passage where relevant.   (15 marks)

(C) (i) What are the main drawbacks to State ownership of firms?   (20 marks)

   (ii) Suggest ways by which firms might benefit from privatisation. Refer to the passage above in your answer.   (20 marks)

(Total = 80 marks)

Applied Business Question
Based on units 4, 5 and 6 for Leaving Certificate 2007/2012

IT SERVICES LTD

Peter Hogan graduated with a Master's Degree in technology. He wanted to be his own boss. In 2002, with financial assistance from his parents, he set up his own company, IT Services Ltd, specialising in advice and back-up service for industrial computer users. Within two years, his business expanded and he employed six 'high-tech' graduates to service his expanding list of customers. He believed in a policy of empowerment so that his staff could give an immediate and better service to the customers. This policy ensures more effective decision making, which is what customers require. It is also good for staff morale as workers are committed, costs are controlled and so profits should increase.

By modern criteria, Peter Hogan would be regarded as a successful entrepreneur. At management meetings, he would regularly refer to the motto 'from local to global'. He researched the concept of a franchise arrangement with a UK software company. If this worked, there would be economies of scale with less dependence on the home market, but he decided it wasn't suitable for his business.

By July 2004, sales were €5m with profits of €1.2m. Business was booming, life was comfortable, but Peter Hogan was anxious to expand his business into the huge Euro market. Having researched the market, he decided to 'go for it'. He had an excellent relationship with his bank and was confident of raising the necessary finance, i.e. €1 million. He approached his bank manager with a request for a 6-year term loan of €1 million. The bank manager requested a copy of his business plan before deciding on the request.

(A) Explain what is meant by empowerment. With reference to the above passage, outline the benefits of empowerment to IT Services Ltd.   (20 marks)

(B) (i) Outline potential benefits of IT Computers Ltd having a franchise arrangement with a UK firm.   (5 marks)

(ii) Why was Peter Hogan wise to establish the business as a private limited company?   (10 marks)

(C) (i) How will the existence of a business plan influence the bank manager?

(5 marks)

(ii) With reference (where relevant) to the above passage, you are required to prepare a business plan which Peter Hogan could submit to his bank manager. You can make appropriate assumptions.   (40 marks)

(Total = 80 marks)

Applied Business Question
Based on units 4, 5 and 6 for Leaving Certificate 2007/2012

McCabe's Transport

Patrick McCabe showed ambition by starting off in business in 2000 operating a 50-seat coach for private hire, which he purchased using redundancy money he had received from Bus Éireann the previous year. In the early years, most of his work came from local groups. In recent years, there has been an increase in requests for sub-contract work from other operators, including Bus Éireann and this has prompted Patrick to lease two more coaches. Patrick employed two full-time and one part-time driver, as well as a receptionist/office assistant.

Up to now, Patrick McCabe has been operating the business as a sole trader. He was happy with the benefits which this form of ownership offered him, particularly the ease of operation and profits. Patrick is, however, conscious of the impending de-regulation of the public transport market. He knows that he will need to expand his operation and increase and modernise his bus fleet if he is to be in a position to bid for commercial routes, which will be made available to private operators. Patrick believes that a different ownership structure will be necessary if the business is to grow and develop in the future. Changing the structure to a Private Limited Company will enable him to become a Managing Director and become more involved in the administration and marketing side of the business. A LTD company structure would also provide him with the benefit of limited liability, something he does not have as a sole trader. He is concerned about the impact that certain economic variables will have on the future of the business.

Patrick has been discussing his options with a friend, who suggested to him that he could expand his business by merging with another transport business. This would give him the additional coaches he needs, along with the necessary staff and an existing client base. Patrick is somewhat apprehensive at the thought of the changes he is considering, but deep down he knows they are essential if the business is to grow. From small beginnings in 2000, Patrick McCabe is about to enter the big competitive world, where there is both uncertainty and potential.

(A) List and explain the types of insurance which you would recommend Patrick should have for his business. Refer to the information contained in the above passage when formulating your answer. (20 marks)

(B) (i) What are the main reasons why Patrick McCabe wishes to expand his business? Refer to the text in your response. (16 marks)

(ii) Indicate which industry this business is involved in. (4 marks)

(C) (i) Outline the benefits to Patrick McCabe of changing the status of his business to a Private Limited Company. Refer to the text in your response. (25 marks)

(ii) Discuss the impact that two economic variables may have on the future of the business. (15 marks)

(Total = 80 marks)

Applied Business Question
Based on units 4, 5 and 6 for Leaving Certificate 2007/2012

MAGAZINE PRINTERS LTD

Deirdre Hayden is the Managing Director of Magazine Printers Ltd, an indigenous company established in Dublin by her father in 1980. The business had grown quite considerably up to the mid-1990's as the demand for general printing increased, but has seen a decline over the last ten years as new and advanced computer software meant that more and more firms were taking to in-house publishing and avoided the need to go outside. Deirdre recognises the problems the firm is facing and is conscious of the need to develop new opportunities for the company if it is to serve and grow in the future. She has weekly meetings with the sales people and also encourages other employees to suggest new product ideas to help the business expand.

The business has been located near the centre of Dublin since its foundation and currently occupies a premises which, due to its location, has a market value of over €2 million. The firm employs 40 people, mostly from the local area, and has actively supported local interests through its sponsorship of a local boxing club and its active involvement with the Inner City Chamber of Commerce. The average weekly wage bill for the firm is €40,000.

Deirdre is considering recruiting a general manager to take over the day-to-day running of the business in an effort to maximise the firm's ability to benefit from new technology. She also hopes that this person will be instrumental in developing new markets for the firm and generating new business which will see the firm grow and prosper. She is undecided, however, whether to promote Jim Carroll who has worked for the firm for the last eight years to this position or recruit an outsider who might have the benefit of valuable experience and contacts and would find it easier to introduce changes which Deirdre feels are required to improve the running of the business.

(A) (i) What is an indigenous firm? (5 marks)

    (ii) Discuss the main benefits of indigenous firms to Ireland's economy. Refer to the above passage in your answer where relevant. (15 marks)

(B) (i) In what ways might Magazine Printers Ltd benefit from an external appointment to the position of General Manager? Refer to the above passage where relevant. (15 marks)

    (ii) What criteria should be used when assessing an applicant for the position of General Manager? (15 marks)

(C) (i) Why is it important for a company to introduce new products? (10 marks)

    (ii) Discuss the main sources of new product ideas available to a company like Magazine Printers Ltd. Refer to the above passage in your answer where relevant. (20 marks)

(Total = 80 marks)

23 Foreign Trade

Objectives

The following topics from **Unit 7** of the syllabus are covered in this chapter:

- Is Foreign Trade Necessary for Ireland?
- Barriers to International Trade
- Balance of Trade and Balance of Payments
- Irish Business and International Trade
- Trading Blocs

Is Foreign Trade Necessary for Ireland?

Foreign trade involves the buying and selling of goods and services between countries. Ireland has an open economy, which means that there are no restrictions on the free movement of goods and services with other countries. Ireland is also a member of the European Union. One of its objectives is the free movement of goods, services, labour and capital between member states. Foreign trade is essential for Ireland for many reasons, for example:

1. Ireland must import essential raw materials and finished goods. Such imports are essential for industrial development, e.g. oil, machinery, cars and components.

2. Irish firms must export in order to achieve high sales, high profit and economies of scale. The home market is too small for such economic benefits to be achieved, e.g. Cement Roadstone, Waterford Wedgewood PLC and Kerry Group PLC.

3. Many firms are depending on exports for growth. If exports decline, it could have an adverse effect on both the exporters and the economy, e.g. sales, profits and job security.

> Can you imagine what it would be like in Ireland if there were no imports or exports?

4. Foreign trade provides competition for importers and exporters. There is a wider choice and lower prices for consumers because of the increased efficiency which results from hectic competition.

5. Foreign trade is essential for economic growth, e.g. increased employment and foreign currency coming into the country to pay for exports.

Barriers to International Trade

Free trade between EU member states did not always exist. Before joining the EU, countries protected their industries by imposing restrictions and barriers on foreign trade. Imports were discouraged by the use of tariffs, quotas and embargoes.

Four barriers to Free Trade:
- Tariffs
- Quotas
- Embargoes
- Subsidies

- **Tariffs** are taxes on imports which make them more expensive than home-produced goods. Some non-EU countries use tariffing, e.g. China.

346

- **Quotas** limit the quantity of a particular product which may be imported in a specified period of time. This has the effect of discouraging imports in order to help the sale of domestic goods.
- When imports or exports of certain products are banned, there is said to be an **embargo** on them, e.g. in 1998 the EU placed an embargo on cattle exports from the UK due to 'mad cow' disease.
- **Subsidies**, i.e. financial assistance, can be paid to manufacturers to help them keep selling prices low.

Reasons for Protection of Domestic Industry

In the past, home industry was protected for the following reasons:

1. To enable firms to compete with low-wage countries, e.g. wage rates in the Philippines are low in comparison to European countries.
2. To protect home employment in firms which cannot compete against cheaper imports.
3. To protect the home industry from dumping by foreign competitors. Dumping involves firms selling their surplus stocks in a foreign country, at a much lower price than is charged in their own country.
4. To protect and help the balance of payments. Tariffs provide revenue for the exchequer.

WORKERS PAY PER WEEK

IRELAND = 400€

PHILIPPINES = 10€

This form of protection has gone because of EU legislation.

Balance of Trade and Balance of Payments

Every business should keep proper records of all business transactions. Likewise, every country should keep a record of all its business dealings (total imports and exports) with the rest of the world. This is referred to as the balance of payments.

Balance of Trade

> **→ Definition of Balance of Trade**
>
> *The balance of trade is when the total value of all goods exported (visible goods) is measured against the total value of all goods imported (visible imports) during the same period of time.*

The balance of trade is only related to visible trade, i.e. physical goods. Invisible trade refers to the export of services, e.g. tourism. If the total value of visible exports is greater than the total value of visible imports, there is a surplus in the balance of trade. If the total value of visible exports is less than the total value of visible imports, there is a deficit in the balance of trade.

> **Balance of Trade**
> ↓
> *Visible Exports*
> *less*
> *Visible Imports*

> **EXAMPLE:**
> Visible Exports   €400m
> Visible Imports   €270m
> Trade Surplus   €130m
> There is a surplus in the balance of trade.

Why do Firms export Goods?

Manufacturers export goods for many reasons:

1. Involvement in exports leaves them less dependent on the small home market.

2. Increased sales lead to increased profits.

3. A combination of both home and export sales enables the manufacturer to benefit from economies of scale. This reduces the unit cost of production, so the firm is more competitive and jobs are more secure.

Why are Imports so High?

The bigger the volume of imports, the smaller the surplus and the greater the deficit in the balance of trade. If consumers switched their purchases from imported goods to home-produced goods, there would be an improved balance of trade and more jobs would be created.

Some imports are essential, e.g. essential raw materials, machinery parts and petrol. Some imports are not essential, e.g. biscuits. Non-essential imports exist because consumers like a wider choice and wholesalers/retailers find some imported goods more profitable to sell than home-produced ones.

Balance of Payments

The balance of payments is the total exports less the total imports of a country. The balance of payments relates to both visible and invisible trade. Invisible exports make up the amount of money earned by this country from foreign sources, e.g. tourist revenue and dividends from foreign investments. Invisible imports refer to the amount of Irish-earned currency spent abroad on services, e.g. spending by Irish people holidaying abroad and interest paid by the Irish Government on foreign loans. When the country receives more than it pays out, there is a surplus in the balance of payments. When the opposite is the case, there is a deficit which the Government must make up, e.g. by borrowing.

> **Balance of Payments**
> ↓
> *Total Exports*
> *less*
> *Total Imports*

EXAMPLE:

Visible Exports	€400m
Invisible Exports	€370m
Visible Imports	€270m
Invisible Imports	€270m

Calculate the Balance of Trade and Balance of Payments

Balance of Trade	= Visible Exports	– Visible Imports	= Surplus/Deficit
	= €400m	– €270m	= €130m Surplus

Invisible Exports	€370m
Invisible Imports	€270m
Surplus on Invisible Trade	€100m

Summary: Surplus on the Balance of Trade	€130m
Surplus on Invisible Trade	€100m
Surplus on the Balance of Payments	€230m

The balance of payments is an important barometer of the financial health of the country. In 2004, the Irish Government had a balance of payments surplus of €8bn.

Irish Business and International Trade

The changing scene in international trade will bring both opportunities and challenges (threats) for Irish industry.

Opportunities for Irish Business in International Trade

1. Due to free trade, Irish firms have direct, unrestricted access to the vast European market. This enables firms to expand, diversify and become more profitable. Some Irish firms, e.g. Smurfit PLC, have become transnational companies because of their ability to profitably compete in international markets.

2. The highly-skilled workforce can be employed to enable firms to avail of the benefits of foreign trade.

3. Ireland is an attractive location for foreign industrialists who wish to invest. They recognise the availability of a skilled labour force and Government grants. They also realise that they would have direct access to the huge free trade European market.

4. Economies of scale, i.e. lower unit costs, are possible due to increased production levels. This should enable firms to become more competitive.

Opportunities include:
- Free Trade
- Proximity
- Language
- Culture
- Green Image

349

5. The service sector in Ireland is now aimed at the global market, e.g. IFSC (International Financial Services Centre), software and tourism.

6. It allows Irish agricultural co-ops to sell surplus produce to countries such as Libya.

Challenges for Irish Business in International Trade

1. Because of the severe open competition, only the efficient firms will survive. Jobs will be lost in the inefficient firms, e.g. firms that are not automated.

2. It is necessary to train and retrain the workforce so the firm can avail of the challenges of the changing markets, e.g. language training.

3. Manufacturing and wage costs are much lower in developing countries. Irish manufacturers must maximise output and sustain high quality in order to remain competitive.

> Challenges include:
> • Competition
> • Distribution costs
> • Payment difficulties
> • Economies of scale
> • Quality of product or service

4. Many skilled employees may be attracted to work in mainland Europe, where wage levels are higher. This may force many Irish employers to increase wages in order to keep employees. This extra cost can reduce the ability of firms to compete.

5. Irish exporters may incur bad debts if they give too much credit to some foreign customers.

The Significance of International Trade for Ireland's Economy

1. Each year, almost 70 per cent of Irish exports are to EU countries.

2. Exports account for an average of two out of three jobs in the Irish manufacturing sector. Almost 59 per cent of jobs in the manufacturing industry are dependent on exports.

3. Food exports are essential to the agri-industry if a high surplus on the home market is to be avoided. The agricultural co-ops play an important role in those exports, e.g. Kerry Group PLC.

4. There has been massive growth in the service industry that has led to a huge increase in invisible trade, e.g. tourism, financial services and computer services. Large numbers of highly-skilled people are employed in these services.

5. The open Irish economy is too small to survive without huge exports. Without exports many Irish manufacturers would not be competitive enough to survive in business.

6. Importing provides Irish consumers with a wider choice of products, e.g. Japanese cars, TVs and videos.

7. Irish industry could not function without importing essential raw materials, e.g. timber, steel and machinery.

8. Certain products, e.g. oil and cars, cannot be produced in Ireland, so they have to be imported.

9. Foreign currency is earned, which is used to pay for imports.

Changing Nature of the International Economy

The ongoing changes in the world economy have a major impact on industry in Ireland. The major changes that have affected the Irish economy include the following:

1. The European Union (EU)

Ireland became a member in 1973. Since 1 January 1993, the citizens of the EU have lived in a borderless Europe. The free movement of goods, services, labour and capital has had a massive impact on industry and employment in the member states. The EU has had a big impact on the agri-industry.

European Union

The main objectives of the European Union, which has 25 member countries, include the following:

(a) Free movement of goods, services, labour and capital between member states.

(b) Common barriers to non-member countries.

(c) Common Agricultural Policy (CAP).

(d) Common Fisheries Policy (CFP).

(e) Common currency – the euro.

(f) Common legislation, e.g. consumer laws.

World Trade Organisation

351

2. World Trade Organisation (WTO)

The WTO is a Geneva-based body that polices the world's trading systems. Established on 1 January 1995, the main functions of the WTO are to promote fair trade among its members and to eventually have a worldwide free-trade area, i.e. no trading barriers, quotas, subsidies etc. Only the powerful and efficient firms will survive in this global market. This explains the reasons for the growth of multinational organisations. This development will cause trading problems for labour-intensive firms, e.g. textile producers, who will find it difficult to compete in the free market. Many of them will eventually close down.

Impact of the WTO on Ireland's Economy

(a) Efficient Irish firms, e.g. Kerry Group PLC, do a lot of profitable business with the USA. This is good for their business, sales, profits, share price and for the job security of their skilled workforce.

(b) The open Irish economy has to face hectic competition from other countries.

(c) The reform of the CAP will adversely affect the income of Irish farmers because of the reduction and eventual elimination of subsidies to the agri-industry.

(d) There will be severe competition on the world market for the service industries. In time, this may affect the International Financial Services Centre in Dublin.

3. Multinational Companies

Multinational companies are formed to maintain a competitive position and avail of the opportunities involved in worldwide free trade. Ireland has encouraged the establishment of multinational firms here because of their positive impact on the economy and employment. It is, therefore, more difficult for indigenous firms to compete, unless they can identify niche markets or enter into international alliances or joint ventures.

4. Technology

Modern developments in technology, e.g. the Internet, have made it possible to be involved in high-tech trading. This speeds up communications and decision making.

5. Growth of Pacific Rim Countries

Since 1960, an increasing number of high quality, low-cost products have been manufactured in Asia. Their non-union, low wage levels have enabled them to export their products to the global markets, thus providing growing competition for home industry. Examples of their products include cars, clothing and footwear. In 2004, 30 per cent of all products produced in the world were produced in Asia. Asia is now the engine of growth for the world economy and this has implications for industry in Ireland.

6. Deregulation

The change from State control to free enterprise has had implications for State firms such as VHI and Aer Lingus. This type of organisation now faces severe competition without subsidies from the taxpayer. The existence of the Single European Market has opened the Irish market to real competition.

7. Collapse of Communism

The changing nature of Eastern Europe has created opportunities and challenges for big firms. For example, some Irish firms, e.g. Cement Roadstone, AIB have set up business in Poland.

Trading Blocs

A trading bloc arises when a number of countries agree to form one free trading area for business purposes. They agree to trade amongst themselves without tariffs or quotas, but to have common trade barriers with non-members.

● Examples of Trading Blocs

1.	The European Union (EU) (see Chapter 24)
2.	The World Trade Organisation (WTO)

The Role of the State in Exporting

Enterprise Ireland is a State agency that assists exporters. The assistance it provides includes the following:

1. Advice on how to identify new market opportunities abroad.

2. Advice on how to market products abroad, e.g. trade fairs and trade missions.

3. Advice on the trade regulations that apply in different countries.

4. Advice on how to overcome difficulties facing exporters, for example:
   (a) Documentation involved.
   (b) Choosing a method of payment.
   (c) Language barriers – language specialists may have to be employed.
   (d) Different currencies and changing exchange rates.
   (e) How to assess the credit rating of a customer.

The head office of Enterprise Ireland is in Dublin and it has support offices in 28 major cities worldwide, e.g. London, New York and Sydney.

Marketing assistance is provided for certain industries by the following State Agencies:

(a) Tourism – Fáilte Ireland

(b) Food – Bord Bia (Ireland's Food Board)

(c) Fishing – Bord Iascaigh Mhara (BIM)

Revision of Important Terms	
• European Union	• Visible Trade
• Imports	• WTO
• Exports	• Multinational Companies
• Barriers to Trade	• Deregulation
• Balance of Trade	• Invisible Trade
• Balance of Payments	• Trading Bloc

Exercises

1. (a) Why is foreign trade important for Ireland?

   (b) Give three examples of essential imports.

2. (a) Outline possible barriers to foreign trade.

   (b) Why was industry in Ireland once protected from imports?

3. (a) Explain what is meant by the balance of trade.

   (b)

	January	February
Visible Imports	€1,000m	€1,200m
Visible Exports	€1,300m	€980m

   Calculate: (i) The balance of trade for January

   (ii) The balance of trade for February

   Why do you think the situation changed in February?

4. (a) Why do Irish firms export goods?

   (b) 'Many of the goods imported into Ireland are not required.'

      Do you agree with this statement? Give reasons for your answer.

   (c) What difference would it make if non-essential imports were reduced?

5. (a) Distinguish between the balance of trade and the balance of payments.

   (b) Analyse the significance of both for Ireland's economy.

6. (a) Mention three examples of visible exports.

   (b) Mention three examples of invisible exports.

Visible Exports	€15,000m
Visible Imports	€10,000m
Invisible Exports	€1,200m
Invisible Imports	€9,000m

   (c) Using the figures above calculate:

      (i) The balance of trade (ii) The balance of payments

7. Outline the changing nature of the international economy and its effect on Irish business.

24 The European Union (EU)

The New Europe

> → **The European Union (EU)**
>
> *The EU is the 'new' regional European block of countries, which provides for closer unification of the economic, social and political systems of the Member States.*

Objectives

The following topics from **Unit 7** of the syllabus are covered in this chapter:

- What is the European Union?
- The Institutions of the European Union
- European Union
- Single Union Social Charter
- Common Agricultural Policy (CAP)
- Common Fisheries Policy (CFP)
- European Union Structural Funds (CFP)
- Role of Special Interest Groups

The European Economic Community (EEC) was established in Rome in 1957. The six original members were Belgium, Germany, France, Italy, Luxembourg and The Netherlands. In 1973, Ireland, Denmark and the UK joined.

In 1991, the Maastricht Treaty was agreed and the European Union (EU) was created.
In October 2004, the total membership became 25 when the EU Constitutional Treaty was signed. The 25 member states in the EU are as follows:

The aim of the EU is to enlarge the scope of co-operation among member states.

Existing Members				
1. Belgium	6. The Netherlands	11. Spain	16. Estonia	21. Czech Republic
2. Germany	7. Ireland	12. Portugal	17. Poland	22. Slovenia
3. France	8. The UK	13. Sweden	18. Slovakia	23. Lithuania
4. Italy	9. Denmark	14. Finland	19. Hungary	24. Latvia
5. Luxembourg	10. Greece	15. Austria	20. Cyprus	25. Malta

Following EU enlargement in 2004, the EU now has 25 member states.

The aims of the EU include the following:

1. Free movement of goods, services, labour and capital between member states.

2. Common barriers to non-member countries.

3. Common Agricultural Policy (CAP).

4. Common Fisheries Policy (CFP).

5. Single European currency called the euro.

6. Common legislation, e.g. consumer law and industrial law.

7. The harmonisation of laws in all the member states in order to ensure no competitive distortion in favour of any one member.

8. To project the Union to the rest of the world through a common foreign and defence policy.

Maastricht Treaty

The Treaty on European Union, known as the Maastricht Treaty, was agreed at the European Council at Maastricht in December 1991 and came into effect in November 1993. The following new objectives were agreed:

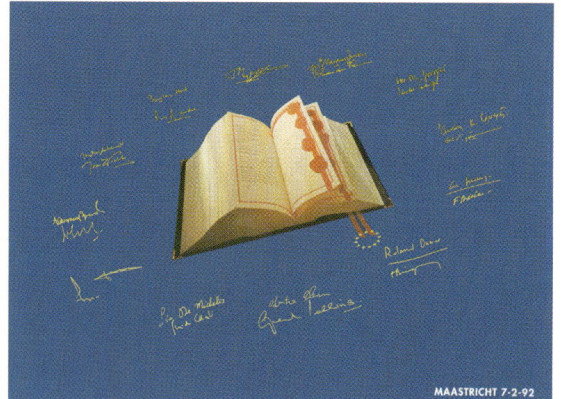

MAASTRICHT 7-2-92

1. A common foreign and security policy, leading eventually to a common defence policy.

2. United economic and monetary systems.

3. A single European market.

4. A charter of social rights.

5. The promotion of economic and social progress, based on free trade throughout the EU.

How Important is EU Membership to Ireland?

The following points clearly highlight the importance to Ireland of being a member of the EU:

1. Industry in Ireland has access to a market of 80 million consumers. Economic growth should continue to increase. This is good for business and employment.

2. Ireland is an attractive location for foreign investors because of accessibility to the huge European market. This explains why many American firms have located in Ireland and have created thousands of jobs, e.g. Intel, Yahoo etc.

3. Irish consumers have the benefit of a wider choice of goods and services at competitive prices.

4. Free trade is beneficial to efficient firms who can compete and expand in the European market.

5. Ireland qualifies for EU grants and loans for the development of the economy, e.g. from The European Investment Bank and The European Structural Fund.

6. The free movement of both capital and labour has benefited the economy. Increased foreign capital investment has helped industry to boom and created thousands of jobs. Many of the jobs are held by people from member states.

EU decisions are made as follows:

1. Proposals for new laws are made by the European Commission.
2. EU Commission proposals are discussed by the European Parliament.
3. Decisions are made by the Council of Ministers.

The Institutions of the European Union

There are six European institutions which play an important role in the operation of the EU:

1.	The European Parliament
2.	The Council of Ministers
3.	The European Commission
4.	The European Court of Justice
5.	The European Court of Auditors
6.	The European Council

There are two community bodies of an advisory nature, i.e. The Economic and Social Committee and the Committee of the Regions. The European Central Bank (ECB) plays a major role in economic and monetary policy.

1. The European Parliament

- The European Parliament is directly elected every five years by the citizens of the member states. It represents the people of the EU. An elected member is called an MEP.

- It has 732 directly elected members, who exercise democratic control at European level.

- Each MEP is a member of at least one of the 20 Euro Parliamentary Committees, which cover areas such as trade, energy, development aid, etc.

- It speaks for its citizens when:

  (a) EU laws are being made.

  (b) EU budgets are being decided.

  (c) EU policies are being implemented.

  (d) EU citizens' rights are at risk.

Role and Functions of the European Parliament (EP)

The role of the European Parliament is to represent the people of the European Union.

The functions of the European Parliament are:

    (a) Legislative

    (b) Budgetary

    (c) Executive control

> *Even though MEPs are directly elected to the European Parliament, the Parliament does not pass legislation. This is known as the Democratic Deficit.*

(a) Legislative

    (i) All proposals for EU legislation and budgets, which are initiated by the European Commission, are sent to the President of the Parliament for discussion and response.

    (ii) The views of the Parliament must be taken into account before new laws or budgets are passed.

(b) Budgetary

    (i) The European Parliament can adopt or reject the annual budget of the EU.

    (ii) It monitors all budgetary expenditure in order to ensure that no money is wasted.

(c) Executive Control

    (i) It has the power to appoint and dismiss the Commission, but not to replace it. In March 1999, the entire European Commission resigned before the Parliament voted to dismiss it. In November 2004, the Parliament refused to ratify the appointment of one of the nominated members, who was eventually replaced.

A sitting of the European Parliament in Strasbourg.

2. The Council of Ministers

- The Council of Ministers is the most powerful institution in the EU. It is made up of 25 members, i.e. one minister from each member state.

- All legislation, proposed firstly by the European Commission and agreed by the European Parliament, must be adopted by the Council of Ministers before it becomes law.

- The Council makes the key economic and political decisions of the EU.

- Unanimous votes of the members are required on important issues, such as taxation policies.

- Each Council member has a right to vote and will use it if the issue under discussion has adverse consequences for the Government and economy that he/she represents.

In 1999, duty-free trading in member-state airports ceased after the decision was agreed by the Council of Ministers.

- The President of the Council is the Minister of the member state currently holding the Presidency of the EU. (Ireland held the EU Presidency for six months in 2004.)

3. The European Commission

The President of the European Commission is chosen by the heads of Government of the member states at a meeting of the European Council. (In November 2004, José Manuel Barroso was appointed President of the European Commission.) Each EU member nominates a member of the Commission. The European Parliament then votes on whether to approve or reject the new Commissioner. In September 2004, the Irish government nominated Charlie McCreevy to be Ireland's European Commissioner. He was given the competition portfolio.

Functions of the European Commission

(a) To implement common policies, e.g. the Common Agricultural Policy (CAP).

(b) To represent European interests common to all member states of the Union.

(c) To represent the EU when conducting international negotiations (e.g. with the World Trade Organisation).

(d) To act as a guardian by ensuring that all EU policy agreements are implemented by member states.

> The European Commission has the authority to impose fines on any business or country that infringes EU rules. Ireland was fined for breaches of agreement in relation to the beef industry. In November 2004, it indicated that legal action would be taken against Greece for providing incorrect data to support its application to join the Euro.

Decisions of the European Commission are taken by simple majority.

The Barruso Commission, 2005 © Audiovisual Library of the European Commission.

4. The European Court of Justice

The European Court of Justice is based in Luxembourg. It is the guardian of all EU laws and treaties, ensuring that they are applied properly throughout the Union. Consisting of 20 judges, the European Court of Justice will give its interpretation of how the laws and treaties should operate. The majority of cases which come before the Court relate to breaches of EU rules relating to free trade.

The role of the European Court of Justice includes the following:

   (a) To supervise the implementation of the provisions of all EU policies.

   (b) To adjudicate on disputes between institutions within the EU, e.g. a dispute between the Council of Ministers and the European Commission.

   (c) To judge on cases which come before it and decide what action is to be taken.

   (d) To settle disputes which could arise in the interpretation and application of the treaties and on all EU legislation.

5. The European Court of Auditors

The Court of Auditors consists of 20 members appointed by the Council for a six-year term. It is responsible for monitoring the management of community finance, i.e. checking that all revenue has been collected and that all expenditure has been carried out in a legal manner. It was established in 1977 and is based in Luxembourg. It checks that all subsidies paid to different member states were justified and properly spent. An annual report is sent to the European Parliament clearly indicating its findings. In July 1999, the Irish Government nominated Máire Geoghegan Quinn to be Ireland's representative in the EU Court of Auditors for the period April 2000–2006.

6. The European Council

The European Council or European Summit is the formal meeting of the Heads of Government of the member states and the President of the European Commission. The Summit has a minimum of two meetings per year, which usually take place in the country currently holding the presidency of the EU. Only important issues affecting the future of the Union and problems facing it are discussed and agreed, e.g. applications for EU membership and foreign policy decisions.

European leaders at the EU enlargement ceremony in Dublin on 1 May, 2004.

European Union Legislation

Every proposal for EU legislation is initiated by the European Commission. The decision-making process is as follows:

1. The Principle of Subsidiarity applies, i.e. the EU will only initiate tasks which are relevant to all the member states and EU institutions, e.g. economic and monetary union.

2. All legislation proposed by the European Commission and agreed by the European Parliament must be adopted by the Council of Ministers before it

can be made law, i.e. the Commission proposes legislation, the Council of Ministers adopts or rejects it.

3. Before adopting legislation, the Council of Ministers will consider the views of the European Parliament.

4. Unanimous voting is required in certain areas, e.g. allowing another country to join the EU.

5. In some cases, a majority vote will be sufficient to pass legislation. This can happen when the Council of Ministers decides to adopt a proposal which was considered on two occasions by the European Parliament. This form of voting is used for legislation relating to the Single Market.

> The Commission proposes legislation
> ↓
> The Council of Ministers adopts or rejects it

All EU laws take precedence over the laws of member states. Each member state implements EU legislation. The following legal instruments are used to ensure the implementation of new EU laws:

1.	Directives
2.	Regulations
3.	Decisions
4.	Recommendations

1. Directives

A directive requires member states to change their national laws to allow for the implementation of EU rules. A directive differs from a regulation in that it is left to each Government to decide how and when to implement a directive. The aim of EU directives is to ensure that identical legislation exists in each member state, e.g. in 1980, an EU directive – the Vredeling Directive – became European Law. This directive requires private companies to publish their accounts. This enables suppliers of goods on credit to find out exact information about the financial position and credit rating of firms they deal with. It also makes it possible to compare businesses in member states.

2. Regulations

These are binding on member states because, in certain areas, it is necessary to have identical laws throughout the EU, e.g. there is an EU regulation making it legal to have a one-shareholder private company with limited liability. The regulations do not have to be made into national laws as they are directly applicable in every member state. The aim of the regulations is to unify laws in member states, e.g. consumer laws.

3. Decisions

Decisions are binding on the party involved in a dispute with the EU, e.g. in 1996, the EU Commission fined Aer Lingus €800,000 because of unfair competitive trading.

4. Recommendations

Recommendations and opinions are not legally binding. They are only a form of advice to the Governments in member states.

Single European Market (SEM)

The existence of the Single European Market (SEM) since 1 January 1993 means that free trade exists throughout the EU. The following measures were implemented to ensure the existence of this barrier-free market:

1. The free movement of goods, persons, services and capital throughout the EU. For example, Irish employees can work in any member state without work permits. Likewise, residents from member states can obtain jobs in Ireland without work permits.

2. The existence of free trade has forced many firms to become more efficient and competitive. Consumers benefit from the lower prices in the competitive market.

3. The harmonisation of tax rates throughout the EU means that the same tax rates apply in each member state, e.g. if the VAT rate on some products in Ireland is 10 per cent, it is also 10 per cent in each EU state. This eliminates any distortion of trade between countries.

4. A Cohesion Fund was set up in 1993 to make huge financial contributions to actions designed to promote cohesion in transport and the environment. Ireland received over €6bn for improvements in roads, airports and harbours and to take steps to reduce the cost of transport.

5. The right of the Irish Government to give all Government contracts to Irish firms was abolished. All Government contracts over €50,000 must be 'put out to tender'. Any European firm can tender for a Government contract, which must then be given to the most competitive firm. This is known as Public Procurement. This change in the granting of Government contracts makes it illegal for the Irish Government to give contracts in order to safeguard jobs in Irish firms.

Impact of the Single European Market on Irish Business

The main changes to Irish business from the SEM include the following:

1. The huge 'Euro' market provides many benefits for Irish firms to expand and become more profitable. Economies of scale are achieved by increased production, which reduces unit costs and makes firms more competitive.

2. The introduction of Public Procurement not only means that firms in other EU states have the right to tender for Irish Government contracts, but also that Irish firms have the right to tender for foreign government contracts. This access to foreign Government contacts puts great pressure on Irish firms to improve all aspects of their design, products and services in order to be able to compete in the barrier-free EU market.

3. Many large businesses from non-EU countries, e.g. Intel and Dell, have located factories in Ireland in order to have access to the barrier-free EU market. These firms have created huge numbers of jobs for the construction industry. The disposable income of many people increased, which has had a spin-off effect on the commercial life of the areas where they are located.

4. The Irish economy has benefited from huge financial assistance from the European Regional Fund, the European Social Fund and the European Structural and Cohesion Fund. The massive amount of money spent on the nationwide infrastructural programme created many thousands of jobs, and improved the network of roads and communication systems. All of these improvements enabled firms to reduce distribution costs and become more competitive.

5. Access to the large EU market has encouraged many profitable firms to invest in research and product development in order to compete abroad. In 1973, Ireland had a trade deficit of €195m with other EU countries. In 1999, Ireland had a trade surplus of €4.9m with other EU countries. This massive impact on the balance of payments has come from the success of Irish firms in the EU market.

Challenges Facing Irish Business because of the SEM

1. Irish-based firms have to compete with large firms offering a service to Irish consumers from their foreign base, e.g. in August 1999 a Scottish-based commercial bank (Bank of Scotland) offered mortgages to Irish people at a lower rate of interest than that charged by Irish banks and building societies. Within two weeks, Irish financial institutions reacted to the new competition by reducing mortgage interest rates below the rate offered by the Bank of Scotland. It is the consumer, of course, who gains from this competition.

2. The inability of Irish firms to secure previously-held contracts from the Irish Government due to Public Procurement can affect their ability to compete

and survive, e.g. on some occasions since 1995, the contract from the Department of Education for the printing of Leaving and Junior Certificate examination papers was given to printing companies in the UK rather than Ireland.

3. Many Irish firms will have difficulty surviving against the hectic competition caused by free trade in the EU. Problems relating to different languages, distribution costs and after-sales

Bank of Scotland headquarters in Edinburgh

service will cost money to sort out. The only realistic solution for some Irish firms to compete and survive is a merger or alliance arrangement.

4. The free movement of labour may attract many Irish employees to work in other EU countries where wage levels are higher. This may force many Irish employers to increase wages in order to keep their employees. Increased wage costs reduce profits and the capability of some firms to compete on both the home and export markets.

European Union Social Charter

The Charter of Fundamental Social Rights of Workers (EU Social Charter) was signed in Strasbourg in 1989. This charter sanctioned the adoption, in all member states, of European directives which stipulated protection standards in many important areas such as working conditions, health, social security, maximum working hours, minimum wages etc. The basic principles of the EU Social Charter are as follows:

1. The right of each person to work in the EU country of his/her choice without requiring a work permit.

2. The right to fair wages, proper working conditions and safety at work.

3. Equal treatment for males and females.

4. The right to social protection.

5. The right to collective bargaining and freedom of association.

6. The protection of children and adolescents.

7. A guarantee of minimum living standards for elderly people.

EU Social Charter Protection standards in:
• working conditions
• health
• social security
• working hours
• minimum wages

Common Agricultural Policy (CAP)

Different member states had different forms of financial support for agriculture. It was decided by the EU that a common development plan for all member states was required. This plan was called the Common Agricultural Policy (CAP).

The word 'agri-business' is used to describe the business of agriculture plus the activities of the other industries which use agricultural output as a source of raw materials.

The products produced by the agricultural industry include milk, butter, baby foods, yoghurt, cattle, poultry, potatoes, sugar beet, wheat and barley.

Objectives

The objectives of the CAP include the following:

1. To increase agricultural productivity and efficiency.

2. To guarantee regular supplies of agricultural products to consumers at reasonable prices in a stable market.

3. To ensure a fair standard of living for those engaged in agriculture.

4. To ensure fair prices for farmers.

5. To have a common level of protection (tariffs) against cheaper imports from outside the EU.

The CAP has been controversial since its inception in 1973 as the agricultural industry has undergone its own revolution. Since 1975, 45 million farmers have ceased farming in Europe. In Ireland, over 150,000 farmers have left the land since 1973. The agricultural market is very important for the Irish economy. It provides industry with essential raw materials and provides full-time employment to over 130,000 farmers. The agricultural industry makes an important contribution to the balance of payments because of its big export market. This guaranteed price support system has been abolished.

Intervention Price

Under the original CAP, farmers were guaranteed minimum prices. If supply exceeded demand, the EU bought the surplus stocks and stored them. The price paid for the surplus stock by the EU was called the intervention price. This guaranteed price support system has been abolished.

New Common Agricultural Policy

From 1 January 2005 a new Common Agricultural Policy was introduced. The new CAP has changed the way that the EU supports the farm sector. The intervention price system, which guaranteed minimum prices to farmers, has been abolished.

The new CAP offers EU farmers the freedom to produce what the market wants. In future, subsidies will be paid independently of the volume of production, i.e. payments have now been de-coupled from production.

By severing the link between subsidies and production, it will make EU farmers more competitive and market-orientated, while providing them with income stablity. More money will be available to farmers for environmental quality or animal welfare programmes by reducing direct payment for bigger farms.

Implications of Changes in the New CAP

1. It will give consumers what they want.
2. It offers taxpayers more transparency.
3. It contributes towards a more market-orientated world farm trade.
4. It allows farmers to become true entrepreneurs.
5. There is now a single farm payment or single payment scheme (SPS) for EU farmers, independent from production.
6. The SPS will be linked to the respect of environmental, food safety, animal and plant health, and animal welfare standards.
7. It is necessary to keep all farm land in good agricultural and environmental condition in order to qualify for the SPS.

Common Fisheries Policy (CFP)

Before Ireland joined the EU in 1973, it was illegal for any foreign trawler to fish within 15 miles (24 km) of the Irish coast. Membership of the EU eliminated such protection for Ireland's fishing industry.

The Common Fisheries Policy is a set of common rules which apply to the fishing industry in each EU member state. It was introduced in 1973. The main provisions in the CFP include the following:

1. To prevent over-fishing, thus preserving fish stocks. This was achieved by the EU stating the quantity of a particular fish that could be caught.
2. To reserve a 19 km fishing zone for each member state's fishing fleets. This rule stopped foreign fishing fleets from over-fishing.
3. Each member state is responsible for enforcing the policy. Severe penalties including fines and confiscation of the fishing vessels can be imposed for breaching the rules.
4. To ensure the economic viability of the European fleets.
5. To protect the marine environment.

6. Under the structure policy of the CFP, grants are available for the construction of new fishing vessels and the modernisation of existing ones. EU funding is also available to modernise port facilities and processing plants.

7. Under its marketing policy, EU standards were introduced to guarantee the quality of fish sold to consumers. A pricing system was introduced to stabilise the income of those working in the fishing industry.

In 2003, the EU confirmed that the 1973 Common Fisheries Poicy was not effective enough in achieving its aims. In particular, it agreed that too many fish were being taken from the sea by fishing, leaving too few adult fish to reproduce and rebuild stocks. Such a situation reduced the income of employees in the industry. It was necessary to introduce changes in order to ensure that the CFP was effective. Some of the changes made in the new Common Fisheries Policy include the following:

1. A better application of the rules, e.g. common sanctions for rule-breakers will help to establish a level playing field throughout the Euro market.

2. A long-term rather than an annual approach to conserving fish stock levels.

3. A new policy for fleets to meet the challenge caused by overcapacity of the EU fleet.

4. A new European Fisheries Fund (EFF) to provide aid to fishermen from 2007 to 2013. This fund will help to finance the changes which are aimed at delivering sustainability to fisheries. The priorities of the new EFF include the following:

   (a) reduction of fishing pressure

   (b) better protection for the marine environment

   (c) processing and marketing of fisheries

The proposed budget for the EFF for 2007–2013 is €4.9 billion. Most of this money will be spent in the new member states.

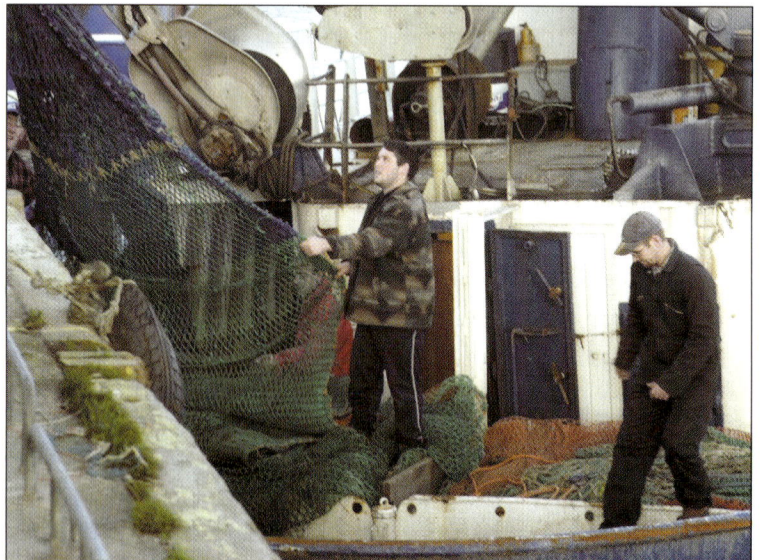

Fishing fleet at dock, Castletownbere, Co. Cork.

European Union Competition Policy

Competition is good for the consumer. Prices are usually lower when competition exists. In September 1999, Ireland's financial institutions all reduced their mortgage rates because of new competition from a Scottish bank. In theory, there is a chance that a large firm will abuse its power, restrict output and maintain high prices. The EU competition policy consists of a set of rules to ensure that there is free and fair competition between all firms in the Single European Market. Article 3 of the Treaty of Rome states that the objective of EU competition policy is to ensure that competition in the EU market is not distorted. Article 85 of the Treaty of Rome outlaws collusive agreements between firms which result in a restriction of competition, i.e. price fixing. Article 86 bans firms from abusing a dominant position, i.e. a large firm using its economic power to prevent effective competition. It is not illegal to achieve a dominant position by being the most successful firm in the market. It is, however, illegal to exploit or abuse the position.

The competition policy of the EU prohibits these practices. Firms who abuse their dominant position or become involved in anti-consumer practices can be fined up to 10 per cent of their annual sales. CRH and other European building firms were fined in this manner.

How can Firms behave in an Anti-consumer Manner?

The following examples relate to anti-consumer behaviour:

1. Forming a Cartel

A cartel is an arrangement where two or more firms agree to curtail the quantity of goods available for sale. This enables these firms to charge high selling prices and earn big profits, e.g. oil.

2. Discriminating Monopoly

This occurs if the goods or services cannot be transferred from one market to another. This means that different prices can be charged to different customers in different areas. This type of situation can only happen when the markets are kept separate.

This is known as a dual pricing policy and means that a firm will charge less in one area to make it difficult for a competitor, whilst in another area the consumer is charged more.

LET'S CURTAIL OUTPUT – KEEP PRICES HIGH...

3. Mergers and Takeovers

The European Commission has the power to prevent or restrict large mergers or takeovers that would restrict competition in the EU. In 1995, the EU investigated the takeover of Quinnsworth by Tesco to make sure that such a deal was not to the detriment of the consumer. It allowed the deal to go ahead. In the early 1990s, Irish Distillers were prevented from taking over Cooley Distillers in Ireland by the Competition Authority. Such a takeover would have given them complete control of the Irish market. In 1999, the EU granted permission for the alliance of Nissan and Renault. The European Commission said that the car market in Europe was very competitive and the alliance posed no threat.

4. Dominant Position

A large firm which abuses its dominant position by manipulating the market to the detriment of the consumer is in breach of EU legislation. In 1996, Greencore was fined €6m by the EU Commission because it abused its dominant position in the Irish sugar market.

Economic and Monetary Union (EMU)

In October 1980, the EU published a report entitled 'One Market, One Monday' about the benefits of economic and monetary union. The EMU was provided for in the Maastricht Treaty in 1991; Ireland joined the EMU in 1999. The adoption of the EMU involved the following:

1. The establishment of a single European currency called the euro and the abolition of each member state's own currency. The value of the Euro is set by the European Central Bank.

2. The setting up of a single monetary policy for the EU. This policy was implemented by the European Central Bank (ECB).

European Central Bank

How does Ireland benefit from the EMU?

The following are the benefits to Ireland from economic and monetary union:

1. Within the EU, the use of the common currency (euro) simplifies financial dealings when exporting. There are no more costs incurred in currency exchanges for business dealings within the single currency area. Exporters to euro customers won't have to worry about being paid in a currency that might fall in value.

2. There is an increase in economic growth and investment because of the reduction of risk and uncertainty caused by currency fluctuations.

3. Inflation and interest rates are similar in member states. This should lead to price and income stability, which is good for the economy as industry should remain competitive and inflation low.

4. Since prices for goods and services in the member states are quoted in the same currency (euro), it is easy for consumers to make a definite comparison and see where the best value is available. This is known as price transparency. This benefits Irish exporters who can quote prices which are cheaper than EU competitors. Consumers also benefit from this information.

5. There can be no devaluation of the euro within the EU by a member state. This is of benefit to exporters and tourists.

European Union Structural Funds

The levels of economic development and unemployment vary among the EU member states. 'Structural funds' is a general title which relates to the financial assistance used to bridge the economic gap between the wealthy and poor regions of the EU.

The reasons for the structural funds include the following:

1. To improve the economic structure of poorer EU regions in areas such as infrastructure, agriculture and industrial development.

2. To promote economic development in areas badly hit by industrial decline.

3. To promote the development of rural areas.

4. To reduce long-term unemployment.

The estimated contribution made to the Structural Funds for Ireland during the period 1994–99 is approximately €5.8bn. The funding from the Structural Funds is allocated to each member state following the submission of a plan to the European Commission.

Different Types of Structural Funds

Four different types of structural fund exist:

1. The European Regional Development Fund (ERDF)

This fund is used to help the very poor regions of the EU by encouraging investment in health, education and enterprise development and improving the infrastructure, e.g. roads. In 1999, 4 per cent of the total investment in the less developed regions of the EU was financed by this fund.

2. The European Social Fund (ESF)

The aim of this fund is to provide extensive financial support for vocational training and retraining to help the long-term unemployed, migrant workers and disabled persons. FÁS receives the majority of its funding from this fund.

3. European Agricultural Guidance and Guarantee Fund (EAGGF)

The aim of this fund is to improve the structures for the processing and marketing of agri-products and to support farm incomes in less developed areas.

4. Financial Instrument of Fisheries Guidance (FIFG)

The aim of this fund is to help the restructuring of the fishing industry by adapting and modernising the fleets and improving port facilities.

Has Ireland benefited from EU Structural Funds?

Ireland was classified as an Objective 1 region, i.e. a region that lagged behind in development. Therefore, the Irish economy benefited greatly from the structural funds. Between 1989 and 1993, Ireland received €3.5bn – this equals €1,000 for every citizen living in the country. This money was spent by the Government on job creation, training, tourism, farming, food-processing and transport infrastructure. Between 1994 and 1999, Ireland received €5.6bn in EU Structural Funds. This money was spent on roads: by-passes, ring roads, dual carriageways and motorways. The Lee Tunnel (Jack Lynch Tunnel) in Cork was financed from these funds. The funding is complemented by public and private sector funding in Ireland for a projected total expenditure of over €10bn.

Jack Lynch Tunnel, Cork

Role of Special Interest Groups

Interest groups are pressure groups who are not elected by the public, but who try to influence those who make decisions, be it at local, national or EU level. These groups have their own agenda and hope to persuade the decision makers that their interests need to be addressed. They want their interests to be reflected in decisions made.

Examples of special interest groups include the following:

1. Irish Congress of Trade Unions (ICTU)

2. Irish Business and Employers Confederation (IBEC)

3. Irish Farmers' Association (IFA)

4. Licensed Vintners Association

5. Irish Hotels Federation

6. Consumers Association of Ireland

How to Influence Decision Makers

Different methods can be used by interest groups to influence EU decisions.

1. Lobby the Irish MEPs, the European Commission and the Council of Ministers to try to influence the outcome of policy making.

2. Set up offices in Brussels with employees based there in order to keep fully up to date with developments. This enables them to react fast to issues that concern them.

3. Use the services of Public Relations (PR) firms to influence public opinions and decision makers.

4. Organise demonstrations and strikes to highlight their serious concerns over the impact of EU decisions on their members.

The EU Constitution Treaty

The EU Constitution Treaty was signed by all 25 heads of Government in Rome on 29 October 2004. This treaty will replace all existing EU treaties when ratified, i.e. it will replace the following:

- The Treaty of Rome 1957, where the six founding members agreed to form a Common Market allowing for free trade between them.
- The Maastricht Treaty 1991, where the single 'Euro' currency was agreed.
- The Single European Act, which promoted the existence of the Single European Market (SEM) from 1 January 1993.

The EU Constitution sets out the EU's values and objectives, its role and powers, its institutions and its decision-making procedures. It includes the following elements:

EU Values and Objectives

The Treaty states that the EU is founded on the the basis of respect for:

• Human dignity	• Justice
• Freedom	• Tolerance
• Democracy	• Non-Discrimination
• Equality	• Pluralism
• Rule of Law	• Respect for Human Rights

Revision of Important Terms	
• European Union (EU)	• Single European Market (SEM)
• EU Objectives	• EU Social Charter
• Maastricht Treaty	• Common Agricultural Policy (CAP)
• Council of Ministers	• Agri-Industry
• European Parliament	• Common Fisheries Policy (CFP)
• Court of Auditors	• Competition Policy
• Court of Justice	• Economic and Monetary Union (EMU)
• European Council	
• Cohesion Funds	• Euro
• Members of the European Parliament (MEPs)	• EU Structural Funds
	• Interest Groups

Exercises

1. (a) Why does the European Union exist?

   (b) Name six countries that are members of the EU.

   (c) When did Ireland join the EU?

2. (a) What are the objectives of the EU?

   (b) What are the aims of the Maastricht Treaty?

3. (a) Why is membership of the EU important to Ireland?

   (b) Outline the work of the European Parliament.

4. Describe the role of each of the following:

   (a) Council of Ministers (b) Court of Auditors (c) European Council

5. (a) What is meant by the SEM?

   (b) Outline three important benefits to business in Ireland of the SEM.

   (c) Describe the functions of the European Commission.

6. (a) Why was the Common Agricultural Policy (CAP) deemed necessary?

   (b) Outline the main objectives of the CAP.

   (c) Why is the CAP important to Ireland?

7. Discuss the Common Fisheries Policy (CFP) and its importance to Ireland.

8. (a) What is the EU competition policy?

   (b) Why is the EU competition policy important?

9. (a) Why is the EMU important to Ireland?

   (b) What are the implications for Ireland of joining the EMU?

10. (a) Why are structural funds important in Europe?

    (b) Name two different types of structural fund.

    (c) How has the Irish economy benefited from the structural funds?

11. (a) How is European law implemented in EU countries?

    (b) What work does the European Commission do?

12. Explain each of the following:

    (a) EU regulations (b) EU directives (c) Euro (d) CAP

13. Explain the importance for Ireland of:

    (a) any two policies of the European Union

    (b) any two institutions of the European Union

14. 'Membership of the SEM brought opportunities and challenges for business in Ireland.' Discuss.

15. (a) How does the decision-making process of the European Union operate?

    (b) Use a diagram to illustrate the decision-making process.

    (c) State two EU policies and outline their importance and impact on Irish business.

16. (a) Why do special interest groups exist?

    (b) What role do special interest groups play in the decision-making process of the EU?

25 International Environment

Objectives

The following topics from **Unit 7** of the syllabus are covered in this chapter:

- Global Business
- Why Do Global Firms Exist?
- Transnational Companies (TNCs)
- Global Marketing
- Information Technology in Globalisation

Global Business

The Single European Market is a huge market with 600 million consumers. All businesses in EU member states have barrier-free access to this market. A major trend in recent decades has been the globalisation of product and service markets.

Globalisation

Globalisation means that the business world is becoming one huge single trading market. Examples of global businesses include the following:

1. Intel – an American company which employs 3,625 people in Ireland and over 80,000 worldwide.

2. Microsoft – an American company with 30,000 employees worldwide.

3. Toyota – a Japanese company with 150,000 employees worldwide.

4. Nike – the largest sports and fitness company in the world.

Characteristics of Global Business

1. It identifies the world market for its standardised product. It then mass produces its products and sells them into both the home and world export markets.

2. The majority of its sales are exports.

3. It benefits from economies of scale (savings) in research, manufacturing, marketing and production as all these activities are planned on a global basis.

4. Its products are globally marketed under a brand name that has worldwide recognition, e.g. Coca-Cola, McDonalds.

5. Its products are globally standardised, e.g. televisions, DVD players, motor cars. Production is flexible to adapt to the needs of different markets, e.g. left- or right-hand drive motor cars.

Factors Giving Rise to Global Companies

Global businesses exist for the following reasons:

1. National markets are too small for some firms. They have standardised products which can be sold throughout the world. If certain firms don't expand, they will miss selling opportunities in other countries.

> Globalisation is a term that refers to the increased competition worldwide between businesses in different countries.

2. The growth in production technology makes mass production possible. Economies of scale that come with the reduced unit cost of mass production mean that firms can compete and expand throughout the world.

3. Institutional investors, e.g. financial institutions, are prepared to invest in large firms which have the potential to establish themselves on the world stage.

4. Companies that want to maximise sales and profits know that this is only possible through worldwide sales.

5. Free trade has eliminated protection for firms. Consumers are demanding a wider choice of goods and services from different countries.

6. Huge improvements in communications worldwide have made it easier to obtain information on goods and services in different countries. The growth of trading on the Internet will have an impact upon businesses, so that location will not be as important as the quality and price of what is sold.

7. Businesses are getting larger due to mergers and alliances. They find it necessary to merge in order to achieve economies of scale in production, promotion and distribution.

8. Political situations have changed, which has enabled big firms to develop new markets in China, Russia, etc.

Globalisation has provided consumers with worldwide choice at lower prices. Firms have to be more efficient and competitive in order to survive. Some firms have merged with foreign firms to succeed in foreign markets. This is one of the reasons for the growth of the multi-sized business, i.e. transnational companies.

Transnational Companies (TNCs)

Transnational companies (multinationals) are big firms that produce and market their products in many countries. They are referred to in business as multinational companies. They produce the products in different countries by setting up fully-owned subsidiary companies that can avail of different wage levels and costs in each country. They also overcome some of the problems of foreign trade such as different languages and currencies.

Example of Irish multinational companies:

- Kerry Group PLC

Example of non-Irish multinational companies:

- Shell

- Nissan

- Nike

Why do Some Businesses become Transnational?

Firms become multinational for a number of reasons which include the following:

1. To be less dependent on one market. By expanding into different countries the business risk is spread.

2. To substantially increase sales and profits. The limited potential in a home market restricts the potential for sales and profits.

3. To manufacture goods in countries like Hong Kong and Poland, where labour costs are very low. It is possible to sell such goods worldwide at profitable prices.

4. To manufacture goods in the market where they will be sold. This greatly reduces warehousing and distribution costs.

5. To overcome the problems of trading barriers, which may exist in some countries and are designed to reduce imports, e.g. the EU has a restriction on the quantity of Japanese cars that can be imported from Japan. To bypass this problem, some Japanese car manufacturers have set up manufacturing facilities in Europe to produce cars for the European market.

6. To avail of the benefits of global standardisation, which is necessary for mass production, e.g. CDs and videos. Global marketing is easier when the products are standardised, e.g. Coca-Cola is a well-known global product. The product is the same whether you buy it in Galway, London or New York. Consumers benefit from global products since the selling price is lower because of savings due to mass production.

● Transnational Companies in Ireland

In March 2005, there were 1,374 foreign-owned businesses operating in Ireland, giving employment to 140,000 people. These large firms were attracted to Ireland for the following reasons:

1. There is access to the huge Single European Market. They can locate a division of their business in Ireland and sell their products into the EU member states.

2. Very attractive grants from the Government are available. Intel received grants in the region of €135m to set up a huge plant in Leixlip, Co. Kildare. In March 2005, Intel employed 3,500 people in its Leixlip plant.

3. The Government offers very attractive tax incentives, originally 10 per cent manufacturing tax, now 12.5 per cent.

4. A highly-skilled workforce is available in Ireland.

5. A very high standard of education exists in Ireland, which is important for high-tech firms.

6. There is a well-developed and improving infrastructure nationwide: telecommunications, roads, etc.

● Impact of Transnational Companies (TNCs) in Ireland

The existence of transnational companies has had a positive effect on the Irish economy. This is borne out by the following:

1. Job Creation
In 2005, 140,000 employees worked for TNCs in Ireland. Unemployment has been reduced, the amount of disposable income has increased and the commercial life of the areas where they are located has improved greatly, e.g. Leixlip in Co. Kildare where Intel is located.

In February 2005, the multinational company Yahoo announced that they were setting up a European operation in Ireland creating 400 jobs.

2. Import Substitution
The domestic manufacture of goods which were previously imported has improved the balance of payments. In some cases, they now source their raw materials in Ireland.

> TNCs in Ireland mean:
> - job creation
> - import substitution
> - increased exports
> - top management
> - job security

This Shell service station is a branch of the Shell multinational.

3. Increased Exports

The growth in Ireland's exports has been linked to the success of the TNCs, whose exports to world markets have greatly improved Ireland's balance of payments through an inflow of foreign currency.

4. Management

They employ top management in order to ensure leadership, top quality training and efficiency.

5. Competition

They are able to resist new competition, so employees have job security.

6. Taxation

TNCs pay 12.5 per cent corporation tax on their profits. In 2004, the Irish Exchequer received over €900m in taxes paid by TNCs. They are also responsible for a huge inflow of PAYE and VAT to the Exchequer.

7. Training

TNCs invest a lot of money in training and developing a skilful workforce.

Risks with Transnational Companies

There are some risks attached to having TNCs in Ireland. They include the following:

1. If they close down their business in Ireland, there are serious social implications, e.g. mass unemployment. Cheaper manufacturing and labour costs in low-wage, developing countries may attract them to relocate to those countries, e.g. Hong Kong and Poland, where wage costs are 60 per cent cheaper than in Ireland.

2. They may abuse their powerful position by demanding extra grants and tax concessions to remain in Ireland.

3. They repatriate their profits to their home country. This means that their profits are not reinvested in the host country. This is referred to as the 'black hole' of the economy and is bad for the balance of payments.

4. They provide severe competition for indigenous firms because of their greater resources in marketing and production. In some cases, the indigenous firm is taken over or forced to close down due to its inability to compete.

Global Marketing

Global marketing, i.e. international marketing, involves marketing a firm's products throughout the world as if it is in one market. It involves using the same brand name, e.g. Coca-Cola. Global marketing is more difficult than home marketing due to major differences in language, culture and legislation. Global marketing will only succeed when there is global standardisation of consumer products, e.g. McDonalds has the same brand identity for its products worldwide.

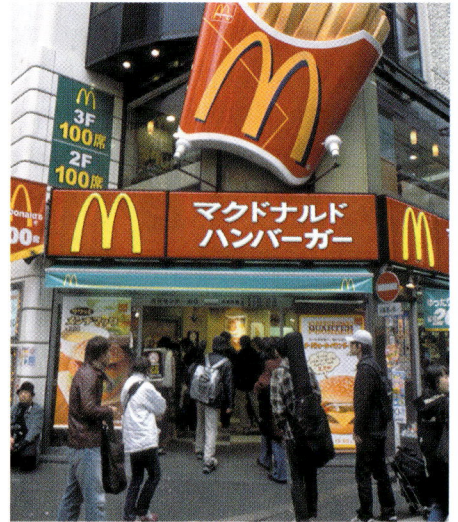

McDonalds' products are the same the world over.

Benefits of Global Marketing to a Business

The following are some of the benefits of international (global) marketing to business:

1. There is no reliance on sales from one market. A drop in sales in one country can be offset against an increase in sales in other countries.

2. Mass production is practical in that the economies of scale reduce unit costs, thus increasing the competitiveness of the global business.

3. International marketing involves visits to foreign markets, personal participation in trade fairs and a good working relationship with distributors. All this activity improves marketing contacts and skills and this is good for global business.

4. The potential size of the global market is much bigger than the home market.

5. It enables a business to be better able to compete with foreign competition in the home market.

6. There is a huge increase in the brand recognition of the firm's products.

Problems in the Global Market

Global growth is good for sales and profits, but global firms encounter problems in the global market that do not exist in the home market. These problems include the following:

1. Additional costs can be incurred in meeting the problem of language. Language specialists may have to be employed and catalogues, order forms etc. may need to be available in different languages.

2. The cultural, legal and political systems in some countries are totally different and this must be understood by the management in the group head office. In time, some of these problems will cease to exist due to the existence of Euro legislation which will be common in all member states.

3. Currency differences and exchange rates have to be taken into consideration when evaluating the cost and value of a foreign-based company in the group. The existence of the Euro will eliminate this problem in the huge Euro market.

4. The management of foreign-based companies is locally situated. Problems can arise if head office policy conflicts with 'local' customers.

5. Due to severe international competition, a global firm may have to reduce its selling price in the foreign markets.

Global Marketing Mix

A vital factor in the success of a global firm is its ability to develop a standardised product. Global marketing involves marketing a firm's products in the world market. A global firm must develop a global marketing mix in relation to the product, price, promotion and place.

> In some cases, it may be necessary to adapt the marketing mix in order to meet the requirements of different customers.

The Global Product

1. This is the standardised product which is mass produced.

2. It can be sold throughout the world because of its brand recognition.

The Global Price

1. Even though the selling price may vary in different countries, it is always seen as fair value by the consumers.

2. The reasons for the non-standardisation of the selling price include the following:

   (a) Different VAT rates

   (b) Distribution costs

   (c) Lack of competition

The Global Promotion

1. This involves informing customers in the global markets of the availability of the products.

2. International TV advertising and sponsorship of major world sports events are costly but effective ways for global firms to promote themselves in mass markets.

● The Global Place

1. This refers to the role of those involved in the channels of distribution.

2. A global firm will use some of the following channels when distributing its goods:

   (a) Manufacturer to the customer, i.e. direct exporting and delivery to the buyer (importer).

   (b) Manufacturer to an agent who is responsible for selling their goods in an agreed area.

   (c) Manufacturer sets up a subsidiary company or branch to sell its products in a country. The locally based operation is responsible for marketing and distribution (and sometimes for producing the product).

Role of Information Technology in Globalisation

Information technology has facilitated the development of global businesses in many ways, for example:

1. It makes it possible for business to directly access information from different parts of the world market. This can be done using IT methods, i.e. video-conferencing and e-mail.

2. Video-conferencing has become a very effective way to facilitate 'link-up' discussions with the management of companies in different countries. The success and effectiveness of this link makes it easier for group management policy to be explained and implemented.

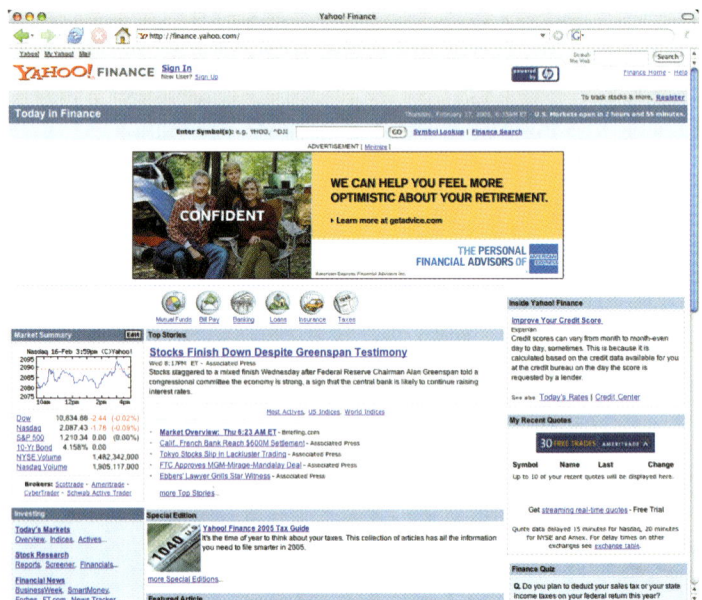

Firms can reach a worldwide audience by advertising on the Internet (The Net).

3. The management in the global head office can be instantly updated on market information from each of its worldwide companies. Important information on sales, trends in sales, market share, profits etc. can be sent from each branch to the group head office daily.

Revision of Important Terms	
• Global Marketing	• Transnational Companies
• Global Business	• Import Substitution
• Global Standardisation	• International Marketing

Exercises

1. (a) What is a global business? Give two examples.

    (b) Why do firms want to become global?

2. (a) What is a transnational company?

    (b) Why do transnational companies invest in Ireland?

3. (a) Why are transnational companies important to Ireland's economy?

    (b) How do firms benefit from international marketing?

4. What problems would a transnational company encounter in the world markets that it would not encounter in its home market?

5. (a) Explain what is meant by the following:

    (i) global business

    (ii) global marketing

    (b) What are the characteristics of a global business?

6. State and explain the components of the marketing mix for a global business.

Applied Business Questions
for Units 5, 6, 7
Leaving Certificate 2008 and 2013

Applied Business Question
Based on units 5, 6 and 7 for Leaving Certificate 2008/2013

CLI-HE LTD (LEAVING CERTIFICATE 2003)

Cli-He is a new brand name in the children's toys and games business. The name is also that of a new business venture that Clodagh has recently established. An engineering graduate with a flair for design, she has, to her credit, won two innovation awards for product development in recent years. Clodagh sees a bright future for a business with original ideas in the growing children's leisure business. The challenges of setting up a new business venture are, however, very significant, especially where to find the necessary resources and expertise.

Clodagh plans to market the Cli-He brand to a niche segment of the 'green' market. This niche market is made up of environmentally conscious consumers, with high disposable income, who have young families. The price of Cli-He products will reflect this environmental premium but the price range will not, however, be as high as its competitors' products.

Clodagh plans that the business will be environmentally conscious in all its production methods and will use raw materials that are sensitive to the environment. Its marketing will make this green range image clear to customers. The Irish base for this new business start-up has been agreed with Enterprise Ireland. Future plans include marketing its products in Europe, the United States of America and other parts of the world through the use of the Internet. Clodagh feels that online trading is the way of the future and is a suitable way to market her new product range to the target market.

(A) Analyse **one** short-term and **one** long-term source of finance available for the Cli-He start-up. (30 marks)

(B) Describe how Clodagh can ensure that **Cli-He** is an environmentally conscious company. (30 marks)

(C) Discuss the challenges facing **Cli-He** in developing markets abroad. Refer to the above text in your response. (20 marks)

(Total = 80 marks)

Applied Business Question
Based on units 5, 6 and 7 for Leaving Certificate 2008/2013

IRISH GLUE PRODUCTS LTD

Irish Glue Products Ltd has been in existence since 1945 as a manufacturer and supplier of glues and solvents for household and industrial use. Due to its existence for over 50 years, the firm operates from a large industrial site in the centre of Dublin, a site which is now surrounded by residential and retail developments. For this reason, the management of IGP have always shown great concern for the local environment, with environmental considerations always to the fore when making business decisions. The firm has for over 20 years operated an environmental committee, which includes not only the managing director of the company, but also four representatives of local community groups.

IGP have recently been approached by International Solvents Inc., a large transnational producer of glues and solvents, with a view to opening discussions on a possible merger. The larger company is very interested in some of the successful products produced by IGP and believes that they could be successfully sold on the global market. Senior management favour such a move, but are concerned about the short-term implications of a merger, once control over decision making is taken away from local level. They are particularly concerned about possible job losses among their loyal staff and the difficulties which the staff may experience working with new managers brought in following the merger. These, as well as the possible effect on motivation and staff morale, must be weighed against the access to new markets, top-class management and greater finance which the merger will provide.

International Solvents Inc. was set up in 1990 and since then has grown into a truly global business with business interests in over 18 countries worldwide. The firm's brands are internationally recognisable and have global appeal. The firm is characterised by a very strong management structure which places a huge importance on the use of technology within their business, as well as excellent communications structures, both within and between all parts of the organisation.

(A) List the characteristics of an environmentally conscious firm in the running of a company such as IGP Ltd. Refer to the example of IGP Ltd in your answer. (20 marks)

(B) What are the main short-term implications to a firm of expansion through merger? (20 marks)

(C) Analyse the reasons why a firm would became a global business. What do you feel are the ingredients for global success? Refer to what you know about International Solvents Inc. in your answer. (40 marks)

(Total = 80 marks)

Applied Business Question
Based on units 5, 6 and 7 for Leaving Certificate 2008/2013

CELLTECH LTD

Established in 1991, Celltech Ltd are currently ranked third largest producer of mobile telephones in the world. They have recently launched on the global market the most modern mobile handset in their range – the Celltech C4. The firm is confident that sales of this product will help the company to become the leading producer of mobile handsets within two years. The Celltech C4 will be sold through a network of independent mobile-phone retailers, as well as in video shops and discount electrical stores. Retailing at €79.99, the mobile phone comes with €30 free call credit, free text alerts and a choice of 30 ring tones. The company has no industrial relations problems and staff turnover and absenteeism is never an issue.

Over the last number of years, Celltech have come under increasing pressure, from community and environmental groups worldwide, to address the issues surrounding the dangers to public health of mobile telephone masts. In response, the company has invested over €1m in researching safer operating systems, as well as researching the impact, if any, of mobile telephone technology on health. This firm has an annual research budget to enable it to keep abreast of all IT developments worldwide. In addition, the firm has come under pressure to supply hands-free kits with every telephone sold, as a step toward reducing accidents caused by people operating mobile phones while driving or walking. Only packaging that can be recycled is used by this firm.

From its headquarters in the United States, where key management executives are based, and its manufacturing plants in Ireland and Spain, Celltech telephone products are sold in 30 countries worldwide. However, despite selling a product with global appeal in a world where people demand the latest and fastest forms of information and communications technology, Celltech have not always found the path of expansion smooth. New foreign markets, though profitable, have presented Celltech management with many problems, both business and cultural along the way. Highly paid linguists and financial controllers are employed in head office to resolve the business problems. Ongoing research is necessary in order to enable the marketing department to be aware of the requirements in the different markets.

(A) With reference to the passage above, analyse the marketing mix for the Celltech C4. (20 marks)

(B) Identify the social responsibilities facing companies today. Make reference to the information contained in the text about Celltech Ltd where appropriate. (30 marks)

(C) Analyse the elements which are essential for the global success of Celltech. In your answer, refer to the problems which expansion may bring to a global business like Celltech. Refer to the information in the ABQ where relevant. (30 marks)

(Total = 80 marks)

Applied Business Question
Based on units 5, 6 and 7 for Leaving Certificate 2008/2013

CEMAC LTD

Cemac Ltd was set up in 1989 by Colm and Edward MacCarthy and, since then, has built itself up to be a major force in the clothing industry. One of the first business decisions the two brothers came to, was to agree on how the new business would be formed and structured. In this regard, neither had any hesitation in deciding to set up a limited liability company. Both believed that an essential element in the long-term success of the business would be its ability to attract top calibre management and staff, and its ability to raise adequate equity finance when needed. They were both aware of the protection benefits of limited liability: in the event of bankruptcy, shareholders cannot be personally sued, although the corporate legal entity can be sued.

Colm MacCarthy's background and training is in accountancy and he is very aware of the importance of good working capital management to a firm like Cemac. Despite the highly competitive environment in which they operate, where selling on credit is a necessity, Colm will only sell on credit to creditworthy customers. Similarly, once a sale is made, ensuring that debtors pay the amount they owe on time becomes a priority for Cemac Ltd, so that creditors/wages can be paid when due.

At a recent meeting of the company board, a lot of consideration was given to the idea of Cemac selling their goods overseas, particularly through the use of their website. Whereas the opportunities presented to the firm by international trade in the form of larger markets, relaxed trading regulations, bigger production output and reduced production costs are obvious to everyone, some board members are concerned about the firm's ability to stand up to the challenges which such a move would present. The absence of any foreign language skills among the existing sales staff, as well as the prohibitive cost of distribution, were two such challenges mentioned at the last meeting.

(A) Analyse the benefits, which Cemac Ltd derive from their status as a limited liability company. In your answer, refer to the points made in the text.   (20 marks)

(B) Why is good working capital management important to a firm? How can Cemac ensure that they manage their working capital well? Refer, where relevant, to the text in your answer.   (20 marks)

(C) Discuss the main opportunities and challenges which international trade will present to Cemac Ltd. Refer to the information contained in the passage when formulating your answer.   (40 marks)

(Total = 80 marks)

AGM	Annual General Meeting	IFA	Irish Farmers Association
APR	Annual Percentage Rate	IFSC	International Financial Services Centre
AOB	Any Other Business	IG	Interest Group
ATM	Automatic Teller Machine	ISO	International Standards Organisation
BEP	Break-even Point		
BIK	Benefit-in-Kind	JIT	Just-in-Time
CAP	Common Agricultural Policy	LRC	Labour Relations Commission
CEB	County Enterprise Board	MBI	Management Buy-in
CFF	Cash Flow Forecast	MBO	Management Buy-out
CFP	Common Fisheries Policy	MNC	Multinational Company
CPI	Consumer Price Index	PAYE	Pay As You Earn
EA	Equality Authority	PLC	Public Limited Company
EAT	Employment Appeals Tribunal	PPS	Personal Public Service Number
ECJ	European Court of Justice	PR	Public Relations
EDI	Electronic Data Interchange	PRO	Public Relations Officer
EFF	European Fisheries Fund	PRSI	Pay Related Social Insurance
EMU	European and Monetary Union	R&D	Research and Development
EPOS	Electronic Point of Sale	ROCE	Return on Capital Employed
ERDF	European Regional Development Fund	ROI	Return on Investment
ESF	European Social Fund	SEM	Single European Market
HRM	Human Resource Management	SWOT	Strength, Weakness, Opportunity, Threat
IBEC	Irish Business and Employers Confederation	TNC	Transnational Company
		TQM	Total Quality Management
ICT	Information and Communications Technology	VAT	Value Added Tax
		WCM	World Class Manufacturing
ICTU	Irish Congress of Trade Unions	WTO	World Trade Organisation
		WWW	World Wide Web

Definitions

Acid Test Ratio

(a) This ratio is used to assess the liquidity position of a firm.

(b) It is calculated by finding current assets – stock : current liabilities. A ratio of 1:1 is seen by interested parties (management, creditors, bank etc.) as satisfactory.

(c) It is a more severe test than the working capital ratio, which shows a firm's ability to pay debts as they fall due. This avoids having to 'lean on the trade'.

Acquisition

(a) This is a costly form of business growth.

(b) It involves a firm taking over another firm by purchasing the majority or all of its shares.

(c) It is often used by firms who want to expand into a foreign market. By taking over a firm which is already in that foreign market, they achieve external growth by acquisition. If a firm acquires a firm in a similar business, it is called a vertical acquisition.

Actuary

(a) This is a specialist employed by an insurance company.

(b) The function of the actuary is to assess the risk to be accepted by the insurer.

(c) The actuary then decides what premium should be charged to the insured. The greater the risk, the higher the premium.

Accounting Ratios (also called Ratio Analysis)

(a) These are ratios used to assess the viability or trading performance of a business.

(b) Important ratios are used to assess the profitability and liquidity of a business. These ratios are calculated from the figures in the Trading Profit & Loss Account and Balance Sheet, hence they are called accounting ratios.

(c) Different parties are interested in different ratios: shareholders are interested in the return on their capital (ROC), while creditors are interested in the liquidity position (i.e. will they be paid on time?) and will look at liquidity ratios such as the working capital ratio and the acid test ratios.

(d) Trends can emerge from the comparison of ratios over a period of time. This can give a clearer picture of the situation, e.g. if the working capital ratio falls from 2:1 in 2004 to 1:1 in 2005, then a continuation of this trend would indicate that the business will have a liquidity problem in 2006.

Agenda

(a) This is a document sent by the secretary of a particular organisation (company, club etc) to all members who are entitled to attend a forthcoming meeting.

(b) It should be sent on official stationery and will state the business proposed to be carried out at a meeting and the order in which it will be done.

(c) It mentions the location, date and time of the meeting and is signed by the secretary.

Agri-Business

(a) This term is used to describe the business of agriculture, as well as the other industries which use agricultural output as a source of raw material.

(b) Products produced by 'agri-business' include milk, sugar, beef and potatoes.

(c) The 'agri-industry' is controlled by the Common Agricultural Policy (CAP) of the EU.

Annual General Meeting (AGM)

(a) Every company, club and organisation holds a special yearly meeting called the AGM. It is a legal requirement for companies to hold an AGM, which all shareholders are entitled to attend. Shareholders are also entitled to speak and vote on issues under discussion.

(b) The purposes of the AGM of a company include the following:

- To enable the directors to explain to the shareholders the financial position of the firm, profits made and the dividends to be proposed.

- To allow shareholders to cross-examine the directors regarding the firm's performance.

- To facilitate the election by the shareholders of the board of directors for the coming year.

Annual Percentage Ratio (APR)

(a) This is the true cost of credit to the consumer and is expressed as an annual percentage of the amount of credit granted by a financial institution.

(b) The APR takes into account:

(i) The interest charged on the loan (called the Flat Rate %).

(ii) Additional costs, e.g. insurance, which have to be taken out with the loan.

(c) By law, all financial institutions must advertise their APR. This allows the consumer to shop around and compare the different APRs available from different financial institutions. A difference of 1 per cent on a €100,000 mortgage would save a person €1,000 p.a. in interest repayments – it pays to shop around.

Arbitration

(a) Arbitration is a way of resolving conflict when both parties to the dispute request a third party to make a decision on the issue. Both sides have agreed in advance to accept this decision.

(b) Many commercial contracts, e.g. a contract to build a house, contain an arbitration clause in order to resolve any major conflict.

(c) Arbitration resolves a conflict quickly without either side incurring high legal costs.

Articles of Association

(a) This document sets out the internal rules and regulations of a company. A model set of Articles of Association called Table A is included in the Companies Acts.

(b) Clauses included in the Articles of Association include:

 (i) Amount of authorised share capital.

 (ii) Voting rights with different classes of shares.

 (iii) Procedure for electing and replacing directors.

 (iv) Procedure for calling meetings of shareholders.

(c) It is one of the documents which has to be registered with the Companies Registration Office when a company is being formed.

Autocratic Leadership

(a) With this style of leadership, instructions and decisions are issued from top management (Managing Director [MD] or Chief Executive [CE]) with no opportunities for subordinates to have a say in decision making.

(b) Instructions are implemented without discussion or query.

(c) No matter how efficient an individual is, it is important for managers to encourage teamwork and goodwill between the staff. This will be difficult to achieve if the 'real boss' is a dictator.

Average Clause

(a) Average clause applies when a partial loss occurs because the risk is underinsured. In the context of the principle of indemnity, average clause is very important.

(b) If property which is worth €200,000 is only insured for €150,000, it is in fact underinsured by 25 per cent. If fire caused damage valued at €60,000, then the insurer will only pay 75 per cent compensation to the insured. The balance of 25 per cent is a loss to be borne by the insured.

(c) The following formula is used to calculate the amount of compensation to be paid where the average clause applies:

$$\frac{\text{Amount Insured}}{\text{Value on Date of Loss}} \times \text{Amount of Partial Damage Caused}$$

Balance of Payments

(a) This is the income and expenditure account of a country. It is a record of the difference between a country's total exports and total imports for the same time period.

(b) Total exports = visible exports (goods) plus invisible exports (services, e.g. tourism).

Total imports = visible imports plus invisible imports

Total Exports	=	€9,000m
Total Imports	=	€5,000m
Surplus on Balance of Payments	=	€4,000m

(c) The balance of payments is an indicator of how an economy is performing. A surplus on the balance of payments is a sign that the economy is booming: the income from foreign currency is greater than expenditure.

Balance of Trade

(a) This is the balance when the total value of all goods exported is measured against the total value of all goods imported during the same time period. It is concerned with visible trade only.

(b) If the total value of goods exported is greater than the total value of goods imported, the balance is a surplus on the balance of trade:

Visible Exports	=	€5,000m
Visible Imports	=	€3,000m
Surplus on Balance of Trade	=	€2,000m

Balance Sheet

(a) This is a statement of the financial position of a business on a specified date (e.g. 01-04-2005).

(b) The purpose of a balance sheet is to show the firm's assets and liabilities. Assets are divided between fixed assets (e.g. buildings) and current assets (e.g. stock). Liabilities are divided between current liabilities (e.g. creditors), long-term liabilities (e.g. debenture loans) and the share capital plus reserves.

(c) By analysing the balance sheet, it is possible to find out if the business is overtrading or highly geared.

Batch Production

(a) This is where identical goods are produced in batches of certain quantities and transferred to the warehouse in anticipation of being sold, e.g. bakery producing bread, cakes etc.

(b) Production must be carefully planned so as to produce the different batches required on time. The constant stopping and restarting of machinery makes this an important task.

(c) Semi-skilled workers can be employed in this form of production. Batch production is practised by the majority of industrial firms of medium size, which means that a wide range of products are produced in this manner, e.g. shoes and clothes.

Benchmark

(a) An important way of measuring ongoing improvement is benchmarking.

(b) Benchmarking involves measuring and evaluating the quality of a firm's goods, services or procedures against the best performing competitor.

(c) Benchmarking enables a firm to know where it stands competitively in its industry and provides management with targets. In a highly competitive industry, the target should be to become the best in the industry with TQM and zero defects.

Benefit-in-Kind (BIK) (also called Fringe Benefits)

(a) This is a way of rewarding employees with benefits additional to their wages.

(b) They are given to employees as a way of recognising their loyalty and contribution to the firm and as a way of improving morale and job status.

(c) BIKs can be monetary (e.g. pension, profit-sharing scheme) and non-monetary (e.g. company car, gift, holiday etc.).

Brainstorming (Meetings)

(a) Often referred to as 'Think Tank' meetings, brainstorming involves the meeting of a group of people to discuss wide-ranging ideas relevant to the future of the business.

(b) The organiser (e.g. MD) will outline the objective of the meeting and ask those present to be creative, objective and wide-ranging in their comments.

(c) It is hoped that from the different comments and suggestions made by those present, some new ideas will emerge that may help to solve existing problems and provide guidelines for new developments.

Branding

(a) A brand is a name, term, design, symbol or feature that clearly distinguishes one seller's goods or service from another's.

(b) A brand name may be a product's only unique characteristic – without it consumers may have difficulty recognising it.

(c) From the viewpoint of consumers, brand names simplify shopping, guarantee an acceptable quality level and enable the consumer to express their preference. Consumers who continually buy the same branded goods are expressing brand loyalty, e.g. Coca-Cola and Polaroid.

Break-Even Analysis

(a) The objective of preparing a break-even analysis is to find out what level of sales is required for a business to be neither making a profit nor incurring a loss, i.e. where total revenue = total costs (i.e. fixed costs + variable costs).

(b) Management should know what the break-even point is. This information is important when making decisions on price increases or reductions.

(c) If variable costs increase (e.g. price increase of 10 per cent for raw materials), management will want to assess the impact this will have on the break-even situation. Management may decide to obtain the raw materials from a cheaper source or buy in the product rather than produce it.

Buffer Stock

(a) Buffer Stock is the name given to the minimum level, below which stocks should not fall.

(b) The existence of a buffer level should ensure that a firm will not lose sales if there is an increase in demand from consumers.

(c) The size of the buffer level will depend on the normal lead time, the normal sales level, the cost of the goods, the storage space available and the nature of the product (e.g. fashions change).

Business Alliance (also called Strategic Alliance)

(a) A business alliance is where two or more firms jointly co-operate for mutual benefit, i.e. all parties increase profits as a result of the arrangement.

(b) Each party to the alliance retains its independence and identity, but as a group they 'pool their resources' for mutual gain, e.g. in 1999 Kodak and Fuji formed an alliance in order to share research and development costs for the production of a new camera film cartridge. This arrangement meant that costs could be shared and controlled rather than increased.

(c) An alliance is easy to establish and dissolve, it will only succeed when there is trust on all sides.

Business Ethics (or Ethical Business Practice or Behaviour)

(a) Business ethics relate to a management policy which is used as a gauge in deciding whether the behaviour of those in the firm is right or wrong.

(b) Ethical behaviour refers to behaviour that conforms to generally accepted standards.

(c) Every business should have a Code of Ethics, i.e. a clear guideline as to what is acceptable behaviour, e.g. is it ethical for a sales manager to own shares in a competing company? Is there a conflict in such a situation?

Business Plan

(a) A business plan is prepared by management. The aim of the plan is to prepare for the future. In preparing the plan it may be necessary and helpful to prepare a SWOT analysis.

(b) The contents of a business plan should answer three important questions:

  (i) What are the goals of the business?

  (ii) What strategy should be adopted to achieve the stated goals?

  (iii) How can these strategies be implemented?

(c) The existence of a business plan will benefit management when seeking finance from a bank or State agency.

Cash Flow Forecast (CFF)

(a) A cash flow forecast should be prepared both by a business and a household.

(b) The purpose of a cash flow forecast is to project future revenue and expenditure in order to ascertain the future liquidity position.

(c) By preparing a cash flow forecast, a firm can determine when there will be a shortfall in the future and when additional finance will be required to meet commitments.

Caveat Emptor

(a) 'Let the Buyer Beware' – this is an implied term in contracts of sale.

(b) The existence of consumer legislation such as the Consumer Information Act 1978 has strengthened the rights of consumers.

(c) The buyer is responsible for ordering the correct product and must act in a responsible manner when making a binding decision. A change of mind by a consumer after buying a non-defective product does not give that person the right to a cash refund.

Chain of Command

(a) This is a management structure within a firm which allows for the passing of instructions from superiors to subordinates.

(b) In a line management structure, the MD has authority over each department. The chain of command eliminates bottlenecks, prevents management from being overloaded and, therefore, creates an environment where the firm can be managed efficiently.

Code of Practice

(a) A code of practice is a collection of agreed rules which are to be followed when dealing with specific issues.

(b) Many firms have a Consumer Code of Practice and this code is the policy of the firm when dealing with customers. The existence of this code should provide the customers with a satisfactory service and hopefully will result in consumer loyalty.

Collective Bargaining

(a) This is where employers and unions negotiate wage increases and conditions of employment.

(b) When an agreement is reached, it is called a collective agreement. The agreement is voluntary, so it is not legally binding.

Commercial Sponsorship

(a) This is where finance or materials for an event are provided by a firm. The event is organised by some organisation, which often seeks out this sponsorship.

(b) If financial support (sponsorship) is given, the firm (sponsor) receives publicity for its product or service in return.

(c) Sponsorship is commonly associated with sporting events.

Common Agricultural Policy (CAP)

The objectives of the CAP include:

(a) Increased agricultural productivity and efficiency.

(b) Free agri-trade between member countries.

(c) Guaranteed regular supplies of agri-products to EU consumers at reasonable prices.

(d) A fair living standard for those engaged in agriculture.

(e) Allowing EU farmers the freedom to produce what the market requires.

(f) Payments to farmers which have been de-coupled from production.

Common Fisheries Policy (CFP)

The objectives of the CFP include:

(a) To prevent over-fishing in Irish waters, thus ensuring adequate stock levels.

(b) To ensure that consumers have regular supplies of fish at reasonable prices.

(c) To guarantee a future livelihood for those working in the fishing industry.

Community Enterprise

(a) This involves undertaking projects in order to develop the commercial life of a local community.

(b) It is achieved through the activities of community-based groups, e.g. Community Councils. They provide finance, advice and support to help projects start up.

(c) Local enterprise is set up to provide jobs (part-time/full-time) in a local area and help develop the local economy.

(d) LEADER Plus and County Enterprise Boards are examples of Government initiatives to develop local enterprise.

Concentrated Marketing

(a) This is where a firm targets a specific market for its product or service by creating and maintaining one marketing mix.

(b) The main advantage of having a strategy of concentrated marketing is that it allows a firm to specialise and concentrate on servicing its target market. It also enables a firm to get the maximum return from its limited marketing resources.

Conciliation

(a) Conciliation is a voluntary attempt by a third party to resolve a conflict by hearing the submissions of both sides and making a recommendation to settle the issue.

(b) One of the functions of the Labour Relations Commission is to provide a Conciliation Service to resolve industrial relations conflicts.

Consideration

(a) This is the price agreed by the parties to a legally binding contract.

(b) The consideration must be real and, in practice, money is the normal form of consideration.

(c) The consideration must be specific and, even though it is accepted, it does not have to be adequate, e.g. X offers to buy Y's house for €150,000. Y accepts the offer. €150,000 is the consideration. As Y accepted the offer from X, an auctioneer's opinion that Y should have received €180,000 is not relevant.

Contract

(a) A contract is an agreement enforceable by law.

(b) A contract exists when the parties, who have the legal ability to make a contract, conclude an agreement that is enforceable by law.

(c) Essential elements must be present to have a valid contract, i.e. offer, acceptance, consideration, capacity, intention and consent. The existence of all the elements are necessary before a contract can be agreed, signed and enforced.

Contribution

(a) If there is over-insurance because a risk is covered with two insurers, the principal of indemnity applies.

(b) The insured is only entitled to recover the full value of the loss suffered and is not allowed make a profit from the loss.

(c) If one insurer pays out in full, this insurer is entitled to recover a certain amount of the pay-out from the other insurer, this is known as the contribution.

Corporate Strategy

(a) This is an action plan that sets out how a firm will achieve its stated objectives.

(b) The strategy may involve reducing selling prices in order to be more competitive and resist competition. Alternatively, the strategy may involve the development of an export market to ensure that the firm is not over-reliant on the home market.

Data Protection Act 1988

(a) This Act was brought about as a result of issues arising from the increased amount of information about individuals which is being kept on computer.

(b) The Data Controller is responsible for ensuring that information which is held on computer disk is accurate, up to date and only retained for as long as necessary.

(c) Individuals have a legal right to access information, have inaccurate information deleted and complain to the Data Protection Commissioner if someone keeping data is in breach of the Act.

(d) The Data Protection Commissioner is responsible for ensuring the implementation of the provisions of the Act. The functions of the office of the Data Protection Commissioner include:

(i) Ensuring that a register of data controllers is kept.

(ii) Issuing enforcement notices where there are breaches of the Act.

(iii) Instigating prosecutions for breaches of the Act.

Debenture

    (a) This is a long-term loan of finance from a financial institution. It carries a fixed rate of interest and has a specified repayment date (maturity date).

    (b) It is recorded in the balance sheet as a long-term liability. It is a form of debt capital.

    (c) A business will have to provide security to obtain a debenture loan.

    (d) When the debt capital is compared to the equity capital, it is possible to assess the gearing position of the business.

Delayering

This involves reducing the number of layers of middle management in a big firm. It gives more authority to those left on the middle management team so instructions are responded to more quickly.

Delegation

This involves giving other people the authority to do certain work, e.g. a managing director appoints a sales manager, who then becomes responsible for running the sales department, i.e. work has been delegated.

Desk Research

    (a) This is a form of market research undertaken to provide information which can be used by the market research manager in the process of decision making.

    (b) It involves examining all internal and external information that is available.

    (c) Internal sources would include the firm's own files and reports from the sales people. External sources would include published reports in magazines, official statistics and information from the World Wide Web.

Deregulation

    (a) This involves a reduction in regulations and Government interference in business activities.

    (b) It means there will be a growth in free enterprise, with no protection for existing firms.

    (c) The taxi industry and our travel industry have both been affected by deregulation. Prior to deregulation, it was very costly to purchase a taxi licence – this is no longer the case.

Development Cycle of a Business

    (a) Every business goes through various stages of growth, each one involving different problems and solutions.

    (b) Stage 1 – the firm commences, raises finance, rents or buys premises, attracts customers etc.

Stage 2 – the firm survives, some profits are reinvested, the organisation improves and it plans for the future.

Stage 3 – the firm expands (grows), it can now afford to take risks, profits are rising etc.

Stage 4 – this may involve further growth, perhaps through diversification or decline, which in some cases leads to closure.

Differential Marketing

(a) This is where a firm has different target markets, so a different marketing approach is required for each target.

(b) Large firms with substantial financial resources can afford differential marketing.

(c) It is only relevant when the different target markets have been identified, the performance of the competition in those markets has been assessed and the product or service in question has the potential to be profitable in the different markets.

Direct Marketing

(a) This is a form of non-store retailing of goods or services. It involves making direct contact with potential (target) customers through direct mail, telesales or direct response brochures.

(b) It has three major advantages:

(i) It is a way of making direct contact with the target market.

(ii) It is a cheaper way of promoting a firm's products.

(iii) It is possible to quantify the results because the sales figures attributed to the campaign can be calculated.

Director of Consumer Affairs

(a) The Director of Consumer Affairs was appointed under the Consumer Information Act 1978.

(b) The functions of the Director of Consumer Affairs include the following:

(i) Enforcing the provisions of the Consumer Information Act.

(ii) Promoting better standards of advertising.

(iii) Instigating legal proceedings against traders involved in misleading advertising.

(iv) Publishing an annual report.

Direct Taxation

(a) Income tax is a direct tax on every person's income, e.g. PAYE.

(b) The employer is responsible for deducting the tax from the employees' wages and remitting it to the tax office. The cost of collecting the tax is therefore low.

(c) It is a progressive tax because the percentage rate of taxation increases as the taxable income increases.

Discretionary Income

(a) This is the amount of income a person is left with after paying taxes and spending on essential items such as food, clothes etc.

(b) Firms that produce and market non-essential products/services will be interested in the level of discretionary income at any one time. During times of economic growth, consumers spend more on discretionary items, e.g. holidays.

Diversification

(a) This is where a firm sells into different markets by offering a wider range of products, e.g. BIC, having experienced huge success with Biro pens, decided to widen its product range by moving into the disposable razor market.

(b) A firm could also diversify by merging with or taking over a firm involved in a different type of business.

(c) Diversification enables a firm to spread its risk, increase sales and profits and benefit from economies of scale.

Economic Variables (or Key Economic Variables)

(a) These are the variables that have an impact on business and the economy.

(b) Examples of economic variables include interest rates, inflation and taxation policies.

(c) An increase in interest rates has many spin-off effects: borrowing costs more, inflation increases, mortgage repayments rise and there may be demands for wage increases.

Economies of Scale

(a) The relationship between cost and production is known as an economy of scale.

(b) When a firm increases its production run, the unit cost will be reduced. This gives a big firm a competitive advantage over a small firm.

(c) Large firms buy raw materials in bulk, thus benefiting from bulk discounts, i.e. the economies of bulk buying. Firms involved in mass production benefit from economies of scale.

Electronic Data Interchange (EDI)

(a) This is the electronic transfer of data from one computer to another using agreed communication standards. It is used for sending purchase orders, paying invoices or transferring business data over a network. It can be used to instruct a bank to pay a specified amount to a creditor. It is used by supermarket chains for purchasing goods from many suppliers.

(b) Benefits to business include a reduction in paper costs, improved stock control and reordering, reduction in administration costs and better use of management time.

E-Mail (Electronic Mail)

(a) This is an electronic system used to send messages to and receive messages from other users on a network, e.g. between staff and between firms.

(b) One of the benefits of e-mail is that a similar message can be sent to many people in one transmission. Once sent, the message is placed in an electronic mailbox for the receiver(s) to access. The sender can see that the message has been accessed and read.

(c) The use of e-mail accommodates a rapid transmission of information, saves on stationery, postage and phonecall costs and allows management to do more work from home.

(d) Most people in business have an e-mail address, e.g. joe.soap@bigfirm.ie, which has been provided by the company's Internet provider.

Empowerment

(a) Empowerment is a process which involves allowing workers to set their own goals, make decisions and solve problems that arise within their area of responsibility and authority.

(b) Empowerment is a form of delegation that is used by management to motivate employees and improve staff morale.

(c) The business benefits from an improved service to customers brought about by a more committed workforce.

Entrepreneur

(a) An entrepreneur is a person who engages in entrepreneurship. This person is a risk-taker by investing private resources in a business venture, hoping to make profit from the process.

(b) Entrepreneurship is the process of planning, organising, staffing, directing, operating and accepting the risk of starting a business venture.

Equity Capital

(a) This is the issued ordinary share capital of a company.

(b) It is a long-term source of finance for a company.

(c) Ordinary shareholders receive dividends from profits.

(d) Ordinary shareholders elect the board of directors.

Exchange Rates

(a) This is the price for which one currency can be exchanged for another.

(b) Exchange rates are very important for firms involved in importing and exporting. A fixed currency exchange rate means that different countries have agreed to an exchange rate for their currencies and have agreed to maintain that rate for a certain period of time. Knowing what a future exchange rate will be is of benefit to both exporters and importers.

Factoring

(a) This is a short-term source of finance which can only be used by a firm that has credit sales and debtors.

(b) Factoring arises when a firm sells its debtors to a financial institution that offers the service of buying debts at a discount. The factor firm collects payment in full from the debtors.

(c) Factoring enables the firm that sold its debts to release cash that is tied up in debtors. It can also reduce the possibility of bad debts if the debts are sold without recourse.

Feasibility Study

(a) This type of study determines whether a business idea is practical and profitable.

(b) It involves checking all the issues involved: R&D, production, finance, logistics and profit.

(c) Results from this study will help management in deciding whether to proceed with or drop the project in question.

Field Studies (or Field Research)

(a) This is a form of market research used by firms to analyse the market before final decisions are made.

(b) Examples of types of field study research include: surveys, sampling, questionnaires and observation.

(c) This type of research is used by TV companies to assess the ratings of TV programmes and channels.

Fiscal Policy

(a) This is the policy which the Government formulates in relation to receipts and expenditure.

(b) If the Government decides to increase taxes, consumers have a reduced net pay and disposable income. In turn, this has an adverse affect on sales and profits. Likewise, an increase in VAT leads to price increases.

(c) Fiscal policy can be used by the Government to increase the revenue from taxation and reduce consumer spending.

Fixed Costs

(a) These are costs which a firm has to pay even when no production occurs, e.g. rent and insurance.

(b) They are costs which are used to provide long-term benefit for the business. They remain the same whether the level of output is high or low.

Franchising

(a) This is an arrangement whereby the franchisor grants a dealer (franchisee) the legal right to sell products in return for some agreed consideration, e.g. sales commission.

(b) The franchisor provides equipment, management advice, marketing advice and branding to the franchisee.

(c) This style of business development is common in retailing.

(d) The franchisee benefits by being able to set up a new business and benefits from the business experience and success of others, e.g. McDonalds.

Gearing (also called Leverage)

(a) This is the relationship between a firm's debt capital and equity capital.

(b) If debt capital exceeds the equity capital, the firm is highly geared. This situation may cause the quoted share price of a PLC to fall.

(c) Information about gearing is available from a firm's Balance Sheet.

Global Business

(a) This is a big organisation that attempts to standardise and integrate its business operations worldwide. The business transcends national boundaries and is not confined to the home country where the head office is based. In reality, it is involved in international business.

(b) The global business succeeds because it is able to identify worldwide markets for its products e.g. Coca-Cola and Ford.

Global Marketing

(a) This occurs when a big firm, with large financial resources, has a total commitment to a policy of international marketing.

(b) The firm applies its financial budgets, products and experience to develop and sustain its marketing strategies on a global scale.

(c) Global marketing can succeed with a brand name and standard packaging and labelling, but it may be necessary to have different selling prices in different markets.

Grant

(a) This is a non-repayable interest free amount of money received by a business from the Government.

(b) Many foreign firms were attracted to Ireland as a place to locate business because of the size of the grants available from the IDA.

(c) A grant would have to be repaid in full or in part if specified conditions relating to jobs, output, etc. are not met.

(d) Since joining the EU, the Irish Government has received huge Euro grants from European funds, e.g. European Regional Development Fund.

Green Consumer

(a) A green consumer is one that considers how the production or disposal of a product affects the environment. When offered a choice of product, they will purchase the one which does the least damage to the environment.

(b) Firms must be aware of potential consumer reaction to products that may harm the environment. A failure to take the views of 'green consumers' into consideration could result in lost sales and profits.

Gross Pay

(a) This is a person's gross earnings before any deductions, (e.g. tax) are made.

(b) Gross Pay is the basic salary plus overtime.

(c) Gross Pay less all deductions equals Net Pay.

Gross Profit

(a) Sales less the cost of sales is a firm's gross profit.

Example: Sales €100,000; Cost of Sales €40,000; Gross Profit €60,000

(b) It is calculated in the Trading Account, which is one of the final accounts of a business.

Hire Purchase

(a) This is a medium-term source of finance often used by business and households.

(b) It is a form of instalment payment and is used to purchase items such as cars and TVs. Items purchased on HP are in the possession of the purchaser after paying the first instalment, but only become the property of the purchaser when the final instalment is paid.

(c) If more than one third of the HP price is paid, the HP firm cannot repossess the goods for further default in payment without a court order.

Human Resource Management – Functions and Responsibilities

(a) Manpower planning involves ensuring that all the human resource needs of each department in the firm are met.

(b) Recruiting new employees involves interviewing, checking references, making job offers and preparing employment contracts.

(c) Industrial relations involves dealing with unions on issues such as discipline of workers, suspensions, redundancy and dismissals.

Indigenous Firms

(a) These are Irish-owned firms that were established in Ireland by Irish people.

(b) Between 1999 and 2004, almost 150,000 jobs were created in Ireland by indigenous firms.

Inflation

(a) Inflation has been defined as a sustained increase in the level of selling prices over a specified period, as measured by the Consumer Price Involver (CPI).

(b) A high rate of inflation is bad for business as firms become less competitive if workers demand a wage increase due to rising prices.

Internet

(a) The Internet is a global computer network that enables the user to access information stored on computers worldwide.

(b) Hundreds of millions of people worldwide use the internet to communicate electronically. It is widely used by firms for advertising their goods to a global market.

(c) Information is accessed through the World Wide Web (WWW). Firms advertise and provide information about their businesses through their 'web page'. Computer users in business or at home can key in the website address using the WWW code, e.g. www.fol.com, and access the information required.

(d) The development of the WWW will have major implications for marketing and retailing in the future.

Intrapreneur

(a) This is a person engaged in entrepreneurial activities from within a firm (or Government department).

(b) This employee is not a risk-taker, but has some of the traits of the entrepreneur, i.e. coming up with new ideas which can be profitably implemented.

(c) Intrapreneurs usually impress top management and are often promoted when vacancies arise.

Job Production

(a) This is the production of a single item to meet the specific requirements of the purchaser. Job-produced products are not placed in stock, they are made to order.

(b) The product is expensive and highly-skilled labour is used in its production e.g. ship- or bridge-building.

Joint Venture

(a) This is where two firms combine certain assets, such as finance and equipment, to form a 'partnership' business entity. They then share management duties, profits and losses. The joint venture may be formed for a specific project and terminated on completion of that project.

(b) A joint venture is also undertaken when an Irish firm invests in a foreign-based firm in order to develop an export market.

Just-in-Time (JIT)

(a) The purchasing manager who adopts this policy orders materials more often and in smaller quantities than one who doesn't. In an ideal situation, the materials ordered arrive just as they are required, i.e. Just-In-Time.

(b) A JIT system reduces a firm's investment in stock levels and storage space. It emphasises the elimination of waste, i.e. anything that increases costs but not value to a product.

(c) A firm will adopt a JIT policy when it has total confidence in its supplier. This policy puts great pressure on the supplier/manufacturer to have a very efficient system of production and distribution.

Labour Relations Commission (LRC)

(a) Under the Industrial Relations Act, the LRC provides a conciliation service to assist in resolving industrial disputes.

(b) It provides an industrial relations advisory service and also nominates Rights Commissioners to investigate disputes involving an individual employee.

(c) It appoints Equality Officers to investigate disputes involving discrimination of some employees.

Leasing

(a) This is a medium-term source of finance used by many firms to acquire assets such as computers and vehicles.

(b) With leasing, a firm does not purchase the asset but 'leases it' (i.e. rents it) from a leasing company (e.g. a bank).

(c) Leasing is good for a firm's working capital and cash flow because only the regular leasing payments have to be made.

Limited Liability

(a) Limited Liability is 'protection' for shareholders in private and public companies.

(b) If a company goes bankrupt, the shareholders only lose the amount of money they invested. None of their private assets (home etc.) can be seized to pay the debts of the company.

(c) The existence of limited liability encourages people to become entrepreneurs and investors.

Liquidity Ratios

(a) These ratios show the relationship between a firm's current assets and current liabilities. They are used when assessing a firm's ability to pay its debts as they fall due.

(b) Examples of liquidity ratios are:

Working Capital Ratio = (Current Assets : Current Liabilities)
2:1 is a good WC ratio

Acid Test Ratio = (Current Assets – stock : Current Liabilities)
1:1 is a good AT ratio

Management Buy-out (MBO)

(a) This arises when the owners of a business agree to sell it as a going concern to its management or employees (or both).

(b) From the viewpoint of the owners, selling to the existing management may be the quickest way of disposing of the business.

(c) A reason for facilitating an MBO is that the owners may want to 'unload' and sell off any business which is not a part of its core enterprise.

Manpower Planning

(a) This is an important function of the human resources manager.

(b) It involves assessing the human resources requirements of each department in the firm.

(c) It involves being up to date with the skills required to perform certain tasks and also the technological developments taking place in manufacturing and computers.

Market Planning

(a) The objective of market planning is to assist management to plan for the future. This can involve a short-term plan and a long-term plan.

(b) A market plan is necessary for a firm to achieve its objectives of sales, growth and profits.

(c) By having a market plan, management will be focused on the future direction of the business. They will be aware of what weaknesses exist and can take steps to eliminate them. By having a market plan, the business can then develop a marketing plan.

Market Research

(a) This is the gathering, recording and analysing of facts and data concerned with the transfer of goods/services from the producer to the final consumer.

(b) Market research involves researching for information which will enable management to make informed decisions. Having accurate information about what the market requires is essential if a firm is planning to make a large investment in a new product.

(c) Spending time and money to obtain accurate market research is a cost-effective investment for any business.

Marketing Concept

(a) Satisfying customers' requirements is the main aim of the marketing concept, i.e. find out what customers want and provide it.

(b) In practice, the marketing concept causes management to recognise that the vital task of a firm is to find out what the customers require and then produce and sell such products profitably and in a superior way to competitors.

(c) The existence of the marketing concept enables a firm to achieve its goal in business, i.e. sales, profit and satisfied customers.

Marketing Mix

(a) The marketing mix relates to product, price, place and promotion.

(b) The above four variables are factors over which a firm has control.

(c) The customer must be kept in mind when considering each of the elements in the mix. The components are important both individually and collectively in order for sales and profits to be achieved.

Marketing Strategy

(a) This involves selecting and analysing a target market and having a marketing mix that will meet the requirements of the consumers in that target market.

(b) A marketing strategy is a form of planning. It enables a firm to be focused and make the best use of its resources and the unique features of its products, e.g. price.

Mass Production

(a) This involves producing large quantities of standardised items, thereby achieving economies of scale in production and reducing the unit cost of production.

(b) It involves high capital expenditure investment by management in order to achieve a low unit cost of production. This enables a firm to be very competitive in the market place.

(c) Huge sales are expected from mass produced goods and so stock levels are also high. Examples include golf balls and biro pens.

Memorandum of Association

(a) This is one of the documents that has to be registered when a company is being formed.

(b) This document defines what the limitations and powers of the company are, for example:

(i) Name of the company – the last word is Ltd or PLC.

(ii) The objects of the company.

(iii) A statement that the company is limited in liability.

These powers show the relationship between the company and the general public.

(c) A company cannot legally carry out any activities not included in the Memorandum of Association. If it does, it is acting *ultra vires,* i.e. outside its authority.

Merchandising

(a) This is where a manufacturer seeks to ensure that the retailer sells the products as quickly and as profitably as possible.

(b) The manufacturer provides advice and assistance to the retailer, e.g. providing display stands at impulse location points, posters, etc. Merchandising leads to impulse buying by customers.

(c) The objective of merchandising is to increase the sales of the products produced by the manufacturer, not all the products in the shop.

Mission Statement of a Business

(a) If a business is to succeed, then everyone in the firm has to be clear about objectives in relation to sales, profits, market share and how these will be achieved.

(b) Some firms clarify their objectives and intentions by having a mission statement which clearly states what the firm hopes to achieve. The mission statement really defines the scope of what management can and should do.

Monetary Policies

(a) These are Government policies which are implemented through the Central Bank.

(b) Monetary policy is implemented when the Government wants to increase or reduce the amount of money being spent in the economy, e.g. if the Government reduces interest rates, it is cheaper for firms and individuals to borrow money. This leads to increased spending, investment and economic growth.

Multi-media

Multi-media involves communicating in more than one way. The term is associated with the WWW.

Text (written data)	The combination of these media makes up the general term multi-media.
Graphics (visual data)	
Sound (speech and/or music)	
Video (picture image)	

Networking

This is the opposite to the entrepreneur working on his/her own. Networking involves making and using contacts in order to develop the business. The aim is to get to know people with influence, e.g. suppliers, local business people and people in key positions, so as to utilise their help and expertise or to pass on information.

Niche Market

(a) An established market is one where normal competition takes place. A niche market, on the other hand, is a segment of a market that is not currently being serviced and exploited. Small firms are better at locating these niches than bigger ones.

(c) Because of the small size of the market there are fewer suppliers, so the competition is not as severe as in established markets.

Open Economy

(a) This is an economy where there is total free trade, i.e. a free movement of goods and services between countries.

(b) No restrictions to trading exist, e.g. tariffs, quotas or import duties.

(c) Within the context of the EU, the Irish economy is an open economy. The Maastricht Agreement ensured free trade between member states.

Opportunity Cost

(a) When making a choice, someone who considers the alternative in order to be sure that it is not worth more than the option being chosen is assessing the opportunity cost of the decision, i.e. the best opportunity which results from the alternative chosen.

(b) In practice, when people are spending they are able to adjust their spending to purchase one product rather than another. A consumer will decide to spend less on one product in order to be able to spend more on another product. The opportunity cost is the value of the benefit that is given up by purchasing one alternative rather than another.

Organisation Structure

(a) This refers to the levels of management and divisions of responsibilities that exist within a firm, i.e. how a firm organises its business activities.

(b) Every business must be organised, otherwise there would be chaos.

(c) A good organisational structure will clearly show who is in charge, i.e. the chain of command. An example of an organisation structure is 'line organisation', where the lines of authority are clearly highlighted for management and staff.

Overtrading

(a) A business is said to be overtrading when it has insufficient current assets to pay its current debts.

(b) This situation is confirmed when a firm's current liabilities are greater than its current assets.

(c) Overtrading can arise for different reasons, for example, overexpansion when the firm is short of money or mis-matching finance, i.e. using a short-term source of finance for a long-term project.

Own Brand Goods (or Labels)

(a) These are initiated and owned by wholesalers or retailers. The manufacturer of the goods is not identified on the product. The wholesaler or retailer bulk buy with their own brand name from the manufacturer.

(b) Wholesalers and retailers use their 'own brand name' to make their advertising more effective and increase sales and profits, e.g. St Bernard brand in Dunnes Stores.

Patent

(a) A patent for an invention is the granting by the State of exclusive rights to manufacture, exploit, use and sell the invention.

(b) To get a patent, an inventor must have something that is new and useful, i.e. it must have an industrial application.

(c) The State grants a patent for a maximum of 20 years.

(d) A firm or person who owns the patent on some product may, for a fee called Patent Royalties, allow others to use the product.

Performance Appraisal (or Appraisal Review)

(a) Some firms relate wage increases to how employees perform during the year.

(b) In large firms, it is the function of the human resource manager to appraise an employee's work. This involves assessing the employee's work in areas such as quality of work, time-keeping, commitment and reaching targets and also suggesting where future improvements can be made.

(c) Based on the result of the performance appraisal, the wage increase will be decided.

Premium Pricing

(a) This policy is associated with high quality and high priced items, e.g. jewellery.

(b) Some consumers expect and are willing to pay high prices for certain items, e.g. fashion clothes. Manufacturers and retailers keep this in mind when deciding the selling price of such products. This is called 'premium pricing' or 'premium mark-up'.

Private Limited Company

The majority of businesses operate as a private limited company with the following characteristics:

(a) Shareholders enjoy the benefit of limited liability.

(b) Shares cannot be issues to the public and are not quoted on the Stock Exchange.

(c) Business can commence on receipt of a Certificate of Incorporation from the Registrar of Companies.

Privatisation

(a) This involves selling a company owned by the State to private enterprise by means of a share issue.

(b) The Government would receive the revenue from the sale of the State firm, e.g. in 1999 eircom was privatised and yielded the Government €3bn. This money can be used by the Government to repay loans, reduce taxes etc.

Product Life Cycle

Products do not last forever, consumers like a change.

(a) The 'product life cycle' describes the different stages a product goes through, from its introduction as a new product to its decline and possible removal from the market by the manufacturer.

(b) The stages are as follows:

(i) The product is developed and introduced onto the market.

(ii) Sales increase, i.e. there is growth.

(iii) Sales reach their peak.

(iv) Sales increase slows down due to competition, i.e. sales mature.

(v) Sales decline as the product is no longer as popular and it may eventually be withdrawn to be replaced by another 'new product'.

Prototype Development

(a) This is the production of one or a small number of units of a new product to enable it to be test marketed.

(b) By producing the product, it will highlight manufacturing problems, costings and enable the firm to test consumer reaction to the selling price required to break-even and then become profitable.

(c) A decision on whether or not to proceed with the new product can be made by management after analysing the results of the test marketing.

Public Limited Company (PLC)

(a) Finance can be raised by issuing shares to the public.

(b) Shareholders have limited liability. This encourages them to buy shares in a PLC.

(c) The shares are quoted on the Stock Exchange.

(d) The accounts of every PLC are published.

Public Relations (PR)

(a) Public Relations is defined as a deliberate, planned and sustained effort to establish and maintain understanding between an organisation and the public.

(b) It involves obtaining good publicity for a firm or organisation, e.g. club.

(c) PR is a function of management. It does not involve direct selling of a firm's products. It really involves influencing people.

Quality Control

(a) Good quality control is essential in order to eliminate the occurrence of faulty goods being produced and sold to consumers.

(b) The level of quality control adopted by a firm will be linked to the quality standards required by consumers and practised by competitors.

(c) Many firms now advertise and display the Q Mark with their products. This is a public confirmation and recognition that the firm has high quality standards and an effective quality control procedure. Quality is more important than price.

Report Writing

(a) A report is a document in which some problem is examined for the purpose of finding out information, reporting findings, putting forward ideas and making recommendations if requested.

(b) The contents of a report must relate to the terms of reference given by those who commissioned the report.

(c) Reports can be formal or informal. Formal reports are often published and are laid out in a standard manner: Title, Name, Contents etc.

Reservation of Title

(a) This is where a contract of sale contains a clause that states that the goods shall remain the property of the seller until they are paid for by the buyer.

(b) If the buyer goes bankrupt before paying for the goods, the seller can recover the goods (if they still exist) or obtain payment for them from the Receiver or Liquidator.

(c) The use of this clause reduces the level of bad debts for firms selling goods on credit.

Rights Commissioners

(a) A Rights Commissioner is appointed under the Industrial Relations Act 1990.

(b) A Rights Commissioner deals with the problems of individual workers as distinct from all workers.

(c) Disputes on issues such as disciplinary procedures and suspension, i.e. issues not involving wages or working hours, are investigated by the Rights Commissioner and a recommendation on how to resolve the conflict is made.

(d) The recommendation can be rejected and appealed to the Labour Court, where a decision is binding.

Risk Management

(a) This is an organised approach to assessing and managing all the potential risks a business or individual can face.

(b) A business has to:

(i) identify the likelihood of some risk occurring or not occurring

(ii) find out the costs of insuring the various risks.

Sales Promotion

(a) These are short-term activities undertaken to support advertising and sales.

(b) Examples of sales promotions aimed at the consumer include:

• Special offers • Price reductions in sales (e.g. 15% off)

• Discount vouchers to be used with future purchases

(c) Sales promotions are short-term incentives that a firm hopes will bring long-term benefits.

Service Industry

(a) This industry is made up of firms that do not manufacture products, but provide services required by business and individuals.

(b) In April 2005, 89 per cent of all the small firms in Ireland were in the service industry.

(c) Employment in the service industry is bigger than in the primary or secondary industries.

Examples: Banks (financial service), taxis (transport service).

Shop Steward

(a) This person is a member of the workforce appointed by his/her colleagues to be the union representative in discussions with management and to act as a contact with the union head-office.

(b) An efficient shop steward is important both to management and workers. This person will work with management to resolve problems within the firm. Workers need to be confident that the shop steward understands their problems, so a satisfactory outcome to issues can be reached without calling in the union.

Single European Market (SEM)

(a) The existence of the SEM since 1 January 1993 means that free trade exists throughout the EU.

(b) It allows the free movement of goods, services and capital. Consumers benefit from the hectic competition and lower prices.

(c) It also involves the harmonisation of taxes throughout the EU, thus eliminating any distortion of trade between member states.

Small Claims Court

(a) The small claim procedure is consumer-orientated and deals with claims for faulty goods and services purchased where the size of the claim does not exceed €1,270.

(b) The aim of the Small Claims Court is to provide a service that is fast, inexpensive and will provide a fair resolution of a minor dispute without the need for legal representation.

(c) Initially, the Registrar will try to resolve the conflict. If this fails, then the case will be heard in the District Court.

Span of Control (also called Span of Management)

(a) This relates to the number of subordinates who report to any one manager or supervisor, e.g. if seven people are reporting to one manager, then the span of control is seven.

(b) The size of the span of control will depend on the type of work, ability of employees, existence of empowerment and the expertise and experience of the person in authority.

(c) Management can delegate authority but not responsibility.

Spreadsheet

(a) It is regularly used in business and provides management with projected answers if different figures are recorded in a computer worksheet.

(b) It enables management to propose 'What If' questions, e.g. if the selling price increased by 5 per cent, what is the potential impact on profit margins?

(c) It is regularly used in business for financial budgeting, statistical analysis and storing information.

Stakeholders

(a) These are the various people involved and interested in how a business is doing.

(b) They are as follows:

- Owners • Consumers • Employees • General public
- Managers • Government

(c) The owners are the unique shareholders because they are also risk-takers, i.e. they invested money to establish and develop the business.

State Enterprise

(a) Some of the biggest businesses in Ireland are owned by the Government. They are called 'semi-state bodies' or 'public corporations' because the State is directly involved in their operation by appointing directors to manage their opportunities.

(b) State enterprise provides many vital services in the areas of transport and electricity, which are capital intensive and may not be profitable for private enterprises.

Examples: ESB, An Post, ACC Bank.

Subrogation

(a) The insured is entitled to compensation from the insurer for a loss suffered that was properly insured.

(b) The insurer, having paid the insured, has the legal right to recover the amount it paid from a third party, which caused the loss, e.g. in car insurance if X is injured by Y's careless driving, X can claim compensation from his/her insurer who, in turn, will recover the loss from Y's insurer.

SWOT Analysis

(a) A SWOT analysis examines a firm's strengths, weaknesses, opportunities and threats.

(b) It is important for a firm when formulating strategy.

(c) By assessing internal strengths and weaknesses, plus external opportunities and threats, a firm is able to exploit opportunities that may arise, counteract threats (e.g. competition), avoid weaknesses and become a stronger and more competitive business.

Synergy

(a) This is the concept that 2 + 2 = 5, i.e. the combined efforts of two firms joining together (through a merger or takeover) will give a greater overall benefit than if the two firms maintained their own entity (and perhaps competed).

(b) If two competing firms merge, there will be no need for two distribution systems, two sets of computers, two sets of sales representatives etc. Only one of every component will be required.

(c) The new business unit is bigger with less competition and so profits should increase.

Tactical Pricing

(a) If price is an important variable, then tactical pricing can be very effective. A firm using this 'tactic' could have a special offer or short-term discount price.

(b) The objective of tactical planning is to attract new customers, encourage existing customers to buy more, get an overall sales increase, reduce stock levels and increase profits.

Tax Credit

(a) A tax credit is the part of your income on which you pay no tax.

(b) Every taxpayer is entitled to tax credits and those depend on personal circumstances, e.g. single or married, etc.

(c) Tax credits are deducted from gross tax to find the amount of tax payable.

Tax Forms

The following are the relevant Tax Forms:

(a) Form P12

(b) Form P45

(c) Form P60

(d) Form P21

} (see page 149)

Teamwork

(a)   Every job requires some form of teamwork. It is impossible to achieve anything in business without the help of others, i.e. colleagues 'members of the team'.

(b)   Firms want employees to feel that they are all part of one big team. They want all employees 'pulling their weight' so that consumers will be satisfied, sales and profit targets will be achieved and the business will succeed.

(c)   Teams may work in certain groups, e.g. sales team, computer team and research team. Though working in separate groups, they are all working for the same employer.

Terms of Reference

(a) These are the instructions given to the report writer by those instigating/commissioning the report.

(b) They usually include the following:

(i) the issues to be discussed in the report

(ii) the time scale in which the report is to be finalised and submitted

(iii) recommendations on what action should be taken when the final report is submitted.

Time Management

(a) This is the most effective use of time available when running a business.

(b) Time should be spent on important issues and not wasted on trivial matters.

(c) Time management is necessary in order to control costs, maximise output and for the firm to maximise its competitive position in the market place.

Tertiary Industry

(a) These are service industries that provide a wide range of vital services to all industry, e.g. telecommunications and banking.

(b) Over two-thirds of the labour force are employed in this sector.

(c) Over 80 per cent of small firms are in this industry and make large tax contributions to the Exchequer.

Theory X

(a) This is part of McGregor's theory of motivation.

(b) It states that the average person dislikes work and tries to avoid it. In turn it means that people have to be pressurised to work and disciplined if deemed necessary.

(c) Management who believe in Theory X are prepared to provide incentives to encourage employees to be interested and committed to the job.

Time Management Skill

(a) This is the most effective use of time available to complete a task. This is necessary for a firm to have a competitive advantage.

(b) It involves setting a 'time target', monitoring it and checking at the end to ensure that the job was done in the specified time.

(c) 'Time is money': if a job takes longer, it costs more. Effective time management will ensure faster deliveries, shorter product cycles and ongoing efficiency levels.

Total Quality Management (TQM)

(a) TQM is a management approach throughout a firm that insists on and ensures total quality throughout the firm. This means that the firm will excel in every area of product and service that is important to customers.

(b) A firm with a TQM policy has excellent teamwork with everyone focused on the job to be done. Everyone realises that ongoing improvements are necessary to satisfy consumers in a competitive market.

Trade Dispute

(a) This is a dispute between employers and workers which is concerned with the employment or non-employment or terms or conditions affecting the employment of a person.

(b) Valid issues for a trade dispute include:

- Dismissal or suspension of an employee
- Trade union recognition • Discrimination

(c) The Industrial Relations Act 1990 sets out what a trade dispute is.

Trade Mark

A trade mark is any sign capable of distinguishing the goods or services of one firm from those of another firm, i.e. trade marks may consist of words, designs, labels, e.g. Coca-Cola, Texaco, Finches.

Transnational Company (TNC) (also called a Multinational Company)

(a) A TNC is a very big corporate organisation with a head-office in one country and subsidiaries in many countries, e.g. Coca-Cola and Shell.

(b) Goods are produced by the subsidiary companies in different countries. These subsidiaries can avail of different wage levels and overcome problems related to different languages and currencies.

(c) The different subsidiary companies in the TNC have a common ownership and economies of scale can be achieved through the global integration of its functional areas.

Ultra Vires

(a) A company (private or public) cannot legally carry out activities not included in its Memorandum of Association.

(b) If the directors authorise any activity not included in its Memorandum of Association they are acting *ultra vires* (outside their authority).

(c) *Ultra vires* contracts entered into by a company are void and cannot be enforced.

Unlimited Liability

(a) Sole traders and partners operate their businesses with unlimited liability. This means that they are personally liable for the debts of their business.

(b) Those operating with unlimited liability are regarded as the ultimate risk-takers as they are also risking their private assets, e.g. their house.

Unsolicited Goods (also called Inertia Selling)

(a) These are goods received by the consumer that were not ordered. An invoice requesting payment comes with the goods.

(b) Under the Sale of Goods and Supply of Services Act 1980, a person who receives unsolicited goods may keep them without payment after giving the sender 30 days' notice that the goods were unsolicited and not required.

Utmost Good Faith *(Uberrimai Fidei)*

(a) Every person seeking insurance must make a full disclosure of all material facts. This is necessary so that the actuary can assess the risk and decide the premium for the insurer to charge.

(b) A failure by the insured to declare all the material facts enables the insurer to declare the contract void and claims by the insured will be rejected.

Variable Costs (also called Direct Costs)

(a) These are costs which vary with the number of items produced or sold.

(b) They are directly related to output, e.g. the more goods that have to be produced, the more raw materials required.

Venture Capital

(a) This is a long-term source of finance, whereby a firm or individual invests finance in an enterprise in return for a minority equity holding and a share of the profits.

(b) Venture capital invested in a new business is called 'seed capital'. Venture capital invested in an established business is called 'development capital'.

Video-conferencing

(a) Video-conferencing involves the visual transmission of live situations to different locations worldwide.

(b) It facilitates corporate meetings between the head office and overseas managers of a transnational company without costly and time-consuming travel.

(c) It enables sellers in one market, who do not have overseas subsidiaries, to demonstrate their products to potential buyers in different countries. This kind of marketing, via video link-up, saves the seller the costs of travel and employing additional marketing people.

Working Capital Management

(a) Working capital management involves managing the ongoing working capital requirements of a business, i.e. managing the stock, debtors, creditors etc.

(b) The efficient management of a firm's working capital will enable a business to avoid operating in an overdraft situation and incurring overdraft interest. It also ensures that creditors are paid on time, thus allowing the firm to avail of discounts.

(c) A firm whose current assets are less than its current liabilities is overtrading. This may be caused by poor working capital management.

World Trade Organisation (WTO)

(a) The WTO came into existence in 1995, replacing GATT (which had 118 member countries).

(b) The WTO promotes the following:

   (i) Open markets with a view to achieving worldwide free trade, i.e. the elimination of all tariffs, quotas and subsidiaries.

   (ii) Greater access to world markets for EU agri-products.

   (iii) Agreed levels to which governments subsidise or provide grant aid for local enterprise.

Business Syllabus – Outcome Verbs

Calculate:	To find out or ascertain by using numerical data, ratios etc.
Contrast:	To display the difference(s) between. To place in opposition in order to show dissimilarities.
Define:	To state the precise meaning of. To set out the meaning of a term or concept.
Demonstrate:	To explain or describe by showing examples, charts, diagrams, graphs etc.
Describe:	To give an account of a person, relationship, event, institution etc.
Distinguish:	To recognise something as distinct from other things, i.e. to point out the difference(s).
Draft:	To draw up a document, letter etc., i.e. to outline in writing, sketch, diagram etc.
Explain:	To make clear in a detailed manner.
Identify:	To show that you recognise something.
Illustrate:	To make clear by means of examples, charts, diagrams, graphs etc.
Interpret:	To give or explain the meaning of. To make clear. To derive a particular understanding of.
List:	To write down a number of names or things that have something in common.
Outline:	To give a short summary of the important features, omitting detail, i.e. the general principles or chief elements of a subject.
Recognise:	To identify something known or perceived before.
Understand:	To grasp something as distinct from other things, i.e. to point out the difference(s).
Analyse: HL	To study a problem in detail by breaking it down into various parts and to examine possible relationships.
Apply: HL	To bring knowledge/skill into use or action, e.g. to use for a particular purpose.
Compare: HL	To examine two or more things in order to discover their likeness and/or differences (similarities and/or dissimilarities).
Differentiate: HL	To distinguish between. To develop separate characteristics.
Discuss: HL	To examine or consider, suggesting a detailed and careful investigation. It may require debating both sides of an argument.
Evaluate:	To find or determine the worth, value, amount or significance of something. To assess. To adjudge.

Index